Autoshaping and Conditioning Theory

Autoshaping and Conditioning Theory

Edited by

C. M. LOCURTO
Department of Psychology
College of the Holy Cross
Worcester, Massachusetts

H. S. TERRACE
Department of Psychology
Columbia University
New York, New York

JOHN GIBBON
New York State Psychiatric Institute
and Columbia University
New York, New York

ACADEMIC PRESS
A Subsidiary of Harcourt Brace Jovanovich, Publishers
New York   London   Toronto   Sydney   San Francisco

COPYRIGHT © 1981, BY ACADEMIC PRESS, INC.
ALL RIGHTS RESERVED.
NO PART OF THIS PUBLICATION MAY BE REPRODUCED OR
TRANSMITTED IN ANY FORM OR BY ANY MEANS, ELECTRONIC
OR MECHANICAL, INCLUDING PHOTOCOPY, RECORDING, OR ANY
INFORMATION STORAGE AND RETRIEVAL SYSTEM, WITHOUT
PERMISSION IN WRITING FROM THE PUBLISHER.

ACADEMIC PRESS, INC.
111 Fifth Avenue, New York, New York 10003

United Kingdom Edition published by
ACADEMIC PRESS, INC. (LONDON) LTD.
24/28 Oval Road, London NW1 7DX

Library of Congress Cataloging in Publication Data
Main entry under title:

Autoshaping and conditioning theory.

    Includes bibliographies and index.
    1. Autoshaping (Psychology) 2. Psychobiology.
3. Paired–association learning. I. Locurto, C. M.
II. Terrace, Herbert S.   III. Gibbon, John

BF319.5.A79A93   156'.23224   80–1102
ISBN 0–12–454480–0

PRINTED IN THE UNITED STATES OF AMERICA

81 82 83 84   9 8 7 6 5 4 3 2 1

Contents

List of Contributors ix
Preface xi

1 *Introduction: Autoshaping and Two-Factor Learning Theory* 1
   H. S. TERRACE

Autoshaping, Related Phenomena, and
  the *Zeitgeist* in which They Emerged 1
Are Autoshaped Keypecks "Superstitious" Conditioned Operants? 3
Is Autoshaped Behavior Classically Conditioned? 4
What Suffices as a Minimal Unit of Conditioning? 10
Future Directions of Research on Autoshaping 13
References 15

I Biological Factors

2 *Response Evocation in Autoshaping: Contributions of Cognitive and Comparative-Evolutionary Analyses to an Understanding of Directed Action* 21
   EDWARD A. WASSERMAN

The Learning–Performance Distinction 22
The Response Evocation Problem 24
Response Evocation in Autoshaping 29
Comparative-Evolutionary Analysis 38
Concluding Comments 45
References 47

3 *Biconditional Behavior: Conditioning without Constraint*   55
DAVID R. WILLIAMS

The Laboratory Phenomenon	57
Autoshaping and the S–S* Relationship	61
A Hypothesis about the Natural Origin of the Phenomenon	65
The Terms of the Classical Paradigm	69
The Associative Aspect of Classical Conditioning	71
The Biological Aspect of Classical Conditioning	72
Autoshaping and Classical Conditioning	74
Autoshaping and the R–S* Relationship	76
Examples of the Analysis of Biconditional Behavior	80
Some General Observations on Biconditional Behavior	91
Conclusion	96
References	97

4 *Contributions of Autoshaping to the Partitioning of Conditioned Behavior*   101
C. M. LOCURTO

Introduction	101
Omission Training	102
Additional Evaluative Procedures	121
Conclusions	129
References	130

II Associative Factors

5 *Second-Order Autoshaping: Contributions to the Research and Theory of Pavlovian Reinforcement by Conditioned Stimuli*   139
MICHAEL E. RASHOTTE

Introduction	139
Some Basic Facts about Second-Order Autoshaping in Pigeons	140
Sources of Variation in the Reinforcing Effectiveness of Conditioned Stimuli	152
Conclusion	174
References	177

6 Effects of Unpredictable Food on the
   Subsequent Acquisition of Autoshaping:
   Analysis of the Context Blocking Hypothesis   181
   ARTHUR TOMIE

Introduction   181
Negative Transfer Effects following Uncorrelated Pretraining   182
Theoretical Interpretations of the Negative Transfer Effect in Autoshaping   186
Experimental Analysis of the Context-Blocking Hypothesis   189
Implications   205
References   210

III Temporal Factors

7 Spreading Association in Time   219
   JOHN GIBBON AND PETER BALSAM

Introduction   219
Trial Spacing   220
Scalar Expectancy   224
Integration   231
Learning Speed   236
Variance   242
Concluding Remarks   247
Appendix A. Trials to Criterion: Deterministic Version   248
Appendix B. Trials to Criterion: Stochastic
   Version—Background Immediate   250
References   253

8 Why Autoshaping Depends on Trial Spacing   255
   H. M. JENKINS, R. A. BARNES, AND F. J. BARRERA

Demonstration of Trial Spacing Effect: Experiment 1   255
Effect Not Due to Local Interference   257
Effect of Long Waits   261
Spacing and Predictive Value   265
Relative Waiting Time Hypothesis   271
Summary of Findings   277
Relation to Theories of Signaling in Classical Conditioning   278
References   283

9 The Contingency Problem in Autoshaping   285
JOHN GIBBON

Introduction	285
Contingency	286
Expectancy	289
Partial Contingencies	293
Relation to Rescorla–Wagner Theory	298
Relation to Relative Waiting Time	304
Appendix A: Rescorla–Wagner Theory	305
References	307

Index   309

List of Contributors

Numbers in parentheses indicate the pages on which authors' contributions begin.

R. A. BARNES (255), Department of Psychology, McMaster University, Hamilton, Ontario L8S 4K1, Canada

F. J. BARRERA (255), Department of Psychology, McMaster University, Hamilton, Ontario L8S 4K1, Canada

PETER BALSAM (219), Department of Psychology, Barnard College, New York, New York 10027

JOHN GIBBON (219, 285), New York State Psychiatric Institute, New York, New York 10032, and Columbia University, New York, New York 10027

H. M. JENKINS (255), Department of Psychology, McMaster University, Hamilton, Ontario L8S 4K1, Canada

C. M. LOCURTO (101), Department of Psychology, College of the Holy Cross, Worcester, Massachusetts 01610

MICHAEL E. RASHOTTE (139), Department of Psychology, Florida State University, Tallahassee, Florida 32306

H. S. TERRACE (1), Department of Psychology, Columbia University, New York, New York 10027

ARTHUR TOMIE (181), Department of Psychology, Rutgers–The State University, New Brunswick, New Jersey 08903

EDWARD A. WASSERMAN (21), Department of Psychology, Spence Laboratories of Psychology, The University of Iowa, Iowa City, Iowa 52242

DAVID R. WILLIAMS (55), Department of Psychology, University of Pennsylvania, Philadelphia, Pennsylvania 19174

Preface

The past decade has been an exciting one for students of animal conditioning and behavior. We have witnessed the development of quantitative models of instrumental and Pavlovian conditioning that describe basic phenomena with increasing sophistication. At the same time, new phenomena—such as taste-aversion learning, adjunctive behaviors, and autoshaping—questioned much of the conventional wisdom of conditioning theory.

The issues raised by these developments have been treated in a number of volumes. The present work is the first to be concerned exclusively with the impact of autoshaping. The impetus for this volume derived from a symposium at the 1976 meeting of the Eastern Psychological Association. Our objective was to summarize the status of autoshaping in the eighth year after the phenomenon was first reported by Brown and Jenkins (1968). This book represents the formal completion of that objective. Contributors to that symposium (Gibbon, Jenkins, Locurto, and Terrace) have been joined by other investigators in compiling this volume.

The book's structure reflects the far-ranging impact of autoshaping, one that has led to reinterpretations of existing phenomena as well as to new experimental and theoretetical issues. Accordingly, this volume will be of interest both to students of traditional animal conditioning phenomena and to investigators concerned with the biological constraints on learned behavior or, more generally, with the nature of associative learning. These topics have foundations in the study of both animal and human behavior.

Chapter 1 by Terrace provides an overview of these varied influences. In Part I the relationship between autoshaping and biological influences on associative learning is explored by Wasserman (Chapter 2), Williams (Chapter 3), and Locurto (Chapter 4). Williams's chapter has had an important impact on workers in this field since its first appearance as an unpublished manuscript. This work was the first to recognize the joint influence of Pavlovian and instrumental contingencies in autoshaping and to specify a new framework for understanding this interaction. Locurto's chapter complements this approach by discussing approaches to evaluate autoshaping within the boundaries of traditional two-factor theory. Part II considers the influence of autoshaping on selected topics in associative learning. The chapters by Rashotte (Chapter 5) on second-order conditioning and Tomie (Chapter 6) on transfer of training provide original theoretical interpretations of existing experimental phenomena. The final section, Part III, is devoted to the influence of temporal factors. It consists of three chapters, Gibbon and Balsam (Chapter 7), Jenkins, Barnes, and Barrera (Chapter 8), and Gibbon (Chapter 9). These authors address some perennial problems in conditioning (e.g., the effects of intertrial interval) with a novel theoretical approach that integrates these issues with the now-familiar notion of "predictiveness" in Pavlovian conditioning.

With some simplification it may be said that any theory of conditioning must address at least two questions: What factors govern the emergence of the first conditioned response? and Why is that response repeated? These are, of course, the fundamental issues of acquisition and maintenance. As the following book demonstrates, the study of autoshaping has provided novel answers to both questions. Therein lies a promise that exciting days are ahead.

H. S. TERRACE 1

Introduction: Autoshaping and Two-Factor Learning Theory

AUTOSHAPING, RELATED PHENOMENA, AND THE *ZEITGEIST* IN WHICH THEY EMERGED

Autoshaping was discovered in a *Zeitgeist* of waning confidence in two-factor learning theory. A steady accumulation of examples of the "misbehavior of organisms" (e.g., Breland & Breland, 1961) made questionable the practice of learning theorist's, originated by Pavlov (1927)—of regarding stimuli and responses as "arbitrary." The observation that a skeletal response such as a pigeon's keypeck can be conditioned by a classical conditioning paradigm (Brown & Jenkins, 1968) and, of equal surprise value, that autoshaped behavior persists when it cancels reinforcement (Williams & Williams, 1969) strengthened this *Zeitgeist* by questioning the theoretical status of an intensively studied example of instrumental behavior.

If a conditioned keypeck is not an "arbitrary" example of shaped instrumental behavior (cf. Skinner, 1953), sensitive to contingencies of reinforcement (cf. Ferster & Skinner, 1957; Skinner, 1969), what is it? The either–or logic of traditional two-factor learning theory led a number of writers, albeit of different theoretical persuasions (e.g., Bindra, 1972; Mackintosh, 1974; Moore, 1973; Skinner, 1971), to regard an autoshaped keypeck as an example of Pavlovian conditioning. In an intriguing exchange with Skinner (1977), Herrnstein (1977a,b) opted for the other factor of two-factor theory and characterized autoshaped keypecks as "self-reinforced" instances of instrumental behavior.

The problem autoshaped behavior poses for two-factor learning theory is but one of many that have been the subject of a considerable body of research and theoretical work during the past 15 years. The autoshaping paradigm, in which a reinforcer (S^*) is signaled by a neutral stimulus (S), provides an opportunity for studying a variety of phenomena that typically have been studied in classical conditioning paradigms in which S^* is an aversive stimulus, for example, second-order conditioning (Rashotte, Chapter 5, this volume), and blocking (Tomie, Chapter 6, this volume). Research on autoshaping has also provided an opportunity for the systematic study, with positive S^*'s, the acquisition of a conditioned response, a process that heretofore has been studied almost exclusively in paradigms employing negative S^*'s. With the possible exception of studies of eyelid conditioning and conditioned emotional responses, studies of autoshaping have provided the most systematic data on the acquisition of conditioned behavior to date, as established by either classical or instrumental conditioning paradigms. (For example, see summaries of the effects of the duration of trial and intertrial intervals and of the probability that S is followed by S in chapters in this volume by Gibbon and Balsam [Chapter 7], Jenkins [Chapter 8] and Gibbon [Chapter 9]).

This book will present some of the many facets of the research on autoshaping that has followed Brown and Jenkin's seminal study. The purpose of this introduction is to evaluate some basic autoshaping phenomena within the framework of two-factor learning theory. These phenomena have been discussed extensively in two thorough reviews (Hearst & Jenkins, 1974; Schwartz & Gamzu, 1977). Accordingly, the following summary of major empirical findings should suffice as background.

1. Pecking at a punctate visual signal is typically conditioned and maintained only when S^* occurs more frequently in the presence of a neutral stimulus than in its absence (Gamzu & Williams 1972, Gibbon, Locurto, & Terrace, 1976; Locurto, Chapter 4, this volume). Initial pecks cannot be accounted for by the operant level of pecking a lit key (Brown & Jenkins, 1968).
2. Responding to S occurs even if it results in the cancellation of S^* (omission training). However, the frequency of responding to S is lower during omission training than when the same frequency of S^* is presented independently of responding (Locurto, Chapter 4, this volume; Schwartz & Williams, 1972; Williams, Chapter 3, this volume).
3. The topography of the keypeck is determined by the nature of the consummatory response (Locurto, Chapter 4, and Wasserman, Chapter 2, of this volume). When S signals a food S^*, the pigeon pecks the key as if it were seizing a grain of food; when S signals a water S^*, the pigeon strikes the key with a drinking motion (Jenkins & Moore, 1973).
4. The rapidity with which an autoshaped response is conditioned varies inversely with the duration of the intertrial interval (Terrace, Gibbon, Farrell & Baldock, 1975). More generally, acquisition varies inversely with the ratio of durations of trial interval to duration of intertrial interval (Gibbon, Baldock, Locurto, Gold & Terrace, 1977; see also [Gibbon & Balsam], Chapter 7, and [Jenkins], Chapter 8, of this volume).

1. INTRODUCTION: AUTOSHAPING AND TWO-FACTOR LEARNING THEORY | 3

In a typical autoshaping experiment, pigeons are trained by the following paradigm. The response key in a standard conditioning apparatus (e.g., Ferster & Skinner, 1957) is illuminated for a brief fixed period of time (usually less than 10 sec). Food is presented at the offset of key illumination. Other variations of this procedure have been used in studies on pigeons with different stimuli and reinforcers. To a lesser extent, and with varying degrees of success, autoshaping has been studied in other organisms, for example, fish (Squier, 1969), chicks (Wasserman, 1973; Zolman, Chadler & Black, 1972), quail (Gardner, 1969), rats (Leslie, Boakes, Linaza & Ridgers, 1979; Peterson, Ackil, Frommer & Hearst, 1972), dogs (Smith & Smith, 1971), and monkeys (Sidman & Fletcher, 1968), as well as in human children (Zeiler, 1972).

ARE AUTOSHAPED KEYPECKS "SUPERSTITIOUS" CONDITIONED OPERANTS?

Particularly because pigeons peck during omission training and thereby cancel programmed reinforcers, autoshaped behavior has been regarded as a "clear violation of the law of effect" (Schwartz & Gamzu, 1977, p. 63). This conclusion was challenged by Herrnstein, (1977a,b), in what appears to be the only attempt to show how the law of effect could account for behavior established by an autoshaping (classical conditioning) paradigm.[1]

In discussing such behavioral anomalies as autoshaped keypecks, Herrnstein hypothesized that the act of pecking is itself reinforcing. If this hypothesis is correct, it obviates the embarrassment posed for the law of effect by responding that cancels food reinforcement: The pigeon pecks during omission training because it feels good. Herrnstein offered similar explanations of other instances of species-specific behavior that seem to violate the law of effect (see, for example, the summary by Seligman and Hager, 1972).

Skinner (1977) criticized Herrnstein's hypothesis concerning the self-reinforcing effect of behavior as gratuitous on the grounds that the behavior it seeks to explain can be accounted for adequately by the phylogeny of that behavior. For our purposes, the failure of Herrnstein's hypothesis to explain some basic facts about autoshaping is of more immediate concern. Most troublesome is the fact that keypecks are conditioned and maintained by an autoshaping paradigm only when the probability that S^* follows S is greater than the probability of S^* during $\bar{S}$. If pecking occurs because of its hedonic value, pecking should occur whether or not there is a contingency between S and S^*. Herrn-

---

[1]Hursh, Naverick, and Fantino (1974) have suggested that the offset of S functions as a secondary reinforcer (because it is followed by the primary reinforcer). Accordingly, pecks to S are reinforced instrumentally. This explanation has not been confirmed empirically (cf. experiments by Brownstein & Balsam, 1975; Herrnstein & Loveland, 1972; and Schwartz, 1972).

stein's hedonic explanation of pecking also fails to explain why pecking occurs only during the signal. The absence of pecking during the intertrial interval (ITI) cannot be explained by the fact that pigeons rarely peck dark keys. Numerous studies (e.g., Brown and Jenkins, 1968; Herrnstein & Loveland, 1972) have programmed, during the intertrial interval a lit key whose color differed from the color of the signal. Responding during the intertrial interval was nil in all of these studies.[2] Another difficulty posed by Herrnstein's account of autoshaping is its limited scope. Herrnstein states that the law of effect is "best reserved as a principle of maintenance (and) not of learning [Herrnstein, 1977b, p. 1014]."

Efforts to explain the first peck(s) observed in autoshaping experiments by appeal to the law of effect have proved similarly unsuccessful. The hypothesis that autoshaped pecks are somehow shaped from operant-level pecks is not plausible since the operant level of pecking appears to be quite low (cf. Brown & Jenkins, 1968; Gibbon, Farrell, Locurto, Duncan, & Terrace, 1980). Explanations that appeal to the adventitious reinforcement of approach behavior or of incipient pecks directed towards the key can be rejected on the grounds that the universal outcome of autoshaping experiments is actual pecking and not the pre-pecking behavior occasionally observed following the onset of the key light (cf. Jenkins, 1973).

IS AUTOSHAPED BEHAVIOR CLASSICALLY CONDITIONED?

The hypothesis that keypecks conditioned in a Skinner box are classically conditioned was not considered seriously prior to the discovery of autoshaping. Longo, Klempay and Bitterman (1964) actually reported the classical conditioning of keypeck (S=key-light; S*=food). But even if these researchers had claimed that the millions of keypecks that have been recorded in operant conditioning laboratories were instances of classical conditioning (a claim they did not make), it would have been difficult to substantiate that view at the time of their study. As Kimble (1961) and others have observed, the use of a classical conditioning paradigm does not guarantee that the outcome will be classically conditioned behavior. Because it is difficult, if not impossible, to prevent instrumental con-

---

[2]In one study (Gibbon, Locurto, & Terrace, 1975), responding occurred during an ITI in which the key light was illuminated. This responding, however, was emitted at a low rate and appears to have been more under the control of stimulus onset (the duration of the ITI was only 1.5 sec) than under the control of the value of the ITI stimulus. Under the noncontingent procedure there was no responding to any of the colors.

tingencies from influencing behavior while a classical conditioning paradigm is in effect, such training could give rise to instrumental as well as to classical conditioning. (It is, of course, equally true that an instrumental conditioning paradigm does not preclude the establishment of classically conditioned behavior.)

As the term they coined implies, Brown and Jenkins (1968) viewed autoshaping as an instrumental process. Brown and Jenkins cautioned, however, that it is "unwise to ignore the possibility that some form of classical conditioning contributes to the result [1968, p. 7]." The view that autoshaped keypecks and perhaps all instances of autoshaped behavior, should be regarded as examples of classical rather than instrumental conditioning (cf. Bindra, 1972; Mackintosh, 1974; Moore, 1973; Skinner, 1971) evolved from three lines of research that were summarized earlier: the similarity between the topographies of the conditioned and unconditioned behavior, the necessity for a contingency between S and S*, and the insensitivity of autoshaped behavior to omission training.

Jenkins and Moore's (1973) demonstration that the topography of autoshaped keypecks could be predicted from a knowledge of the topography of the consummatory responses elicited by the US was consistent with Pavlov's view that classical conditioning could be explained as stimulus substitution: By virtue of pairing the CS and the US, the CS comes to elicit a response similar to that elicited by the US. Rescorla's (1967) observation that a contingency between S and S* (as opposed to their mere continguity) was a necessary condition for the occurrence of classical conditioning was confirmed by studies that showed that autoshaped behavior can be conditioned and maintained only if a contingency exists between S and S*. As will be discussed below, however, the contingency between S and S* (a procedural factor) does not force the conclusion that autoshaped behavior is classically conditioned. Williams and Williams's (1969) demonstration of the refractoriness of keypecks to an instrumental omission contingency was the first reported example of a skeletal response that, in its insensitivity to such a contingency, resembled autonomically mediated behavior (cf. Sheffield, 1965). Typically, studies of omission training presuppose a conditioned response (e.g., pecking the key or approaching it; see Locurto, Chapter 4, and Williams, Chapter 3 this volume, for further discussion). Accordingly, they are more relevant to theories concerned with the maintenance of behavior than they are to theories of acquisition.

Acquisition

At first glance, similarities between the topographies of the CR and UR appear to provide the most telling evidence of the role that classical conditioning plays in the acquisition of autoshaped behavior. Such similarities, which support the view that the CS comes to serve as a substitute for the US, have been noted in a variety of examples of autoshaped behavior. Aside from Jenkins and Moore's (1973) observation of "food" and "water" pecks, Rackham (1971) has shown that a male pigeon will exhibit courtship behavior to a CS that signals the availability of its mate. Wasserman (1973) has shown that young chicks will peck at a light, in a low-temperature environment, that signals the activation of a heat lamp. The UR to the heat lamp consisted of one or more of the following: a reduction in activity, "twittering" sounds, lowering of the body, extension of the wings, and rubbing the floor beneath the lamp with the chest. Some components of the UR (e.g., the "twittering" vocalization and body lowering) accompanied key pecking; others did not. In a strict sense Wasserman's autoshaping study did not produce a CR that resembled the UR. However, some observations by Hogan (1974) lend credence to the view that the CR and the UR of Wasserman's chicks were similar. According to Hogan, young chicks often initiate contact with the mother hen by pecking and snuggling up to her.

Other examples of classically conditioned and autoshaped behavior pose more problems for stimulus substitution theory. The literature on classical conditioning contains exceptions to the generalization that the CR resembles the UR (cf. Gormezano & Moore, 1969; Terrace, 1973). Even when the full scope of changes in behavior that define the CR are examined, the CR often turns out to be quite different from the UR (e.g., heart deceleration vs. heart acceleration). While Wasserman's data on the differences between the CR and UR can be regarded as equivocal, a study of autoshaping in rats by Timberlake and Grant (1975) provides a telling exception to the principle of stimulus substitution as applied to autoshaped behavior. When a block of wood sliding down a chute signaled the occurrence of food, the CR consisted of gnawing at S. When another rat served as the CS, the CR consisted of social behavior toward S.

A variation of stimulus substitution theory, suggested by Hearst and Jenkins (1974), construes S as a surrogate, rather than as a substitute for S^*. This idea is especially relevant to directed skeletal responses that are characteristic of autoshaped behavior. Direction need not (indeed cannot) be specified in the case of autonomically mediated reflexes such as salivation, heart rate, and change in skin resistance. In the case of autoshaped behavior it is often the direction of the CR per se that is an exception to the principle of stimulus substitution theory. Autoshaped keypecks, for example, are directed at S and not at the food magazine (as called for by stimulus substitution theory). If, however, S is regarded as a surrogate of S^*, one would expect the pigeon to approach and peck the key as if it were grain.

To emphasize that autoshaped behavior is directed toward a stimulus by virtue of that stimulus's relationship with a reinforcer, Hearst and Jenkins (1974) referred to such behavior as *sign tracking*. The term *sign* calls attention to the importance of the relationship between S and S^* during the conditioning and the maintenance of autoshaped responses. The term *tracking* calls attention to an organism's "orientation, approach and contact responses directed towards signs of particular reinforcers" (Hearst and Jenkins, 1974, p. 4) as well as to such related phenomena as feature-positive and feature-negative discriminations. Hearst and Jenkins also noted that the term *sign tracking* avoids the erroneous suggestion (implied by the term *autoshaping*) that autoshaped behavior can be explained by the law of effect.

Hearst and Jenkins have also applied the concept of sign tracking to situations in which an organism comes to move *away* from a stimulus that signals the nonoccurrence of food. Wasserman, Franklin and Hearst (1974) for example, performed a study in which, for one group of subjects, S was explicitly unpaired with food. Those subjects spent more time on the side of the chamber *opposite* the key than did either an explicitly paired group or a group to which only S was presented. The explicitly paired group approached S; the S-only group showed no tendency either to approach or to withdraw from S.

The interesting observation that an organism distances itself from a stimulus that is negatively correlated with a reinforcer is consistent with the concept of sign tracking. At the same time, however, it reveals a difficulty in equating sign tracking with many traditional instances of classically conditioned behavior. When a reflex ($S^* \rightarrow R^*$) occurs, R^*, by definition, is elicited by some S^*. In the case of "negative" sign tracking it is unclear how withdrawal can be elicited by $\bar{S}^*$ or by a negative contingency between S and S^*. Even if one were to argue that, in the case of a positive contingency between S and S^*, approach behavior to S is the same as approach behavior elicited by S^*, the argument that S, as defined in the contingency, $S-\bar{S}^*$, *elicits* withdrawal from S is implausible.

The concepts of surrogation and sign tracking emphasize correctly the association (either positive or negative) that develops between S and S^* by virtue of the autoshaping paradigm. However, such a formulation of autoshaped behavior cannot specify the nature of the CR, given the nature of the UR. Nor does it follow that the association in question is the product of classical conditioning. To make that argument is to define classical conditioning as nothing more than a learned association between two stimuli. The weakness of such a definition is its inability to specify the form of the CR (cf. Osgood, 1953, p. 391; see also Wasserman, Chapter 2 of this volume, for a fuller discussion of this problem).

In answering the question as to whether autoshaped behavior is classically conditioned, our point of departure was the inability of the law of effect to account for the acquisition of such behavior. Given that autoshaped behavior is conditioned by means of a classical conditioning paradigm, and given the inadequacy of the remaining factor of two-factor learning theory to explain the acquisition of autoshaped behavior, it seems logical (within the framework of that theory) to conclude that autoshaped behavior is classically conditioned. We have seen, however, that stimulus substitution, the only theoretical process offered to explain classical conditioning, cannot predict many important aspects of behavior conditioned by Pavlovian conditioning procedures. Before pursuing alternative formulations of such behavior, it would be helpful to consider the role of $S-S^*$ contingencies in the maintenance of autoshaped behavior.

Maintenance

Studies of omission training pose an obvious problem: Why would a pigeon peck at a stimulus that normally signals food when pecking results in the cancellation of food?

That autoshaped behavior is not completely insensitive to the law of effect was shown by two studies, both of which employed within-subject designs. Schwartz and Williams (1972) compared choice and rate of responding under $S-S^*$ and $R-S^*$ contingencies in which the frequencies of S^* were matched. Jenkins (1977) showed that the relaxation of *either* the $S-S^*$ or the $R-S^*$ contingencies in an $S(R-S^*)$ paradigm led to similar decrements in responding of keypeck and head-positioning responses in the pigeon.

In the Schwartz and Williams study, two stimuli were alternated successively; one was associated with an omission contingency, (S1), the other (S2) was not. Each stimulus signalled food in a conventional autoshaping paradigm. The frequency of reinforcement that occurred in the presence of both signals was matched as follows. When the omission contingency was in effect, the frequency of reinforcement was related inversely to the probability of pecking S1. The frequency of reinforcement obtained in the presence of S2 was determined solely by performance on the omission key. Following an omission trial in which one or more pecks occurred, reinforcement was cancelled on the next trial in which S2 was presented, irrespective of the subject's performance on that trial. Omission trials on which pecking did not occur insured that reinforcement would be obtained on a subsequent non-omission trial—again, irrespective of the subject's behavior on that trial.

Even though the omission contingency did not eliminate pecking, Schwartz and Williams (1972) showed that their subjects were sensitive to its presence. The rate of pecking to S1 was lower than the rate of pecking to S2. When the two keys were presented simultaneously, the pigeons preferred the key that was not associated with the omission contingency. Since the densities of reinforcement obtained in the presence of each stimulus were matched, these differences could be attributed directly to the presence or absence of the omission contingency.

Jenkins's (1977) study directed attention to two important assumptions that have been implicit in most studies of omission training. One is that if an $R-S^*$ contingency has no effect on autoshaped behavior [in particular, an $\bar{R}-S^*$ (omission) contingency], the adventitious $R-S^*$ contingency that is inherent in a typical autoshaping paradigm also has no effect.

Jenkins questioned this assumption on both logical and empirical grounds. Before examining the data that bear on this question it would be helpful to consider a second, more general, assumption that Jenkins questioned, one that he referred to aptly as the *origin hypothesis:* The contingency in effect at the time of occurrence of the initial CR is crucial in defining whether the CR is an instance of operantly conditioned behavior (that is controlled by an $R-S^*$ contingency) *or* an instance of classically conditioned behavior (that is controlled by an $S-S^*$ contingency). As we shall see later, the origin hypothesis was an important feature of the first formulations of two-factor theory (Konorski & Miller, 1937; Miller & Konorski, 1928; Schlosberg, 1937; Skinner, 1935).

Jenkins (1977) compared the effect of different contingencies on the relative frequency of two responses—a keypeck that was conditioned by an autoshaping paradigm and a head-positioning response that had to be conditioned by the instrumental method of reinforcing successive approximations of the desired responses. The head-positioning response was defined as the interruption of a pair of infrared photo-cell beams (neck-high) at right angles to one another in the center of the chamber. Reinforcement for head-positioning occurred only in the presence of an auditory discriminative stimulus (white noise). Unlike the autoshaped keypeck, the head-positioning response could not be established by an $S-S^*$ contingency. Also, it was not directed at the signal for food and it was not a natural component of food-obtaining behavior.

In comparing the keypeck and head-positioning responses, Jenkins sought to evaluate the extent to which a response is sensitive to contingencies other than the one used to condition it. According to the either–or logic of the origin hypothesis, a response conditioned by a classical conditioning paradigm should be sensitive only to $S-S^*$ contingencies and a response conditioned by an instrumental conditioning paradigm should likewise be sensitive only to $R-S^*$ contingencies. Consistent with this point of view are the assertions that responses mediated by the autonomic nervous system are insensitive to $R-S^*$ contingencies and that skeletal responses are insensitive to $S-S^*$ contingencies. At the very least, studies of autoshaping have shown the latter assertion to be false.

If a conditioned response is sensitive only to the contingency employed at the outset of conditioning, one would not expect keypecks established by an $S-S^*$ contingency to be sensitive to the presence or absence of an $R-S^*$ contingency. Likewise, one would not expect a head-positioning response established by an $R-S^*$ contingency to be sensitive to the presence or absence of an $S-S^*$ contingency. Studies of omission training provide empirical support for this view in that they show that responses that are conditioned by an $S-S^*$ contingency are relatively insensitive to an $R-S^*$ contingency.

Having conditioned the keypeck and the head-positioning responses, Jenkins placed *both* responses on a joint $S(R-S^*)$ contingency: Responding was reinforced only in the presence of a signal (the key light for keypeck birds and noise for head-positioning birds) and only if the required responses occurred. In order to test for the influence of $S-S^*$ and $R-S^*$ contingencies, Jenkins relaxed the $S(R-S^*)$ contingency, in different phases of the experiment, in one of two ways. During the $S-S^*$ phase, the $R-S^*$ contingency was not in effect. Food was contingent only on the occurrence of S. This condition makes explicit the implicit $S-S^*$ contingency that arises from the $S(R-S^*)$ contingency. During the $R-S^*$ phase, the $S-S^*$ contingency was removed by presenting food during the ITI at the same rate as in the presence of S. (In the presence of S, the $R-S^*$ contingency was in effect.)

Both pecking and head-positioning were influenced similarly by variations of the original $S(R-S^*)$ contingency. When the $R-S^*$ contingency was eliminated, the relative frequency of both head-positioning and keypecking responses decreased; head-positioning decreased somewhat more than keypecking relative to the baseline rate that obtained under the joint $S(R-S^*)$ contingency. The rate of both responses also decreased when the $S-S^*$ contingency was removed; the relative frequency of keypecks was somewhat higher than the frequency of head-positioning responses. While these results did not allow Jenkins to identify the actual role of the various contingencies he manipulated, they do show why it is erroneous to conclude that $R-S^*$ relations do not influence autoshaped behavior.

Keypecking was shown to be supported by an $R-S^*$ contingency even though it is known that it is difficult to suppress that response during omission training. Although Jenkins did not employ an omission training procedure in this experiment he assumed that "the outcome would certainly demonstrate that the system was sensitive to a response-reinforcer relation. [That]... would not, of course, mean that the response was being supported solely by, or even predominately by, positive $R-S^*$ relations that existed prior to the introduction of the omission contingency [Jenkins, 1977, p. 61]."

In noting that the joint $S(R-S^*)$ contingency has properties similar to that of the behavioral unit that Skinner refers to as a *discriminative operant* ($S^D:R \rightarrow S^R$), Jenkins concluded that autoshaped behavior cannot be accounted for by appeal to a correlation between a *single* pair of stimuli. Just as the discriminative operant is not reducible to a pair of contingencies between S^D and S^R and between R and S^R, an account of behavior maintained by an autoshaping paradigm requires a specification of all three terms of the $S(R-S^*)$ contingency, along with the two subordinate contingencies ($R-S^*$ and $S-S^*$).

WHAT SUFFICES AS A MINIMAL UNIT OF CONDITIONING?

A major thrust of the empirical and theoretical literature on autoshaping can be construed as negative: It was generally concluded that $R-S^*$ (as compared with $S-S^*$) contingencies contributed minimally to the conditioning of autoshaped behavior (see, e.g., Bindra, 1972; Moore, 1973; and Williams and Williams, 1969). This state of affairs has left a void that the logic of two-factor learning theory tried to fill by invoking $S-S^*$ contingencies to explain autoshaping. As we have seen, however, this logic is hampered by the absence of a universally applicable theory of just how a particular response becomes conditioned by virtue of an $S-S^*$ contingency. It is widely recognized that, except for the limited concept of stimulus substitution, an $S-S^*$ theory cannot predict how an organism's behavior will reflect knowledge of an $S-S^*$ association. Designating the behavioral manifestation of an $S-S^*$ association as a problem of "performance" merely relabels the phenomena in question. What is needed is a theoretical formulation of conditioning and conditioned behavior that includes the CR; without the latter, of course, there would be no basis for asserting that conditioning actually occurred (see Locurto, Chapter 3, and Wasserman, Chapter 4 of this volume, for other approaches to this problem).

A major obstacle to the realization of such a theory is the seemingly reasonable strategy of trying to isolate a *single* pair of elements in explaining an instance of conditioned behavior. Although the appeal of such minimal units is obvious there are many lines of evidence (aside from the literature on autoshaping) that suggest that isolated $S-S^*$ and $R-S^*$ associations cannot capture the complexities of the many phenomena they seek to explain (cf. Catania, 1971; Rescorla & Solomon, 1967).

Given such evidence, it is of interest to review Skinner's classic argument in support of a mutually exclusive two-factor theory. In his early formulation of operant conditioning, Skinner (1937) discounted as irrelevant the prevailing stimulus conditions. Though he later modified his position to recognize the role played by "discriminative stimuli" in exerting "stimulus control" (Skinner, 1953, 1974; Terrace, 1966, 1970), Skinner consistently denied that a stimulus that precedes an operant functions as an eliciting stimulus:

> There is ... a kind of response which occurs spontaneously in the absence of any stimulation with which it may be specifically correlated. ... It does not mean that we cannot find the stimulus that elicits such behavior, but that none is operative at the time the behavior is observed. It is the nature of this kind of behavior that it should occur without an eliciting stimulus, although discriminative stimuli are practically inevitable after conditioning [Skinner, 1937, p. 274].

Skinner denied the eliciting function of stimuli that precede a conditioned operant, in order to avoid certain "difficulties": "The introduction of the notion of the operant clears up many difficulties. ... It eliminates the implausible assumption that all reflexes ultimately conditioned according to Type R may be spoken of as existing as identifiable units in unconditioned behavior and substitutes the simple assumption that all operant responses are generated out of undifferentiated material [Skinner, 1937, p. 380]." During recent years, the literature that has accumulated under the heading of "biological constraints" suggests that much of what Skinner referred to as *Type R* behavior does in fact exist as "identifiable units in unconditioned behavior" (see Wasserman, Chapter 2 of this volume, for additional discussion; also see Skinner, 1966, for a discussion of the phylogeny, as opposed to the ontogeny, of behavior).

Consistent with Skinner's early view that antecedent stimuli are not basic to the specification of a conditioned operant is his term *pseudo-reflexes*, for arrangements in which antecedent stimuli do appear to exert an influence (Skinner, 1935). Even when a neutral stimulus elicits a response, and the frequency of that response is increased by virtue of an instrumental contingency, Skinner regards S as incidental to the conditioning process. An interesting example is Skinner's analysis of Konorski and Miller's (1937) demonstration that a dog can be conditioned to flex its leg by first eliciting flexion with a mild electric shock and then reinforcing flexion with food. Prior to its reinforcement with food, the occurrence of the flexion response was controlled exclusively by the administration of electric shock. Skinner nevertheless regarded the conditioned flexion response maintained by food as a conditioned operant.

The paradigm used by Konorski and Miller bears an important similarity to the autoshaping paradigm. In both cases a response is elicited by a stimulus and then followed by reinforcement. While the factors responsible for the occurrence of the response may differ in each case (shock in one case, the signaling of reinforcement by a small visual stimulus in the other), the outcome appears to be the same.

Konorski and Miller's study and the recent literature on autoshaping suggest that the operations used to produce conditioning are of minimal importance in specifying the nature of the conditioning process. Imagine, for example, some mechanical procedure for getting a pigeon to position his head in the manner required of Jenkins' head-positioning subjects. (Possible procedures include a mild shock to the base of the neck that elicits the desired response when the bird is appropriately positioned in the chamber or a gentle pulling of one of more strings attached to the pigeon's head.) It is doubtful that the subsequent control exerted by $R-S^*$ or $S-S^*$ contingencies would reflect the origin of the head-positioning response, that is, whether it was elicited or shaped.

Quite clearly, the "difficulties" Skinner hoped to avoid by ignoring stimuli antecedent to R can be ignored only at the price of oversimplification. We have seen that a description of an $R-S^*$ contingency that does not include antecedent stimuli is incomplete for two reasons. Skinner (1937) himself recognized one reason in his analysis of pseudo-reflexes: The omission of the antecedent stimuli yields an incomplete specification of the stimulus conditions under which an $R-S^*$ contingency is in effect. A second reason is the unavoidable potential of uncontrolled $S-S^*$ contingencies for exerting some influences on any conditioning procedure.

The origin hypothesis has served as a major obstacle to the view that a conditioned response is controlled jointly by $S-S^*$ and $R-S^*$ contingencies. The notion that only certain classes of responses are susceptible to particular contingencies (e.g., skeletal versus autonomic responses) further strengthened the view that conditioned behavior could be dichotomized into two nonoverlapping types. Evidence against the origin hypothesis includes the fact that responses such as the keypeck and the bar-press can be elicited (or *released*, to use the term favored by Williams; cf. Chapter 3, this volume) and that, as shown by Jenkins's experiment, $S-S^*$ and $R-S^*$ contingencies exert similar influences on responses established by one or the other contingency.

If one's purpose in analyzing the learning process is simply to reveal the different types of contingencies that can exert an influence on learning, it is reasonable to adopt the strategy of Skinner and other two-factor learning theorists of focusing on $S-S^*$ or $R-S^*$ contingencies separately. However, as the literature on autoshaping clearly shows, a minimal description of the learning process requires a specification of the *joint* influence of $S-S^*$ and $R-S^*$ contingencies. These contingencies enjoy separate existences only as analytic abstractors (see Locurto, Chapter 4 this volume).

An alternative to the approach of considering only one of two mutually exclusive contingencies is Williams's formulation of autoshaping, which makes provision for the joint and simultaneous influence of $S-S^*$ and $R-S^*$ contingencies (see Chapter 3, this volume). Prior to the first keypeck one need only specify the $S-S^*$ contingency and "biological factors" that influence what response systems will be evoked. But after the response in question has been conditioned, the influence of what Williams refers to as a "piggy-back" contingency between R and S^* has to be recognized.

Once the ontogeny of the CR is dropped as a defining characteristic of the conditioning process, the question of interest is what determines the relative influence of different types of contingencies. As noted by Wasserman (Chapter 2, this volume) certain species-specific responses may prove to be more sensitive to $S-S^*$ contingencies (cf., Solomon & Turner, 1962). Other types of response may prove to be maximally sensitive to $R-S^*$ contingencies. This state of affairs should not be regarded as an anomaly but rather as a continuum of sensitivity to different types of contingencies. An important contribution of the literature on autoshaping has been to help define the nature of this continuum.

FUTURE DIRECTIONS OF RESEARCH ON AUTOSHAPING

A case has been made that a major contribution of research on autoshaping has been to discredit the notion than an independent $S-S^*$ or $R-S^*$ contingency can fully describe an instance of conditioned behavior. As, the contents of this book will reveal, however, studies of autoshaping have the potential of making many positive contributions to our understanding of the learning process.

One issue, which Williams (Chapter 3) refers to as the *biology of association*, has to do with what responses in what organisms can be autoshaped and with what reinforcers. It was noted earlier that the subjects of most studies of autoshaping have been pigeons and that the stimuli used in these studies have been punctate visual stimuli. While it is easy to understand the appeal of the highly developed technology for automatically presenting visual stimuli and reinforcers and for recording keypecks, the disproportionate amount of effort that has been invested in such studies runs the risk of yielding information about autoshaping that is of a limited generality. Attention must obviously be paid to variations in the susceptibility of different response systems in different organisms to autoshaping and omission training paradigms. Powell and Kelly (1976) for example, suggest that crows are not easily autoshaped and that crow's keypecks (established by reinforcing successive approximations) are highly responsive to the effects of omission training. This and related issues are amenable to study within the framework of autoshaping.

An important example of the role that the biology of association plays can be seen in the relationship between autoshaping and behavioral contrast. The role of autoshaping in positive contrast has been described by the *additivity hypothesis* (cf., Rachlin, 1973; Schwartz and Gamzu, 1977). Following baseline training to two alternating stimuli (S1 and S2), each associated with identical schedules of reinforcement, a differential reinforcement procedure is instituted in which reinforcement is available only in the presence of S1. The usual result is positive contrast, an increase in the rate of responding to S1 that accompanies the decrease in the rate of responding to S2 (Reynolds, 1961; Terrace, 1963). The additivity hypothesis draws attention to the similarity of the procedure used to produce positive contrast and that used to produce autoshaped pecking. Numerous studies (e.g., Gamzu and Schwartz, 1973) have shown that pecks can be autoshaped only when $p(S^* \mid S1) > p(S^* \mid S2)$, a contingency inherent in the differential reinforcement paradigm used to produce positive contrast. Rachlin (1973) and Gamzu and Schwartz (1973) argued that the increase in the rate of responding to S1 observed in studies of positive contrast could be accounted for by the "autopecks" engendered by the differential reinforcement procedure. While positive contrast cannot be accounted for completely by appeal to autopecks, (cf. Hamilton & Silberberg, 1978; Hemmes, 1973; Whipple & Fantino, 1979; Ziriax & Silberberg, 1978), the free-operant multiple schedule serves as an important example of how $S-S^*$ and $R-S^*$ contingencies can jointly influence conditioned behavior.

Because of their reliability in establishing conditioned behavior, autoshaping paradigms provide an unusually good opportunity to obtain parametric data on variables that influence the acquisition of such behavior, an issue that Williams refers to as the *psychophysics of association*. Several chapters in this book address that question. Gibbon and Balsam (Chapter 7) present a model that encompasses a large body of data concerning the influence of the durations of trial and intertrial intervals and of the probability that a trial will terminate with reinforcement on acquisition. The way an organism times the durations of trial and intertrial intervals and uses that information is the focus of chapters by Jenkins (Chapter 8) and Gibbon (Chapter 9). Rashotte, discussing second order conditioning, (Chapter 5) and Tomie, discussing blocking, (Chapter 6) also provide data of general interest regarding the associative process. Now that the phenomenon of autoshaping has shown how the law of effect and two-factor learning theory need to be qualified, the autoshaping paradigm appears to be making another, independent contribution to learning theory in the opportunity it provides for systematic study of the nature of the associative process.

REFERENCES

Bindra, D. A unified account of classical conditioning and operant training. In A. H. Black & W. F. Prokasy (Eds.), *Classical conditioning II: Current theory and research.* New York: Appleton-Century-Crofts, 1972.

Breland, K., & Breland, M. The misbehavior of organisms. *American Psychologist*, 1961, 16, 681–684.

Brown, P. L., & Jenkins, H. M. Auto-shaping of the pigeon's keypeck. *Journal of the Experimental Analysis of Behavior*, 1968, 11, 1–8.

Brownstein, A. J., & Balsam, P. D. A search for conditioned reinforcement effects in negative automaintenance of keypecking. *Bulletin of the Psychonomic Society*, 1975, 6, 165–168.

Catania, A. C. Elicitation, reinforcement, and stimulus control. In R. Glaser (Ed.), *The nature of reinforcement.* New York: Academic Press, 1971.

Ferster, C. B., & Skinner, B. F. *Schedules of reinforcement.* Englewood Cliffs, New Jersey: Prentice-Hall, 1957.

Gamzu, E., & Schwartz, B. The maintenance of keypecking in stimulus-contingent and response-independent food presentation. *Journal of the Experimental Analysis of Behavior*, 1973, 19, 65–72.

Gardner, W. M. Auto-shaping in bobwhite quail. *Journal of the Experimental Analysis of Behavior*, 1969, 12, 279–281.

Gibbon, J., Baldock, M., Locurto, C., Gold, L., & Terrace, H. S. Trial and intertrial durations in autoshaping. *Journal of Experimental Psychology: Animal Behavior Processes*, 1977, 3, 264–284.

Gibbon, J., Farrell, L., Locurto, C. M., Duncan, H. S., & Terrace, H. S. Partial reinforcement in auto-shaping. *Animal Learning and Behavior*, 1980, 8, 45–59.

Gibbon, J., Locurto, C., & Terrace, H. S. Signal-food contingency and signal frequency in a continuous-trials auto-shaping paradigm. *Animal Learning and Behavior*, 1976, 3, 317–324.

Gormezano, I., & Moore, J. W. Classical conditioning. In M. H. Marx (Ed.), *Learning: Processes.* London: Macmillan, 1969.

Hamilton, B. E., & Silberberg, A. Contrast and autoshaping in multiple schedules varying reinforcer rate and duration. *Journal of the Experimental Analysis of Behavior*, 1978, 30, 107–122.

Hearst, E., & Jenkins, H. M. Sign tracking: The stimulus–reinforcer relation and directed action. *Monograph of the Psychonomic Society*, 1974.

Hemmes, N. S. Behavioral contrast in pigeons depends on the operant. *Journal of Comparative and Physiological Psychology*, 1973, 85, 171–178.

Herrnstein, R. J. The evolution of behaviorism. *American Psychologist*, 1977, 32, 593–603. (a)

Herrnstein, R. J. Doing what comes naturally: A reply to Professor Skinner. *American Psychologist*, 1977, 32, 1013–1016. (b)

Herrnstein, R. J., & Loveland, D. H. Food-avoidance in hungry pigeons, and other perplexities. *Journal of the Experimental Analysis of Behavior*, 1972, 18, 369–383.

Hogan, J. A. Response in Pavlovian conditioning studies. *Science*, 1974, 186, 156–157.

Hursh, S. R., Navarick, D. J., & Fantino, E. "Automaintenance": The role of reinforcement. *Journal of the Experimental Analysis of Behavior*, 1974, 21, 112–124.

Jenkins, H. M. Effects of the stimulus reinforcer relation on selected and unselected responses. In R. A. Hinde & J. S. Hinde (Eds.), *Constraints on learning*. New York: Academic Press, 1973.

Jenkins, H. M. Sensitivity of different response systems to stimulus-reinforcer and response-reinforcer relations. In H. Davis & H. M. B. Hurwitz (Eds.), *Operant–Pavlovian interactions*. Hillsdale, New Jersey: Erlbaum, 1977.

Jenkins, H. M., & Moore, B. R. The form of the auto-shaped response with food or water reinforcers. *Journal of the Experimental Analysis of Behavior*, 1973, 20, 163–181.

Kimble, G. A. *Hilgard and Marquis conditioning and learning*. Englewood Cliffs, N.J.: Prentice-Hall, 1961.

Konorski, J., & Miller, S. On two types of conditioned reflex. *Journal of Genetic Psychology*, 1937, 16, 264–272.

Leslie, J. L., Boakes, B. A., Linaza, J., & Ridgers, A. Autoshaping using visual stimuli in the rat. *The Psychological Record*, 1979, 29, 523–546.

Longo, N., Klempay, S., & Bitterman, M. E. Classical appetitive conditioning in the pigeon. *Psychonomic Science*, 1964, 1, 19–20.

MacKintosh, N. J. *The psychology of animal learning*. London: Academic Press, 1974.

Miller, S., & Konorski, J. Sur une forme particulière des reflexes conditionnels. *Compte Rendu Hebdomadaire dea Séances et Memoires de la Societé de Biologie*, 1928, 99, 1151–1157.

Moore, B. R. The role of directed Pavlovian reactions in simple instrumental learning in the pigeon. In R. A. Hinde & J. S. Hinde (Eds.), *Constraints on learning*. New York: Academic Press, 1973.

Osgood, C. E. *Method and theory in experimental psychology*. New York and London: Oxford Univ. Press, 1953.

Pavlov, I. P. *Conditioned reflexes*. New York and London: Oxford Univ. Press, 1927.

Peterson, G. B., Ackil, J., Frommer, G. P., & Hearst, E. Conditioned approach and contact behavior toward signals for food or brain-stimulation reinforcement. *Science*, 1972, 177, 1009–1011.

Powell, R. W., & Kelly, W. Responding under positive and negative response contingencies in pigeons and crows. *Journal of the Experimental Analysis of Behavior*, 1976, 25, 219–225.

Rachlin, H. Contrast and matching. *Psychological Review*, 1973, 80, 217–234.

Rackham, D. *Conditioning of the pigeon's courtship and aggressive behavior*. Unpublished master's thesis, Dalhousie University, 1971.

Rescorla, R. A. Pavlovian conditioning and its proper control procedures. *Psychological Review*, 1967, 74, 71–80.

Rescorla, R. A., & Solomon, R. S. Two-process learning theory: Relationships between Pavlovian conditioning and instrumental learning. *Psychological Review*, 1967, 74, 151–182.

Reynolds, G. S. Behavioral contrast. *Journal of the Experimental Analysis of Behavior*, 1961, 4, 57–71.

Schlosberg, H. The relationship between success and the laws of conditioning. *Psychological Review*, 1937, *44*, 379–394.
Schwartz, B. The role of positive conditioned reinforcement in the maintenance of key pecking which prevents delivery of primary reinforcement. *Psychonomic Science*, 1972, *28*, 277–278.
Schwartz, B., & Gamzu, E. Pavlovian control of operant behavior. In W. K. Honig & J. E. R. Staddon (Eds.), *Handbook of operant behavior*. Englewood Cliffs, New Jersey: Prentice-Hall, 1977.
Schwartz, B., & Williams, D. R. The role of the response-reinforcer contingency in negative automaintenance. *Journal of the Experimental Analysis of Behavior*, 1972, *17*, 351–357.
Seligman, M. E. P., & Maser, J. L. (Eds). *Biological boundaries of learning*. Englewood Cliffs, N.J.: Prentice-Hall, 1972.
Sheffield, F. D. Relation between classical conditioning and instrumental learning. In W. F. Prokasy (Ed.), *Classical conditioning*. New York: Appleton-Century-Crofts, 1965.
Sidman, M., & Fletcher, F. G. A demonstration of auto-shaping with monkeys. *Journal of the Experimental Analysis of Behavior*, 1968, *11*, 307–309.
Skinner, B. F. Two types of conditioned reflex and a pseudo type. *Journal of Genetic Psychology*, 1935, *12*, 66–67.
Skinner, B. F. Two types of conditioned reflex: A reply to Konorski and Miller, *The Journal of General Psychology*, 1937, *16*, 272–279.
Skinner, B. F. *The behavior of organisms*. New York: Appleton-Century-Crofts, 1938.
Skinner, B. F. *Science and human behavior*. New York: Macmillan, 1953.
Skinner, B. F. The phylogeny and ontogeny of behavior. *Science*, 1966, *153*, 1205–1213.
Skinner, B. F. *Contingencies of reinforcement*. New York: Appleton-Century-Crofts, 1969.
Skinner, B. F. Autoshaping. *Science*, 1971, *173*, 752.
Skinner, B. F. *About behaviorism*. New York: Knopf, 1974.
Skinner, B. F. Herrnstein and the evolution of behaviorism. *American Psychologist*, 1977, *32*, 1006–1012.
Smith, S. G., & Smith, W. M. A demonstration of auto-shaping with dogs. *Psychological Records*, 1971, *21*, 377–379.
Squier, L. H. Auto-shaping key responses in fish. *Psychonomic Science*, 1969, *17*, 177–178.
Terrace, H. S. Discrimination learning with and without "errors." *Journal of the Experimental Analysis of Behavior*, 1963, *6*, 1–27.
Terrace, H. S. Stimulus control. In W. K. Honig (Ed.), *Operant behavior: Areas of research and application*. Englewood Cliffs, N.J.: Prentice-Hall, 1966.
Terrace, H. S. Towards a doctrine of radical behaviorism. Review of Skinner's *Contingencies of reinforcement: A theoretical analysis*. *Contemporary Psychology*, 1970, *15*, 531–535.
Terrace, H. S. Classical conditioning. In J. A. Nevin (Ed.), *The study of behavior*. Glenview, Ill.: Scott, Foresman, 1973.
Terrace, H. S., Gibbon, J., Farrell, L., & Baldock, M. D. Temporal factors influencing the acquisition and maintenance of an autoshaped keypeck. *Animal Learning and Behavior*, 1975, *3*, 52–62.
Timberlake, W., & Grant, D. L. Auto-shaping rats to the presentation of another rat predicting food. *Science*, 1975, *190*, 690–692.
Wasserman, E. A. Pavlovian conditioning with heat reinforcement produces stimulus-directed pecking in chicks. *Science*, 1973, *181*, 875–877.
Whipple, W., & Fantino, E. Unpublished manuscript cited in Fantino, E., & Logan, C. A., *The Experimental analysis of behavior*. San Francisco: Freeman, 1979, p. 133.
Williams, D. R., & Williams, H. Auto-maintenance in the pigeon: Sustained pecking despite contingent nonreinforcement, *Journal of the Experimental Analysis of Behavior*, 1969, *12*, 511–520.

Zeiler, M. D. Superstitious behavior in children: An experimental analysis. *Advances in Child Development and Behavior*, 1972, 7, 1-29.

Ziriax, J. M., & Silberberg, A. Discrimination and emission of different key-peck durations in the pigeon. *Journal of Experimental Psychology: Animal Behavior Processes*, 1978, 4, 1-21.

Zolman, J. F., Chandler, S. D., & Black, D. Visual discrimination learning of the young chick: Key-pecking conditioning with heat-light reinforcement. *Developmental Psychobiology*, 1972, 5, 181-187.

Biological Factors

I

EDWARD A. WASSERMAN

Response Evocation in Autoshaping: Contributions of Cognitive and Comparative-Evolutionary Analyses to an Understanding of Directed Action[1]

Few phenomena have proven so provocative in recent years as *autoshaping*—the conditioning of directed locomotor and manipulative behaviors with response-independent reinforcement procedures. Autoshaping has been important in reappraising the operant–respondent distinction, in evaluating the generality of the laws of learning, and in providing new insights into persistent problems in the stimulus control of behavior (Hearst & Jenkins, 1974; Lajoie & Bindra, 1976; Schwartz & Gamzu, 1977).

The intent of this chapter is to put autoshaping into a rather different light. Instead of emphasizing the associative conditions that are necessary for autoshaping, I will stress the factors that promote the expression of autoshaped behaviors after learning has occurred. Since the factors responsible for response evocation reside both in the external environment of the organism and in its inherited response equipment, situational and evolutionary determinants of response production will each be discussed.

Before considering the issue of response production in autoshaping, however, it will be useful to place the problem in the broader realm of response evocation in behavior theory. Since the issue of response production was brought into bold relief by the distinction between learning and performance, it is to that distinction that I turn first.

---

[1] The preparation of this chapter as well as the research it discusses were supported by grants from the National Science Foundation (BNS 75-15905) and the National Institute of Mental Health (MH-24482). The work was further facilitated by an exchange visit to the Soviet Union sponsored by the National Academy of Sciences, 1976.

THE LEARNING–PERFORMANCE DISTINCTION

> [Although] the distinction between learning and performance is in fact often used, explicitly or implicitly, in the formulation of experimental problems, there has been relatively little systematic concern with the determiners of performance as distinguished from the conditions of learning [Postman, 1968, p. 556].

When certain kinds of changes in the environment lead to certain kinds of changes in the activities of an organism, learning may be said to have occurred. Of course, the occurrence of learning must be inferred because learning is not a thing, but a construct—a construct invented to embrace specific environment–behavior interrelations. We are entitled to conclude that an organism has learned when a reliable and durable change in its behavior has resulted from a change in its environment. But should we conclude that an organism has failed to learn if particular environmental changes have been ineffectual in modifying a specific category of its behavior? What if other action systems had been monitored? What if the conditions of motivation or reinforcement had been otherwise? And even if reliable changes in behavior did result, could they have been produced by other alterations in the environment that are thought not to promote learning, thus raising the question as to whether learning had taken place?

The above queries led the early behavior theorists Lashley and Tolman to distinguish learning from performance. According to this distinction, *learning* denotes the process whereby environmental changes make a relatively permanent imprint on the organism, whereas *performance* concerns the expression of learning through changes in overt behaviors.

Undoubtedly, the learning–performance distinction has been of great value in elucidating many otherwise puzzling phenomena including latent learning and extinction, sensory preconditioning, overtraining effects, and learning under the influence of paralyzing or incapacitating drugs. However, the distinction between learning and performance has also had a rather serious negative effect, as noted in the opening quotation from Postman. For several decades behavior theorists have directed their considerable talents to analyzing the learning process, virtually neglecting to examine the principles of performance.

One aim of the present chapter is to alert contemporary researchers to this empirical and theoretical oversight and to call upon them to redirect their efforts toward a fuller account of the principles of performance. The study of autoshaped behaviors may help to formulate those principles, as we will see later. The next two sections outline the essentials of the learning–performance distinction.

Learning

A striking simplification in the interpretation of many learning phenomena is achieved at a stroke if we conceive the result of an organism's experiencing a sequence of events to be, not simply the strengthening or weakening of the constituent stimulus–response connections, but rather the establishment in memory storage of a representation of the entire sequence, so that later recurrences of earlier members of the sequence lead to anticipation of the later members [Estes, 1969, p. 186].

When unfettered from the requirement of overt response expression, learning is usually thought to involve the formation of an internal representation of a sequence of events—be they stimuli, responses, or reinforcers. The above opinion of Estes is characteristic of the theoretical approach, dubbed "cognitive," that views association formation as (*a*) separable from overt response performance; (*b*) dependent on interevent contiguity; (*c*) independent of any special effects of reward or punishment; and (*d*) the rapid result of an active organism interacting with its surroundings (for critical discussions of this viewpoint see Spence, 1950; Spiker, 1977).

Within the cognitive approach, associations have usually been thought to be of the stimulus–stimulus variety, whether the stimulus events are biologically indifferent or biologically significant to the organism at the moment. The importance of response–stimulus connections is more problematical (for a denial of their importance see Bindra, 1978). However, at least one recent author (Bolles, 1972) joins Tolman (1932) in incorporating response–stimulus associations into a cognitive formulation.

The conditions of association formation have been of primary importance to theorists and researchers in the field of animal psychology for some 80 years. Nonetheless, controversy still surrounds the issue of what are the necessary and sufficient conditions for learning (Gray, 1975; Honig & Staddon, 1977; Mackintosh, 1974). In what follows, I will focus principally upon stimulus–stimulus association, assuming conservatively that temporal contiguity is necessary but not always sufficient for association formation.

Performance

> Perhaps... the question is less one of what is *learned* than it is... of what an organism will *do*?... [We] are inclined to use performance criteria of learning; and with this we are back at the point of having to be able to predict and explain *behavior* in order to talk meaningfully about *learning* [Mowrer, 1960, p. 340].

According to cognitive behavior theories, an organism that has been exposed to a series of events and has formed an internal representation of the events and their order of occurrence has learned (Wasserman & Larew, 1978; Weisman & Dodd, 1979). But this learning will remain latent until something triggers overt action. Here, we come to a difficult and critical problem for cognitive behavior theories: namely, how learning is transformed into performance.

The typical response to this problem is to appeal to motivational constructs that would energize learned behaviors. Unfortunately, cognitive theories (and others as well) usually fail to specify what particular responses will be energized in any given context. Thus, the critical question is not *whether* some behavioral indicant will disclose learning in a conditioning situation—by definition some change in behavior is necessary for inferring that learning has occurred—but *what* particular behaviors will be expressed. This question is central to the response evocation problem.

THE RESPONSE EVOCATION PROBLEM

> Most of the really interesting problems of psychology... will eventually find their place... under the heading of complications in the principles of performance [Tolman, 1955, p. 325].

Despite this pronouncement late in Tolman's career, he was—and most contemporary behavior theorists still are—interested mainly in studying the process of association formation (but see pp. 45–47). In trying to find evidence of learning, investigators commonly adopt a rather curious tactic. *They* choose the response system to be monitored; *they* expose the organism to a change in its environment; and *they* then decide whether changes in the chosen response system were sufficiently reliable and appropriate to claim that learning had occurred. Actually, it is the *organism*, in conjuction with its stimulus surroundings, that selects the behaviors in which it engages as learning unfolds. The experimenter's task is to pick, by whatever means are at hand, those response systems that unequivocally divulge the subject's learning. It is precisely at this point in our current ignorance of how learning maps into performance that we stumble in our efforts to erect viable theories of learning and behavior.

In this light, an issue of considerable importance becomes communication between human experimenter and animal subject. A learning experiment that fails may do so because of: (*a*) failure of the experimenter to communicate clearly to the subject the particular environmental changes to be learned about and (*b*) failure on the part of the subject to report clearly to the experimenter that it has learned. Although we may damn the stupid beasts that we study for not confirming our theories, it is considerably more constructive that we at least tentatively accept the blame for conducting an ambiguous experiment or for having been insensitive to the means that the animal has at its disposal for communicating to us that it has learned. As Skinner (1977) has so often stated, "the basic rule in animal research [is] that the organism is always right. It does what it is induced to do by its genetic endowment or the prevailing conditions [p. 1007]." Animal psychology has always sought out more effective ways of "looking into the minds of animals [Griffin, 1976]." It must continue to do so.

A final comment in this context concerns the currently popular notion of "constraints on learning." According to advocates of this viewpoint, whether, when, what, and how an animal learns depends upon certain species-typical dispositions and limitations (Hinde & Stevenson-Hinde, 1973; Seligman & Hager, 1972). Without questioning the ultimate validity or utility of this notion, I do question whether all of the purported constraints on *learning* are truly due to associative limitations. It is equally plausible to propose that the failure of a specific environmental change to effect a reliable modification in behavior is not due to an associative limitation at all, but to ambiguous learning conditions or to insensitive behavioral assays. To reiterate, learning may take place but not be manifested in performance. Too few researchers today seriously entertain the possibility that their results actually reveal constraints on *performance* (but for a growing appreciation of this possibility see LoLordo, 1979; Shettleworth, 1979).

Respondent Conditioning

[The] widespread implicit assumption of the existence of independently conditionable response components and the urge toward exact measurement have led to too exclusive emphasis upon precise registration of the particular effector component selected for observation, and to relative neglect of the experimental determination... of its behavioral and physiological organization in the total pattern of activity [Zener & McCurdy, 1939, p. 321].

The familiar case of respondent conditioning may take place when a signaling stimulus (conditioned stimulus, or CS) reliably precedes an event of biological importance (unconditioned stimulus, or US). Just how an experimenter goes about discovering if such learning has occurred is a complicated matter because a signal of reinforcement may come to be an eliciting stimulus, a motivating stimulus, or a conditioned reinforcing stimulus (Brown & Farber, 1968). Different experimenter operations are necessary to disclose the possibly multiple capabilities that a CS has acquired after pairing with reinforcement.

Historically, the notion of respondent conditioning is more strongly tied to the response-evoking capability of a CS than to its motivating or reinforcing properties. Within this sphere, the reflex tradition in experimental psychology has promulgated a highly constrained view of the associative process in respondent conditioning, wherein a specific component reaction to the US is elicited by the CS after paired presentations. Of course, such an approach guarantees that conditioned and unconditioned responses will be similar if conditioning is successful.

A less restrictive, cognitive view of respondent conditioning requires only that some change in responding to the CS accompany pairings of CS and US (e.g., Hilgard & Marquis, 1940). This approach grew out of studies conducted by

Zener (1937) and others that questioned the thesis that respondent conditioning reflects the process of *stimulus substitution*—a process whereby the CS comes to stand as a surrogate for the US and to evoke reactions replicating those elicited by the US (Hilgard 1936a,b; Wasserman, 1978a; Williams, 1929). Zener's observations of dogs undergoing salivary conditioning led him to conclude that an entire behavioral system, not just an isolated component reaction, was being modified in the course of conditioning (also see Timberlake & Grant, 1975). The end result of this process was that an animal now responded to the CS in a number of new ways—some similar to the unconditioned response (salivating) and some quite different (approaching the CS, becoming restless). The conditioned response was thus considerably more plastic and preparatory than the reflex account suggests.

Despite the plausibility of his thesis and the forcefulness of his exhortations to adopt new experimental strategies (see the quotation at the beginning of this section), Zener's polemic against the reflex approach seems generally to have had but slight impact on the study of respondent conditioning. Recently, however, investigators from two diverse orientations have begun systematically to explore the effects of conditioning operations on a multitude of reaction systems. Ethologically oriented researchers have most often observed a host of overt skeletal reactions during conditioning (e.g., Holland, 1977; Jensen, 1970; Reynierse, Scavio, & Ulness, 1970), whereas physiologically oriented researchers have principally monitored a number of neural and autonomic reactions throughout conditioning (e.g., John, 1967; Schneiderman, 1972). Although studies from these two approaches differ greatly in methodology, their collective results suggest the following conclusions: (*a*) The speed with which different reaction systems change in responsivity during conditioning varies dramatically; (*b*) some reaction systems—even those intimately affiliated with the US—fail to change during conditioning; and (*c*) those reaction systems that do undergo modification seem intimately affiliated with either the CS, US, or both.

Theories of response production in respondent conditioning make selective use of these facts. Pavlov's (1927) original notion of "drainage" from one cerebral locus to another (and the subsequent emendations of this notion by Asratyan [1965; personal communication, 1976] and other Pavlovians) holds that neural connections between the afferent centers of CS and US are elaborated during conditioning. Since the range of directly elicited reactions is held to be a positive function of US strength, and since the CS only indirectly excites the US center after conditioning, an established CS should elicit but a subset of the reactions elicited by the US. This view is then a modified version of the stimulus substitution hypothesis, wherein the US is not only an element of the S–S associative connection but is also the prime determiner of conditioned response performance (see Estes, 1973, for a similar, but cognitively worded proposal). Naturally, other factors such as the organism's current need state may alter the reactivity of the neural center affiliated with the US to stimulation by either the CS or the US. Thus, one implication of this approach is that an ineffective CS under a low level of motivation may be measurably effective if the motivational level is increased. A US that is just capable of evoking a behavioral reaction may, therefore, not necessarily support conditioned responding. A second implication is that overt response elicitation by the US during conditioning is not necessary for association formation between CS and US. Contiguous excitation of CS and US neural centers and their final efferent paths still takes place even if overt responses to the US are prevented (Kimble, 1961; Mackintosh, 1974).

Other theorists have stressed the importance of reactions related to the CS in determining the form of the conditioned response. Bindra (1978), Dykman (1965, 1967), Weisman (1976), Wyrwicka (1972), and Zener (1937) have all proposed that the established conditioned response may represent an amalgamation of both CS- and US-related behaviors. Two very different lines of research support this proposal. First, Holland (1977) has systematically observed a number of overt reactions during either light–food or tone–food training with rats. His results clearly showed that the total pattern of behavioral change during conditioning differed dramatically when lights versus tones were used as CSs. Control groups indicated that this response specificity depended on each of the two CSs having been paired with food.

Second, Thompson and his associates (1976) have investigated the neural substrate of the nictitating membrane response in rabbits. They found that the excitability of motoneurons in the abducens nucleus (the final common path for extension of the nictitating membrane over the eyeball) was enhanced by the sounding of a brief tone. Furthermore, the form of the interstimulus interval function for abducens excitability closely paralleled the familiar CS–US interval conditioning function for this response system. This functional correspondence could be due to the novel tone CS intrinsically biasing certain reaction systems to becoming conditioned responses or to the tone CS being a subthreshold elicitor of the unconditioned response.

The combined results of Holland (1977) and Thompson (1976) thus indicate not only that the CS may be an important determiner of the form of the conditioned response but that temporal and intensive properties of the CS may contribute to quantitative features of conditioning (like the interstimulus interval function and stimulus intensity dynamism) usually ascribed only to associative processes. A rather more significant role may then be played in conditioning by the CS than that of merely informing the organism of an upcoming US. Consideration of the importance of the CS in response production may greatly alter our current conceptions of respondent conditioning (Rescorla, 1978).

Operant Conditioning

> There is no evidence which shows that only pleasant consequences of acts produce learning, much less that unpleasant consequences weaken learning. Rather the

animal learns in all cases to associate the consequences of an act with the act. This learning results in the avoidance of acts which produce unpleasantness and the repetition of acts which produce pleasantness. The consequences thus determine the preference and are not a condition for learning [Maier & Schneirla, 1935, pp. 432-433].

The problem of response evocation has been treated quite differently by theorists of respondent and operant conditioning. In the case of respondent conditioning the problem has generally been unrecognized; in the case of operant conditioning it has largely been taken for granted. Because the contingencies of reinforcement stipulate the behavioral class that directly produces or removes rewards or punishers, it seems obvious that these contingencies necessarily select that response class above all others for modification.

Nonetheless, many problems plague such simplistic applications of the law of effect. Maier and Schneirla, as quoted at the onset of this discussion, note that response–consequence learning is dissociable from overt response performance, the latter being in their opinion a motivational rather than an associative matter. More recently, Staddon (1975; Staddon & Simmelhag, 1971) has suggested that the logic of reinforcement needs to be reversed: Rewards do not selectively strengthen the responses they follow; these responses rise in probability because other, ineffective behaviors are weakened by nonreward (also see Harlow, 1959). Staddon relates the persistence of effective behaviors in operant conditioning (reinforcement) to the survival of fit individuals in the struggle for existence (natural selection), and suggests that borrowing the concepts of variation and selection from the latter may help us to understand the former (Ghiselin, 1969).

Segal (1972) has productively discussed the provenance of operants after recognizing that little attention has been given to the principles of response variation or to the raw behavioral material from which operant behavior is selected. She concludes that much of the arbitrariness that is thought to typify operant behavior soon vanishes when the organism's pre- and postlearning behaviors are carefully examined. Situational and motivational factors evidently combine to promote the expression of the specific behaviors that constitute the basic response repertoire from which successful operant behaviors are selected. In a surprising number of cases, the form and direction of operant behaviors can be predicted on the basis of current motivational and situational conditions, without reference to response–reinforcer relations. This finding raises the strong possibility that the response–reinforcer contingency may be of much less importance in operant conditioning than has usually been thought (Herrnstein, 1977; Seligman, 1970).

Indeed, Bindra (1978) has recently gone so far as to deny that response–reinforcer factors participate in operant conditioning. According to his formulation, the issue of learning must first be separated from the issue of response production. Learning in operant or respondent conditioning involves association of a signaling stimulus with a hedonic or motivating stimulus. After learning, the signaling stimulus indirectly excites the motivational state affiliated with the hedonic stimulus. The learned behaviors that will be produced then depend upon the nature of the induced motivational state (appetitive or aversive) and the nature of the signaling stimulus (the behaviors that it actively promotes or permits). For example, in the case of a rat given food for lever pressing, the lever becomes a signal for food. Sight of the lever later permits the expression of salivation and other nondirected ingestive and emotional reactions, and actively promotes the expression of directed approach, contact, and lever-pressing behaviors; the former response set seems reinforcer-related, the latter manipulandum-related (Wasserman, 1978a).

According to Bindra, the selective recording of either autonomic (salivation) or skeletal behaviors (lever pressing) has contributed to the mistaken conclusion that there are two distinct learning processes—respondent conditioning in the first case and operant conditioning in the second—when in reality these two forms of reaction are merely different reflections of the same learned association. A fuller understanding of the principles of response expression may thus hasten the demise of already failing two-process theories of learning (Hearst, 1975a).

RESPONSE EVOCATION IN AUTOSHAPING

Consider the conventional method of autoshaping the pigeon's keypeck. A hungry pigeon is placed in a conditioning cubicle and given sequential pairings of a lighted key and food. After a number of such pairings, the bird comes to approach the lighted key and to peck it. What determines the form of the autoshaped response? What determines its direction? Potential answers to these questions come from considerations of the nature of the unconditioned stimulus (pp. 29–35), the conditioned stimulus (pp. 35–37), and the species of organism (pp. 37–38) studied in an autoshaping experiment.

Unconditioned Stimulus

Aside from the matter of response direction, the original demonstration of autoshaping by Brown and Jenkins (1968) suggested that the phenomenon might be placed in the domain of respondent conditioning; consistent with the principle of *stimulus substitution*, both conditioned and unconditioned responses involved vigorous pecking. This proposal gained added support from later observations by Jenkins and Moore (1973), who found that the form of the key contact response differed when food or water was the US; in the former case key contacts were forceful and brief, whereas in the latter case they were weak and sustained. Hungry and thirsty pigeons appeared to respond to key light CSs as though they were food and water, "eating" and "drinking" them, respectively.

In most autoshaping work, food and water USs are made available independently of the pigeon's behavior. However, the bird is required to approach, contact, and ingest the reinforcing substances, thereby raising the possibility that similar responses directed toward the key light might simply reflect the process of stimulus generalization (see the original suggestion by Logan, 1971 and later data of Sperling, Perkins, & Duncan, 1977). Considerable evidence strongly argues against this stimulus-generalization notion (in addition to the following discussion, see Jenkins & Moore, 1973, Experiments 4 and 5).

Woodruff and Williams (1976) implanted an oral fistula in the pigeon's bill through which small quantities of water could be injected directly into the mouth (see Lucas, Vodraska, & Wasserman, 1979 for detailed descriptions of the method). When water injection was scheduled to occur shortly after response key illumination, pigeons came to approach and contact the lighted key and to make drinking movements on it. Randomly presented key light and water stimuli failed to produce key-directed behaviors. Because the water US was directly applied to the pigeon's oral receptors, the performance of directed approach and contact behaviors to the key light CS could not be attributed to stimulus generalization of magazine behaviors—there were none. Furthermore, directed approach to and contact with the CS in this experiment is of added analytical importance because these facets of the conditioned response were not components of the bill and throat movements elicited by direct application of the water US. Thus, these results are not easily reconciled with the stimulus substitution hypothesis.

Additional evidence contrary to both stimulus substitution and stimulus generalization interpretations comes from experiments autoshaping the key peck of young chicks given key light–heat pairings in a refrigerated chamber (Wasserman, 1973b; Wasserman, Deich, Hunter, & Nagamatsu, 1977; Wasserman, Hunter, Gutowski, & Bader, 1975). Here, diffuse thermal stimulation produced generally unenergetic and undirected postures that often entailed head raising, body lowering, napping, and wing extension (Figure 2.1). In contrast, key illumination occasioned vigorous, stimulus-directed pecking (Figure 2.1e) that, in a small proportion of the subjects, drifted toward less effortful snuggling (Figure 2.1f). The dissimilarity of conditioned and unconditioned responses is again to be noted as is the successful autoshaping of the avian peck under circumstances that preclude the involvement of generalized magazine behaviors.

More recently, robust second-order conditioning has been obtained in our laboratory with the heat reinforcement preparation (unpublished experiments by J. Deich, J. Deitchler, S. Cohen, & E. Kalb). As shown in Figure 2.2, when no

---

Figure 2.1. Unconditioned responses of chicks to heat stimulation including (*a*) head raising; (*b*) body lowering; (*c*) napping; and (*d*) wing extension. Conditioned responses of chicks to a heat-paired key light including (*e*) key pecking and, less commonly, (*f*) snuggling. (See facing page.)

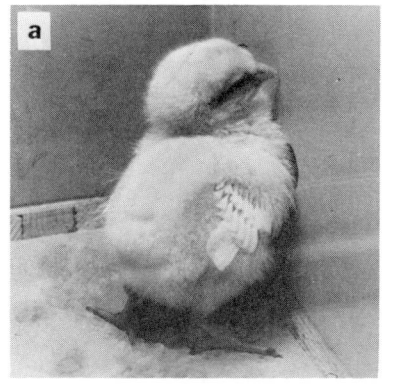
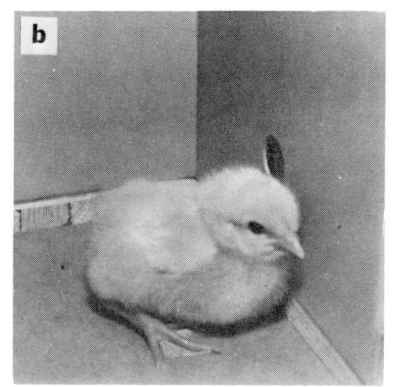
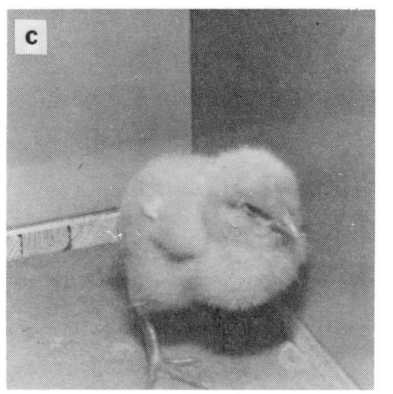
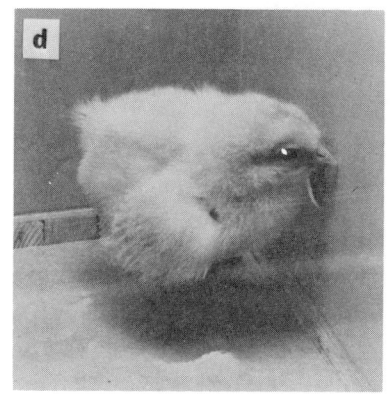
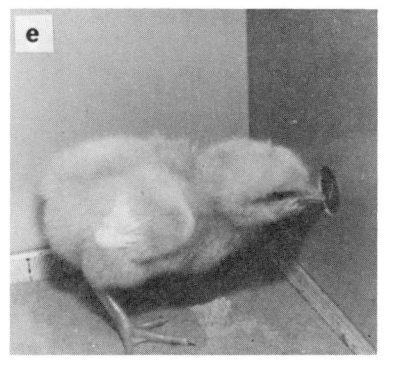
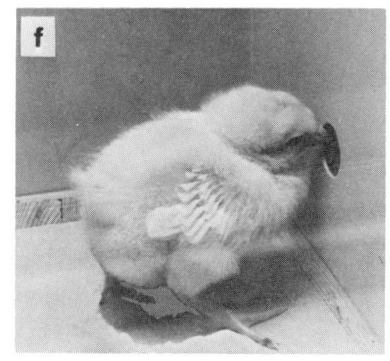

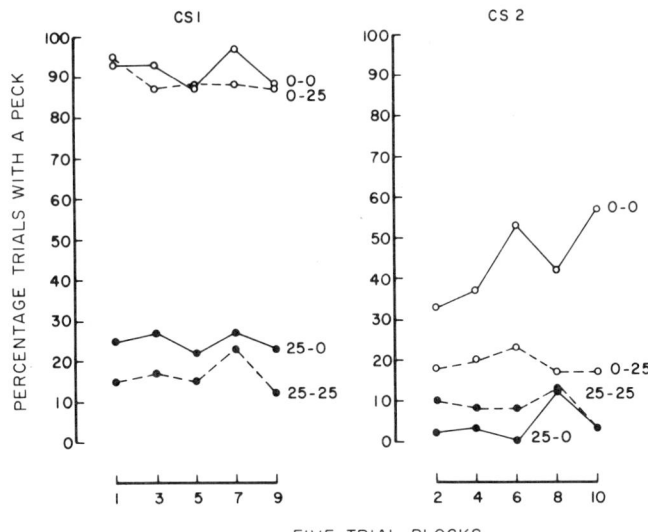

Figure 2.2. Second-order autoshaping of the chick's key peck with heat reinforcement (US). After 2 days of first-order autoshaping of the key peck to CS1 (not shown), 48 chicks were given alternating blocks of first-order (CS1–US) and second-order (CS2–CS1) conditioning trials for 2 additional days. The four groups ($n = 12$) that are shown represent the factorial combination of 0-sec or 25-sec delays separating offset of CS1 and onset of US on first-order trials (the first digit of the two-digit group labels) and of 0-sec or 25-sec delays separating CS2 offset and CS1 onset on second-order trials (the second digit of the two-digit labels). The figure separately portrays mean performance to CS1 and to CS2 for the four groups of subjects.

delay was imposed between CS1 offset and US presentation or between CS2 offset and CS1 presentation (Group 0–0), responding to a second-order key light stimulus (CS2) on second-order trial blocks rose to about 50% trials with a peck; responding to a different, first-order key light stimulus (CS1) that had earlier been paired with heat reinforcement remained near 90% trials with a peck on alternating first-order trial blocks. Second-order responding was much lower when a 25-sec delay separated CS1 offset and US presentation or when 25 sec separated CS2 offset and CS1 presentation (Groups 0–25, 25–0, and 25–25). These results support the conclusion that second-order conditioning in this situation depends upon both the positive relationship between CS2 and CS1 plus the positive relationship between CS1 and US (Rescorla, 1973). Furthermore, second-order autoshaping of the chick's key peck occurred under conditions in which both CS1 and CS2 failed to evoke reactions elicited by the heat US. This finding is then at odds with Konorski's (1948) variant of the stimulus substitution hypothesis, which proposed that, after CS1–US and CS2–CS1 pairings, CS2 comes to excite an internal representation of the US and to elicit the attendant component reactions of the unconditioned response (also see Rashotte, Griffin, & Sisk, 1977).

Although further evaluation of the stimulus substitution and stimulus generalization accounts of autoshaping could come from research involving aversive stimuli, relatively little work in autoshaping has been concerned with the control of locomotor and contact behaviors by noxious events. What evidence is available suggests that the effect of following key illumination with electric shock is to direct the pigeon away from the key light stimulus (Dunham, Mariner, & Adams, 1969; Green, 1978; Green & Rachlin, 1977; Schwartz, 1973b; Wesp, Lattal, & Poling, 1977). In other circumstances, directed attack may be provoked by a shock-associated key light (Rachlin, 1969).

If it is assumed that the nonoccurrence of food in the context of otherwise scheduled food delivery is aversive, then evidence portrayed in Figure 2.3 from a study by Wasserman, Franklin, and Hearst (1974, Experiment 2) parallels the prominent findings with shock USs (Jenkins & Boakes, 1973; Wasserman & Anderson, 1974). This study monitored locomotor reactions in addition to key contact responses (Brown, 1968; Hearst & Franklin, 1977) while subjects received key-light and food stimuli that were positively, randomly, or negatively correlated with one another. It can be seen that approach (tracking scores greater than 50) to a key-light CS positively correlated with food reinforcement arose in experimentally naive pigeons (Phase 1) and in subjects previously exposed to random and negative correlations of key light and food (Phase 2). Subjects exposed to a random correlation of key light and food were neither strongly attracted to the key-light CS nor repelled by it (tracking scores near 50). And subjects given training with the key light negatively correlated with food delivery stayed away from and moved away from the CS (tracking scores less than 50), whether they were experimentally naive (Phase 1) or had been given prior training with positively or randomly correlated key-light and food stimuli (Phase 2).

These findings with signals of nonreward not only parallel those with shock USs but address prevalent theories of autoshaping. Because there are no behaviors that an animal must perform in order to receive the nonoccurrence of a reinforcer (except perhaps to expect it) and because no directed responses are plausibly evoked by the nonoccurrence of a reinforcer (frustration is usually thought to be a nondirected, emotional reaction [Amsel, 1958]), stimulus generalization and stimulus substitution interpretations fail to account for this negative counterpart to autoshaping.

Another facet of the findings reported in Figure 2.3 deserves mention here. This figure depicts keypecking on more than 25% of the scheduled trials by the filled symbols. It can be seen that reliable approach was frequently shown by several pigeons even in the absence of appreciable keypecking; this was especially true of subjects previously given the negative CS–US correlation in Phase 1

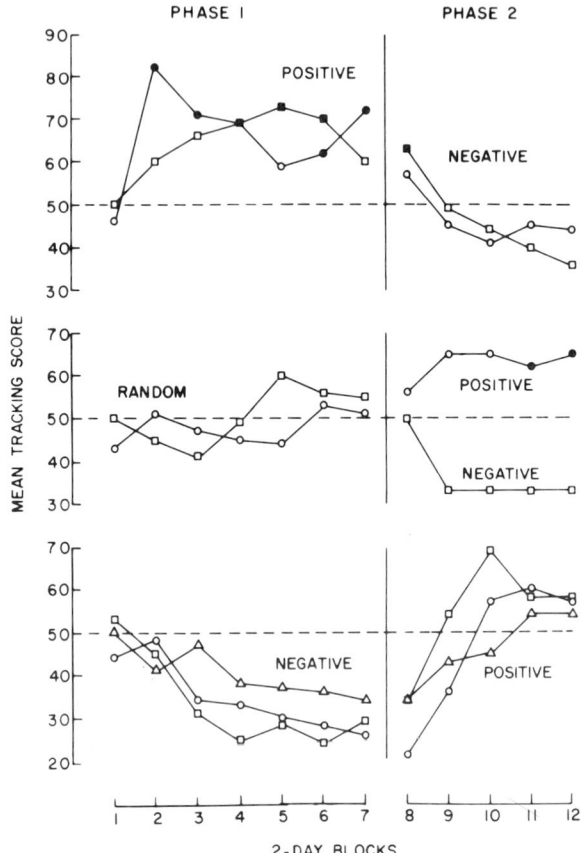

Figure 2.3. Mean tracking scores over successive blocks of sessions for seven individual pigeons. The tracking scores were calculated by the formula: total time on the same side of the chamber as the key-light CS ÷ total CS time × 100. A score of 50 would indicate that the pigeon's movements were not controlled by the key-light CS. Scores near 100 or near 0 would indicate very strong approach or withdrawal, respectively. Filled symbols indicate that, during the 2-day block, the pigeon pecked the lighted key on 25% or more of its presentations. Each pigeon was first exposed to a Positive, Random, or Negative key light-food relation during Phase 1 (14 days) and then switched to another key light-food relation during Phase 2 (10 days). (From Wasserman et al., 1974. Copyright © 1974 by the American Psychological Association. Reprinted by permission.)

(Browne, 1976; Wasserman & Molina, 1975). Thus, not only is CS-approach a logical precursor to CS-contact but, in this context, it is demonstrably the more sensitive dependent variable of the two. Perhaps because of the popularity of the keypecking response or because of its ease of recording, few investigators have studied autoshaping from a broader behavioral perspective (Lucas, 1975; Wessells, 1974). This is indeed unfortunate; research and theory have been severely constrained by this empirical narrowness. As succeeding discussion will reveal, I strongly disagree with the comment of an anonymous reviewer who claimed that "the contact response is the hallmark of autoshaping."

In summary, approach-with-contact and withdrawal behaviors are produced by CSs associated with appetitive and aversive events, respectively. These results substantially extend the range of behavioral reactions usually encountered in autoshaping experiments, from manipulation of objects (pecking) to directed locomotor and orienting behaviors (approach–withdrawal). Additionally, topographical details of the behaviors that make contact with reinforcer signals may often be related to the reinforcer, even when redirection of magazine behaviors is prevented by direct reinforcer application. Further analysis of these results will be delayed until other determinants of the autoshaped response are delineated.

Conditioned Stimulus

Earlier discussion centered on the increasing explanatory role that is being given to the CS in determining the form and character of conditioned responses. The importance of the CS in conditioned response evocation has been especially emphasized by Bindra (1978) who refers to reinforcer signals as "eliciting stimuli" in order to stress their generally neglected behavioral potency.

Historically, investigators of conditioning have been interested in how the rate of learning is influenced by such physical parameters of the CS as its intensity, duration, and intermittency. However, from a biological standpoint, other properties of the conditioned stimulus may be of much greater significance in controlling conditioned responses. Recent attention has thus been given to the modality of CS reception in determining the relative associability of CSs with USs. Several lines of evidence here support the conclusion that different modalities of CSs are differentially associable with particular kinds of USs (LoLordo, 1979), although we should again note with caution the persistent predilection of researchers in this area to equate learning with performance.

Other properties of stimulus reception might well affect the nature of conditioned responses. For instance, external stimulus sources may or may not make contact with the body surface in order to permit detection. In the former class belong tactual and gustatory stimuli, whereas in the latter class belong visual, auditory, and olfactory stimuli. Along a somewhat orthogonal dimension might be ranked stimuli of varying physical extents—from diffuse to localized.

Considerable interest in autoshaping initially arose because the conditioned pecking response of pigeons was aimed directly at the localized visual CS. It was thought that the directionality of the behavior had no precedent in respondent conditioning, wherein such nondirected behaviors as salivation, respiration, and blinking were produced in response to such widespread stimuli as changes in ambient illumination and noise level. That distinguishing autoshaped behaviors and conditioned respondents on the basis of response direction is fundamentally unsound was suggested by the early observations of CS-directed behaviors by Pavlov (1934) and Zener (1937). Interestingly, Skinner (1935) originally held that what he later called *respondents* and *operants* could be distinguished on the basis of the nature of supporting environmental stimuli; respondents "require no external point of reference in their elicitation or description," whereas operants "require points of reference for their elicitation which are not supplied by the organism itself, but by the stimulus [p. 68]."

Consideration of the role of CS localizability suggests that (*a*) association of CS and US arises regardless of the spatial extent of the CS and (*b*) that the mode of expression of this CS–US association may very well depend on the locatability of the CS. Locomotor and manipulative behaviors might then be expected only if the source of the CS is discretely locatable; nondirected secretory and autonomic reactions might occur regardless of this physical property of the CS (Wasserman, 1978a,b,c). Thus, the presumed differences in associative processes among autoshaping, respondent conditioning, and operant conditioning may simply be reducible to differences in performance under different environmental circumstances.

Evidence collected in autoshaping is consistent with the above analysis. Approach-with-contact of the CS rarely occurs when widespread visual stimuli accompany response-key illumination (Hearst, 1975b; Wasserman, 1973a) or when generally diffuse auditory stimuli are used as CSs (Bilbrey & Winokur, 1973; Schwartz, 1973a; Wasserman, 1972). Further supportive evidence comes from CS-superimposition and behavioral contrast experiments with visual and auditory CSs (Bottjer, Scobie, & Wallace, 1977; Hearst & Gormley, 1976; LoLordo, McMillan, & Riley, 1974; Redford & Perkins, 1974; Schwartz, 1975, 1976).

How strong is the control of directed actions by highly localized CSs? In the case of autoshaping young chicks, pecking arises to a punctate, visual CS even though the diffuse, thermal US elicits seemingly incompatible behaviors and postures (Figure 2.1). This fact indicates that the response eliciting properties of a CS can, under certain circumstances, overshadow control over conditioned response form and direction by the US.

Another characteristic of CSs that, from a biological standpoint, should markedly influence the form of conditioned responses is whether the CS is animate or inanimate. Timberlake and Grant (1975) signaled the response-independent delivery of food to rat subjects either by the presentation of another rat or by the presentation of a block of wood. The animate "rat CS" more strongly supported approach and contact behaviors than did the inanimate "wood CS." Furthermore, the form of the contact response with the "rat CS" was decidedly social in nature, rather than ingestive, again supporting the thesis that the topography and direction of autoshaped behaviors are strongly controlled by physical and biological properties of the CS.

Species of Organism

Within autoshaping, the role of species membership has been considered in regard to two questions: Does a particular species of organism autoshape? And, how are the form and direction of autoshaped responses related to the natural repertoire of the species? Tentative answers to these questions have been provided for several species of fish, reptiles, birds, and mammals. However, considerable caution should be exercised in evaluating these results because of the importance of CS and US factors discussed in the two preceding sections.

Approach-and-contact of small visual stimuli paired with food has been obtained with the goldfish (Brandon, & Bitterman, 1979; Woodard & Bitterman, 1974) and the tilapia fish (Squire, 1969), as well as with the monitor lizard (Loop, 1976). These cold-blooded animals most often contact the CS with biting and other feeding behaviors.

In addition to the pigeon, the pecking response of avians has been autoshaped with food reinforcement including the domestic chick (S. McCracken & L. Mazula, unpublished observations in our laboratory) and the bobwhite quail (Gardner, 1969). The avian peck has also successfully been autoshaped with water (Jenkins & Moore, 1973; Woodruff & Williams, 1976) and heat reinforcement (Wasserman, 1973b). Aside from these positive results, Powell, Kelly, and Santisteban (1975) have reported that two species of crows (common crow and fish crow) failed to show much autoshaped key pecking. And Wilson (1978) has found that, after autoshaping, the key pecking of three species of corvids (carrion crow, rook, and jay) fell to very low levels.

Several experimenters have studied the behavior of rats toward a lever inserted into the chamber just prior to food delivery (Atnip, 1977; Locurto, Terrace, & Gibbon, 1976; Peterson, Ackil, Frommer, & Hearst, 1972; Stiers & Silberberg, 1974). After a number of lever–food pairings, rats approach and contact the lever with the mouth (licking and gnawing) or forepaws (touching and pressing). Approach and contact of a lever CS also occurred when the US was electrical stimulation of the brain, although relatively less oral responding and more sniffing was observed (Peterson *et al.*, 1972). As noted earlier, rats approach and contact a "rat CS" paired with food, but not a "wood CS" (Timberlake & Grant, 1975). In light of the success of the insertion of a small lever as CS, the failure of rats to contact a much larger wooden block as CS may be related to the generally stronger tendency of highly localized stimuli to support autoshaped behaviors (although it should be noted that Timberlake and Grant's inanimate "wood CS" was about the same size as the animate "rat CS"). Another rodent species, the guinea pig, has also been reported to approach and contact a lever paired with food delivery (Poling & Poling, 1978).

Food-deprived cats learned to approach and contact a small loudspeaker that was the source of food-paired sounds (Grastyan & Vereczkei, 1974). Behaviors directed to the CSs included searching, sniffing, pawing, and biting.

Pavlov (1934) originally noted that dogs occasionally approached and licked a localized visual CS paired with food delivery. However, the generality of his incidental observations was in considerable doubt despite some supportive evidence of Zener (1937). Therefore, Wasserman (1978b,c) studied the secretory and motor behaviors of loosely tethered dogs in a standard Pavlovian conditioning experiment. The results of this study revealed that, although the light panel CS reliably elicited salivation and CS-approach, CS-contact failed to occur. In freely moving dogs, Jenkins, Barrera, Ireland, and Woodside (1978) also observed relatively stronger approach to audio-visual CS sources than contact of such sources (see also Stepien, 1974).

Finally, the occurrence of autoshaping in primates has been verified. Approach-and-contact of a light-panel CS has been observed in rhesus (Likely, 1974; Sidman & Fletcher, 1968) and squirrel (Gamzu & Schwam, 1974) monkeys. Here, it has been noted that the form of food-ingestive responses may differ from the form of CS-contact responses. Likely (1974) noted that key-contact responses usually involved biting, licking, and palpation; however, delivery of the food-pellet reinforcer produced neither licking nor fondling, but instead produced pellet seizing, prompt placement in the mouth, chewing, and swallowing.

In summary, most species that have been studied have been autoshaped to approach and contact a localized CS paired with an appetitive US—from fish to monkeys. Not surprisingly, the forms of the CS-contact responses observed in these studies are "species-typical" in character, but they do not always mimic the form of the unconditioned response to the reinforcer.

COMPARATIVE-EVOLUTIONARY ANALYSIS

The comparative analysis of behavior has as a central aim the delineation of similar and dissimilar behavioral processes in existing animal forms (Ratner, 1970; Waters, 1960). The evolutionary analysis of behavior is concerned principally with reconstructing the histories of the various behaviors now performed by different animal species (Hinde & Tinbergen, 1958; Lorenz, 1958).

Despite the rather unfortunate past debate between proponents of these two approaches, it now appears that systematic study along both lines may produce valuable and complementary data on the causation and function of behavior

(Hinde, 1970; Hodos & Campbell, 1969; Lockard, 1971; Tinbergen, 1965). Of immediate relevance to the current topic are several concepts and distinctions that have arisen in the course of studying animal behavior from comparative and evolutionary perspectives. These concepts and distinctions elucidate the behavioral processes involved in the evocation of autoshaped behaviors.

Appetitive versus Consummatory Behavior

Early considerations of comparative anatomy and behavior led Sherrington (1906) and Craig (1918) to distinguish between two classes of behavior that are ordinarily integrated into elaborate sequences of species-typical responses; *appetitive* behaviors come at the beginning of response sequences and continue until a particular stimulus or situation occurs that may then trigger a sequence-terminating *consummatory* behavior. Thus, in the case of feeding, appetitive behaviors would correspond to food-getting patterns, and consummatory behaviors would correspond to food-eating patterns.

Appetitive behaviors are characteristically variable, excited, and effortful, and they are often outwardly directed by locomotion or orientation toward objects or places that have previously been associated with reward or relief. During the appetitive phase, learned behaviors predominate, but incipient consummatory behaviors may also occur. The searching, appetitive phase ceases when the appeted stimulus is received, often (but not always) instigating a highly stereotyped instinctive reaction and consummating the behavioral sequence. The appetitive–consummatory distinction has not only survived the test of time (Denny & Ratner, 1970; Tinbergen, 1951), but physiological investigation has moved toward disclosing the bodily basis of the integration of appetitive and consummatory behaviors (Ewert, 1974; Kupfermann, 1974; Randall, Trulson, & Parsons, 1976).

Analysis of avian feeding behavior along the lines of the appetitive–consummatory distinction might proceed as follows: When deprived of food, the hungry bird becomes active and starts seeking food (Andrew, 1976; Croze, 1970). In its search, it is directed to those places that, in the past, have been associated with food (see Wasserman, Carr, & Deich, 1978 for a laboratory analog of this situation). Spotting a kernel of grain, the bird approaches it, pecks and seizes it in its bill, and finally swallows it. Within this behavioral sequence we see the progressions from general to specific activity and from learned to innate behavior suggested by the appetitive–consummatory analysis. But can we be more precise as to how the integration of these component responses comes about? And how does autoshaping fit into this scheme?

Consider the bird limiting its search to those places where food has been found earlier. Clearly, this narrowing of search results from learning. Although it is not yet possible to say whether the animal searches area A rather than area B because it is attracted to area A and/or repelled by area B, such directed locomotor behavior is a prime feature of the autoshaping phenomenon (Wasserman et al., 1974). When food is spotted, the pigeon moves directly toward and pecks it. Here, the punctate stimulus (the kernel of grain itself) has repeatedly been paired with favorable nutritive consequences in the life of the pigeon (Hogan, 1973). This learning guides the pigeon toward food-paired stimuli and possibly away from non-food stimuli of similar shape and size. Again, autoshaping directs the pigeon's locomotor and pecking behavior toward the sources of reinforcement.

One might ask why the pigeon pecks only when food is spotted, rather than when a food site is encountered. Two possibly interacting factors may be involved. First, the spatial landmarks directing the pigeon to particular places where food has been found may not provide the bird with appropriate target stimuli for pecking; target stimuli are provided by kernels of grain in the natural world or by lighted keys in the laboratory world. A second factor may be the more remote associative relation holding between spatial stimuli and ingestion than between grain stimuli and ingestion. Because grain stimuli are more contiguous with nutritional consequences than place stimuli, they may come to be more effective conditioned signals for pecking (see the greater responding to CS1 than CS2 at the end of second-order autoshaping in Figure 2.2 and the higher rate of pecking to CS1 than CS2 in CS2–CS1–US serial compound autoshaping observed by Newlin & LoLordo, 1976; Ricci, 1973; and Wasserman et al., 1978).

There are still further ways in which the appetitive–consummatory distinction is relevant to autoshaping. The classical work of Lorenz and Tinbergen (1957) on the egg-retrieving behavior of the greylag goose revealed that it is possible to disentangle appetitive from consummatory response components in species-typical behavior sequences. In the case of pigeon autoshaping, evidence exists that the approach–keypeck linkage may be broken (contrary to the look–peck hypothesis of Brown & Jenkins, 1968 and the related proposal of Herrnstein, 1977). As shown in the bottom portion of Figure 2.3, Wasserman et al. (1974) found that after negative correlation of key light and food, pigeons came to approach (albeit less than without pretraining) but not to peck the lighted key when the stimulus was later positively correlated with food delivery.

Interestingly, even though approaching and pecking can be uncoupled by pretraining procedures, other evidence indicates that a very strong sequential dependency exists in birds between approach to a localized visual stimulus and pecking it. Wasserman et al. (1975, Experiments 2, 3, and 5) conditioned baby chicks in a cooled chamber into which a wire-mesh screen was placed. This screen permitted the chicks to approach to within 1 in. of the visible response key during 3 days of key light–heat pairings, but prevented the chicks from contacting the key. When the barrier was later removed during an extinction test, 96% of 23 subjects (in Experiments 2 and 3) pecked the lighted key during the

30-trial test; 74% of the chicks first pecked the key within the first five illuminations; and 48% of the birds pecked the key on its very first illumination!

As mentioned earlier, the linkage between pecking and swallowing can be broken by surgical means (Lucas et al., 1979; Woodruff & Williams, 1976). Delivery of water directly into the pigeon's mouth elicits mandibulation and deglutition. Nonetheless, when direct water injection follows response-key illumination, approach and contact of the lighted key arise as conditioned responses. This result holds not only for adult birds, whose ingestive behavior is already the product of a long developmental history, but for baby chicks, who also approach and contact a lighted key that signals intraoral food or water delivery (Woodruff & Starr, 1978). Again, strong sequential dependencies exist between the bird's locomotor, pecking, and intraoral activities that may be strongly influenced by evolutionary as well as by developmental organization (Premock & Klipec, 1980).

Eliciting versus Directing Stimuli

Within the ethological approach to the study of animal behavior, a distinction between eliciting and directing stimuli is often made (Fraenkel & Gunn, 1961; Tapp, 1969; Tinbergen, 1951): Whereas some stimuli instigate a response, others may guide or steer responses toward or away from specific loci. In the case of the bird's feeding or autoshaped behaviors, the same stimulus that elicits the peck also directs it. Far from being an anomaly, the avian peck is a prototype of adaptive behavior.

The functional coincidence of eliciting and directing stimuli in one and the same object represents an important ecological reality; signals of rewards and punishers are usually located at the source of reward and punishment (Campbell, 1963; Lorenz, 1957). Indeed, Eibl-Eibesfeldt (1970) coined the term "object orientation" to denote the directed quality of behaviors that are oriented toward or away from biologically significant objects. The implications of this coincidence of signal and reinforcer for the evolution of brain and behavior have been carefully articulated by Campbell (1963), and many of the following points are derived from his astute analysis.

Unlike reflexive behavior, most adaptive behaviors of mobile organisms are guided by such distal stimuli as sights, noises, and odors, whether or not learning strongly participates in response performance. It is obvious why distal stimuli are so important in the control of adaptive behaviors: The fact that these stimuli are at a distance enables the organism to make behavioral and internal adjustments before physical contact with the objects takes place. Herein lie the ecological forces that have shaped the behavioral complexities of extant species.

Naturally, the evolution of behavioral complexity has a structural basis. Here, it is of interest to note that Sherrington's (1906) original distinction between appetitive and consummatory behavior arose from his considerations of the role of distance receptors in the evolution of brain and behavior. Sherrington speculated that the brain was the part of the central nervous system that was built and evolved upon the organs of distance reception. Thus, both neural and behavioral complexities promoting survival sprang from the pressing exigencies of the natural environment.

A simple situation exemplifies the role that the demands of survival play on appetitive behavior oriented by distal stimuli. Consider a cat tracking a mouse. The mouse is both signal and reward; its distinctive sights, sounds, and smells signal flesh to the cat. The cat therefore does not run away from, but toward the mouse. In an opposite fashion, the mouse's behavior is guided away from, but not toward the cat, which to the mouse is both signal and punisher. Because of their respective object orientations, the behaviors of predator and prey appear goal-directed when in reality they are simply stimulus-directed (Bindra, 1959).

Despite its experimental merits, the conditioning laboratory is an extremely abnormal environment. Here, reinforcing stimuli are often spatially distinct from guiding or directing stimuli. Indeed, it is just this feature of the autoshaping situation that permits important insights into behavioral integration to be made: in the autoshaping experiment, a lighted key stands for food in place of the more natural food signal, the sight of a kernel of grain (Pavlov, 1927, p. 22). That appetitive and consummatory behaviors may be elicited and directed by such an unnatural food signal as a lighted key strongly suggests that similar behavioral processes are normally at work in the organization of avian feeding (Hailman, 1969; Hogan, 1973; Woodruff & Starr, 1978).

As the earlier discussion of the species generality of autoshaping revealed, this is not an isolated behavioral phenomenon. The tendency of organisms to approach and contact appetitive signals and to withdraw from aversive signals is widespread in vertebrates. "It seems a fair extension of selective survival mechanisms in the evolutionary perspective to predict that the capacity with the greatest general ecological usefulness will have emerged first and have remained most basic in the functioning of organisms [Campbell, 1963, pp. 142-143]."

Thus it is of considerable interest that the early behaviorist Jennings was among the first to recognize the adaptive significance of distal, signaling stimuli. Jennings introduced the concept of *representative stimuli* in 1906 to account for the tendency of organisms to respond to inherently "indifferent" stimuli as though these stimuli were beneficial or harmful. Representative stimuli acquire this capability due to pairing with beneficial or injurious agents. Locomotor behavior is then oriented by these representative stimuli in a manner appropriate to the signaled event.

> This reaction to representative stimuli is evidently of the greatest value, from the biological standpoint. It enables organisms to flee from injury even before the injury occurs, or to go toward a beneficial agent that is at a distance [Jennings, 1962, p. 297].

Although the evidence is not yet strong, the localizability of a signaling stimulus would appear to be positively related to the directedness of behavior. Marler and Hamilton (1966) have suggested that distal stimuli can be ordered with respect to the ease of localization. Such an ordering for birds might proceed in descending order from visual, to auditory, to olfactory stimuli: A punctate visual stimulus apparently is a maximally effective one, capable in certain circumstances of both triggering and targeting pecking (Nye, 1973; Wasserman, 1973b; Woodruff & Starr, 1978; Woodruff & Williams, 1976). In other species, a different ordering may hold with olfactory (rat, dog) or auditory (cat, monkey) stimuli most strongly directing behavior (Downey & Harrison, 1972; Grastyan & Vereczkei, 1974; Jenkins et al., 1978; Wasserman, 1978b,c). (In light of this discussion, the reader may wish to reexamine the evidence reviewed on pages 29–35 and 37–38).

Approach versus Withdrawal Behavior

Prior discussion of the directing function of stimuli stressed the orientation of movements toward or away from particular stimulus objects. As indicated in the last section's quotation from Jennings, approach and withdrawal behaviors are vital to the survival of most organisms—from protozoans to primates. Correspondingly, several writers (e.g., Denny, 1971; Glickman & Schiff, 1967; Schneirla, 1959) have proposed that approach and withdrawal are innate behavioral dispositions to appetitive and aversive objects, respectively. From such an evolutionary viewpoint, localized signaling stimuli are hypothesized to produce approach or withdrawal behaviors because ancestral animals that were so directed were more likely to survive and reproduce than were those that were not; these evolutionary misfits must have had quite a time obtaining nourishment, fleeing from predators, and courting prospective mates!

Support for the proposal that directed actions are innately based comes first from studies showing that organisms approach and withdraw from reinforcer signals in the absence of response-dependent reinforcement for such actions (e.g., Haraway, Wirth, & Maples, 1974; Jenkins & Boakes, 1973; Wasserman et al., 1974), and second from studies obtaining stimulus-directed actions in spite of response-dependent nonreinforcement (e.g., Peden, Browne, & Hearst, 1977; Williams & Williams, 1969).

An issue still not resolved concerns the specific reinforcement or feedback mechanisms at work in directing organisms toward or away from meaningful stimulus objects. Here, two possibilities can be sketched. According to the first, a stimulus that is paired with an appetitive or an aversive consequence acquires conditioned reinforcement value. Therefore, the animal performs those movements that effectively increase (positive reinforcement) or decrease (negative reinforcement) stimulation by the distant object (Skinner, 1953). Because the reinforcement mechanism automatically and arbitrarily connects response and reinforcer, any equally probable response should function as the effective behavior; therefore, animals ought to be able to be trained to move forward or backward in order to change (up or down) the intensity of a distal signal (Skinner, 1974, p. 41). According to the second notion, organisms are genetically programmed to move toward distant appetitive stimuli and to move away from distant aversive stimuli. Here, strong constraints are placed on the direction of movement and any correlated changes in external stimulation; approach should continue as long as the distal stimulus is too far away, and withdrawal should continue as long as the distal stimulus is too near (Powers, 1973).

In a clever test of these two possibilities, Hershberger (1962) attempted to train baby chicks to move toward or away from a food dish in order to move the dish close enough to permit eating. In the first group, every step toward the food dish moved it nearer and every step away from the dish moved it farther away; in the second group, these conditions were reversed (see Bateson & Wainwright, 1972 on a similar technique applied to imprinting). Although the first group of chicks adapted to the contingencies of reinforcement, the second was notably unsuccessful in reaching food; chicks in the latter group would occasionally turn and walk away from the food dish for a brief period (thereby moving it closer), but then they would whirl toward the dish and avidly chase it away! In short, the chicks behaved in the cybernetic fashion described by the feedback hypothesis instead of in a way consistent with the reinforcement hypothesis.

Direct versus Indirect Approach

An organism will move directly toward a distant, appetitive object. The apparent intelligence of this behavior is put to the test when a transparent barrier is placed between the animal and the object. Now, the organism must move away from the visible object for some distance if it is ever to reach it. Whereas the unobstructed goal requires only *direct* approach for contact, the obstructed goal requires *indirect* approach (thus the name "detour" for this type of problem). Interestingly, some animals fail to circumvent the barrier and continue to make futile, direct approaches toward the goal object. On the basis of these findings, it is not goal-direction but rather the flexibility of goal-direction that best qualifies as a behavioral criterion of intelligence (Bindra, 1976).

Of course, the classical investigations of Kohler (1925) were the first to study this spatial attribute of intelligence from a comparative perspective. Kohler observed the behavior of human children, chimpanzees, dogs, and chickens in the detour problem (for more recent results see Thorpe, 1962). On the basis of their performance, Kohler felt that these four ordered species possessed decreasing degrees of intelligence.

Prior discussion of the autoshaping literature led to the conclusion that locomotor and manipulative responses aimed directly toward or away from locatable stimuli represented a general behavioral disposition found in most mobile species. The prevalence and potency of autoshaping is certainly in keeping with the conclusion that this is a very basic form of learning (Bindra, 1976; Campbell, 1963; Jennings, 1962). The present discussion suggests that indirect approach behavior is a more recently evolved and advanced adaptation, one based upon more complicated survival demands than those promoting direct approach behavior. It is interesting then to reconsider some possible exceptions to the prevalence and potency of autoshaping. Recall that crows and dogs have been reported not to contact reinforcer signals with the reliability or durability of other species (pp. 37–38). Perhaps if tested on the detour problem, these animals would also show more successful circumvention of imposed obstructions than other species. Furthermore, despite autoshaping of the panel press in primates, Gamzu and Schwam (1974) have reported that squirrel monkeys promptly stop pressing when panel contacts omit scheduled food deliveries (pigeons of course continue to approach and peck under optimal "omission" training conditions; Peden et al., 1977; Williams & Williams, 1969). And no one would be surprised to learn that primates can cope with the detour problem. Thus tests of both direct (autoshaping) and indirect (detour problem) approach behavior might prove to be very instructive in assessing one aspect of the relative intelligence of animal species.

In this connection, the popular "omission" training procedure can be seen to represent something of a hybrid between direct and indirect approach tasks. Here, signal and reinforcer are paired unless a criterion directed response occurs, thereby omitting the reinforcer. As in the detour problem, direct approach behavior fails to permit access to the reinforcer; successful omission performance requires withholding of the approach response or redirecting it toward some other site (Barrera, 1974; Wasserman, 1972). However, unlike the detour problem, the omission procedure permits the subject unobstructedly to complete the approach response with the prescribed negative consequence or to execute incipient or incomplete approach responses with impunity.

CONCLUDING COMMENTS

By way of summary, the present chapter has reviewed the learning–performance distinction in behavior theory so that the determiners of response evocation in autoshaping might be more clearly understood. Available evidence indicates that the unconditioned stimulus, the conditioned stimulus, and the species of organism all importantly influence the form and direction of autoshaped behaviors. The contribution of these multiple influences on conditioned responding was also placed in a comparative-evolutionary perspective. Although tentative, perhaps the best conclusion here would be that the form of the conditioned response reflects the organism's unique sensorimotor organization, whereas the outward direction of the response does not. While response form is usually species-specific in character, response direction typically reflects the species-general dispositions to approach positively valued objects and to withdraw from negatively valued ones.

As was indicated in earlier discussion, behavior theorists have generally paid much less attention to the problem of response evocation than to the conditions of association formation. Thus, at present there is little more that can be said of the determiners of learned performance than that the unconditioned stimulus, the conditioned stimulus, and the species of organism must all be considered. However, at this point I would like to introduce some early thoughts of Tolman (1922, 1926, 1933) that bear upon this issue of response production and may represent the seeds of a theory of performance.

According to Tolman, the to-be-conditioned stimulus in an autoshaping (or any conditioning) experiment is not behaviorally inert. Rather it has what today we might call discriminative and evocative potential; that is, it is potentially discriminable from the context in a number of ways (size, shape, color, brightness, location, etc.), and each discriminative property is capable of supporting or evoking certain species-specific locomotor and manipulative responses. Such response potentialities are, of course, not actualized until the conditioned stimulus is associated with a motivating event. This association arises from stimulus–reinforcer pairings and is called an expectancy: After pairings, the organism is said to expect the reinforcer when the conditioned stimulus is presented. What does the animal do to evince this expectancy? Here, the discriminative nature of the conditioned stimulus permits the anticipatory activation of autonomic arousal, and the evocative nature of the conditioned stimulus (in conjunction with the appetitive or aversive character of the anticipatory arousal) calls forth particular directed skeletal behaviors:

> Appetites and aversions plus external stimuli constitute the final determiners of behavior [Tolman, 1926, p. 357].
>
> [The] internal [emotional–motivational] stimuli release the acts and determine the type, but... the external stimuli provide the specifying control and regulation [Tolman, 1922, p. 151].
>
> Not only does the organism "sense"... [conditioned stimulus] objects as presenting ... discrimination-possibilities, but ·further he also "perceives" in these objects... manipulation-possibilities [Tolman, 1933, p. 410].
>
> [Since] the types of possible motor manipulation will vary with the structure of the species, one and the same objective environment often must offer quite different manipulanda to different species of organisms [Tolman, 1933, p. 397].

Thus, the conditioned stimulus, the unconditioned stimulus, and the species of organism all can be seen to be incorporated in Tolman's analysis of response production.

Of course, Tolman also held that means–end or response–reinforcer relations participate in learned performance. And research in autoshaping (Hearst & Jenkins, 1974; Schwartz & Gamzu, 1977) has revealed that such relations do play a small, but reliable role in autoshaped behavior. I have chosen to focus on the stimulus–reinforcer relation and on particular determiners of performance simply because they seem to account for most of the data in autoshaping.

However, at this time, undue speculation about these theoretical matters seems pointless; research into the causation and function of directed actions has only just begun. Much still needs to be learned about how the environment influences the form and direction of conditioned responses, about how development and evolution participate in organizing sequences of directed action, and about how various biological mechanisms guide bodily movements.

Elucidation of these and related problems could take considerable time. Perhaps much more time than necessary will be taken if experimental psychologists continue in their narrow quest for the principles of learning. Wider investigation of the determinants of performance and the attendant amplifications of situational and evolutionary influences will move the study of learning closer to more biological approaches to the study of behavior. Future research into autoshaping and directed action may then not only greatly extend our understanding of the principles of adaptive behavior; it may also bring together scientists now needlessly separated by historical, theoretical, and semantic barriers.

ACKNOWLEDGMENTS

The author wishes to thank J. D. Deich, R. A. Hancock, G. A. Lucas, B. R. Moore, K. R. Nelson, W. L. Randall, and W. Timberlake for their contributions of valuable ideas and suggestions.

REFERENCES

Amsel, A. The role of frustrative nonreward in noncontinuous reward situations. *Psychological Bulletin*, 1958, 55, 102–119.

Andrew, R. J. Attentional processes and animal behaviour. In P. P. G. Bateson & R. A. Hinde (Eds.), *Growing points in ethology*. London and New York: Cambridge Univ. Press, 1976.

Asratyan, E. A. *Compensatory adaptations, reflex activity, and the brain*. Oxford: Pergamon, 1965.

Atnip, G. W. Stimulus- and response-reinforcer contingencies in autoshaping, operant, classical, and omission training procedures in rats. *Journal of the Experimental Analysis of Behavior*, 1977, 28, 59–69.

Barrera, F. J. Centrifugal selection of signal-directed pecking. *Journal of the Experimental Analysis of Behavior*, 1974, 22, 341–355.

Bateson, P. P. G., & Wainwright, A. A. P. The effects of prior exposure to light on the imprinting process in domestic chicks. *Behaviour*, 1972, 42, 279–290.

Bilbrey, J., & Winokur, S. Controls for and constraints on auto-shaping. *Journal of the Experimental Analysis of Behavior*, 1973, 20, 323–332.

Bindra, D. *Motivation: A systematic reinterpretation.* New York: Ronald, 1959.
Bindra, D. *A theory of intelligent behavior.* New York: Wiley, 1976.
Bindra, D. How adaptive behavior is produced: A perceptual–motivational alternative to response-reinforcement. *Behavioral and Brain Sciences,* 1978, *1,* 41–52.
Bolles, R. C. Reinforcement, expectancy, and learning. *Psychological Review,* 1972, *79,* 394–409.
Bottjer, S. W., Scobie, S. R., & Wallace, J. Positive behavioral contrast, autoshaping, and omission responding in the goldfish (*Carassius auratus*). *Animal Learning and Behavior,* 1977, *5,* 336–342.
Brandon, S. E., & Bitterman, M. E. Analysis of autoshaping in goldfish. *Animal Learning and Behavior,* 1979, *7,* 57–62.
Brown, J. S., & Farber, I. E. Secondary motivational systems. *Annual Review of Psychology,* 1968, *19,* 99–134.
Brown, P. L. Auto-shaping and observing responses (R_o) in the pigeon. *Proceedings, 76th Annual Convention, American Psychological Association,* 1968, 139–140.
Brown, P. L., & Jenkins, H. M. Auto-shaping of the pigeon's key-peck. *Journal of the Experimental Analysis of Behavior,* 1968, *11,* 1–8.
Browne, M. P. The role of primary reinforcement and overt movements in autoshaping in the pigeon. *Animal Learning and Behavior,* 1976, *4,* 287–292.
Campbell, D. T. Social attitudes and other acquired behavioral dispositions. In S. Koch (Ed.), *Psychology: A study of a science* (Vol. 6). New York: McGraw–Hill, 1963.
Craig, W. Appetites and aversions as constituents of instincts. *Biological Bulletin,* 1918, *34,* 91–107.
Croze, H. Searching image in carrion crows. Hunting strategy in a predator and some anti-predator devices in camouflaged prey. *Zeitschrift für Tierpsychologie,* 1970, *5,* 1–86.
Denny, M. R. Relaxation theory and experiments. In F. R. Brush (Ed.), *Aversive conditioning and learning.* New York: Academic Press, 1971.
Denny, M. R., & Ratner, S. C. *Comparative psychology: Research in animal behavior.* Homewood, Ill.: Dorsey, 1970.
Downey, P., & Harrison, J. M. Control of responding by location of auditory stimuli: Role of differential and non-differential reinforcement. *Journal of the Experimental Analysis of Behavior,* 1972, *18,* 453–463.
Dunham, P. J., Mariner, A., & Adams, H. Enhancement of off-key pecking by on-key punishment. *Journal of the Experimental Analysis of Behavior,* 1969, *12,* 789–797.
Dykman, R. A. Toward a theory of classical conditioning: Cognitive, emotional, and motor components of the conditional reflex. In B. A. Maher (Ed.), *Progress in experimental personality research.* New York: Academic Press, 1965.
Dykman, R. A. On the nature of classical conditioning. In C. C. Brown (Ed.), *Methods in psychophysiology.* Baltimore: Williams & Wilkins, 1967.
Eibl-Eibesfeldt, I. *Ethology: The biology of behavior.* (E. Klinghammer, trans.) New York: Holt, 1970.
Estes, W. K. New perspectives on some old issues in association theory. In N. J. Mackintosh & W. K. Honig (Eds.), *Fundamental issues in associative learning.* Halifax, Canada: Dalhousie Univ. Press, 1969.
Estes, W. K. Memory and conditioning. In F. J. McGuigan & D. B. Lumsden (Eds.), *Contemporary approaches to conditioning and learning.* Washington, D.C.: Winston, 1973.
Ewert, J. P. The neural basis of visually guided behavior. *Scientific American,* 1974, *230,* 34–42.
Fraenkel, G. S., & Gunn, D. L. *The orientation of animals: Kineses, taxes, and compass reactions.* New York: Dover, 1961.
Gamzu, E., & Schwam, E. Autoshaping and automaintenance of a key-press response in squirrel monkeys. *Journal of the Experimental Analysis of Behavior,* 1974, *21,* 361–371.
Gardner, W. M. Auto-shaping in bobwhite quail. *Journal of the Experimental Analysis of Behavior,* 1969, *12,* 279–281.

Ghiselin, M. T. *The triumph of the Darwinian method.* Berkeley: Univ. of California Press, 1969.
Glickman, S. E., & Schiff, B. B. A biological theory of reinforcement. *Psychological Review*, 1967, 74, 81–109.
Grastyan, E., & Vereczkei, L. Effects of spatial separation of the conditioned signal from the reinforcement: A demonstration of the conditioned character of the orienting response or the orientational character of conditioning. *Behavioral Biology*, 1974, 10, 121–146.
Gray, J. A. *Elements of a two-process theory of learning.* London: Academic Press, 1975.
Green, L. Are there two classes of classically-conditioned responses? *Pavlovian Journal of Biological Science*, 1978, 13, 154–162.
Green, L., & Rachlin, H. On the directionality of key pecking during signals for appetitive and aversive events. *Learning and Motivation*, 1977, 8, 551–568.
Griffin, D. R. *The question of animal awareness: Evolutionary continuity of mental experience.* New York: Rockefeller Univ. Press, 1976.
Hailman, J. P. How an instinct is learned. *Scientific American*, 1969, 221, 98–106.
Haraway, M. M., Wirth, P. W., & Maples, E. G. Contiguous approach conditioning: A model for positive reinforcement. *Psychological Reports*, 1974, 34, 127–130.
Harlow, H. F. Learning set and error factor theory. In S. Koch (Ed.), *Psychology: A study of a science* (Vol. 2). New York: McGraw-Hill, 1959.
Hearst, E. The classical–instrumental distinction: Reflexes, voluntary behavior, and categories of associative learning. In W. K. Estes (Ed.), *Handbook of learning and cognitive processes: Conditioning and behavior theory* (Vol. 2). Hillsdale, N.J.: Erlbaum, 1975. (a)
Hearst, E. Pavlovian conditioning and directed movements. In G. H. Bower (Ed.), *The psychology of learning and motivation* (Vol. 9). New York: Academic Press, 1975. (b)
Hearst, E., & Franklin, S. R. Positive and negative relations between a signal and food: Approach–withdrawal behavior toward the signal. *Journal of Experimental Psychology: Animal Behavior Processes*, 1977, 3, 37–52.
Hearst, E., & Gormley, D. Some tests of the additivity (autoshaping) theory of behavioral contrast. *Animal Learning and Behavior*, 1976, 4, 145–150.
Hearst, E., & Jenkins, H. M. *Sign-tracking: The stimulus–reinforcer relation and directed action.* Austin, Tex. The Psychonomic Society, 1974.
Herrnstein, R. J. The evolution of behaviorism. *American Psychologist*, 1977, 32, 593–603.
Hershberger, W. A. Experimentally induced positive feedback in locomotor behavior (Doctoral dissertation, University of Colorado, 1962). *Dissertation Abstracts International*, 1962, 23, 2219–2220. (University Microfilms No. 62–6276.)
Hilgard, E. R. The nature of the conditioned response: I. The case for and against stimulus-substitution. *Psychological Review*, 1936, 43, 366–385. (a)
Hilgard, E. R. The nature of the conditioned response: II. Alternatives to stimulus-substitution. *Psychological Review*, 1936, 43, 547–564. (b)
Hilgard, E. R., & Marquis, D. G. *Conditioning and learning.* New York: Appleton-Century-Crofts, 1940.
Hinde, R. A. *Animal behaviour: A synthesis of ethology and comparative psychology* (2nd ed.). New York: McGraw-Hill, 1970.
Hinde, R. A., & Stevenson-Hinde, J. *Constraints on learning.* London: Academic Press, 1973.
Hinde, R. A., & Tinbergen, N. The comparative study of species-specific behavior. In A. Roe & G. G. Simpson (Eds.), *Behavior and evolution.* New Haven, Conn.: Yale Univ. Press, 1958.
Hodos, W., & Campbell, C. B. G. Scala naturae: Why there is no theory in comparative psychology. *Psychological Review*, 1969, 76, 337–350.
Hogan, J. A. How young chicks learn to recognize food. In R. A. Hinde & J. S. Hinde (Eds.), *Constraints on learning.* New York: Academic Press, 1973.
Holland, P. C. Conditioned stimulus as a determinant of the form of the Pavlovian conditioned response. *Journal of Experimental Psychology: Animal Behavior Processes*, 1977, 3, 77–104.

Honig, W. K., & Staddon, J. E. R. *Handbook of operant behavior.* Englewood Cliffs, N.J.: Prentice-Hall, 1977.
Jenkins, H. M., Barrera, F. J., Ireland, C., & Woodside, B. Signal-centered action patterns of dogs in appetitive classical conditioning. *Learning and Motivation,* 1978, *9,* 272–296.
Jenkins, H. M., & Boakes, R. A. Observing stimulus sources that signal food or no food. *Journal of the Experimental Analysis of Behavior,* 1973, *20,* 197–207.
Jenkins, H. M., & Moore, B. R. The form of the autoshaped response with food or water reinforcers. *Journal of the Experimental Analysis of Behavior,* 1973, *20,* 163–181.
Jennings, H. S. *Behavior of the lower organisms.* Bloomington: Indiana Univ. Press, 1962.
Jensen, D. D. Polythetic biopsychology: An alternative to behaviorism. In J. H. Reynierse (Ed.), *Current issues in animal learning: A colloquium.* Lincoln: Univ. of Nebraska Press, 1970.
John, E. R. *Mechanisms of memory.* New York: Academic Press, 1967.
Kimble, G. A. *Hilgard and Marquis' conditioning and learning* (2nd ed.). New York: Appleton-Century-Crofts, 1961.
Kohler, W. *The mentality of apes.* New York: Harcourt, Brace, 1925.
Konorski, J. *Conditioned reflexes and neuron organization.* London and New York: Cambridge Univ. Press, 1948.
Kupfermann, I. Dissociation of appetitive and consummatory phases of feeding behavior in *Aplysia:* A lesion study. *Behavioral Biology,* 1974, *10,* 89–97.
Lajoie, J., & Bindra, D. An interpretation of autoshaping and related phenomena in terms of stimulus-incentive contingencies alone. *Canadian Journal of Psychology,* 1976, *30,* 157–173.
Likely, D. G. Autoshaping in the rhesus monkey. *Animal Learning and Behavior,* 1974, *2,* 203–206.
Lockard, R. B. Reflections on the fall of comparative psychology: Is there a message for us all? *American Psychologist,* 1971, *26,* 168–179.
Locurto, C., Terrace, H. S., & Gibbon, J. Autoshaping, random control, and omission training in the rat. *Journal of the Experimental Analysis of Behavior,* 1976, *26,* 451–462.
Logan, F. A. Incentive theory, reinforcement, and education. In R. Glaser (Ed.), *The nature of reinforcement.* New York: Academic Press, 1971.
LoLordo, V. M. Selective associations. In A. Dickinson & R. A. Boakes (Eds.), *Mechanisms of learning and motivation: A memorial volume to Jerzy Konorski.* Hillsdale, N.J.: Erlbaum, 1979.
LoLordo, V. M., McMillan, J. C., & Riley, A. L. The effects upon food-reinforced pecking and treadle-pressing of auditory and visual signals for response-independent food. *Learning and Motivation,* 1974, *5,* 24–41.
Loop, M. S. Auto-shaping—A simple technique for teaching a lizard to perform a visual discrimination task. *Copeia,* 1976, *3,* 574–576.
Lorenz, K. The conception of instinctive behavior. In C. H. Schiller (Ed.), *Instinctive behavior.* New York: International Universities, 1957.
Lorenz, K. The evolution of behavior. *Scientific American,* 1958, *199,* 67–83.
Lorenz, K., & Tinbergen, N. Taxis and instinctive action in the egg-retrieving behavior of the greylag goose. In C. H. Schiller (Ed.), *Instinctive behavior.* New York: International Universities, 1957.
Lucas, G. A. The control of keypecks during automaintenance by prekeypeck omission training. *Animal Learning and Behavior,* 1975, *3,* 33–36.
Lucas, G. A., Vodraska, A., & Wasserman, E. A. Technical note: A direct fluid delivery system for the pigeon. *Journal of the Experimental Analysis of Behavior,* 1979, *31,* 285–288.
Mackintosh, N. J. *The psychology of animal learning.* London: Academic Press, 1974.
Maier, N. R. F., & Schneirla, T. C. *Principles of animal psychology* New York: McGraw-Hill, 1935.
Marler, P., & Hamilton, W. J. *Mechanisms of animal behavior* New York: Wiley, 1966.
Mowrer, O. H. *Learning theory and behavior.* New York: Wiley, 1960.

Newlin, R. J., & LoLordo, V. M. A comparison of pecking generated by serial, delay, and trace autoshaping procedures. *Journal of the Experimental Analysis of Behavior,* 1976, *25,* 227–241.

Nye, P. W. On the functional differences between frontal and lateral visual fields of the pigeon. *Vision Research,* 1973, *13,* 559–574.

Pavlov, I. P. *Conditioned reflexes.* New York and London: Oxford Univ. Press, 1927.

Pavlov, I. P. An attempt at a physiological interpretation of obsessional neurosis and paranoia. *Journal of Mental Science,* 1934, *80,* 187–197.

Peden, B. F., Browne, M. P., & Hearst, E. Persistent approaches to a signal for food despite food omission for approaching. *Journal of Experimental Psychology: Animal Behavior Processes,* 1977, *3,* 377–399.

Peterson, G. B., Ackil, J. E., Frommer, G. P., & Hearst, E. S. Conditioned approach and contact behavior toward signals for food or brain-stimulation reinforcement. *Science,* 1972, *177,* 1009–1011.

Poling, A., & Poling, T. Automaintenance in guinea pigs: Effects of feeding regimen and omission training. *Journal of the Experimental Analysis of Behavior,* 1978, *30,* 37–46.

Postman, L. Association and performance in the analysis of verbal learning. In T. R. Dixon, & D. L. Horton (Eds.), *Verbal behavior and general behavior theory.* Englewood Cliffs, N.J.: Prentice-Hall, 1968.

Powell, R. W., Kelly, W., & Santisteban, D. Response-independent reinforcement in the crow: Failure to obtain autoshaping or positive automaintenance. *Bulletin of the Psychonomic Society,* 1975, *6,* 513–516.

Powers, W. T. Feedback: Beyond behaviorism. *Science,* 1973, *179,* 351–356.

Premock, M., & Klipec, W. D. The effects of modifying consummatory behavior on the topography of the autoshaped pecking response in pigeons. *Journal of the Experimental Analysis of Behavior,* 1980, in press.

Rachlin, H. Autoshaping of key pecking in pigeons with negative reinforcement. *Journal of the Experimental Analysis of Behavior,* 1969, *12,* 521–531.

Randall, W., Trulson, M., & Parsons, V. Role of thyroid hormones in an abnormal grooming behavior in thyroidectomized cats and cats with pontile lesions. *Journal of Comparative and Physiological Psychology,* 1976, *90,* 231–243.

Rashotte, M. E., Griffin, R. W., & Sisk, C. L. Second-order conditioning of the pigeon's keypeck. *Animal Learning and Behavior,* 1977, *5,* 25–38.

Ratner, S. C. Comparative psychology. In A. Gilgen (Ed.), *Contemporary scientific psychology.* New York: Academic Press, 1970.

Redford, M. E., & Perkins, C. C. The role of autopecking in behavioral contrast. *Journal of the Experimental Analysis of Behavior,* 1974, *21,* 145–150.

Rescorla, R. A. Second-order conditioning: Implications for theories of learning. In F. J. McGuigan & D. B. Lumsden (Eds.), *Contemporary approaches to conditioning and learning.* Washington, D.C.: Winston, 1973.

Rescorla, R. A. Some implications of a cognitive perspective on Pavlovian conditioning. In S. H. Hulse, H. Fowler, & W. K. Honig (Eds.), *Cognitive processes in animal behavior.* Hillsdale, N.J.: Erlbaum, 1978.

Reynierse, J. H., Scavio, M. J., & Ulness, J. D. An ethological analysis of classically conditioned fear. In J. H. Reynierse (Ed.), *Current issues in animal learning.* Lincoln: Univ. of Nebraska Press, 1970.

Ricci, J. A. Key pecking under response-independent food presentation after long simple and compound stimuli. *Journal of the Experimental Analysis of Behavior,* 1973, *19,* 509–516.

Schneiderman, N. Response system divergencies in aversive classical conditioning. In A. H. Black & W. F. Prokasy (Eds.), *Classical conditioning II: Current research and theory.* New York: Appleton-Century-Crofts, 1972.

Schneirla, T. C. An evolutionary and developmental theory of biphasic processes underlying approach and withdrawal. In M. R. Jones (Ed.), *Nebraska symposium on motivation* (Vol. 7). Lincoln: Univ. of Nebraska Press, 1959.

Schwartz, B. Maintenance of key pecking by response-independent food presentation: The role of the modality of the signal for food. *Journal of the Experimental Analysis of Behavior*, 1973, 20, 17–22. (a)

Schwartz, B. Maintenance of keypecking in pigeons by a food avoidance but not a shock avoidance contingency. *Animal Learning and Behavior*, 1973, 1, 164–166. (b)

Schwartz, B. Discriminative stimulus location as a determinant of positive and negative behavioral contrast in the pigeon. *Journal of the Experimental Analysis of Behavior*, 1975, 23, 167–176.

Schwartz, B. Positive and negative conditioned suppression in the pigeon: Effects of the locus and modality of the CS. *Learning and Motivation*, 1976, 7, 86–100.

Schwartz, B., & Gamzu, E. Pavlovian control of operant behavior: An analysis of autoshaping and its implications for operant conditioning. In W. K. Honig & J. E. R. Staddon (Eds.), *Handbook of operant behavior*. Englewood Cliffs, N.J.: Prentice-Hall, 1977.

Segal, E. F. Induction and the provenance of operants. In R. M. Gilbert & J. R. Millenson (Eds.), *Reinforcement: Behavioral analyses*. New York: Academic Press, 1972.

Seligman, M. E. P. On the generality of the laws of learning. *Psychological Review*, 1970, 77, 406–418.

Seligman, M. E. P., & Hager, J. L. *Biological boundaries of learning*. New York: Appleton-Century-Crofts, 1972.

Sherrington, C. S. *The integrative action of the nervous system*. New Haven, Conn.: Yale Univ. Press, 1906.

Shettleworth, S. J. Constraints on conditioning in the writings of Konorski. In A. Dickinson & R. A. Boakes (Eds.), *Mechanisms of learning and motivation: A memorial volume to Jerzy Konorski*. Hillsdale, N.J.: Erlbaum, 1979.

Sidman, M., & Fletcher, F. G. A demonstration of auto-shaping with monkeys. *Journal of the Experimental Analysis of Behavior*, 1968, 11, 307–309.

Skinner, B. F. Two types of conditioned reflex and a pseudo-type. *Journal of General Psychology*, 1935, 12, 66–77.

Skinner, B. F. *Science and human behavior*. New York: Macmillan, 1953.

Skinner, B. F. *About behavorism*. New York: Knopf, 1974.

Skinner, B. F. Herrnstein and the evolution of behaviorism. *American Psychologist*, 1977, 32, 1006–1012.

Spence, K. W. Cognitive versus stimulus–response theories of learning. *Psychological Review*, 1950, 57, 159–172.

Sperling, S. E., Perkins, M. E., & Duncan, H. J. Stimulus generalization from feeder to response key in the acquisition of autoshaped pecking. *Journal of the Experimental Analysis of Behavior*, 1977, 27, 469–478.

Spiker, C. C. Behaviorism, cognitive psychology, and the active organism. In N. Datan & H. W. Reese (Eds.), *Life-span developmental psychology: Dialectical perspectives on experimental research*. New York: Academic Press, 1977.

Squire, L. H. Auto-shaping key responses with fish. *Psychonomic Science*, 1969, 17, 177–178.

Staddon, J. E. R. Learning as adaptation. In W. K. Estes (Ed.), *Handbook of learning and cognitive processes: Conditioning and behavior theory* (Vol. 2). Hillsdale, N.J.: Erlbaum, 1975.

Staddon, J. E. R., & Simmelhag, V. L. The "supersition" experiment: A reexamination of its implications for the principles of adaptive behavior. *Psychological Review*, 1971, 78, 3–43.

Stepien, I. The magnet reaction, a symptom of prefrontal ablation. *Acta Neurobiologiae Experimentalis*, 1974, 34, 145–160.

Stiers, M., & Silberberg, A. Lever-contact responses in rats: Auto-maintenance with and without a negative response-reinforcer dependency. *Journal of the Experimental Analysis of Behavior*, 1974, 22, 497–506.

Tapp, J. T. Activity, reactivity, and the behavior-directing properties of stimuli. In J. T. Tapp (Ed.), *Reinforcement and behavior*. New York: Academic Press, 1969.
Thompson, R. F. The search for the engram. *American Psychologist*, 1976, *31*, 209–227.
Thorpe, W. H. *Learning and instinct in animals*. London: Methuen, 1962.
Timberlake, W., & Grant, D. L. Auto-shaping rats to the presentation of another rat predicting food. *Science*, 1975, *190*, 690–692.
Tinbergen, N. *The study of instinct*. New York and London: Oxford Univ. Press, 1951.
Tinbergen, N. Behavior and natural selection. In J. A. Moore (Ed.), *Ideas in modern biology*. Garden City, N.Y.: The Natural History Press, 1965.
Tolman, E. C. Can instincts be given up in psychology? *Journal of Abnormal and Social Psychology*, 1922, *17*, 139–152.
Tolman, E. C. A behavioristic theory of ideas. *Psychological Review*, 1926, *33*, 352–369.
Tolman, E. C. *Purposive behavior in animals and man*. New York: Appleton-Century-Crofts, 1932.
Tolman, E. C. Gestalt and sign-gestalt. *Psychological Review*, 1933, *40*, 391–411.
Tolman, E. C. Principles of performance. *Psychological Review*, 1955, *62*, 315–326.
Wasserman, E. A. Auto-shaping: The selection and direction of behavior by predictive stimuli (Doctoral dissertation, Indiana University, 1972). *Dissertation Abstracts International*, 1972, *32*, 6704B. (University Microfilms No. 72-15, 935.)
Wasserman, E. A. The effect of redundant contextual stimuli on autoshaping the pigeon's keypeck. *Animal Learning and Behavior*, 1973, *1*, 198–206. (a)
Wasserman, E. A. Pavlovian conditioning with heat reinforcement produces stimulus-directed pecking in chicks. *Science*, 1973, *181*, 875–877. (b)
Wasserman, E. A. Bindra's theory: Some successes and precursors. *Behavioral and Brain Sciences*, 1978, *1*, 80–81. (a)
Wasserman, E. A. Interrelations between motor and secretory reactions in classical alimentary conditioning. *Journal of Higher Nervous Activity*, 1978, *28*, 493–497. (in Russian) (b)
Wasserman, E. A. The relationship between motor and secretory behaviors in classical appetitive conditioning. *Pavlovian Journal of Biological Science*, 1978, *13*, 182–186. (c)
Wasserman, E. A., & Anderson, P. A. Differential autoshaping to common and distinctive elements of positive and negative discriminative stimuli. *Journal of the Experimental Analysis of Behavior*, 1974, *22*, 491–496.
Wasserman, E. A., Carr, D. L., & Deich, J. D. Association of conditioned stimuli during serial conditioning by pigeons. *Animal Learning and Behavior*, 1978, *6*, 52–56.
Wasserman, E. A., Deich, J. D., Hunter, N. B., & Nagamatsu, L. S. Analyzing the random control procedure: Effects of paired and unpaired CSs and USs on autoshaping the chick's key peck with heat reinforcement. *Learning and Motivation*, 1977, *8*, 467–487.
Wasserman, E. A., Franklin, S. R., & Hearst, E. Pavlovian appetitive contingencies and approach versus withdrawal to conditioned stimuli in pigeons. *Journal of Comparative and Physiological Psychology*, 1974, *86*, 616–627.
Wasserman, E. A., Hunter, N. B., Gutowski, K. A., Bader, S. A. Autoshaping chicks with heat reinforcement: The role of stimulus-reinforcer and response-reinforcer relations. *Journal of Experimental Psychology: Animal Behavior Processes*, 1975, *1*, 158–169.
Wasserman, E. A., & Larew, M. B. *Retention of stimulus order by pigeons*. Paper presented at the annual meeting of the American Psychological Association, Toronto, August 1978.
Wasserman, E. A., & Molina, E. J. Explicitly unpaired key light and food presentations: Interference with subsequent auto-shaped key pecking in pigeons. *Journal of Experimental Psychology: Animal Behavior Processes*, 1975, *1*, 30–38.
Waters, R. H. The nature of comparative psychology. In R. H. Water, D. A. Rethlingshafer, & W. E. Caldwell (Eds.), *Principles of comparative psychology*. New York: McGraw-Hill, 1960.
Weisman, R. G. On the role of the reinforcer in associative learning. In H. Davis & H. M. B. Hurwitz (Eds.), *Operant-Pavlovian interactions*. Hillsdale, N.J.: Erlbaum, 1976.

Weisman, R. G., & Dodd, P. W. D. The study of association: Methodology and basic phenomena. In A. Dickinson & R. A. Boakes (Eds.), *Mechanisms of learning and motivation: A memorial volume to Jerzy Konorski*. Hillsdale, N.J.: Erlbaum, 1979.

Wesp, R. K., Lattal, K. A., & Poling, A. D. Punishment of autoshaped key-peck responses of pigeons. *Journal of the Experimental Analysis of Behavior*, 1977, 27, 407–418.

Wessells, M. G. The effects of reinforcement upon the prepecking behaviors in pigeons in the autoshaping experiment. *Journal of the Experimental Analysis of Behavior*, 1974, 21, 125–144.

Williams, D. R., & Williams, H. Auto-maintenance in the pigeon: Sustained pecking despite contingent non-reinforcement. *Journal of the Experimental Analysis of Behavior*, 1969, 12, 511–520.

Williams, K. A. The conditioned reflex and the sign function in learning. *Psychological Review*, 1929, 36, 481–497.

Wilson, B. *Autoshaping in pigeons and corvids*. Unpublished doctoral dissertation, The University of Sussex, 1978.

Woodard, W. T., & Bitterman, M. E. Autoshaping in the goldfish. *Behavior Research Methods and Instrumentation*, 1974, 6, 409–410.

Woodruff, G., & Starr, M. D. Autoshaping of initial feeding and drinking reactions in newly hatched chicks. *Animal Learning and Behavior*, 1978, 6, 265–272.

Woodruff, G., & Williams, D. R. The associative relation underlying autoshaping in the pigeon. *Journal of the Experimental Analysis of Behavior*, 1976, 26, 1–13.

Wyrwicka, W. *The mechanisms of conditioned behavior*. Springfield, Ill.: Thomas, 1972.

Zener, K. The significance of behavior accompanying conditioned salivary secretion for theories of the conditioned response. *American Journal of Psychology*, 1937, 50, 384–403.

Zener, K., & McCurdy, H. G. Analysis of motivational factors in conditioned behavior: I. The differential effect of changes in hunger upon conditioned, unconditioned, and spontaneous salivary secretion. *Journal of Psychology*, 1939, 8, 321–350.

DAVID R. WILLIAMS | 3

Biconditional Behavior: Conditioning without Constraint[1]

Psychobiology and learning theory have finally noticed each other, and the important problem now is to bring about their union and make it a productive one. In an effort to go beyond mere pointing out of the need for such a merger, this paper will begin with a detailed analysis of what began as a bewildering phenomenon of the laboratory: hungry pigeons pecking persistently and tenaciously at the response key of an operant conditioning chamber, when the only discernible effect of such pecking was to prevent an opportunity to eat (Williams & Williams, 1969). The phenomenon itself—a laboratory peculiarity similar to the "misbehaviors" described by the Brelands (1961)—has already played a role in several efforts to relate psychobiology and learning theory (Rozin & Kalat, 1971; Seligman, 1970; Shettleworth, 1971; Staddon & Simmelhag, 1971). The discussion in this chapter differs from such treatments in that it does not set out to restructure or delimit the traditional framework of learning theory: It offers an analysis of the phenomenon itself, not a revision or retreat from theory.

The major thesis to be put forth is that the harmonious operation of the ordinary laws of conditioning provides a surprisingly powerful basis for the development and maintenance of behaviors that are both species-typical and sensitive to the particulars of an individual's experience. The development of this thesis demands a functional orientation to conditioning: It will be assumed that a given behavioral phenomenon may reflect the joint operation of several different conditioning processes. Functional analysis of this sort is a customary step in behavioral analysis, where, for example, drive and reward are seen as joint determiners of a response, even though they constitute separate processes. A

---

[1]Preparation of this manuscript was aided by Grant GB 35319X from the National Science Foundation.

corresponding step will be taken in the present treatment, but some confusion may arise because the "joint determiners" of interest both involve conditioning. Specifically, we will treat, as separate but direct determiners of the behavior, the mechanisms involved in *respondent* and *operant* conditioning. It is easy to separate these sources of control operationally: One class of determiners arises from stimulus–reinforcer (S–S*) relations, the other from response–reinforcer (R–S*) relations.[2]

It is necessary to emphasize the adoption of this strategy of analysis at the outset, because S–S* and R–S* relations have often been used to classify rather than to analyze. The critical difference lies in what is implied when, for example, it is shown that a behavioral pattern is influenced by its consequences (i.e., by R–S* relationships). The assumption will be made here that such a demonstration *does not preclude* the possibility that S–S* relationships also effect the behavioral pattern directly. This assumption implies that classification of the pattern as an operant or a respondent is misleading, since such classification is normally taken to preclude the simultaneous operation of multiple sources of control, including respondent (i.e., S–S*) control for operants, or operant (i.e., R–S*) control for respondents. Obviously, the pluralism of principles that this step makes possible risks the danger of confusion and needless complexity. From an analytic point of view, however, the *availability* of a principle does not produce complexity; simplicity or complexity inhere in the phenomena themselves.

The underlying purpose of this chapter is to contribute to the useful interaction of learning theory and psychobiology by illustrating the utility of an analytic approach based on the fundamental conceptions of learning. The coordination of learning principles that constitutes the heart of this approach seems most likely to be appropriate in the study of behaviors that express the reactions of a species to laboratory and nonlaboratory situations. It may be through analysis of the mechanisms of conditioning at work in such instances that learning theory and psychobiology can most gracefully merge. Doubtless many species have developed unique and important mechanisms relevant to learning in their natural environments. However, an effective integration of psychobiology and learning theory is most likely to start with a consideration of how the best-understood mechanisms of learning normally coordinate in the occurrence of species-typical behaviors.

[2]Conditioning theory partitions any setting into four classes of events: conditional stimuli and responses, and unconditional stimuli and responses. Following Bolles' (1972) recent suggestion, these four classes will be called S, R, S*, and R*, as a shorthand for "conditional stimulus," "conditional response" or "operant," "unconditional stimulus" or "reinforcer" and " unconditional response." Operationally, operant or instrumental conditioning is concerned with relationships between R and S*, while respondent or classical conditioning arises from S–S* relationships.

THE LABORATORY PHENOMENON

At the heart of this discussion is a phenomenon that grew out of Brown and Jenkins' (1968) technique for *autoshaping* the pigeons' keypeck. Brown and Jenkins' shaping procedure was remarkably direct: After first training a hungry pigeon to accept grain from the grain hopper in a standard operant conditioning chamber, a series of Pavlovian delay conditioning trials was administered as shown in Figure 3.1 (*a*). Following an intertrial interval during which the chamber was normally illuminated, the response key was transilluminated for 8 sec, and then 4 sec access to grain was provided. Illumination of the response key corresponds to presentation of S in a Pavlovian delay conditioning paradigm, and access to grain constitutes presentation of S*. Brown and Jenkins found that after somewhere between 4 and 200 trials (with a mean around 45), pigeons began pecking at the illuminated key. In Brown and Jenkins' experiments, pecks were usually reinforced immediately, in completion of the autoshaping procedure. They also reported that presenting reinforcers in the presence of an illuminated key was not sufficient to engender pecking, and that flashing the key in the absence of reinforcement was not effective either.

The autoshaping procedure has obvious merit as a simple means of training pigeons to peck response keys (cf. Ferster & Skinner, 1957). Among operant

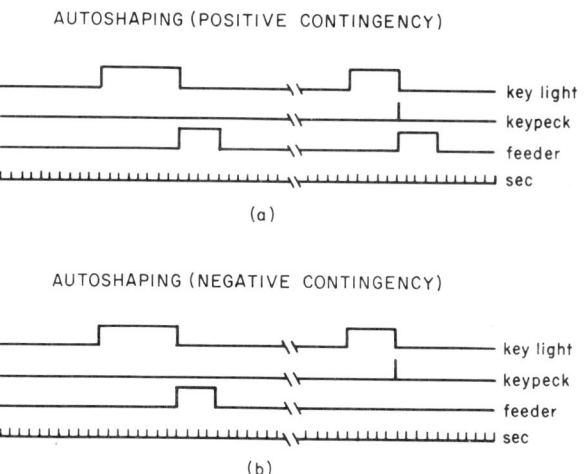

Figure 3.1. Two basic autoshaping procedures. Upward deflection of the line signals the onset of the event labeled at right. With (*a*) a positive contingency, autoshaping involves presentation of the reinforcer after a set period of key exposure or immediately after a key peck response. By contrast, with (*b*) the negative contingency, the reinforcer is presented after a set period of key exposure if there is no peck, but a peck turns off the key, prevents reinforcement, and starts the interval between trials.

procedures, it is truly remarkable—and virtually unique—in that it depends for its effectiveness on the pigeon's making an uncoerced contribution to the situation. Prior to the occurrence of the first keypeck, the experimenter does nothing that makes keypecking an advantageous or special behavior, yet pigeons reliably and steadfastly begin keypecking. Given the paradigm of classical delay conditioning, it may not come as a surprise that *something* is conditioned in pigeons; but it seems like remarkable good luck that the "something" should be skeletal behavior, directed at the response key and apparently identical to the behavior that constitutes the classic example of a free operant.

The procedure illustrated in Figure 3.1 (*b*) illustrates just how strong this remarkable good luck is. As diagrammed, conditions are the same as those of Brown and Jenkins' autoshaping procedure on trials where no peck occurs; on trials where a peck occurs, however, the key is turned off and no reinforcer is presented. In this new procedure, there is a *negative* relationship between pecking and the reinforcer: Instead of producing reinforcement, pecks prevent or (in an operational sense) avoid it. Under these new conditions, pecking is "functional" in the sense that it blocks the opportunity to feed; any behavior other than pecking during the time of key illumination is compatible with the subsequent presentation of food. Under this procedure, as with Brown and Jenkins', there is a positive correlation or contingency between key illumination and reinforcement; in contrast to their procedure, however, there is negative correlation between keypecking and presentation of the reinforcer. Just how often key-illumination is followed by food depends, inversely, on how often the pigeon pecks the key when it is illuminated.

Results from the use of this procedure were unequivocal (Williams & Williams, 1969): Food-deprived pigeons peck reliably at the key—and thereby prevent the presentation of food—on a substantial fraction of all trials presented. The effect holds up over a series of sessions comprising hundreds (and in later experiments, thousands) of trials. Figure 3.2 shows results from the first 13 birds studied under this procedure, and Figure 3.3 reproduces detailed performances of 4 of the birds. Results of this character have been obtained subsequently in dozens more pigeons under a variety of conditions, and it seems inescapably clear that sustained keypecking can be maintained under conditions where pecks prevent reinforcement.

Schwartz (1972) modified the paradigm of Figure 3.1 (*b*) so that pecking did not turn off the key—even though it prevented reinforcement at the time of key offset—and also studied a procedure under which key illumination overlapped the period of food presentation. Both of these maneuvers were designed to control for the possibility that peck-produced key offset might be responsible for at least some of the pecking observed. Neither of these alterations of the paradigm of Figure 3.1 (*b*) gave any evidence of reducing the tendency to peck the key; if anything, levels of responding were enhanced. Thus, an explanation of the sustained responding based on consequences of peck-produced stimulus change,

3. BICONDITIONAL BEHAVIOR: CONDITIONING WITHOUT CONSTRAINT | 59

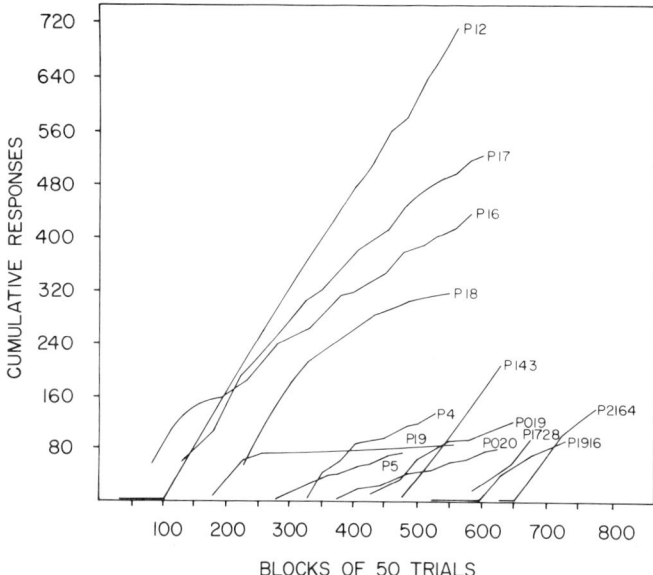

Figure 3.2. Cumulative responses per session for the first 13 pigeons trained on autoshaping with a negative contingency. Curves for the various birds are displaced along the abscissa. (From Williams & Williams, 1969. Copyright © 1969 by the Society for the Experimental Analysis of Behavior. Reprinted with permission.)

or on secondary reinforcement from peck-correlated key offset, does not seem to account adequately for the sustained responding observed under the negative contingency of Figure 3.1 (b). Herrnstein and Loveland (1972) have recently come to a similar conclusion.

The intermediate levels of responding shown in Figures 3.2 and 3.3 are similar to results reported by Sheffield (1965) for the omission-training procedure of classical conditioning, and to findings from conventional studies of avoidance learning. In these cases, responding never wholly disappears, but it never becomes perfectly established either. In the case of avoidance learning, such an intermediate state of affairs is readily understood: If an avoidance response occurred on every trial, then the shocks that maintain the behavior would occur on none of the trials, and the actual procedure would be that of experimental extinction. As soon as extinction does set in, however, under a conventional avoidance procedure shocks are readministered and the response again increases in likelihood. Sheffield has offered a similar account for the fact that salivation occurs at intermediate levels when the omission procedure is used with an appetitive reinforcer in salivary conditioning. A similar analysis seems appropriate in the present case. Under the negative contingency, trials where no peck

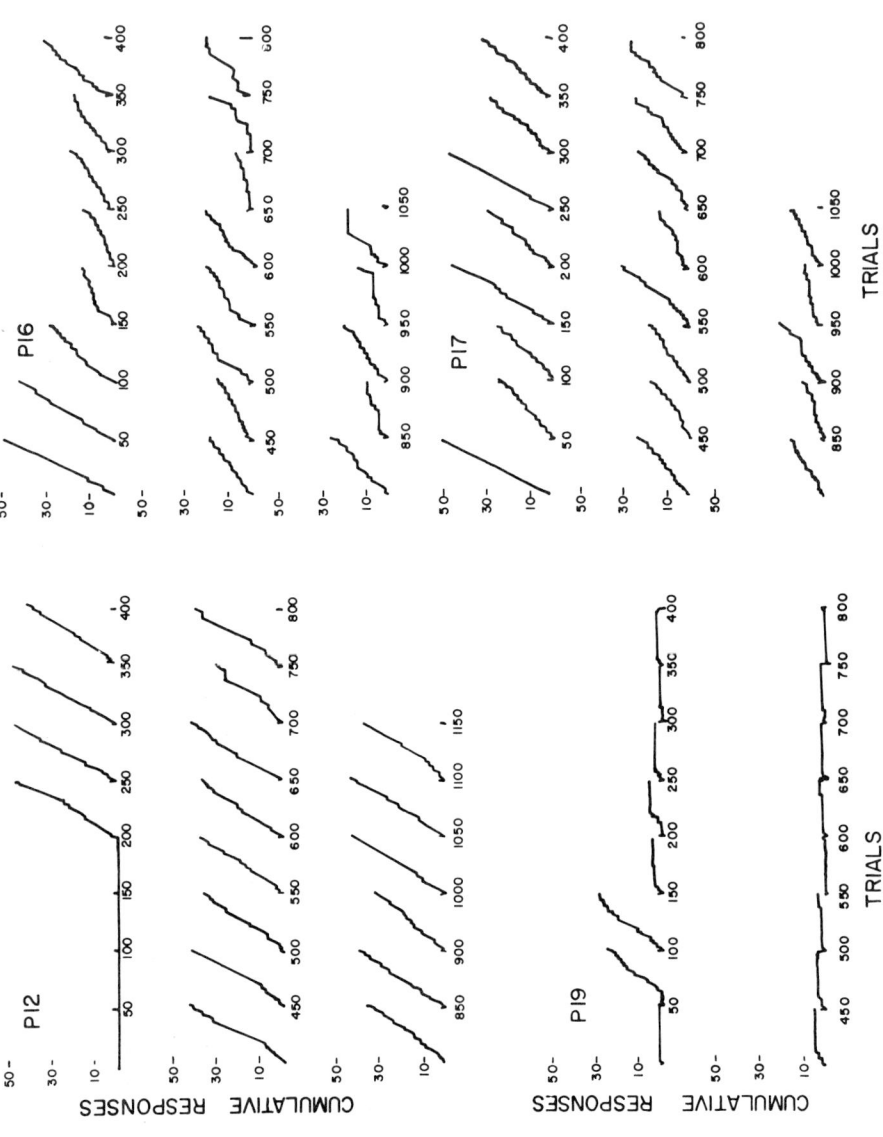

Figure 3.3. Cumulative responses for four birds within daily sessions of 50 trials each. Pecking of Pigeons 16 and 17 (P16 and P17) had previously been reinforced, while that of Pigeons 12 and 19 (P12 and P19) had not. Throughout these sessions, each peck terminated the trial and prevented reinforcement. (From Williams & Williams, 1969. Copyright © 1969 by the Society for the

occurs are of the sort that Brown and Jenkins used to autoshape the pigeon's keypeck in the first place: On these trials a key is illuminated and followed after some seconds by a grain reinforcer. However, pecking turns off the key and prevents reinforcement; operationally, this is a case of experimental extinction. Procedurally, then, the negative contingency combines trials on which extinction conditions are present (namely, those where a peck occurs) with trials of a type that can engender the initiation of pecking (namely, trials followed by reinforcement because no peck occurred).

This is the phenomenon as initially encountered. The remainder of the chapter will explore its origins, significance, and implications.

AUTOSHAPING AND THE $S-S^*$ RELATIONSHIP

In our laboratory, an insight into the critical $S-S^*$ relationship in autoshaping began with an unsuccessful series of pilot experiments carried out in collaboration with Elkan Gamzu. Operationally, the goal of those experiments was to unconfound two aspects of key illumination in the autoshaping procedure, namely, the role of key illumination as a Pavlovian S and its status as a visual display toward which pecking could be directed. We attempted to unconfound these two functions in the most straightforward fashion possible: We used an auditory stimulus (1000-Hz tone) as a Pavlovian S, and presented the key only sporadically. We tried a number of procedures whose common element was as follows: A 6-sec tone was paired with food in the Pavlovian manner for some number of trials, and from time to time the tone and an illuminated key were presented in conjunction. If classical delay conditioning, plus an opportunity to peck, were sufficient to produce autoshaping, this procedure should suffice to produce the result. Sustained keypecking never developed, however, and we concluded that autoshaping was not merely a happy conjunction of classical conditioning, restricted feeding, and an opportunity to peck.

These exploratory experiments did not, in and of themselves, yield much information: The failure to obtain a result may arise for many reasons, some of which are not at all interesting. An experiment by Allaway, also carried out in our laboratory, brought the matter into sharper focus. Allaway (1971) adapted a procedure devised by Egger and Miller (1962) for manipulating the "informativeness" of a stimulus associated with a reinforcer. Allaway's study was based on the hunch that the S for autoshaping had to be both peckable and "informative," and that the failure of the procedures Gamzu and I had tried lay in the fact that the tone carried information about grain presentation but the pecking key did not. Allaway's experiment explored this point directly, and also controlled for the possibility that the tone was, for some unsuspected reason, an unsuitable stimulus for use in autoshaping situations. Allaway's experiment involved a comparison of the keypecking development by three procedures outlined in Figure 3.4. One group of pigeons received standard conditioning trials on which a response key was presented for 6 sec and followed by food (key-only condition); for a second group, trials consisted of an 8-sec tone presentation that overlapped a 6-sec key presentation, so that on every trial tone onset *preceded* key onset by 2 sec (redundant condition); for the third group, reinforced trials occurred exactly as in the redundant condition, but these trials were administered in the context of an equal number of trials on which a tone was presented alone and followed neither by the key nor by presentation of the grain reinforcer (tone-irrelevant condition).

Allaway found that the tone-irrelevant procedure engendered the greatest amount of pecking, the key-only procedure an intermediate amount, and the key-redundant condition the smallest amount. Indeed, when the key-redundant condition was the first one presented, circumstances were found under which the development of pecking was blocked entirely. This fact is particularly significant because it demonstrates that, in the supposedly "visual" pigeon, information in the auditory modality can mask redundant information in the visual modality, even for a response that is visually guided. These results suggest that what counts in the autoshaping of pecking is the *information* conveyed by a peckable S about the forthcoming presentation of the grain reinforcer, and not mere feeding plus an available response key.

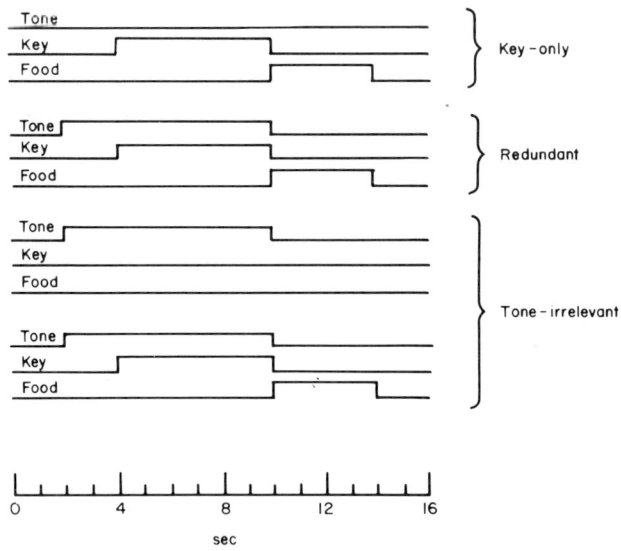

Figure 3.4. Procedural diagrams for the three conditions in the Allaway experiment. The tone-irrelevant procedure involved a mixed sequence of both procedures shown.

To probe the "information" issue further, Gamzu and I (1971, 1973) explored a classical paradigm similar to one developed by Rescorla (1967). In our adaptation, an experimental session consisted of a series of trials during which a response key was illuminated for 8-sec periods, with a mean interval between presentations of 30 sec. The independent variable was the rate of delivery of grain reinforcers when the pecking key was illuminated versus the rate of reinforcement delivery when the key was not illuminated (intertrial interval). As Rescorla has argued, S carries no information about presentation of the reinforcer when these two probabilities are the same, even though reinforcement is sometimes delivered in its presence. When the two probabilities are different, however, S does provide at least general information about reinforcement presentation: it indicates prevailing temporal frequency for reinforcement, even though it does not signal the specific time of arrival of reinforcers.

Gamzu and I found that when reinforcers were presented in a differential procedure, in the presence of the illuminated key and never in the absence of key illumination, key-pecking developed and was maintained at rates in excess of 60 pecks per min, as shown in the left-hand portion of Figure 3.5. Pecking subsided rapidly in the nondifferential procedure, where the rate of reinforcement when the key was darkened was made equal to the rate of reinforcement when the key was illuminated. This state of affairs can be brought about either by withholding reinforcement entirely, or, as we did, by introducing reinforcement during the intertrial interval at an equal rate of one reinforcer per 30 sec. Our finding from this latter procedure is shown in the right hand portion of Figure 3.5. The rapid decline in responding that we observed is remarkable because (a) it takes place when there has been no alteration in the key–reinforcer relationship during periods of key illumination; and (b) the cessation is brought about by adding reinforcement (to the intertrial interval) rather than by withdrawing it from the situation. Thus, this experiment demonstrates that sporadic feeding in a situation that involves occasional presentations of a response key is not sufficient to engender substantial pecking, and also that the specific signaling relationship between key presentation and reinforcement that characterizes the delay conditioning paradigm is not an essential aspect of the autoshaping procedure.

An informal working hypothesis in light of these results might take the following form: Pigeons will autoshape only to stimuli that are associatively linked to reinforcers. "Associatively linked" refers to that body of S–S^* relationships that is necessary and sufficient for classical conditioning in general. A hypothesis of this sort is consistent with Hearst and Jenkins' (1974) concept of *sign-tracking*, and with the experimental work they describe as well as with the work of Jenkins and Sainsbury (1969, 1970).

The intent of this section has been to show that S–S^* relationships, as conventionally met in the literature of classical conditioning, appear to operate in autoshaping. In concluding this section, it may be wise to emphasize that the

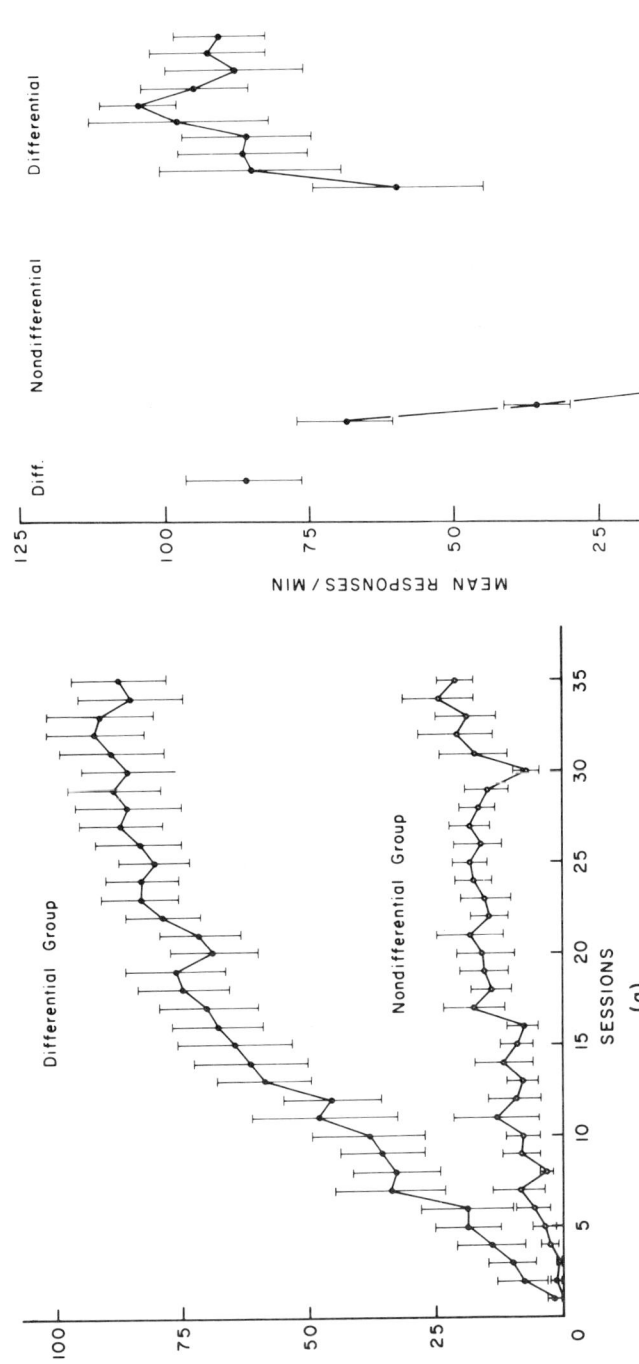

Figure 3.5. (a) Acquisition of keypecking when food was randomly presented only during illuminated key trials. (b) Reduction of established key pecking when food is presented randomly during both trials and intertrial intervals. In both figures, the standard error of the mean number of responses per minute of key illumination is indicated by vertical bars. (From Gamzu & Williams, 1973. Copyright © 1973 by the Experimental Analysis of Behavior. Reprinted with permission.)

involvement of S–S* relationships does *not* imply that pecking is respondent, rather than operant behavior. The reason has been brought forth above: To assert S–S* control is not to *deny* categorically R–S* control; the matter requires experimental resolution, and both forms of control may be operative. The question of response categorization will be considered in detail further below.

A HYPOTHESIS ABOUT THE NATURAL ORIGIN OF THE PHENOMENON

Thus far, the analysis of autoshaped keypecking has focused exclusively on variables important to traditional concepts of classical conditioning. This is because the S–S* relationship has obvious importance in the autoshaping situation. To appreciate *why* S–S* relationships might be involved, it is useful to step out of the confines of the autoshaping situation and consider a mechanism that appears to operate in the natural acquisition of ingestive patterns in birds; subsequently, we will relate that mechanism to the S–S* aspect of the autoshaping phenomenon.

Hunt and Smith (1967) studied the emergence of drinking responses in young domestic fowl. They noted that naive chicks—who have never contacted or ingested water—apparently make no drinking response to any substance, whether food, water, or a nonnutritive object. Apparently, *prior* experience arising from an accidental encounter with a drop of water is required before a complete drinking response is emitted. In the course of a detailed observational study of naive chicks learning to drink, Hunt and Smith found that 17 of 57 chicks "followed the initial peck with further pecking and were not seen to use any other response over a period in which they took several drops.... Within a few pecks 16 changed to a peck-and-hold drinking response; the remaining 24 changed to this response in their second peck [p. 234]." Droplets of water are presumably reinforcing to thirsty chicks: indeed, encountering droplets leads to further consummating behavior. If we assume that the receipt of water is a positively reinforcing consequence of pecking and believe that the *outcome* of pecking governs its form, the rapid shift in response topography is puzzling. Receipt of a reinforcing water drop would reasonably be expected to strengthen the topography that produced it. This expectation was not confirmed by Hunt and Smith, however. These investigators report that the receipt of water caused a subsequent systematic, holistic, *shift* of original pattern. Even if it is assumed that the drinking topography is most effective or efficient for ingesting water, it seems implausible to suppose that so many chicks would shift topographies so rapidly if the mechanism of change were based on the differential reinforcement of more and more efficient patterns. An alternative hypothesis—that stimuli that are followed by whatever factors identify water become *learned releasers* for the drinking topography—seems far more attractive (cf. Shettleworth, 1971). At the core of the learning mechanisms must be some form of association between the visual aspect of a water drop (S) and whatever mandibular factors identify it as water (S^*). Whether or not the S–S^* relationship involved here is identical to that normally occurring in classical conditioning remains to be analyzed; nevertheless, Hunt and Smith's observations provide unambiguous evidence for some form of direct S–S^* control over a directed skeletal response.

The concept of acquired S–S^* control over ingestive patterns in chicks receives added support from some incidental observations of Moseley (1925). She reported that sometimes, after extended force-feeding by hand, chicks, "pecked at the experimenter's hands instead of pecking at the grains. In addition, they gave the food-twitter there which is ordinarily given only when eating [Moseley, 1925, p. 92]." In this instance, it appears that association of the experimenter's hands with subsequent insertion of food into the mandibles resulted in the development to the hands themselves, of a directed feeding pattern that was capable of overriding a tendency to peck at the normally effective stimulus pattern furnished by grain.

These observations suggest the following partial account of the development of functionally appropriate ingestive patterns in chicks. Whenever an (S) in a chick's environment is pecked at and enters the mandibles, it is subjected to an analysis on the basis of mandibular cues (S^*). If the mandibular cues are positive, a consummatory response (R^*), such as swallowing, takes place. Through the operation of a learning mechanism, objects similar to S acquire the ability to engender *appropriate* directed feeding or drinking reactions (R) on future occasions, regardless of the kind of reaction—appropriate or otherwise—with which the process began. In this fashion, chicks develop normal and effective responses to objects on the basis of some form of S–S^* learning, without any necessary involvement of R–S^* outcome learning.

By this account, the R–S^* relation is important primarily because it arranges for an association between S and S^*; presumably, if this association could be arranged in some other way, as Moseley apparently did, the normally appropriate ingestive response would nevertheless be learned. The biological advantage of such a mechanism over a law-of-effect or R–S^* learning principle is that the S–S^* principle guarantees the development of appropriate ingestional behavior to new classes of objects regardless of the coincidence by which the class is first sampled and subjected to mandibular analysis. If, in the ecological niche of the species, nourishing food is normally in the form of small peckable grains, and water is commonly a liquid (both subject to local variations in specific appearance, such as muddy versus clear water), the holistic appearance of a well-formed ingestive pattern carries with it an efficiency of execution that has apparent survival value, compared with the gradual development of such a pattern through a trial-and-error shaping process. (cf. Bolles' [1970] argument about,

3. BICONDITIONAL BEHAVIOR: CONDITIONING WITHOUT CONSTRAINT | 67

species-specific defense reactions, or SSDR's.) In particular, a chick that had to learn—by a process of shaping—to peck, to close the bill, to move the tongue forward, to sample the contents of whatever was grasped in the bill, and to raise the head and swallow, if appropriate, would almost certainly die of starvation before these elements were smoothly and effectively integrated, even if the chance level of occurrence of the elements were high enough to produce just a few complete learning "trials."

Hogan (1973) has recently reported a fascinating investigation into the way chicks learn to recognize food. Hogan's treatment begins where the present one leaves off: His primary concern is with the mandibular and post-mandibular factors that establish effective feeding reactions. Thus, he treats most intensively what are included in the present treatment as the S^* and R^* events.

The key features of this account are summarized in the left hand portions of Figure 3.6. Each circle contains an example of a member of one of the categories discussed—that is, S, S^*, etc. The arrows connecting the circles represent the relationships suggested as critical in the development of ingestional patterns. The

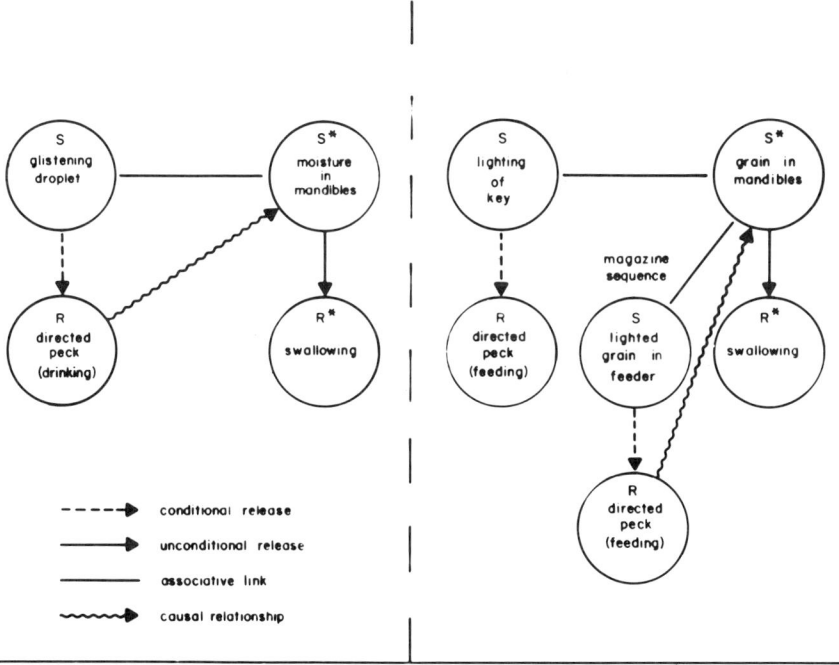

Figure 3.6. The left-hand-portion of this figure contains a hypothesis about the critical events in a chick's learning to drink. The right-hand-portion shows a related hypothesis about the events critical to autoshaping. The terms within each circle are merely illustrative conjectures; the actual properties are not known.

relationship of conditional release between S and R depends on the status of the association between S and S*; the relationship of unconditional release between S* and R* depends only on the S* event itself. The wavy arrow between R and S* indicates the normal result of an occurrence of the response R. No other relationship between R and S* is depicted in the diagram, and none is needed to account for the acquisition or maintenance of efficient, goal-oriented pecking, since occurrences of R in the presence of S can be expected to maintain the critical S–S* bond. Thus, it is possible to account for the apparently "purposive" behavior of a chick's approaching a water droplet and drinking it without appeal to means-end or law-of-effect (i.e., R–S*) relationships. The S–S* relationship (which, in this instance, may or may not be Pavlovian) is given priority in the figure in order to account for observations such as Moseley's and Hunt and Smith's; direct experimental analysis is required before the possible involvement of the R–S* relationship in the natural situation can be known with certainty.

The right hand portion of Figure 3.6 shows a similar diagram, with the specific components relabeled to pertain to the autoshaping situation. Here the chain of events by which S and S* are associated is more complicated: It involves the "magazine events" interposed between R and S*. Setting aside this complication for a moment, it is possible to account for autoshaping in a manner parallel to that for development of ingestional patterns in chicks: Directed pecking is released by an available stimulus (the illuminated response key) when an associative relationship obtains between the key and an S* event. That this account is *sufficient* is shown by the fact of autoshaping with a negative response–reinforcer contingency: Apparently, the pairing of S and S* engenders pecking even when any possible contribution of an R–S* relationship is blocked by experimental intervention.

How important is the "complication" of the magazine sequence? Recent experiments that Woodruff and I (1976) have carried out indicate that this variation on the ingestive mechanism itself does not alter the characteristics of the autoshaping situation. Woodruff placed cannulas in the upper mandible of adult pigeons, and carried out an autoshaping procedure that was standard in every way except that the S* event was provided by water introduced directly into the mandibles. In this way the normal magazine sequence was circumvented. Within a normal number of trials, birds approached and operated the key with a drinking pattern, much as reported by Jenkins and Moore (1973) when autoshaping is carried out with water delivered through a magazine. Since water entered the mandibles directly, there was no behavioral approach–drink sequence. Empirically, then, it appears that the magazine sequence does not seriously alter the similarity of the two diagrams in Figure 3.6.

Figure 3.6 represent a hypothesis about the process underlying autoshaping of the pigeon's keypeck: Pigeons autoshape through the operation of the same mechanism by which chicks (and presumably pigeons as well) learn to identify external stimuli as food, water, etc. In the autoshaping case, the functional relationships that describe the associative link between S and S* have been shown experimentally to be like those of classical conditioning generally. At present, postulation of similar relationships for the associative bond in the feeding case would be speculative but not implausible. Other aspects of Figure 3.6 do not normally figure in discussions of classical conditioning: the conditional release arrow between S and R, and the identification of R as directed, are two examples. To clarify the status of these aspects of the analysis, it is necessary to turn briefly to an examination of what is involved in conventional classical conditioning.

THE TERMS OF THE CLASSICAL PARADIGM

Zener's (1937) classic inquiry into the nature of the R in Pavlovian conditioning broadened the traditional view of the Pavlovian paradigm. Zener noted that most studies of classical conditioning had focused on a single bit of behavior—for example, the occurrence of salivation in an appetitive conditioning situation. He argued that a wide range of behaviors was influenced and controlled during conditioning experiments and that restricted observational techniques underestimated the breadth and impact of the procedure. When Zener supplemented traditional salivary recording techniques with visual observation and cinematographic recording, he was able to demonstrate that a diverse array of behaviors was controlled by a well-conditioned S. There were behaviors that occurred only to S (for example, glancing at the auditory stimulus, prancing, and staring fixedly into the food dish); behaviors that occurred to both S and S* (such as salivation, and licking or chewing movements); and behaviors that occurred only when S* was presented (for example, moving the head into the dish, masticating, and swallowing). Whether or not one accepts Zener's own theory of the conditioning process, his experiments serve to emphasize the scope and magnitude of the behavioral changes that accompany classical conditioning.

Zener's observations may be summarized as shown in Figure 3.7, which partitions behavior that systematically occurs during presentation of a previously associated S and S*. Behavior is partitioned into three distinct subsets: behaviors that occur in response to the S alone, behaviors that occur in response to both S and S*, and behaviors that occur in response to S* alone. Both portions of the R-set are assumed to depend on the associative bond between S and S*; unless the bond is maintained, this "conditional" set of behaviors will not be systematically controlled by presentation of S.

How shall we describe the behaviors listed in Figure 3.7? They all depend on presentation of S, and are, in that sense, R's. But do the same relationships govern all of them in the same way? Do the same laws that apply to salivation

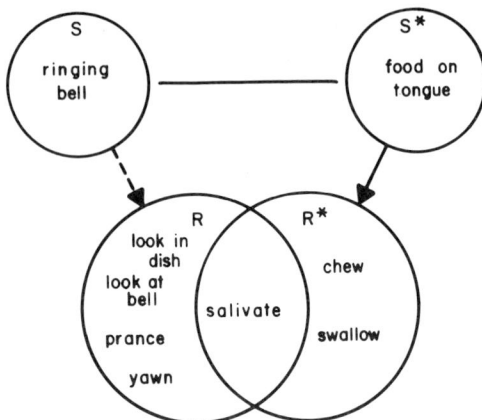

Figure 3.7. A representation of Zener's findings in the salivary conditioning experiment. Again, entries within the circles are illustrative only. The figure shows that in a salivary conditioning experiment some behaviors are related to S only, some S^*, and to both.

apply to prancing as well? Certainly the mere occurrence of a behavior in a classical conditioning experiment does not serve as a basis for classification, and clearly we cannot appeal to the dog's anatomy—in terms of striped versus smooth muscle, for example—for an answer. What we can ask about any behavior we observe here is to what degree it is controlled by an $S-S^*$ relationship, by an $R-S^*$ relationship, and by other factors such as novelty and time of exposure to the situation. From this point of view, to note that the peck in the diagram of Figure 3.6(b) is a member of the R-set but not the R^* set, and that the peck appears to be related directly to the $S-S^*$ bond, would seem consistent with observations and questions that must be asked within the framework of any classical conditioning experiment.

The aim of Figure 3.7 is to do more than conventionalize the autoshaping diagram of Figure 3.6(b), however. Figure 3.7 is also intended to distinguish clearly between two orthogonal aspects of classical conditioning experiments. One aspect is represented by the associative bond: Consideration of the bond involves questions about the necessary and sufficient conditions relating S and S^* if S is to gain control over a response set. The second aspect is represented by the four sets: For particular S and S^* elements, and for a particular species, what behaviors will be found in the R and R^* sets? To consider this second aspect, it is necessary that an associative bond be formed, but knowing only that an $S-S^*$ associative relationship has been established provides no basis for filling in the contents of the R and R^* sets. Specification of the members of these sets depends in part on the specific stimuli involved, and in part on the species under study. A full understanding of the changes brought about by a classical conditioning procedure requires consideration of both aspects of the situation: the associative aspect, concerned with the relationships governing the $S-S^*$ associative link, and the biological aspect, concerned with the particular R and R^* behaviors.

It is remarkable that, after seven decades of study, no definitive statement can be made about either the biological or the associative aspect of classical conditioning. Obviously, seven decades of work have yielded an enormous body of useful and scientifically exciting information. However, although many particulars have been firmly established, broad generalizations are still controversial. Doubtless this uncertain state of affairs is a major impediment blocking productive interchange between learning theory and psychobiology. In the present instance, it even stands in the way of confidently relating the two parts of Figure 3.6. It may nevertheless be helpful to make some broad comments about both the associative and the biological aspects of classical conditioning. At the least, these will help clarify the status of autoshaping with regard to classical conditioning. It is to be hoped that these observations will prove more broadly useful in bringing our knowledge of conditioning to bear on psychobiological problems.

THE ASSOCIATIVE ASPECT OF CLASSICAL CONDITIONING

A great deal of the early work on classical conditioning was guided by the notion that conditioning involved the formation of special "reflexes", similar to unconditional reflexes, arising from the conjunction of neutral stimuli with biologically potent ones. More modern work, however, has emphasized the predictive nature of the $S-S^*$ relationship (Gibbon, Berryman, & Thompson, 1974; Perkins, 1968, 1971; Rescorla & Solomon, 1967; Zener, 1937). Indeed, beginning with Rescorla's (1967) analysis of the proper control procedures for classical conditioning experiments, efforts have been made to bring together concepts of conditioning and the abstract idea of information or "contingency" between S and S^* events. Empirically, it has been shown that relationships between S and S^* *alone* do not provide an adequate statement of the necessary and sufficient conditions for the formation of an $S-S^*$ association; it is also necessary to consider the occurrence of S^* in the absence of S (Rescorla, 1967).

In general terms, these modern developments in conditioning theory can be seen as developing a *psychophysics of association*. The quantitative formations cited above are readily viewed as efforts to develop an adequate metric for the "physical" stimulus presented by events (S and S^*) whose relationship is temporal rather than spatial. The "psychological" component in the psychophysical relationship would be the associative strength of given correlation engenders. Discussing the necessary and sufficient conditions for the formation of $S-S^*$ associations in terms of psychophysics and detection may initially be jarring, perhaps because correlations across time are not "physical stimuli" in the conventional sense. But this may be more a matter of custom than of principle:

Spatially separated stimuli are often perceived as a related whole, apparent movement is perceived from a series of discrete images, and causality itself is intuitively inferred from the temporal sequence of events (Michotte, 1963). Whatever the bearing of these perceptual phenomena on the detection of environmental contingencies, they do illustrate the point that spatial–temporal integration is commonplace, and little confusion is likely to be introduced by extending the idea of perceptual integration to the larger temporal domain of associative conditioning.

THE BIOLOGICAL ASPECT OF CLASSICAL CONDITIONING

The behaviors that are brought about by an S that is associatively linked to an S^* represent the biological aspect of conditioning. A pigeon and a human might obey similar psychophysical rules in detecting a nonrandom relationship between illumination of a response key and feeder presentation, but the behavioral consequences of such detection would be entirely different. Using the terminology introduced above, these differences could be said to represent alternative compositions of the R-set controlled by an effectively associated S. In general, the constitution of the R-set may reflect the nature of S, the nature of S^*, and the species involved; for this reason, its composition seems properly treated as a matter of the organism's biological endowment.

Is any general characterization of the elements of the R-set possible? Not at the present time, if the definition of the R-set is taken to include all consequences of an effective S–S^* association. Potentially, the set might involve such emotional responses as fear, a variety of visceral changes, and skeletal behaviors such as those Zener reported for the dog. It cannot be said, a priori, whether such behaviors are classically conditioned or respondent, since there is no basis for supposing that direct control by the S–S^* relationship precludes an effect of the R–S^* relationship as well.

A number of current papers have recently advanced the concept that highly organized and flexible response patterns are controlled by brainstem motor systems (Glickman & Schiff, 1967; Valenstein, Cox, & Kakolewski, 1970; von Holst & von Saint Paul, 1963). The response-patterns are often best described in molar terms and, even when elicited by direct electrical stimulation of the brain, depend for their occurrence on characteristics of the environment as well. These patterns are commonly species-characteristic, and their execution may be rewarding. This latter observation suggests that at least many such patterns are appropriately considered as members of the R^*-set, elicited by S^* events. Hoarding, copulating, fighting, and possibly some social-play behaviors, are instances of the sort under consideration.

Two characteristics of such patterns seem worthy of note in the present context. The first is that these patterns are highly organized, and involve the coordinated operation of visceral and skeletal effectors; they are not simply autonomic, or reflexive. The second point is that these patterns are quite dependent in their execution on the context provided by environmental stimuli: Most are directed, and in addition, behaviors that involve grabbing, clasping, or gnawing, for example, are perforce closely toned to local characteristics of the milieu in which they take place. Yet these behaviors are centrally organized at a low level of the nervous system and are often stimulus-bound.

It would seem reasonable to endow members of the conditioned R-set with the same sophistication and sensitivity of organization that is appropriate for putative members of an R^*-set. As Zener pointed out, the punctate, disorganized character of Rs as often conceived with learning theory may be an artifact of the experimenter's recording techniques. Zener showed a far more integrated and extensive pattern of changes when broader spectrum-recording techniques were used, and there seems no good reason to deny admission to the R-set to the nonvisceral elements he observed (being careful to consider, as will be pointed out below, their possible biconditionality). In this spirit, neither the directedness nor the skeletal character of the pigeon's keypeck would seem grounds to dismiss it from membership in the R-set of behaviors established in the pigeon by certain $S-S^*$ pairings. Most importantly, the fact that it is more easily aroused by an illuminated key than by a tone does no violence to its status as a conventional member of the R-set. R^* behaviors are also situation-dependent.

Labeling complex and integrated patterns, or identifying them as part of a species' biological endowment, is of course not the same as providing a scientific account. In the context of past learning–theoretic treatments of the response issue, however, it seems important to free the concept of biological aspects of conditioning from the notion that elements of the R-set should be less organized or complex, or freer of a close dependence on the eliciting stimulus, than are species-typical reactions or R^* (that is, members of the R^*-set). An adequate understanding of the nature and organization of behavior patterns is needed in the domains of conditional and unconditional behavior alike; prejudgment of the characteristics of either set is best avoided.

In pulling back from the question of the composition of the R-set in classical conditioning, we are retreating from a problem that has been worked and reworked, with dedication and ingenuity, since Pavlov's initial formulation. The retreat seems strategically wise: What it provides is the opportunity to ask a functional rather than a categorical question, to test experimentally the relative influence of $S-S^*$ and $R-S^*$ relationships on all members of the R-set. Functional questions of this sort may be of greater immediate utility in promoting interchange between learning theory and psychobiology than traditional questions of obvious learning–theoretic interest.

AUTOSHAPING AND CLASSICAL CONDITIONING

Autoshaping uses the procedures of classical conditioning to establish and maintain a keypeck response. It was suggested above, in conjunction with Figure 3.6, that there is a "natural" reason why autoshaping works in pigeons: The procedure invokes an associative mechanism that normally operates in food-getting behavior. Specifically, it was hypothesized that the identification of an object as "food" or "water" involves the *association* of that object with subsequent S^* events that take place once mandibular contact is established. Once an object, through an associative $S-S^*$ link, is identified as food, it elicits a feeding response, namely a peck. If the object is a grain of corn, pecking will be directed at grains of corn; if the object is a response key, pecking will be directed to the response key. The fact that pecking is the response is a matter of the *biology* of association; the fact that a procedure works in setting up an $S-S^*$ link involves the psychophysics of association. Both aspects are involved in the autoshaping procedure.

This treatment of autoshaping and classical conditioning stands in marked contrast to a *stimulus substitution* view. The central idea in the stimulus substitution view of classical conditioning is that S takes command of responses formerly governed by the S^* alone: When stimulus substitution is taken to be the mechanism operative in classical conditioning, the R-set is supposed to contain only elements that are also in the R^*-set. Moore (1973) has used this idea to account for autoshaping and for the differential consequences of using food or water as S^* events. Thus, when Moore (1973) and Jenkens and Moore (1973) studied the topography of keypecking autoshaped to food or to water, it was noted that forms of keypecking appropriate to each reinforcer were established: Pecking occurred with a grain reinforcer, but water served to establish a drinking-like response pattern to the key. Moore interpreted these observations as "indicating that the response topographies were indeed due to associative learning," which he took to be a "simple Pavlovian process [p. 187]," by which the S comes to evoke the response previously engendered by S^*. The simplicity of this approach, however, may be more apparent than real, since it is doubtful whether pecking is a member of the R^*-set at all. To include pecking in the R^*-set it is necessary to identify the S^* event that elicits it. The mere sight of grain, however, does not suffice to elicit pecking unconditionally: In our laboratory we have found that birds cease pecking to visually presented grain if it is covered with a clear sheet of acrylic so that mandibular contact is blocked. It would appear, then, that the S^* event in the case of grain *follows* the pecking response, rather than preceding it, as an eliciting stimulus must. The situation is similar to Hunt and Smith's (1967) observation that water drops do not *unconditionally* elicit a drinking response; some form of experience is required. If pecking is not a member of the R^*-set, however, its representation in the R-set cannot be explained by stimulus substitution. By contrast with a stimulus substitution analysis, the present account maintains that keypecking takes place for the same reasons that grain-pecking does: In both cases, a visual S is associated with the subsequent occurrence of an S^* event, the latter occurring *after* the pecking response has placed the object in the mandibles. The fact that an $S-S^*$ association produces pecking in *both* cases is a matter of the biology of association.

Pavlov's (1927) own observations with regard to salivary conditioning are instructive in discussing this distinction. Pavlov stated that "the sound of the metronome is the signal for food, and the animal reacts to the signal in the same way as if it were food. . . . That the effect of sight and smell of food is not due to an inborn reflex, but to a reflex which has been acquired in the course of the animal's own individual existence, was shown by experiments [1927, p. 22]. Thus, it is not the *presentation* of the physical S^* that constitutes the S^* event in the salivary experiment but the presence of food on the tongue. In the case of autoshaping, it is not the *presentation* of grain but the presence of grain in the mandibles or beyond. Later Pavlov (1927) states:

> Formerly we made a distinction between 'natural' reflexes and 'artificial' conditioned reflexes, 'natural' reflexes being those which appeared to be formed spontaneously as a result of the natural association of, for example, the sight and smell of food with the eating of food itself. . . , while 'artificial' reflexes were those which could be formed as a result of artificially associating . . . stimuli which in the ordinary course of events have nothing in common with food. . . . At the present time, however we know that there is not the slightest difference in properties between all these reflexes [p. 49].

Pavlov's point is that the dog salivates to the presentation of food (prior to its receipt on the tongue) for the same reason that it salivates to a tone, namely, because each of these stimuli is paired with the effective (i.e., unconditional) S^* event. Similarly, we argue that the pigeon pecks at the key for the same reason that it pecks at grain: Key and grain are both S-events that are associated with a mandibular S^*.

Pavlov's own treatment of the salivary conditioning situation sheds light on another aspect of the analyses in Figure 3.6. In salivary conditioning as well as in autoshaping, pairing of the S-event with S^* commonly requires the intervention of a motor chain that begins with presentation of the S^*. Actual occurrence of the truly unconditional stimulus takes place only after the motor chain is completed. The troublesome question of whether this makes most Pavlovian experiments a matter of higher-order conditioning (presentation of the S^* being of the first order) is a matter beyond the reach of this discussion.

The directedness of pecking is another aspect of autoshaped pecking that requires comment. Many of the responses that are maintained by $S-S^*$ relations are *not* directed: Salivation is an obvious example, as are most other autonomic responses. Some striped-muscle activities ought also be included, such as the eyeblink to shock on the cheek and the tail-flexion response in rats (Schlosberg, 1934). On the other hand, Wasserman (1972, 1973) has carefully documented the fact that when localized environmental stimuli predict appetitive events, animals are drawn to and approach these stimuli. He notes Pavlov's observations that dogs orient to the direction of S (cf. Zener, 1937), and most directly, Jenkins' "feature-tracking" experiments, which show that pigeons direct pecks to the positive cue of a complex visual display. In terms of the present analysis, the directedness of pecking in the autoshaping situation reflects a biological aspect of certain $S-S^*$ associations in pigeons. Wasserman's suggestion, like that of Hearst and Jenkins (1974), that directed approach is a common characteristic of the R-set, seems well taken. The treatment developed here differs from theirs in only one major particular, namely, whether the key in the autoshaping experiment is a "sign" for the "significate" of forthcoming grain. The position taken here is that it is not: Key and grain particles alike are S events; the grain itself is not an S^*. Both key and grain, therefore, are pecked for the *same* reason: They are S-events associatively linked with S^* that occurs *after* the peck and that elicits such internally-directed behaviors as swallowing. A more thorough discussion of this point will be possible after $R-S^*$ relations have been explicitly discussed and the concept of biconditionality introduced.

AUTOSHAPING AND THE $R-S^*$ RELATIONSHIP

Thus far, we have considered only the operation of the $S-S^*$ relationship in autoshaping and have seen (*a*) that it is, by itself, sufficient to engender and maintain pecking; (*b*) that the associative relationships that are effective in classical conditioning generally seem to describe effective $S-S^*$ relationship in autoshaping as well; and (*c*) that the capability of $S-S^*$ relations to engender keypecking in pigeons makes biological sense, in terms of learned components in birds' feeding behavior. It was suggested at the outset of this paper, however, that the importance of the $S-S^*$ relationship does not suffice, a priori, to rule out an effect of the $R-S^*$ relationship as well; the matter requires experimental evaluation. In the case of the pigeon's keypeck, there is an obvious basis for considering the matter. Pigeons can be trained by instrumental means to peck at keys enduringly and persistently without support from any obvious external source of $S-S^*$ relationships, as for example with simple variable-internal reinforcement (Ferster & Skinner, 1957).

Schwartz and Williams (1972a) carried out an experiment to determine whether, within the context of an autoshaping situation, anything other than the $S-S^*$ relationship was involved. Their procedure involved a comparison of response rate and preference between two keys, distinguished by color, that differed with regard to possible R–S^* relationships, while identical S–S^* relationships were maintained. In their procedure, when a key was illuminated with red light, a "fixed trial, negative contingency" trial was in force: the key was illuminated for a fixed duration of 6 sec, regardless of whether or not any responding took place, but it terminated without reinforcement if one or more pecks were made to it, and it terminated with reinforcement only when no peck occurred throughout the full duration of its illumination. Thus, no direct facilitation of pecking due to R–S^* relationships was possible on trials signaled by the red key. When the key was illuminated with green light, however, another schedule, "fixed trial, no contingency" was in force. Here, responses had no bearing at all on whether the trial would terminate in reinforcement; that matter was decided by the outcome of a previous red-key trial on which the negative R–S^* contingency had been in force. The yoking procedure equated "red key" and "green key" trials with regard to the variables important for S–S^* relationships of classical conditioning—key duration and percentage of key food pairings—but permitted the keys to differ with regard to the R–S^* relationship of instrumental conditioning: On the yoked trials, pecking was compatible with the subsequent presentation of reinforcement. If the R–S^* relationship of instrumental conditioning can influence performance that is governed primarily by an S–S^* relationship, that possibility would be shown by differences in rate of responding to the two keys and by a preference for the yoked green key on unreinforced, "probe" choice trials when both keys were illuminated together.

In eight birds tested with this procedure, there was a strong difference in both rate and preference measures favoring the yoked key on which R–S^* instrumental facilitation was possible. Although the birds pecked a substantial fraction of the time on the "fixed-trial, negative contingency" key, they responded at a higher rate to the yoked "fixed-trial, no contingency" key when it was presented alone, and they developed a preference ratio of almost 2:1 for the yoked key on choice trials. The experiment clearly demonstrates that the R–S^* relationship of instrumental conditioning can influence keypecking in a situation where the S–S^* relationship of classical conditioning is sufficient to engender and maintain pecking in its own right. Apparently, classical and instrumental conditioning are simultaneous and directly operative in controlling keypecking in the pigeon.

The Schwartz and Williams (1972a) study clearly demonstrated that keypecking is susceptible to both S–S^* and R–S^* conditioning relationships within the framework of a single procedure arrangement. Apparently it is not the case that the discrete-trials Pavlovian paradigm in some way operates to blot out operant relationships. Rather, it seems that keypecking in the pigeon is sensitive to direct S–S^* relationships, and maintains a sensitivity to R–S^* operant linkages as well. Thus, pecking is sensitive to the conditional S–S^* relationship of classical conditioning and also to the conditional R–S^* relationship of operant or instrumental conditioning.

In light of these findings, it seems appropriate to refer to key-pecking as "biconditional" behavior, because its strength depends on both the conditional $S-S^*$ link of classical conditioning, and the conditional $R-S^*$ link of instrumental conditioning. A full account of its occurrence must take *both* sources of conditional control into account.

Although the discovery that keypecking could be engendered and maintained by an $S-S^*$ relationship led to a series of investigations probing the extent of similarity to $S-S^*$ relationships in classical conditioning situations generally, a similar program of research is not required by the demonstration of $R-S^*$ influences on keypecking; the matter is already well-researched (Ferster & Skinner, 1957). As with classical conditioning, however, the wealth of factual material available has not been codified into a generally accepted statement of the laws in instrumental or operant $R-S^*$ control: We do not know, in general, the necessary and sufficient conditions for effective $R-S^*$ control. It may be useful to review this matter briefly, however, in order to point out a fundamental similarity between the conceptual issues involved in $R-S^*$ control, and those already discussed with regard to $S-S^*$ control. If the two sets of problems are seen as analogous, the remarkable complementarity of the two branches of the biconditional relationship becomes readily apparent.

When discussing autoshaping and $S-S^*$ conditioning in an earlier section, the central question focused on whether "contingency" or "pairing" of S and S^* was fundamental; the evidence made it clear that a *contingent* relationship, by which S in some way provided information about S^*, seemed sufficient for classical conditioning in general and autoshaping in particular. With regard to the $R-S^*$ relationship of operant conditioning, the same question may be posed: how must S^* relate to R in order to reinforce R effectively?

Fortunately, the issue has recently been considered at length in several excellent papers, and it is possible to make use of their conclusions directly here (see Gibbon & Balsam, Chapter 7; Gibbon, Chapter 9). Baum (1973), for example, has reviewed evidence from a number of studies on contingencies of reinforcement and has concluded that "the correlation between responding and reinforcement stands out as the essential ingredient in instrumental behavior [p. 144]." By *correlation* Baum refers to a quantitative relationship between responding and the frequency of occurrence of reinforcers; specifically, this relationship does not take account of such contiguity factors as $R-S^*$ pairing or $R-S^*$ delay. Herrnstein (1970) has come to a similar conclusion, and Gibbon *et al* (1974) have explicitly drawn the parallel between correlation (or as they call it, *contingency*) and contiguity in $S-S^*$ and $R-S^*$ cases, while adducing persuasive evidence for the effectiveness of correlation alone.

Explicitly, what these theoretical treatments of the law of effect mean is that traditional formulations, according to which single $R-S^*$ pairings (with or without delay) determine response strength, must be revised to include a more general correlational or contingent relationship. Just as Rescorla's experiments indicated that it was the S–S* correlation that was essential for respondent conditioning and not S–S* pairing, so the evidence reviewed, for example, by Baum and by Gibbon et al. makes it appear that it is the R–S* correlation, not R–S* pairing, that constitutes the minimal sufficient relationship for operant conditioning.

This shift in emphasis on the sufficient condition for reinforcement is important, particularly in connection with the dynamics of biconditional behavior, but it is not so radical a shift as to undermine former conceptions of the fundamental law of reinforcement. This is because all instances of pairing or contiguity imply a correlation, even though all instances of correlation need not imply pairing. (See Baum, 1973, for a full treatment of the logical difficulties involved.) The point is that the correlation, or contingency, view represents a relaxation and generalization of the instrumental reinforcement concept and not a fundamental revision of it. The new rule admits all instances governed by the old one.

There is a further point to be brought out as well: Logically, *both* R–S* correlation and pairing might have an independent influence. Thus, holding the *R–S* correlation* constant, it might be possible to manipulate delay of reinforcement and find important effects (indeed, discrete-trials delay-of-reinforcement studies would seem to involve just this possibility). There is no fundamental reason why *both* correlation and contiguity might not contribute separately to response strength. The issue is an empirical one, not a logical one, and direct evidence is not yet sufficient (see, however, Woodruff, Connor, Gamzu, & Williams, 1977). The same issue, it should be noted, can be raised in connection with Rescorla's *contingency* versus *pairing* distinction in classical conditioning: A fixed S–S* interval (as in delay conditioning) might, in some circumstances, provide stronger conditioning than another arrangement of Ss and S*s that involved an equal S–S* contingency. Such an outcome would not detract from the force of Rescorla's position, which was that pairing per se does not provide a sufficient basis for conditioning. These considerations go to the question of the completeness of statement of the fundamental laws of conditioning and are matters for empirical resolution. They are introduced here to provide an indication of the similar status of the correlation–contiguity question in respondent and operant conditioning.

The diagram of Figure 3.6, which represented the S–S* influence in autoshaping, can be generalized as shown in Figure 3.8. A_s refers to the associative relationship between S and S*; the magnitude of A_s refers to the degree of association actually formed between S and S* as a result of their temporal relationship. The effect of A_s on a given reaction pattern is itself a function of A_s; for different combinations of S, S*, and R, this function, and thus the effect of an S–S* association, might be different. A similar treatment is given the other

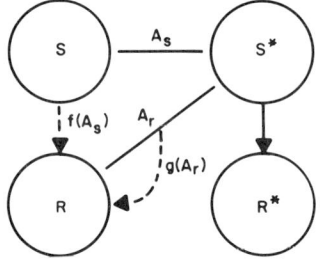

Figure 3.8. Schematic outline of the critical events underlying biconditional behavior. For a "pure" or arbitrary operant, $f(A_s)=c$, whereas $f(A_r)=c$ for a "pure" or absolute respondent. A_s and A_r represent the psychophysical aspect of conditioning, while $f(A_s)$ and $f(A_r)$ represent the biological aspect, with respect to a particular R.

relationship, R–S*. Here, A_r describes the degree of association actually formed between R and S*, again as a result of their temporal relationship. The function $g(A_r)$ indicates the amount of strengthening of R that accrues from a given A_r. The interplay of A_s and A_r in biconditional relationships, as expressed in general terms in Figure 3.8, will be illustrated below in the context of several concrete examples of biconditional behavior.

EXAMPLES OF THE ANALYSIS OF BICONDITIONAL BEHAVIOR

Murray (1973) recently studied S–S* and R–R* factors controlling components of the display pattern in the fighting fish *betta splendens*. Murray first replicated earlier observations of Thompson and Sturm (1965a, 1965b) and Adler and Hogan (1963), showing that four separately identifiable components of the complex display pattern would condition to the presentation of a visual S when the reinforcer consisted of elicitation of the whole pattern by means of presentation of a mirror in which the fish could see itself. Fin erection conditioned very quickly, and reached a level well above 90% probability of occurrence per trial within the first 100 trials. Frontal approach showed an initial increment in the first 20 trials, and then a gradual increase to a maximum probability near 100 percent after more than 200 conditioning trials. Gill extension and undulating movements conditioned at a rate similar to each other and intermediate between fin erection and frontal approach. After roughly 200 trials all four components of the pattern were reliably elicited by a presentation of S.

Further observations of this group of fish, and a full scale experiment on a new group of 18 fish, clearly demonstrated control of these elements was actually biconditional. Fish were divided into three main groups, each of which comprised an experiment similar to the Schwartz and Williams study (1972a) just described. In one of the three main groups, three fish were placed on a procedure under which S–S* pairings were administered *unless* fin erection took place; if fin erection took place, the trial terminated after the 10 sec S presentation, and no S^* was presented. Thus, for this group, fin erection was on a negatively contingent schedule similar to the schedule used for keypecking in pigeons under conditions of negative automaintenance. The other components of behavior—gill extension, undulating movement and frontal approach—were recorded on all trials but had no programmed consequences. For each of the fish under the negatively contingent procedure, a second fish was tested with the same sequence of S–S^* presentations. This "yoked control" condition also resembled that used in the Schwartz and Williams study just described. A second set of six fish was also divided into experimental and yoked-control groups, but this time the negative contingency was on gill extension. In a third main group of six fish, the negative contingency was on frontal approach. When asymptotic performance appeared to have been reached, the experimental versus yoked-control status of each fish was shifted and a new series of observations was carried out.

Data from this experiment are summarized in Figure 3.9:

1. In each group of fish, the negative contingency had a substantial effect, and the frequency of occurrence of the component to which the negative contingency was applied was considerably lower than the frequency of the corresponding component under yoked-control procedure.

2. In no case did the negative contingency completely suppress occurrences of the component behavior to which it was applied. The overall percentages of reinforcement (which are the complement of the percent occurrence of the component to which the negative contingency is applied) were nearly equal in the fin erection and gill-extension groups: Both received reinforcement during approximately two-thirds of the trials. Nearly complete control by the negative contingency was shown in the case of the frontal approach subjects, however, which were reinforced on an average of approximately 94% of all trials.

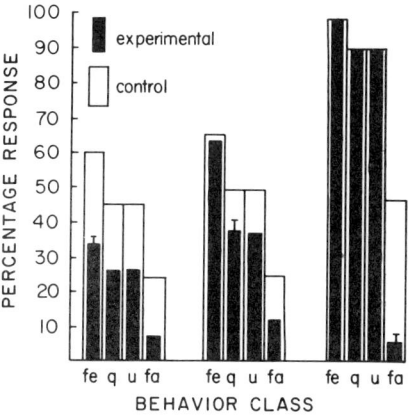

Figure 3.9. Results obtained by Murray (1973). Each group of bar graphs represents mean percent response in an experiment in which one of the four components of the display (*fe*, or fin erection; *g*, or gill extension; *u*, or undulating movement; *fa*, or frontal approach) is placed under a negative contingency. The target behavior is indicated by a dash over the bar.

3. The order of arrangement of components along the abscissa of Figure 3.9 represents the order of difficulty of conditioning. It is noteworthy that components to the right of the behavior suppressed by the negative contingency are also depressed, but components to the left are virtually unaffected. Thus, the components of the display pattern do not appear to be entirely independent of each other: Whether gill extension is suppressed or not, for example, seems to depend on whether the reinforcement is negatively contingent upon either it *or* upon fin erection.

The data indicate that all four components of the display pattern of *betta splendens* can be educed by an S–S* generative relationship. The reason is similar to the reasoning used above in the case of the pigeon's keypeck: Even under a procedure (far more stringent than ordinary classical conditioning) that insures that no R–S* relationship can contribute to the maintenance of behavior, the behavior in question nevertheless occurs. It is also clear that the strength of the generative S–S* relationship is different for various components of the display pattern. Thus, the negative contingency is almost sufficient to wipe out occurrences of frontal approach, whereas fin erection occurs on a substantial fraction of trials even when reinforcement is negatively contingent upon it. Because of the inverse relationship between frequency of occurrence of the target response and frequency of reinforcement, we must assume that whatever generating S–S* processes were available for frontal approach were stronger when nonreinforcement was contingent on frontal approach than they were when nonreinforcement was contingent on fin erection. Nevertheless, there are fewer occurrences of frontal approach where it is the target response than anywhere else in the experiment. Thus, a major point illustrated by the Murray investigation is that different components of an integrated pattern of response may differ in their sensitivity to S–S* and R–S* relationships. A second point illustrated by the Murray study is the internal organization of the behavior pattern: It is almost certain that the concept of biconditional control will need to be taken into account *experimentally* to analyze the interdependence of components revealed in Figure 3.9. Moreover, if the concept is experimentally important, it seems likely that it will be of conceptual importance in the elucidation of this complex act as well.

The biconditional structure of the display pattern of *betta splendens* is summarized in Figure 3.10. Because the strength of the S–S* bond has not itself been systematically varied, it is not yet possible to conjecture relationships among g_1 through g_4 of A_r; experimental differences of Figure 3.9, however, provide assurance that the g-functions are neither constant nor equal to zero. The arrows connecting the various elements of the R-set are tentatively placed, and serve only to indicate that these components are not independent.

The internal structure of elements of the display pattern of *betta splendens* is

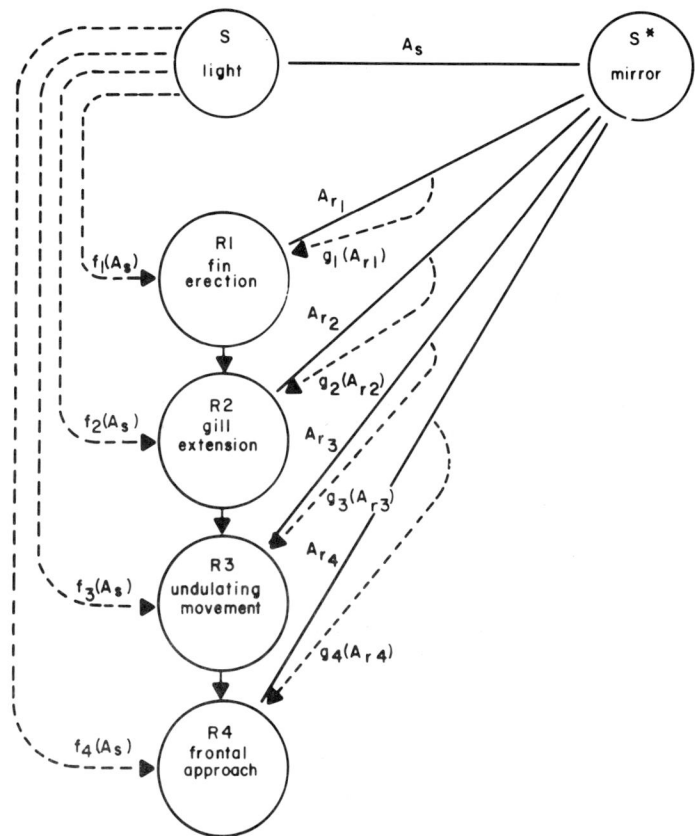

Figure 3.10. Schematic diagram of the elements of the display pattern of *betta splendens*, considered biconditional behavior. The A_r's must be distinguished, since they are subject-controlled, unless a full negative contingency is introduced.

in some ways reminiscent of the relationship Schwartz and Williams (1972b) found among keypecks of different durations: Specifically, they reported that short-duration pecks appeared to be predominantly under S–S* control, while long-duration pecks were predominantly related to R–S* influence. Further, they conjectured that the appearance of long-duration pecks might in some way depend on the strength of the class of short-duration pecks. These possibilities are expressed in Figure 3.11, where short-duration and long-duration pecks are treated as topographically different components of the R-set. The algebraic expressions illustrate the relationships Schwartz and Williams (1972b) demonstrated: generation of short-duration pecks by the S–S* link, and modification of long-duration pecks by the R–S* link. The possibility of some contribution of A_s to the strength of long-duration pecks, and the structural contribution of short-to

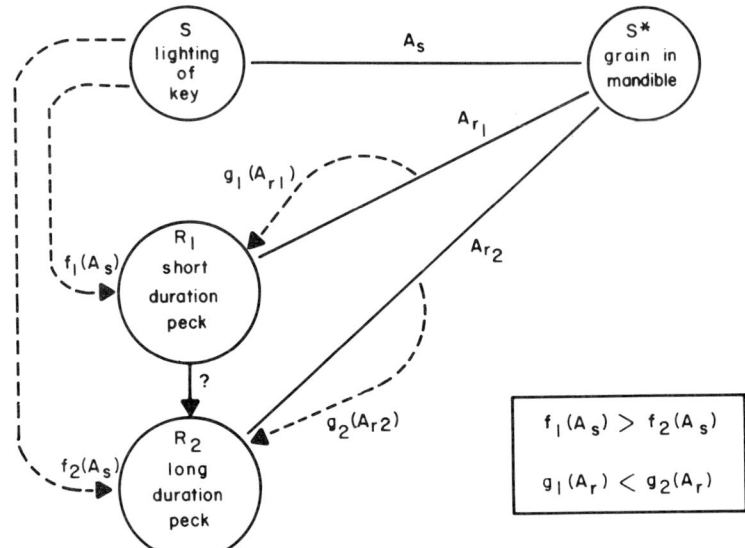

Figure 3.11. Schematic diagram of short- and long-duration pecking topographies, considered as biconditional behaviors. The inequalities in the inset summarize the findings of Schwartz and Williams (1972b). The question mark connecting R_1 and R_2 indicates uncertainty about the precise nature of the relationship between pecks with short- and long-duration topographies.

long-duration pecks, remains to be analyzed experimentally, presumably by experimentally altering A_s, and by different combinations of A_r and A_s. However, these relationships are finally established, it seems likely that the biconditional formulation expressed in Figures 3.10 and 3.11 will contribute to the analysis.

The main points brought out in Murray's work have also been illustrated in a recent experiment by Morrison and Williams (1974), who autoshaped pigeons using a water reinforcer. Like Jenkins and Moore (1973), Morrison and Williams found that pigeons began pecking a response key that reliably signaled forthcoming water reinforcement. Morrison and Williams also found that the nearly exclusive force of the S–S* relationship in producing keypecking that characterizes food S*s was not at all characteristic of the water S*. With water as the reinforcing S* event, the probability of pecking fell to nearly zero within 500–1000 trials. Observation of the birds indicated that in addition to keypecking, several other patterns of behavior emerged, including "bowing" in front of the key with a downward motion of the bill, and "rooting" in the vicinity of the water magazine. Morrison and Williams found that *any* of the three behaviors would decline to near-zero frequency when placed on the negative contingency. However, one of the other behaviors would appear to replace it. If pecking, rooting,

3. BICONDITIONAL BEHAVIOR: CONDITIONING WITHOUT CONSTRAINT | 85

and bowing were *all* placed on the negative contingency, however, the birds' versatility appeared exhausted: At least one of the three behaviors—typically pecking—took place with a frequency such that reinforcement was aborted on a substantial majority of the trials. Thus it appears that the Morrison and Williams pigeons could not learn to do nothing, even though they could learn to shift among several independent behaviors, only one of which involved keypecking. These relationships are summarized in Figure 3.12.

It appears then, that the biology of association may produce a number of behaviors when an $S-S^*$ association is formed. When this happens, the behavior that is actually observed depends not only on the evocative $S-S^*$ relationship, but also on the operant $R-S^*$ relationship. In this case, contingencies of reinforcement are seen to be genuinely selective: Given that a generating $S-S^*$ base exists for a number of behaviors, the relative frequency of occurrence of the various possibilities is a function of their association with reinforcement ($R-S^*$ link). An account of the occurrence of a behavior demands consideration of both branches of the biconditional relationship, $S-S^*$ and $R-S^*$. Thus, the Murray and the Morrison and Williams investigations bring out the *selective* aspect of the $R-S^*$ relationship more clearly than the original autoshaping phenomenon, because these later studies involve co-observation of strong alternative behaviors.

The generative strength of the $S-S^*$ relationship for pecking when food consti-

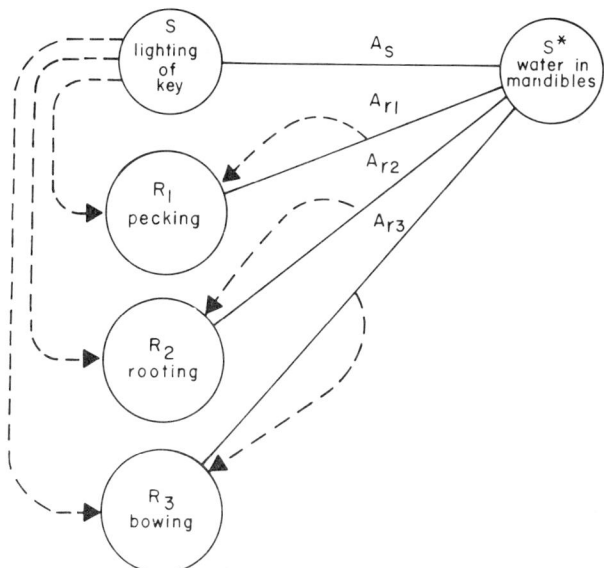

Figure 3.12. Schematic diagram of three major components of the autoshaped drinking pattern, considered as biconditional behavior.

tutes the S^* event appears to be unusually strong, so that, with a food S^* and pecking-key S, $S-S^*$ links generating other behaviors are not very prominent. Because of this relative imbalance, the facilitation of alternative behaviors by $R-S^*$ control never becomes possible. If this reasoning is correct, then a procedure that maximized the selective control or the $R-S^*$ relationship while minimizing $S-S^*$ generation of pecking might ultimately prevent pecking even under normally effective parameters of the negative autoshaping situation. A procedure suitable for doing this appears to have been devised by Hitzing (1972), who used a discrete trials differential reinforcement of other behavior (DRO) schedule, under which, after a relatively modest intertrial interval, a pecking key was illuminated and followed by reinforcement after 6 sec without a keypeck had elapsed. Each keypeck "reset" the 6-sec period, so that the actual duration of presentation of the key light was variable. Hitzing found that early in training, owing to autoshaping, birds pecked consistently at the key and thus extended trial durations considerably. Eventually, however, birds seldom pecked the key. Thus, using a fading procedure, Hitzing was ultimately able to train birds virtually to withhold pecking from the key even when its 6-sec period of presentation was followed by grain.

A theoretical account of the effectiveness of Hitzing's procedure can be conjectured as follows. The relative duration of the intertrial interval may be assumed to affect A_s (Ricci, 1973; Terrace, Gibbon, Farrell, & Baldock, 1975). Since pecking prolonged trial durations, occurrences of pecking reduced A_s. Furthermore, since reinforcement was given only when pecking had been so weakened that it did not occur for a 6-sec period, there was potentially an $R-S^*$ bond to any behavior other than pecking that occurred on a trial. The combination of these two factors—weakening of the generating link A_s as a function of strength of generated tendency to peck, and strengthening of any other behavior that might be generated by means of the operant link A_r—might well establish a condition under which some behavior other than keypecking could (owing primarily to the $R-S^*$ link) eventually be established and compete with pecking. Provided that the combined contribution of A_s and A_r to this other behavior was greater than the effect of A_s acting alone on the keypeck, such a procedure would instate some behavior other than keypecking during the time S was presented. By this line of reasoning, Hitzing's (1972) procedure might be effective where the ordinary negative automaintenance procedure would not be successful, because it reduces the generative bond for pecking to the point where other behaviors have a chance to intrude and compete. Additionally, in contrast to the all-or-nothing procedure of negative autoshaping, Hitzing's procedure provides for reinforcement of a competing R on every trial (even if keypecks also occur). In the Morrison and Williams (1974) study, where the keypeck engendered by a water S^* did seem sensitive to the negative contingency, such heroic measures may not have been necessary because the water S^* does not so exclusively control a particular response—an apparent fact of the biology of association in the pigeon.

We have carried out a study (unpublished) based on this analysis. Hitzing's discrete trials DRO condition was instituted for four food-deprived pigeons as subjects. Four "yoked" subjects received similar training with regard to deprivation, intertrial interval, key-presentation, and reinforcement, but their behavior had no programmed consequences. This pair of conditions is illustrated in the top part of Figure 3.13, which shows a yoke between the associative bonds in the experimental and control conditions. In the control conditions, pecking is not systematically separated by the DRO procedure from S^*, so we may expect to find an $R-S^*$ bond—in some degree—established between pecking and S^*, as well as between other behavior and the S^* event. In the experimental condition, the $R-S^*$ bond to pecking is blocked by the procedure. Therefore, pecking in the yoked control condition should be stronger than it is in the experimental condition.

To test this analysis further, the conditions illustrated in the lower part of Figure 3.13 were also explored. Once again, a design using four experimental

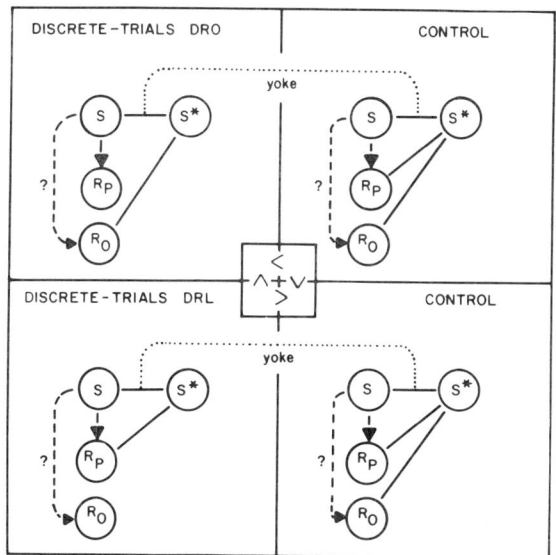

Figure 3.13. Schematic diagram of four experimental conditions, from the standpoint of a biconditional analysis. For convenience, the indicated relationships are not labeled, but the relative effectiveness of the linkage is indicated by the width of the corresponding lines. Neither R_o, nor its dependence of the $S-S^*$ link, can confidently be described; hence the question marks. The inequalities inserted in the center of the figure show the expected outcomes of this experiment, in terms of response strength.

and four yoked control pigeons was used. In this experiment, however, the experimental schedule was a discrete-trials differential reinforcement of low rate (DRL). Under this condition, reinforcement was delivered for the first keypeck that occurred either 6 sec after the start of a trial or, if the trial had started and a peck had occurred too soon, 6 sec or more after the last peck. This procedure is similar to the discrete-trials DRO in that pecking prolongs the duration of key illumination prior to reinforcement, and thus weakens the $S–S^*$ link. It differs from the discrete-trials DRO procedure, however, in that *pecking* rather than not-pecking is reinforced on every trial. Thus the $R–S^*$ link is strongest between pecking and S^*, and not between some other behavior and S^*. The $S–S^*$ bond is held equal for the experimental and control condition, and both pecking and other behaviors can maintain some associative strength through the $R–S^*$ link. Under this new pair of conditions, the theoretical expectation is opposite to that for the DRO pair. Under discrete-trials DRL, the pecking response is strengthened both by the $S–S^*$ link and by the $R–S^*$ link; the $S–S^*$ link is the same in the control condition, but the $R–S^*$ link to pecking is weaker.

A number of specific predictions about response rates under these procedures can readily be made. Under discrete-trials DRO (top of Figure 3.13), experimental subjects should respond less frequently than yoked control subjects, while under discrete-trials DRL (lower portion of Figure 3.13) experimental subjects should respond more vigorously than their yoked controls. This prediction also has implications for between-groups comparisons of the yoked control subjects: since at the end of training the discrete-trials DRO stimulus duration should be shorter than the discrete-trials DRL stimulus duration, and since the relative stimulus duration is presumed to affect the generative strength of the $S–S^*$ link, the yoked control subjects in the DRO condition should respond more frequently than the yoked control subjects in the DRL condition. These predictions are illustrated qualitatively in the small table in Figure 3.13.

Eight randomly constituted pairs of pigeons were run under the conditions described in Figure 3.13. The DRO schedule involved a 6-sec criterion: Once the key came on a reinforcer was presented as soon as 6 sec had elapsed without response. Under the DRL condition, reinforcement was given for the first keypeck that occurred 6 or more sec from the start of the trial or the time of last keypeck. (In the event of 12 sec without any peck, reinforcement was automatically delivered. This obviated the need for a special pretraining or handshaping of performance. After the first few sessions, rates of responding were established such that almost no reinforcers were presented by this concurrent 12-sec autoshaping schedule.) Four pairs of birds were tested under either the DRO or the DRL condition for approximately 1200 trials, and then switched to the opposite condition for approximately 2800 more trials. Finally they were returned to the original DRO condition for approximately 4500 trials. The status of experimental and control birds did not change throughout this extended training. Another group of four pairs of pigeons was first tested under one experimental condition for approximately 2500 trials and then tested under the other condition for approximately 7000 additional trials. The data presented in Figure 3.14 represent average responding on the last 200 trials under each condition for each pair of subjects in the experiment. It is obvious from the figure that rate of responding was higher under the DRL than under the DRO condition for the experimental subjects, by a factor of approximately three. This is a within-bird comparison, and the difference held for all eight subjects studied: Each bird's average terminal performance under DRL showed a higher rate than under DRO, regardless of which schedule was learned first. Two other manifestations of the greater tendency to respond seen under the DRL schedule are reflected in the following statistics. First, under DRL there was an average of 3.5 *excess* pecks per trial—that is, pecks that did not produce reinforcement but rather delayed it. Under DRO there was only an average of .56 excess pecks per trial (all pecks being excess in this case). This is borne out in the mean trial duration for the trials represented in Figure 3.14. Under DRL, the mean asymptotic trial duration was 18.22 sec whereas under DRO it was 7.01 sec. This difference in mean trial duration is almost certainly responsible for the differences in rate under the yoked control groups (for which there was never any explicit R–S^* contingency in force and for which the change from DRO to DRL did not involve any change of procedure). For the yoked subjects, responses per minute reached a high of 25 under the DRO condition and fell to 6.2 under DRL, in line with expectations.

This experiment demonstrates the importance of evaluating both the S–S^* and R–S^* aspects of biconditional behavior. Under the DRO experimental condition, where the possible influence of the R–S^* link was minimized (and its applicability to other behavior was maximized), rate of responding was lowest. The considerably higher rates seen under DRL reflect the power of the R–S^* link when applied to the pecking response; operationally, this manipulation of the peck/grain contingency is the only distinction between the two experimental groups. Further evidence for the importance of the R–S^* link in this situation is found in the difference between experimental and yoked control DRL subjects: here, the strength of the S–S^* is matched between the two groups, but the R–S^*

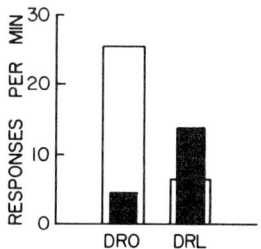

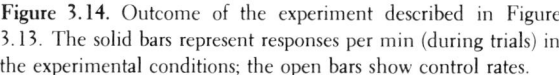

Figure 3.14. Outcome of the experiment described in Figure 3.13. The solid bars represent responses per min (during trials) in the experimental conditions; the open bars show control rates.

link is principally attached to the pecking response in the experimental condition. In the case of experimental and control DRO subjects, the S–S* links are again equated, but now a contribution to pecking by the R–S* link is procedurally minimized in the case of the experimental group; the difference in response rate reflects this exclusion. Finally, there is the substantial difference in rates between the two yoked-control conditions: Presumably, this reflects the relatively longer trial duration (perhaps in conjunction with a fixed-mean ITI) that occurred under DRL, and provides experimental support for the theoretical contention that trials of extended duration diminish the effectiveness of the S–S* link.

In these three experiments on biconditional behavior, the coordinated operation of S–S* and R–S* links has been considered. The last example to be presented introduces another aspect of biconditional dynamics, namely the interdependence of S–S* and R–S* links themselves. A rigorous treatment of this interdependence would be possible if the basic laws determining S_s and A_r were known. A qualitative treatment is possible, however, to bring out an aspect of biconditional relationships that might otherwise readily be overlooked.

To illustrate this property of interdependence of S–S* and R–S* links, let us return to the Gamzu and Williams (1971, 1973) experiment (Figure 3.3) in which keypecking was established by presenting reinforcement sporadically in the presence of the key (on an average of once per 30 sec) and withholding it when the key was not illuminated. When this procedure had succeeded in establishing pecking at high rates, Gamzu and Williams explored the effect of introducing reinforcement at the same rate during the intertrial interval, while continuing to present reinforcement as before when the key was illuminated. The result of this procedure was that responding rapidly diminished in the presence of the key even though there were no experimental alterations of any sort during the trial period. Although this result contributed strongly to the demonstration that S–S* relationships of the sort characteristic of classical conditioning can also engender keypecking, the result also raises a problem in the biconditional context that cannot be ignored: If keypecking is biconditional and reflects the operation of R–S* relationships as well as S–S* relationships, why does adding reinforcement to the intertrial interval produce a rapid cessation of responding? It would seem reasonable to suppose that the R–S* relationship would be sufficient to maintain responding for some extended period of time even during the nondifferential period. This reasonable argument suggests either that pecking is not biconditional after all, or that the nature of the R–S* relationships must more clearly be identified. It is to this latter task that we now turn.

In the Gamzu and Williams procedure, the R–S* link has its origins in the following process. First, a procedure is used by which the key (S) is associatively linked to a reinforcer (S*) capable of engendering pecking. It is, of course, the illuminated key that constitutes S. Once pecking begins, pecking is nonrandomly associated with the occurrence of reinforcement. This is, of course, not a causal relationship, but an artifactual type, arising from the fact that pecking is associated with key illumination and key illumination is associated with reinforcement: Therefore, pecking is associated with reinforcement. By the considerations discussed above regarding the necessary and sufficient conditions for the development of A_r, this differential association of R and S^* should contribute to the strength of R.

This state of affairs changes when reinforcement is added to the intertrial interval. Now, as discussed above, the key is no longer differentially associated with reinforcement. Therefore, even though pecking is differentially associated with the key, the key itself is not differentially associated with reinforcement; thus pecking also is not differentially associated with reinforcement. A nondifferential $R-S^*$ relationship is, of course, an extinction condition for the $R-S^*$ link. Thus the rapid decline of pecking reported by Gamzu and Williams involves simultaneous withdrawal of $S-S^*$ and $R-S^*$ linkages, the second being withdrawn as inconspicuously as it was introduced in the first place, namely through its piggyback relationship to the underlying $S-S^*$ linkage.

This account of extinction is capable of experimental test. What is required is that the $R-S^*$ linkage be strengthened beyond the point maintained by the association with the $S-S^*$ linkage. That could be done, for example, by making reinforcement actually contingent on pecking prior to the introduction of extinction. Such a maneuver, essentially introducing a zero delay of reinforcement of keypecking, would be expected to enhance $R-S^*$ control. Under this new procedure, it should be possible to maintain keypecking with a substantial rate of reinforcement in the intertrial interval.

SOME GENERAL OBSERVATIONS ON BICONDITIONAL BEHAVIOR

It is a fundamental tenet of this paper that behavior is not, in general, uniquely determined by one or another form of control—for example, by exclusively operant or respondent conditioning. Ideally, it may be possible to find examples of behaviors controllable by one means exclusively so that $S-S^*$ and $R-S^*$ laws can be studied in isolation. The force of this paper, however, is to argue that care and experimental effort must be expended in ascertaining that possible candidates are in fact uniconditional or, alternatively, in arranging situations where the impact of $S-S^*$ and $R-S^*$ links is minimized. Only in this way can a straightforward experimental analysis of associative laws proceed. It does not seem reasonable any longer to declare by fiat that a certain behavior is an operant (and thereby unsusceptible to direct $S-S^*$ control), or a respondent (and thereby unsusceptible to $R-S^*$ control). The matter is an experimental question, not a legislative one.

Common to several of the examples of biconditional control that were discussed above was the selective interaction of S–S* and R–S* links. These examples underscore an important point: biconditional relationship may operate even when control by one link is not so lopsided as it is in the case of the S–S* link that engenders keypecking for food. The failure of the negative contingency to halt pecking in the original experiments (Williams & Williams, 1969) was sufficiently conspicuous as to call attention to the existence of biconditional control, but that case is hardly representative of biconditional relationships in general.

The proposal that experiments take into account the susceptibility of a bit of behavior to joint S–S* and R–S* control is not, one hopes, a call for the mere "botanizing" of behavior. The term *botanizing* has recently been used by Herrnstein and Loveland (1972) to describe a call to survey what laws apply in particular response–species–reinforcer situations. The presumption is that an inchoate patchwork of special cases may be found. The perplexity of "food avoidance in the pigeon," that is, the bewilderment engendered by the phenomenon of negative autoshaping, led to these researchers' call for a consideration of botanizing. It is to be hoped that the present analysis of pecking as biconditional behavior will put that call to rest. If pecking is analyzed as biconditional behavior it is seen as behavior that follows two concurrently operative sets of laws, and not just one. From the biconditional point of view, systematic work on the nature and interaction of S–S* and R–S* relationships is called for, not an abandonment of principled research. Obviously it is of enormous importance to survey a wide variety of behavioral situations, situations that have been chosen, one hopes, with more respect for their biological significance than has often been the case in the past. But learning theory will never make its needed contribution to a genuine psychobiology of learning if it chooses to abandon its principles, rather than use them in experimental analysis.

The idea of biconditional behavior is in general agreement with Staddon and Simmelhag's (1971) analysis of mechanisms involved in learned behavior. The concepts developed here, like Staddon and Simmelhag's, both assume that a particular activity is regulated by "generative" and "selective" factors, and that the results of behavioral experiments require taking both sources of control into account. Staddon and Simmelhag devised a general stance with regard to learned behavior, however, and were concerned with stressing the diversity of generative sources that might be operative (their *principles of variation*). In contrast, the present treatment considers only one generative source, namely that arising from S–S* association. There is, however, nothing inherent in the biconditional approach that would argue *against* the operation of other generative sources; again, that is a matter for experimental determination. The importance of biconditional control vis-à-vis other, nonassociative, forms (as might operate, for example, with SSDRs: see Bolles, 1969) will depend primarily on the ubiquity of biconditional phenomena.

3. BICONDITIONAL BEHAVIOR: CONDITIONING WITHOUT CONSTRAINT   93

The biconditional analysis represents an attempt to outline one specific manifestation of the general orientation Staddon and Simmelhag proposed. It seems likely that biconditional analysis will apply most directly to "terminal behaviors" and in that manner complement Staddon and Simmelhag's focus on problems raised by "interim activities" such as displacement behaviors and adjunctive behaviors. The reason is that generative principles that are associatively based probably have a maximal effect as the moment of reinforcement approaches: certainly selective principles have their most important impact then. The generative and selective factors in biconditional analysis are thus focused on the target behaviors in learning experiments. It is doubtful that interim activities are generated associatively in the manner of a response such as the pigeon's keypeck, or that biconditional analysis, as such, will apply to them.

Biconditional situations appear to involve a complication with regard to the matter of "superstition" that was not anticipated in Staddon and Simmelhag's treatment. In essence, these authors argue that a selective reinforcement operates only by weakening unreinforced behaviors, not by strengthening reinforced ones (the purely selective role for reinforcement). Since selection cannot occur on a random basis, they conclude that adventitious reinforcement is not a tenable construct. The ability of generative relationships to strengthen response tendencies, while selective relationships do not, is a major asymmetry in Staddon and Simmelhag's approach, and sets it apart from the biconditional framework, where $S-S^*$ and $R-S^*$ links are afforded parallel treatment. The matter is in part an empirical one. Thus, regarding their position that selective ($R-S^*$) links do not actually strengthen response tendencies, Staddon and Simmelhag point out that their failure to find the consistent difference in rate of observed or defined pecking between the response-dependent and response-independent conditions of the present superstition experiment supports their view. The experiment of Figure 3.13, however, contains a comparison of response rate under DRL (response-dependent) and yoked control (response-independent) conditions. The rate under DRL was considerably higher than the yoked-control rate, even though $S-S^*$ and other generative factors were carefully equated. The difference between the present study and Staddon and Simmelhag's may lie in the relatively weaker generative link in the DRL experiment reported here: Control rates were not nearly as high. Although it is a matter of guesswork at the present time, it does not seem unreasonable to suppose that the high rates of responding observed by Staddon and Simmelhag were near a ceiling-of-response rate, and that their failure to find the difference between response-dependent and response-independent reinforcement was due to a problem of measurement, and not to a "purely selective" operation of an $R-S^*$ link. Work by Fenner and me (1974), repeating and extending Staddon and Simmelhag's experiment, is consistent with this interpretation. Results reported by Williams (1966) also suggest that reinforcement of a behavior (in that case, locomotion in rats) can directly strengthen it. In Williams' study the speed of running was related to magnitude or reinforcement for running whether or not there was any instrumental relationship between speed and reinforcement. Ultimately of course, the question of whether or not an $R-S^*$ link can lead to a strengthening of behavior depends on the availability of a metric for response strength, and no generally accepted scale is available or in view. Although treatment of the question of superstition is complicated by the assumption that $R-S^*$ links, like $S-S^*$ links, can strengthen behavior, such a complication should not obscure the fundamental accord between the concept of biconditional behavior and Staddon and Simmelhag's original approach.

The fact that pecking and drinking behaviors in chicks and pigeons are under $S-S^*$ generative control is an expression of what was called the *biology of association*. It is here that a major contribution of psychobiology to conditioning theory is to be found: It is surely not haphazard that an $S-S^*$ link to food, established in a pigeon subject, leads to pecking rather than flying away. A consideration of the biology of association raises the question of whether such behaviors are "prepared," in Seligman's (1970) sense.

Seligman (1970) suggests that "preparedness" can be operationally interpreted in terms of "the amount of input (e.g., number of trials, pairings, bits of information, etc.) which must occur before that output (responses, acts, repertoire, etc.) which is construed as evidence of acquisition, reliably occurs [p. 409]." Seligman hopes that using "preparedness" as a dimension will make it possible to establish, at the very least, a set of learning laws broadly applicable in each segment of the "preparedness" continuum. He also hopes that it may be possible to find one or a few parameters of a generalized association learning model that will have different loci on the preparedness continuum and thus provide a truly general set of learning laws. The central focus of Seligman's concept is on the rate of formation of associations—essentially a matter of the psychophysics of association—and not on the specific characteristics of the R-set. Unfortunately, without taking these characteristics and their possible biconditionality into account, it may not be possible to use even the operational tests on which the concept rests. An example may help clarify the nature of the problem.

Seligman takes the negative autoshaping phenomenon to indicate that a pigeon's keypeck is highly prepared and the (putative) difficulty of finding negative automaintenance in rats' lever-pressing to indicate that the latter is relatively unprepared. In line with this, Seligman (1970) states that "a typical rat will ordinarily learn to bar-press for food after a few dozen exposures to the bar-press/ food contingency . . . on the other hand pigeons require a key-peck in the lighted key/grain situation even when there is no contingency at all between key-pecking and grain [p. 413]." In effect, Seligman is asserting that pigeons learn to peck keys more readily than rats learn to press levers. Factually, however, this possibility does not seem to be the case. Skinner (1938) ably documented the fact that a *single reinforcement* is often sufficient to establish a high rate of lever pressing in rats, provided only that magazine training has been carefully carried out. By contrast, autoshaping experiments typically require 20–200 trials before the first peck emerges. With regard to rate of acquisition then, it would seem that lever pressing in rats might be even more highly prepared than keypecking in pigeons is, depending, to be sure, on the choice of metric. Such a conclusion would present a paradox for Seligman's position, however, if we assume that pigeons' keypecking is more readily maintained in the absence of an $R-S^*$ link than is rats' lever pressing.

The difficulties arise because the preparedness approach considers neither the nature and variety of mechanisms of learning nor their coordination. As Staddon and Simmelhag (1971) point out, "no inferences about 'speed of conditioning' can be drawn on the basis of speed of acquisition without information about frequency and pattern of a given behavior to be expected in a given situation (which may include predictable delivery of reinforcement) *in the absence of contiguity* between that behavior and reinforcement [p. 37]." Thus Seligman's identification of preparedness with quantitative properties of S–R associations seems unanalytic, unweildy, and premature. More generally, it seems clear that a distinction between the biology of association and the psychophysics of association may be helpful in the analysis of specific situations and that the coordination of learning mechanisms, those of biconditional behavior as well as others, must be analyzed experimentally if a useful fusion of learning theory and psychobiology is to take place. Pigeons would almost certainly be better prepared than people to fly from perch to perch to escape shock, if the operational test of preparedness were applied. A clear understanding of the reason, however, obviously demands further inquiry into the particulars of the situation than learning-rate data would provide. It does not seem likely that *less* analysis is called for when the critical features of a comparison are less conspicuous.

Suggesting that a fusion of learning theory and psychobiology requires an analytic application of conventional conditioning principles does not, of course, argue that a biconditional framework requires or implies an *equipotentiality of association* assumption. On the contrary, just as the psychophysics of loudness threshholds does not require that incremental energy be the same at all points on the frequency continuum, so also the psychophysics of association do not in any way require that the rate of formation of an $S-S^*$ or $R-S^*$ bond be independent of the specific nature of S, R, or S^*, or of the species involved. Seligman's doubt about the equipotentiality of association seems well founded; apparently it is only the preparedness continuum per se that leads to difficulties. The biconditional framework provides a clear indication of where those difficulties may lie and how, in some instances, they may be circumvented. The question of how general the laws of learning may prove to be requires experimental analysis of the laws operating in a variety of situations. The usefulness of learning laws in guiding such analysis, and the final results of inquiry, will provide the only adequate answer to the question of generality, and the only real indication of the usefulness of yet another metastructure to house them.

CONCLUSION

The overarching aim of this chapter has been to contribute to the integration of learning theory and psychobiology by illustrating the analytic utility of the process and laws of conditioning. Although this was done primarily in the context of a single laboratory preparation, the aim can be reached only if the approach carries beyond this particular instance.

A major theme running through this chapter is that the ordinary concepts and laws of learning represent a powerful analytic tool for inquiry into behaviors of psychobiological relevance. Such a claim is not tantamount to asserting the universal applicability of one or another theory of learning, any more than asserting the general utility of the laws of motion is tantamount to asserting a cosmology. Experimental analysis operates best from a footing above mere chaos, but well below universality of principle. The challenging task for behavioral biology at the present time may be one of detailed analysis of specific phenomena guided by principles that seem to apply in a variety of instances. It may well be that a general picture will emerge where the job of analysis has carried out repeatedly; it seems of only philosophical interest to contemplate the question now.

This chapter takes a major step beyond the conventional use of conditioning concepts in asserting biconditional control over behavior. Certainly this step is in opposition to the use of "operant" and "respondent" as categorical concepts (i.e., as mutually exclusive and possibly exhaustive "types" of behavior to which only $S-S^*$ or only $R-S^*$ laws apply). Although the idea of biconditional control is unconventional, it seems to do little violence to anything other than a gratuitous step in theory construction. There is nothing inherently illogical in the notion that two sets of laws may apply to a single phenomenon; if anything, exclusive control by one source of influence would seen the exception, particularly in the biological domain. In any event, the question of joint control appears to be an experimental one, and the case of pigeon's pecking appears to be one clearly affirmative instance.

Hand-in-hand with the departure from categorical thinking goes the suggestion that behavior be analyzed experimentally, not used as an indicator of the validity of one or another theory. The status of conditioning principles of both $R-S^*$ and $S-S^*$ varieties as tools of analysis is too often overlooked, possibly because categorical thinking has led to the unfounded assumption that at most one set must apply. It would be of considerable interest, for example, to see whether emotional responses such as fear, which are ordinarily considered from an S–S* or classical conditioning point of view, can also be altered by R–S* relationships. Can fear be strengthened by positive consequences? The possibility that emotional states constitute biconditional behavior deserves evaluation; certainly it would help make sense of a number of psychosomatic complaints. The tools for experimental analysis are available—they have only to be applied.

Biconditional behavior is, of course, only one case of an interaction of multiple sources of control over behavior. In his analysis of SSDRs as nonassociatively evoked behaviors sensitive to their outcomes, Bolles has postulated another case. Falk (1971) has made a strong case that *adjunctive behaviors* are directly generated in experimental situations by mechanisms that lie outside the biconditional framework of interlocking S–S* and R–S* relations. It may well be, as Staddon and Simmelhag suggest, that there are many generative sources of behavior, and therefore many ways in which principles of control interact. The important contribution of psychobiology is to identify types of species-relevant behavioral phenomena where experience appears to play a role. Learning theory, if it sticks to its principles and applies them analytically, can then share productively in the labor of answering the riddles of biologically significant behavior.

REFERENCES

Adler, N., & Hogan, J. A. Classical conditioning and punishment of an instinctive response in *Betta splendens. Animal Behavior,* 1963, *11,* 351–354.
Allaway, T. A. *Information, attention and autoshaping.* Unpublished doctoral dissertation, University of Pennsylvania, 1971.
Baum, W. M. The correlation-based law of effect. *Journal of the Experimental Analysis of Behavior,* 1973, *20,* 137–153.
Bolles, R. C. Species-specific defense reactions and avoidance learning. *Psychological Review,* 1970, *77,* 32–48.
Bolles, R. C. Reinforcement, expectancy, and learning. *Psychological Review,* 1972, *79,* 394–409.
Breland, M., & Breland, K. The misbehavior of organisms. *American Psychologist,* 1961, *16,* 681–684.
Brown, P., & Jenkins, H. M. Autoshaping of the pigeon's key-peck. *Journal of the Experimental Analysis of Behavior,* 1968, *11,* 1–8.
Egger, M. D., & Miller, N. E. Secondary reinforcement in rats as a function of information value and reliability of the stimulus. *Journal of Experimental Psychology,* 1962, *64,* 97–104.
Falk, J. L. The nature of determinants of adjunctive behavior. *Physiology and Behavior,* 1971, *6,* 577–588.
Fenner, D., & Williams, D. R. Personal communication, University of Pennsylvania, 1974.
Ferster, C. B., & Skinner, B. F. *Schedules of Reinforcement.* New York: Appleton-Century-Crofts, 1957.
Gibbon, J., Berryman, R., & Thompson, R. L. Contingency spaces and measures in classical and instrumental conditioning. *Journal of the Experimental Analysis of Behavior,* 1974, *21,* 585–605.
Gamzu, E., & Williams D. R. Classical conditioning of a complex skeletal response. *Science,* 1971, *171,* 923–925.

Gamzu, E., & Williams, D. Associative factors underlying the pigeon's key pecking in autoshaping procedures. *Journal of the Experimental Analysis of Behavior*, 1973, *19*, 225-232.

Glickman, S. E., & Schiff, B. A biological theory of reinforcement. *Psychological Review*, 1967, *74*, 81-109.

Hearst, E., & Jenkins, H. M. *Sign-tracking: The stimulus-reinforcer relation and directed action.* Monograph of the Psychonomic Society, Austin, Tex., 1974.

Herrnstein, R. J. On the law of effect. *Journal of the Experimental Analysis of Behavior*, 1970, *13*, 243-266.

Herrnstein, R. J., & Loveland, D. H. Food-avoidance in hungry pigeons, and other perplexities. *Journal of the Experimental Analysis of Behavior*, 1972, *18*, 369-383.

Hitzing, E. W. *Auto-maintenance: An analysis of the contingent non-reinforcement control procedure.* Paper presented at Southeastern Psychological Association, Atlanta, Georgia, April, 1972.

Hogan, Jerry A. How young chicks learn to recognize food. In R. A. Hinde & J. S. Hinde (Eds.), *Constraints on learning.* New York: Academic Press, 1973.

Hunt, G. L., & Smith, W. J. Pecking and initial drinking responses in young domestic fowl. *Journal of Comparative and Physiological Psychology*, 1967, *64*, 230-236.

Jenkins, H. M., & Moore, B. R. The form of the autoshaped response with food or water reinforcers. *Journal of the Experimental Analysis of Behavior*, 1973, *20*, 163-181.

Jenkins, H. M., & Sainsbury, R. S. The development of stimulus control through differential reinforcement. In N. J. Mackintosh & W. K. Honig (Eds.), *Fundamental issues in associative learning.* Halifax, Canada: Dalhousie Univ. Press, 1969.

Jenkins, H. M., & Sainsbury, R. S. Discrimination learning with the distinctive feature on positive of negative trials. In D. Mostofky (Ed.), *Attention: Contemporary theory and analysis.* New York: Appleton-Century-Crofts, 1970.

Michotte, A. *The perception of causality.* New York: Basic Books, 1963.

Moore, B. R. The role of directed Pavlovian reactions in simple instrumental learning in the pigeon. In R. A. Hinde & J. S. Hinde (Eds.), *Constraints on Learning.* New York: Academic Press, 1973.

Morrison, G., & Williams, D. R. Unpublished observations, University of Pennsylvania, 1974.

Moseley, D. The accuracy of the pecking response in chicks. *Journal of Comparative Psychology*, 1925, *5*, 75-97.

Murray, C. S. *Conditioning Betta splendens.* Unpublished doctoral dissertation, University of Pennsylvania, 1973.

Pavlov, I. P. *Conditioned reflexes.* New York and London: Oxford Univ. Press, 1927.

Perkins, C. C., Jr. An analysis of the concept of reinforcement. *Psychological Review*, 1968, *75*, 155-172.

Perkins, C. C., Jr. Reinforcement in classical conditioning. In H. H. Kendler & J. T. Spence (Eds.), *Essays in neobehaviorism: A memorial volume to Kenneth W. Spence.* New York: Appleton-Century-Crofts, 1971.

Rescorla, R. A. Pavlovian conditioning and its proper control procedures. *Psychological Review*, 1967, *74*, 71-80.

Rescorla, R. A., & Solomon, R. L. Two-process learning theory: relationships between Pavlovian conditioning and instrumental learning. *Psychological Review*, 1967, *74*, 151-182.

Ricci, J. A. Classically conditioned key-pecking to simple and compound stimuli of long duration. *Journal of the Experimental Analysis of Behavior*, 1973, *19*, 509-516.

Rozin, P., & Kalat, J. W. Specific hungers and poison avoidance as adaptive specializations of learning. *Psychological Review*, 1971, *78*, 459-486.

Schlosberg, H. Conditioned responses in the white rat. *Journal of Genetic Psychology*, 1934, *45*, 303-335.

Schwartz, B. The role of positive conditioned reinforcement in the maintenance of key-pecking which prevents delivery of a primary reinforcement. *Psychonomic Science*, 1972, *28*, 277-278.

Schwartz, B., & Williams, D. R. The role of the response–reinforcer contingency in negative automaintenance. *Journal of the Experimental Analysis of Behavior*, 1972, *17*, 351-357. (a)

Schwartz, B., & Williams, D. R. Two kinds of key-peck in the pigeon: Some properties of responses maintained by negative and positive response-reinforcer contingencies. *Journal of the Experimental Analysis of Behavior*, 1972, *18*, 210-216. (b)

Seligman, M. E. P. On the generality of the laws of learning. *Psychological Review*, 1970, *77*, 406-418.

Sheffield, F. D. Relation between classical conditioning and instrumental conditioning. In F. W. Prokasy (Ed.), *Classical conditioning*. New York: Appleton-Century-Crofts, 1965.

Shettleworth, S. Constraints on learning. In D. S. Lehrman, R. A. Hinde, & E. Shaw (Eds.), *Advances in the study of behavior*. Vol. 4. New York: Academic Press, 1971.

Skinner, B. F. *The behavior of organisms*. New York: Appleton-Century-Crofts, 1938.

Staddon, J. E. R., & Simmelhag, V. L. The "superstition" experiment: A re-examination of its implications for the principles of adaptive behavior. *Psychological Review*, 1971, *78*, 3-43.

Terrace, H. S., Gibbon, J., Farrell, L., & Baldock, M. D. Temporal factors influencing the acquisition of an autoshaped response. *Animal Learning and Behavior*, 1975, *3*, 53-62.

Thompson, T. I., & Sturm, T. Classical conditioning of aggressive display in Siamese fighting fish. *Journal of the Experimental Analysis of Behavior*, 1965, *8*, 397-404. (a)

Thompson, T. I., & Sturm, T. Visual-reinforcer color and operant behavior in Siamese fighting fish. *Journal of the Experimental Analysis of Behavior*, 1965, *8*, 341-346. (b)

Valenstein, E. S., Cox, V. C., & Kakolewski, J. W. Reexamination of the role of the hypothalamus in motivation. *Psychological Review*, 1970, *77*, 16-31.

von Holst, E., & von Saint Paul, U. On the functional organization of drives. *Animal Behavior*, 1963, *11*, 1-20.

Wasserman, E. A. Auto-shaping: The selection and direction of behavior by predictive stimuli. (Doctoral dissertation, Indiana University, 1972.) *Dissertation Abstracts International*, 1972, *32*, 6704B. (University Microfilms No. 72-15, 935.)

Wasserman, E. A. The effect of redundant contextual stimuli on auto-shaping of the pigeon's key-peck. *Animal Learning and Behavior*, 1973, *1*, 198-206.

Williams, D. R. Relation between response amplitude and reinforcement. *Journal of Experimental Psychology*, 1966, *71*, 634-641.

Williams, D. R., & Williams, H. Auto-maintenance in the pigeon: Sustained pecking despite contingent non-reinforcement. *Journal of the Experimental Analysis of Behavior*, 1969, *12*, 511-520.

Woodruff, G., Connor, N., Gamzu, E., & Williams, D. R. Associative interaction: Joint control of keypecking by stimulus-reinforcer and response-reinforcer relationships. *Journal of the Experimental Analysis of Behavior*, 1977, *28*, 133-134.

Woodruff, G., & Williams, D. R. The associative relation underlying autoshaping in the pigeon. *Journal of the Experimental Analysis of Behavior*, 1976, *26*, 1-13.

Zener, K. The significance of behavior accompanying conditioned salivary secretion for theories of the conditioned response. *American Journal of Psychology*, 1937, *50*, 384-403.

C. M. LOCURTO

Contributions of Autoshaping to the Partitioning of Conditioned Behavior

Scientific discovery consists of the interpretation for our convenience of a system of existence which has been made with no eye to our convenience at all [Norbert Wiener, 1954, p. 7].

INTRODUCTION

The study of conditioned behavior has consisted principally of a series of attempts to specify the correspondence between Pavlovian and instrumental conditioning. The problem is made difficult by the fact that at the level of description the laws of conditioning are necessarily stated as relations between behavior and environmental events. As a result, the laws derived from these two forms of conditioning must per force be different, even if the respective outcomes are found to be indistinguishable (cf. Rescorla & Solomon, 1967).

Autoshaping emerged during a period of reassessment of the relationship between Pavlovian and instrumental learning, a period initiated most directly by the demonstration of autonomic instrumental conditioning (see, e.g., Miller, 1969). Oddly, it was not its first demonstration, by Brown and Jenkins (1968), that established the theoretical significance of autoshaping. For it had long been recognized that Pavlovian procedures may contain sources of instrumental reinforcement. In autoshaping, a stimulus–reinforcer relation is programmed, but that arrangement does not prevent close temporal pairings between response to the signal and delivery of the reinforcer. The first account of autoshaping relied strongly upon these adventitious pairings between pigeons' keypecking and food:

> The bird notices the onset of the light and perhaps makes some minimal motor adjustment to it. The temporal conjunction of reinforcement with noticing leads to

orienting and looking toward the key. The species-specific look-peck coupling eventually yields a peck to the trial stimulus [Brown & Jenkins, 1968, p. 7. Copyright © 1968 by the Society for the Experimental Analysis of Behavior, Inc.].

This interpretation may be viewed as consistent with other contemporary attempts to integrate Pavlovian conditioning within the framework of instrumental behavior (cf. Gormezano & Coleman, 1973; Kimmel & Burns, 1975). However, that explanation was soon questioned, as a result of the demonstration by Williams and Williams (1969; see also Chapter 3) that autoshaped keypecking might be engendered and maintained when pecking prevented food delivery. In their omission training procedure, food was delivered only following trials (6-sec illuminations of the response key) during which a keypeck did not occur (cf. Sheffield, 1965). Any keypeck during the trial terminated the keylight and cancelled food delivery. As a result, there could be no adventitious reinforcement for pecks and from an instrumental viewpoint keypecking should be reduced to pre-experimental levels. Should responding persist in this procedure, it can apparently only be explained by the Pavlovian stimulus–reinforcer pairings that result in trials in which no responses occur. Examination of the cumulative response curves for the first 13 pigeons run under the Williamses' omission procedure (see Williams, Chapter 3, Figure 3.2) reveals that despite variability among these subjects only one bird ceased to respond during extended training. The remaining animals continued to lose a substantial percentage of the programmed reinforcers.

The omission procedure has been characterized as a criterion test for evaluating the relative contributions of Pavlovian and instrumental contingencies to the maintenance of a response (e.g., Gamzu & Schwam, 1974; Mackintosh, 1974; Sheffield, 1965). As a result, the persistence of autoshaped responding in this procedure has been cited as the strongest evidence that autoshaping is not reducible to an instance of instrumentally controlled behavior (e.g., Hearst & Jenkins, 1974; Schwartz & Gamzu, 1977). Indeed, were it not for the data on omission training it is doubtful that autoshaping would have created quite the impact it has among psychologists interested in the study of animal learning.

In what follows, the reliability and generality of the Williams's demonstration are examined, as are the results of analytic experiments that have attempted to identify the factors controlling responding within the omission procedure. These data are compared to the results of related procedures that also bear on the nature of the mechanism(s) underlying autoshaping.

OMISSION TRAINING

Reliability

Numerous studies followed the initial application of the omission procedure to autoshaping. Although these experiments do not form an integrated program of inquiry, many share at least the use of the same *response system* employed in the Williamses' (1969) study—pigeons' keypecking, a visual conditioned stimulus, and food. Table 4.1 provides an overview of this work. The table lists the temporal parameters used in each experiment, the subjects and their experimental histories, the length of omission training and an estimate of response probability, indexed as the proportion of trials with at least one keypeck. It should be noted that for several studies response levels were estimated from published figures. Also, in cases where a study involved several experimental treatments, the data have been summarized only for subjects' first exposure to omission training (e.g., Hursh, Navarick, & Fantino, 1974; Lucas, 1975; Schwartz, 1973).

The average response probability for all studies combined was .44. The range of response probability was 0–.95 for individual subjects and .10–.75 for different experiments. To a first approximation, the outcomes of these experiments fall into three categories. In some studies little or no maintenance under the omission contingency was noted (Barrera, 1974; Herrnstein & Loveland, 1972; Hursh et al., 1974; Powell & Kelly, 1976). In others, relatively high response levels were observed (Balsam, Brownstein, & Shull, 1978; Griffin & Rashotte, 1973; Schwartz & Williams, 1972a; Woodard, Ballinger, & Bitterman, 1974). The majority of studies reported moderate response levels of approximately .30–.50.

Doubtless, procedural differences (see footnotes to table 4.1) contributed importantly to the variability between studies. For example, subjects' past histories varied greatly, as did the amount of exposure to omission training (and, hence, the base from which averages were computed), with a range of 120–5880 trials. These studies also differed with respect to the consequences of a keypeck in addition to cancelling food: Some studies used the Williamses' response-terminated trials (RTT) format while others used a fixed-trial (FT) procedure in which keypecking did not affect trial duration.

In some studies, a subject's previous experience has been found to be critical. Unfortunately, experimental histories often have not been systematically controlled; subjects range from those that are experimentally naive to those that have had extensive prior training involving autoshaping, omission training, or various schedules of instrumental reinforcement. Moreover, in those cases where this variable has been studied a clear picture does not emerge. Barrera (1974) reported that subjects with prior autoshaping training maintained lower levels of responding than was evident for naive subjects. However, Powell and Kelly (1976) observed that subjects with a history of intermittent instrumental reinforcement exhibited greater persistence under the omission procedure than did naive subjects. Other studies have noted no consistent differences between naive and experienced subjects (Herrnstein & Loveland, 1972; Williams & Williams, 1969; see also, Peden, Browne, & Hearst, 1977).

Additional factors such as the temporal parameters used in training do not provide a firm basis for sorting the results of these studies. In all cases but one, a narrow sample of temporal values–those quite favorable to conditioning—have

TABLE 4.1
Summary of Omission Training Studies [a]

Study	Intertrial/trial durations (sec)	Subject status	Number of training trials	Mean response level	Response level range
Williams & Williams (1969): Experiment I	30/6 RTT [b]	13 naive and experienced	1000 (average)	.40 (over entire study)	.10–.90
Herrnstein & Loveland (1972): Experiment IV		23 naive and experienced	5880 (average)	.10 (median)	0–.65
Schwartz & Williams (1972a)	30/6 FT	8 naive and experienced	1800	.64 (last 600 cycles)	.36–.87
Schwartz (1972)	30/6 [c]	4 naive	18 sessions (trials/session unknown)	.57 (over entire study)	.47–.66
Schwartz (1973)	40/6 FT	3 experienced	350	.54 (last 150 trials)	.40–.76
Griffin & Rashotte (1973)	120/6 FT	4 naive	720	.75 (last 150 trials)	.60–.83
Hursh, Navarick, & Fantino (1974)	30/6 RTT	8 naive and experienced	917 (average)	.22 [d] (last 250 trials)	0–.83
Woodard, Ballinger, & Bitterman (1974)	60/8 FT	6 naive	120	.75 (last 500 trials)	individual data not reported
Barrera (1974): Experiments I & II	30/8 RTT	12 naive and experienced	3250 (experiment I) 1000 (experiment II)	.25 .10 (last 250 trials)	0–.45 0–.30

Study				
(1975)			1200	.53
Lucas (1975)	30/6 FT	3 experienced	1000 (average)	.03–.92 (last 200 trials)
Powell & Kelly (1976)	30/6 RTT	8 naive and experienced		.25 (last 250 trials)
Wilke (1976)	15–240/5 FT	5 experienced	1858/intertrial interval (average)	.32 not available (last 300 trials)
Peterson, Lyon, Stone, & Scott (1977)	33/6 [h]	20 naive	first 1000 trials used	.45 0–.95 (last 250 trials)
Balsam, Brownstein, & Shull (1978): Experiment I	30/8 FT	8 naive and experienced	400	.63 not available (last 200 trials)
Rosenthal & Matthews (1978)	60/7.5 FT	5 naive and experienced	450	.57 .45–.81 (over entire study)

[a] RTT = response-terminated trial; FT = fixed-trial.
[b] The procedure consisted of a 59.5 sec "trial" followed by a .5 sec "signal." Any response during the trial cancelled food and had various stimulus-change consequences. Data were determined by averaging across several procedures.
[c] For two subjects a keypeck terminated the trial, for two others trial duration was fixed. On trials without a response the keylight terminated with the end of reinforcement.
[d] Data are summarized only for those subjects exposed first to omission training. Six of these subjects responded at near-zero levels, two others at approximately .80.
[e] In Experiment II, 40 sessions of autoshaping preceded omission training.
[f] Three conditions were compared: response-terminated trials, fixed trials, and response-feedback trials. As responses between these conditions did not differ, data have been pooled.
[g] Omission training continued until two consecutive sessions in which at least .50 reinforcers were obtained. Except for subjects with extensive histories of intermittent reinforcement, all subjects met the criterion within five sessions. Each session was 45 min long.
[h] On trials without a response, a 6 sec conditioned stimulus was followed by 4 sec of a different colored stimulus preceding food. Subjects were exposed to various manipulations involving presenting or withholding this 4 sec stimulus on trials with a response in response-terminated and fixed-trial omission procedures.
[i] Subjects were exposed to pre-feeding on one-half of the sessions; data were summed only for sessions without pre-feeding.

been used (cf. Gibbon, Baldock, Locurto, Gold, & Terrace, 1977). The one exception, a study by Wilkie (1976), reported that variations in intertrial interval over a range of 15–240 sec had no consistent effect upon the level of omission responding. It is also evident that average response levels did not depend simply on amount of training. Substantial responding was noted in studies that consisted of extensive training, as well as those with relatively brief exposure to the omission procedure (cf. Schwartz & Williams, 1972a, with Schwartz, 1973).[1]

Studies that reported low maintenance levels involved departures from the standard training format. For example, Herrnstein and Loveland (1972) followed a procedure in which a cycle of 60 sec consisted of one keylight color (the "trial") for 59.50 sec followed by a second color for .50 sec. Any peck during the "trial" cancelled food delivery (see footnote *a* to Table 4.1). Barrera (1974) used a two-key procedure in which a 3.2 sec pretrial stimulus was followed by an 8-sec trial. A peck to either key cancelled food. The study by Hursh et al. (1974) has been faulted on several grounds due to the wide variety of manipulations introduced to examine maintenance during omission training (see Peden et al., 1977). However, the data reported from this study in Table 4.1 were taken only during subjects' initial exposure to a standard omission procedure (see footnote *c* to the table).

These findings leave little doubt that with this response system keypecking persists under an omission contingency. To assess the significance of this level of responding, and to characterize the mechanisms underlying it, two strategies have been followed: Omission responding has been compared to various control conditions, and the effects of introducing alterations in the standard omission procedure have been studied.

Analytic Experiments

Comparisons with Control Procedures

Few studies have systematically compared the level of omission responding to extinction or to a random-control procedure (Rescorla, 1967). Studies in which

---

[1]One might expect response probability to vacillate during extended training; that is, periods of responding (trials without a reinforcer) should be followed by periods of no responding (trials with reinforcers), which should in turn generate responding, and so on. Disconfirming evidence is found in an analysis of the sequential dependencies during omission training compiled by Balsam, et al. (1978). The conditional probability of a peck given N prior trials without a peck decreased with increases in N. Similarly, the conditional probability of no-peck given N prior trials with a peck also decreased with increases in N. Both functions peaked at $N=0$. Thus, once responding or not responding the pigeon tended to remain in that state. If response strength were directly related to the number of prior successive pairings, conditional probability should have increased as N increased. Similar data have been reported by Shapiro and Herendeen (1975) in omission training of the salivation response in dogs (see also Solomon & Wynne, 1953, for similar considerations derived from avoidance training).

these comparisons were made have yielded conflicting results (cf. Herrnstein & Loveland, 1972, with Woodard *et al.* 1974). However, in view of the maintenance levels summarized in Table 4.1, it would appear that the average level of keypecking under an omission contingency is greater than would be expected from these control procedures.[2]

A different type of comparison was conducted by Schwartz and Williams (1972a), who studied the responding maintained by an omission-correlated stimulus to a stimulus yoked to the omission stimulus in terms of percentage reinforcement. Since responding to the yoked stimulus has no effect on delivery of the reinforcer, it may be influenced both by stimulus–reinforcer relations and by adventitious pairings between responses and reinforcers. As a result, if higher response probabilities are maintained by the yoked stimulus one may infer that autoshaped keypecking, which is engendered by Pavlovian relations in omission training, is also susceptible to instrumental control. No difference in the responding supported by these two stimuli would indicate the predominance of Pavlovian relations (cf. Moore & Gormezano, 1961).

Higher response levels were associated with the yoked stimulus, as was a preference for that stimulus on choice trials. Unfortunately, these findings do not reveal why intermediate levels of responding are observed in omission training. It may be that keypecking is sensitive to the negative instrumental contingency and, therefore, is weakened by omission training. Yet it is also possible that the levels of omission responding do not reflect the sensitivity of keypecking to its consequences, but only the debilitating effects of partial, Pavlovian reinforcement (cf. Gormezano & Moore, 1969; Terrace, 1973). From this perspective, the yoked/omission difference may be due solely to the strengthening of keypecking in the yoked treatment by the positive instrumental relation. Of course, a combination of these factors cannot be ruled out: This pattern may be the result of both the suppressive effects of the omission contingency and the positive effects of adventitious instrumental pairings in the yoked condition (see Stiers & Silberberg, 1974).

Conditioned Reinforcement

One potential source of a direct influence of instrumental relations in omission training is conditioned reinforcement. On trials without a response, trial-offset is followed by food. Thus, trial-offset may be established as a conditioned

---

[2]These results are similar to those observed for the prototypical Pavlovian reflex, dogs' salivation and a food reinforcer. Sheffield (1965), in the initial study of omission training, reported that one dog continued to salivate under an omission contingency, losing approximately .50 of the scheduled reinforcers. Recent work has demonstrated that although an omission contingency may maintain salivation somewhat better than extinction, response probability is reduced to low levels in both procedures, averaging approximately .15 to .30 (Herendeen & Shapiro, 1975; Shapiro & Herendeen, 1975).

reinforcer. This possibility is an important one because it questions the primacy of Pavlovian relations in omission training as well as the use of the procedure as a criterion test of stimulus–reinforcer control.

A common experimental strategy has been to compare the responding supported by a fixed-trial omission procedure to that of a response-terminated procedure. In the former case, responses bear an unprogrammed relationship to trial offset, whereas in the latter procedure the first response during a trial is paired with trial-offset. The results of several studies using pigeons have confirmed that there are few differences between these procedures (Brownstein & Balsam, 1975; Schwartz, 1972; see also Peterson, Lyon, Stone, & Scott, 1977). The one exception comes from the study by Hursh *et al.* (1974). These workers noted that responding was virtually eliminated during omission training if keypecks delayed the end of a trial, thereby insuring that responses would not be paired with trial offset. In only one in twelve subjects was the keypeck acquired and maintained under the omission procedure when this and related manipulations were introduced. Unfortunately, this procedure also has the effect of increasing trial duration, and it is not possible to separate the effects of these changes from those produced by the omission contingency (see also Herrnstein & Loveland, 1972, for evidence of stimulus-change influences in autoshaping and omission training).

Overall, these studies provide no evidence that for this response system responding during omission training is the result of some subtle conditioned reinforcement process.

Dual-Unit Hypothesis

It is difficult to reconcile the observation of persistent keypecking in omission training with the obvious susceptibility of this response to instrumental contingencies of reinforcement. These data seem to contradict the assumption of two-factor theory that the responses controlled by Pavlovian contingencies are different in kind from those amenable to instrumental reinforcement. To preserve the theory one might argue that keypecking does not represent a unified response class but is composed of qualitatively different subclasses of responses. Comparable arguments have been advanced with respect to the leg flexion response in dogs (Schlosberg, 1937; Wahlsten & Cole, 1972).

The dual-unit hypothesis was adopted by Schwartz and Williams (1972b) who noted that keypecks engendered under an omission contingency were distinguished by their shorter duration (averaging approximately 20 msec) from those observed in autoshaping (averaging nearly 40–50 msec). These duration differences were independent of whether subjects experienced the omission contingency before or subsequent to autoshaping. It was also noted that in conventional instrumental procedures such as continuous reinforcement (CRF) and variable-ratio (VR) schedules, as well as in autoshaping, response durations were invariably short early in training. With extended training, long-duration responses emerged and predominated in these procedures. Most important, these differences in duration reflected functional distinctions. Only long-duration responses appeared to be sensitive to instrumental reinforcement. Responses of shorter duration were not increased in frequency when reinforcement was made contingent on their occurrence.

Two subsequent sets of experiments extended these findings (Schwartz, 1977a, b). The occurrence of short-duration pecks on fixed-interval (FI) and fixed-ratio (FR) schedules of reinforcement appeared to parallel bursts of salivation in dogs exposed to similar schedules (i.e., during the early portions of the FI and during the latter portions of FR cycles; cf. Williams, 1965). In a differential reinforcement of low rate procedure (DRL), short latency responses—those failing to meet the reinforcement criterion—were of short duration, whereas responses of longer latency were longer in duration. Also, the effects of punishment on keypecks of short and long duration were found to be asymmetrical. Long- but not short-duration pecks were suppressed by punishment. The punishment of short-duration pecks resembled only the effects produced by response-independent shocks (i.e., shocks delivered independently of response duration).

These data have been interpreted as indicating the existence of two different types of keypecks, indexed by differences in duration. Short-duration responses appear to be insensitive to instrumental relations and are instead controlled exclusively by Pavlovian relations. Hence we find that responding persists in omission procedures despite the negative response–reinforcer relation. It was further suggested that these short-duration responses correspond to what Skinner (1966) has labeled *minimal units*, phylogenetically based response units that serve as the foundation from which responses sensitive to instrumental control (i.e., long-duration keypecks) emerge. This explains why short-duration responses are found early in instrumental training and in autoshaping procedures (see also Kimmel & Burns, 1975; Wahlsten & Cole, 1972, for similar dual-response accounts derived from different experimental procedures).

The dual-unit hypothesis is by far the most provocative to emerge in autoshaping and has attracted several challenges. Perhaps the strongest comes from a recent study by Ziriax and Silberberg (1978). Although this study was not concerned with autoshaping, it bears on the the dual-unit hypothesis. These workers used a conditional discrimination procedure to study the pigeon's sensitivity to both the emission and discrimination of short- and long-duration pecks. In one experiment, the pigeon emitted a keypeck and was then required to report its duration by pecking one of three keys corresponding to either no peck, short duration, or long duration. In a second experiment, the presentation of one of two colors signified which type of keypeck duration was required for reinforcement. Their data provided clear evidence that the pigeon is quite successful at both tasks for each type of response.

These results suggest that it is not possible to make functional distinctions between short-duration and long-duration pecks. It did not appear that the pigeon was insensitive to the occurrence of short-duration pecks, or that short-duration pecks were controlled solely by the stimuli that precede them (i.e., by Pavlovian relations). As an alternative to the dual-unit hypothesis it was suggested that duration serves simply as an index of response strength. Figure 4.1 illustrates this alternative and summarizes the results of a variety of studies compiled by Ziriax and Silberberg. It can be seen that various experimental procedures, ranging from omission training through various schedules of instrumental reinforcement, can be rank-ordered with respect to a characteristic response duration, latency, and rate. On this scale, omission training occupies a position of relatively low strength.

Interestingly, these authors also argued that the original peck duration data reported by Schwartz and Williams (1972b) were inconsistent with the dual-unit hypothesis. For example, autoshaping, a Pavlovian conditioning procedure, supports long-duration pecks, whereas a CRF schedule even after extended training is associated with durations that are shorter than those observed on FI or FR schedules. Moreover, to explain why short-duration responses were apparently insensitive to instrumental reinforcement, Ziriax and Silberberg pointed out that Schwartz and Williams used a VR–5 schedule to generate keypecking. Long-duration responses predominate on this schedule and, as a result, the "insensitivity" of short-duration responses may be due simply to their low frequency of occurrence.[3]

A second challenge, not unrelated to the first, was initiated by Moore (1973) in reporting an unpublished study by Warren wherein the differential reinforcement of short- or long-duration responses was factorially combined with food or water reinforcement. On the average, little learning was evidenced except in the case of water reinforcement for long-duration responses. Moore suggested that this one instance of successful learning appeared to capitalize on the pigeon's natural tendency to "slurp" the key when water was the reinforcer, thereby producing long-duration key contacts (see Jenkins & Moore, 1973). In those infrequent cases in which individual subjects evidenced learning, it appeared to be more the redirection of a topography than the selective control over two different kinds of keypeck (see also Lajoie & Bindra, 1976, for the argument that short- and long-duration responses index different points in the consummatory sequence).

[3]Figure 4.1 also questions Schwartz's (1977a) conclusion that short latency pecks predominate in omission training. The omission latency data for Figure 4.1 were taken from Brownstein and Balsam (1975) who reported latencies averaging 6.10 sec in a nominal 8 sec trial (or as transformed in Figure 4.1, -0.78 log mean latency^{-1}). In addition, Williams and Williams (1969) observed that latencies under a discrete-trial FR-1 schedule were shorter than those engendered by an omission procedure. It seems reasonable that in discrete-trial procedures latency is inversely related to response strength.

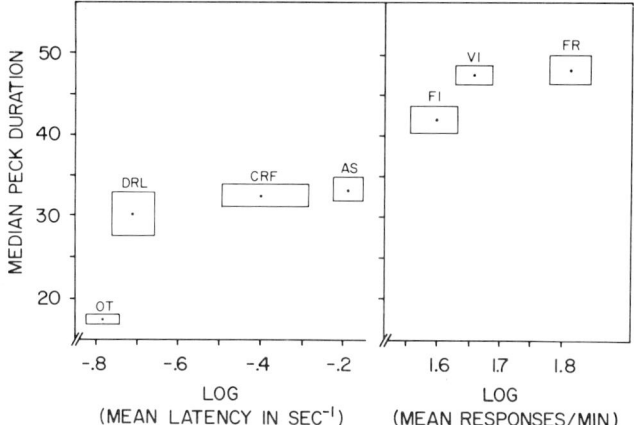

Figure 4.1. Summary of keypeck duration data, plotted as a function of latency and response rate. The rectangles encompassing each data point represent plus and minus one standard error. Various experimental procedures are shown including omission training (OT), autoshaping (AS) and several schedules of instrumental reinforcement. (Redrawn from Ziriax & Silberberg, 1978. Copyright © 1978 by the American Psychological Association. Redrawn with permission.)

The re-direction of behavior in the omission procedure was systematically studied by Barrera (1974), who made careful observations of pigeons' behavior during trials. In omission training keypecking was reduced substantially in all subjects, particularly in those with prior autoshaping training (see Table 4.1). However, pecking per se was not reduced in frequency but was re-directed to other features of the test chamber, as approximately only 1% of all pecks resulted in key closures. Moreover, these high levels of off-key pecking were specific to omission training and were not observed during autoshaping.

The redirection of pecking during omission training was the result of subjects' repositioning themselves with respect to the key. In cases where autoshaping had preceded exposure to the omission contingency, this repositioning was more dramatic than for naive subjects and often resulted in withdrawals from the front area of the chamber. Moreover, in most cases the topographies evident during omission training consisted of forms not previously observed in these animals; also, they were unlike those observed during extinction where subjects tended to remain in close proximity to the key (cf. Terrace, 1966). Thus, the adoption of these topographies would not appear to be simply the result of changes in the rate of food delivery.

These data were characterized as indicating the birds' sensitivity to the omission contingency. Indeed, they closely resemble those changes noted during response-contingent punishment or in conflict situations (e.g., Dunham, Mariner, & Adams, 1969; Hinde, 1970). In addition, the topographical changes during omission training suggest that short peck durations merely reflect these shifts in the locus of pecking. That is, keypecks during omission training consist of those responses that accidently strike at oblique angles to the key, thereby producing brief closures. The fact that Schwartz and Williams found these short-duration pecks to be insensitive to instrumental reinforcement may be due to the fact that on their baseline VR–5 schedule pecks were not redirected but were almost exclusively key-directed (i.e., long-duration pecks).

This redirection hypothesis is not without problems. For one, Schwartz (1977b) argued that if the inaccuracy of pecking produced short-duration responses one would expect more variability early in training under, say, a CRF schedule than following extended training. However, just the reverse pattern is observed. In addition, omission training and shock might be expected to have similar effects in creating conflict and, as a result, oblique-angle pecks. But Schwartz noted that response-contingent punishment of long-duration pecks (35–50 msec) produced pecks not of shorter duration but of even longer duration).

These data would appear to be more consistent with the dual-unit hypothesis than with the redirection alternative. At the very least they argue for a more deterministic mechanism than Barrera's "glancing pecks" notion. It is also the case that the redirection hypothesis is embarrassed by the finding that a sequential patterning is evident in the pigeon's omission responding (see footnote 1). More generally, the question remains as to why responding persists, albeit at moderate levels, during omission training. The dual-unit hypothesis suggests a straightforward answer to this question: Responding in omission training consists exclusively of Pavlovian-controlled pecks. Yet Barrera's topographical data, along with the conditional discrimination work of Ziriax and Silberberg, are consistent with the conclusion that the short-duration responses observed during omission training are sensitive to their consequences. Barrera's work also suggests that responding may persist to some extent in omission procedures because components of the behavior sequence resulting in keypecks (e.g., approaches, key-directed pecks) may continue to occur and be reinforced on trials in which keypecks do not occur. If one considers these components of the keypeck sequence to be nonindependent, then the adventitious reinforcement of the precursors of the keypeck may be sufficient to insure that keypecking occurs at some nonzero level during omission training.

Components of the Keypeck Sequence

It will be recalled that Brown and Jenkins (1968) proposed a similar mechanism to account for the development of the first autoshaped response. This strategy is consistent with a long-standing interest in the study of the components of conditioned behavior sequences (e.g., Pavlov, 1941; Razran, 1971; Staddon & Simmelhag, 1971; Zener, 1937). Applying the strategy to autoshaping raises two questions: (a) how is the sequence of behavior culminating in the keypeck organized?; (b) to what extent does adventitious reinforcement of the precursors of keypecking contribute to the maintenance of responding under an omission contingency?

The first question has been answered through the observations of several workers which indicate that an orderly sequence of behavior, namely, orientations, approaches and key-directed pecks, often precedes the first recorded keypeck (e.g., Brown & Jenkins, 1968; Rachlin, 1969; Wessells, 1974). The second question is far more difficult to assess. A common strategy has been to subject selected precursors of the keypeck to an omission contingency.

As first studied by Wessells (1974), approaches to within a specified distance of the response key (as judged by the experimenter) resulted in termination of the trial and cancellation of food. This procedure resulted in the elimination of previously conditioned approach responses in each of two subjects, although orientations to the key persisted. The maintenance of orientations suggests that the stimulus–reinforcer relation was detected even after approaches ceased. Wessells also showed that approaches did not invariably lead to a keypeck once initiated, but depended instead upon the value of the conditioned stimulus present during an approach. For example, if after an approach were initiated a stimulus previously correlated with the absence of reinforcement were presented, the approach was immediately aborted. These data support an interpretation of omission training that focuses not only on the influence of Pavlovian relations on sustained responding, but also on the effects of adventitious reinforcement of components of the keypeck sequence.

Subsequent work has not confirmed these findings. Lucas (1975) placed keypecks and then pre-keypecks (i.e., key-directed pecks that fell short or to the side of the key) on an omission contingency. As did Barrera (1974), Lucas noted that under the omission contingency keypecks were reduced but pecking per se remained at high levels. When these off-key pecks were subjected to the omission procedure, keypecks were eliminated but pre-keypecking continued on about .40 of omission trials, a finding inconsistent with Wessells' observations concerning the elimination of approaches under omission training. Interestingly, these data suggest that the effects of the omission contingency may at times be most evident on behavior following the target response. That is, omission for pre-keypecking eliminated keypecks but not pre-keypecks.

The most extensive series of studies concerning the sensitivity of approach behavior to food omission was conducted by Peden et al. (1977). In their procedure, approaches were automatically recorded as depressions in the floor. The results of one of their manipulations are presented in Figure 4.2. It can be seen that approaches persisted during .35–.45 of the omission trials for most subjects. (In additional experiments, these workers replicated Wessells's experimenter-judged procedure, with results identical to those shown in Figure 4.2.) Although

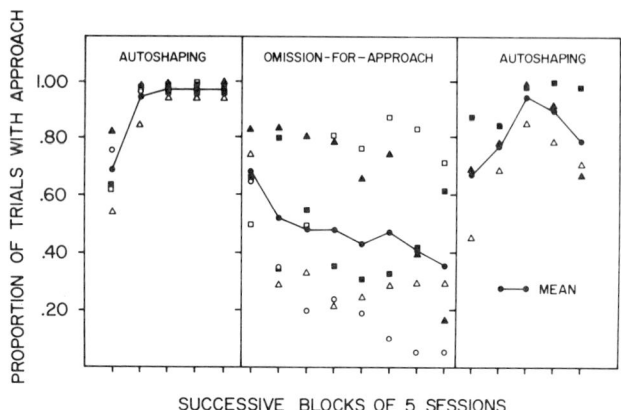

Figure 4.2. Probability of an approach response for individual subjects (each represented by a different symbol) in the Peden et al. study (Experiment I) during autoshaping and omission-for-approach training. The solid line represents the group mean response level. During the last phase of the experiment (right panel) three of the five original pigeons were re-exposed to autoshaping. (From Peden et al., 1977. Copyright © 1977 by the American Psychological Association. Reprinted with permission.)

these data contradict Wessells's results, the omission contingency was not without effect: Levels of approach were higher for yoked subjects as compared to omission subjects (Peden et al., 1977, Experiment IV).[4]

It is difficult to reconcile these findings with those of Wessells. Peden et al. were systematic in attempting to replicate Wessells' work: They studied a much larger sample and used a wider variety of experimental treatments. It seems reasonable to conclude that at least under some conditions, approach behaviors in the pigeon are maintained under an omission contingency.

Recall that these studies were initiated to evaluate the role played by the adventitious reinforcement of the components of the keypecking sequence to the maintenance of keypecking under an omission contingency. Peden et al. concluded that their data were incompatible with an adventitious reinforcement interpretation, since this account relies on the sensitivity of approaches to in-

---

[4]An unusual feature of Peden et al.'s (1977) data concerned the keypecking performance of their subjects. For subjects receiving autoshaping following omission-for-approach training (three of which are shown in Figure 4.2) only three of nine keypecked at above-zero levels. One could argue, as did Lucas (1975), that the omission contingency has its strongest effects on the subsequent response component, in this instance, keypecking. However, for the five subjects in Figure 4.2 exposed initially to autoshaping, only two of five keypecked at above-zero levels. This level of keypecking is far below that typically observed on autoshaping procedures (e.g., Brown & Jenkins, 1968). Interestingly, since approach behaviors did occur at high levels during autoshaping, these data suggest that approach behaviors and keypecking may be more independent than has been assumed by other investigators.

strumental relations and predicts elimination of this response during omission-for-approach training. Instead they favored an interpretation that focused on perception of the Pavlovian stimulus–reinforcer relation.

It must be recognized that although these data are consistent with that position they do not necessitate it. The demonstration that approaches persist under an omission contingency does not indicate to what extent the adventitious reinforcement of approaches during omission-for-keypecking procedures, or in autoshaping, contributes to *keypecking* maintenance (see footnote 4). It has been shown that approaches occur during omission training trials when keypecking does not, and that approaches exhibit some sensitivity to instrumental relations. These factors form the necessary conditions for an explanation of omission responding that includes the adventitious reinforcement of keypeck-related behaviors. Conversely, elimination of approaches under an omission procedure would not guarantee that adventitious reinforcement of approaches contributed to keypeck maintenance in the usual omission procedure.

Generality

According to Hinde (1970), the term *comparative* may refer to comparisons between species or to different response systems within the same species. In autoshaping, researchers have attempted to study response systems in the pigeon that do not consist of keypecking and food. Boakes (1977) autoshaped pigeons using food reinforcement and a small loop suspended from the ceiling as the conditioned stimulus. Pigeons autoshaped with this arrangement and displayed omission effects similar to keypecking in that responding occurred on about .25 of the trials. One might question the difference between this response and keypecking, but Boakes reported that the pigeon grasped the loop with its beak and pulled it down.

Woodruff and Williams (1976) autoshaped pigeons to keypeck a visual stimulus that preceded water injected directly into the mandibles. They noted that while keypecking was engendered with this procedure, for three subjects subsequently exposed to the omission procedure, responding fell to near-zero levels after 25 sessions (range: 0–.10). During omission training responding appeared to be redirected away from the key, and new responses including bowing and rooting were directed at the floor or parts of the test panel.

A small number of studies have investigated autoshaping in species other than the pigeon. The most extensive experiments have centered upon the rat, the common preparation consisting of the delivery of food pellets signaled by the presentation of a retractable lever (Peterson, Ackil, Frommer, & Hearst, 1972). Locurto, Terrace, and Gibbon (1976) studied responding under omission training as compared to control procedures in naive subjects and those receiving prior autoshaping training. As can be seen in Figure 4.3, rats reliably contacted the

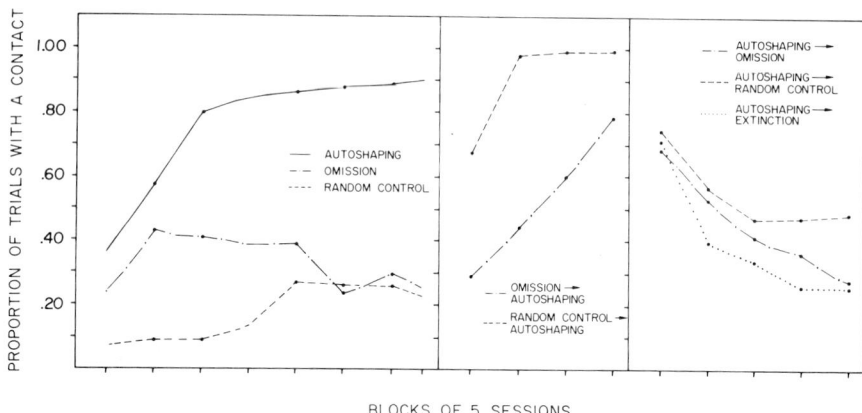

Figure 4.3. Group mean functions from Locurto et al. (1976). Subjects whose data are shown in the left panel were experimentally naive at the initiation of training. Naive omission and random-control subjects were exposed to autoshaping (center panel) following the last session of training summarized in the left panel. The functions in the right panel represent the performance of subjects exposed first to autoshaping. (Individual data can be found in Locurto et al., 1976. Copyright © 1976 by the Society for the Experimental Analysis of Behavior. Redrawn with permission.)

lever under an autoshaping procedure. However, the responding maintained by the omission contingency was no greater than that engendered by a random-control procedure, with the exception of the early portions of training for experimentally naive subjects (left panel). Moreover, prior exposure to omission training retarded the subsequent development of autoshaping as compared to prior random-control training (center panel). For subjects previously exposed to autoshaping (right panel), omission training sustained responding no better than simple extinction or the random-control. (See also Atnip, 1977; Stiers & Silberberg, 1974, for results indicating somewhat greater response maintenance under an omission contingency.)

A subsequent study by these workers (Locurto, Terrace, & Gibbon, 1978) reported that substantially lower response levels were maintained by an omission contingency than by a yoked condition in naive rats and in those with prior autoshaping training. In addition, higher levels of responding were noted in a response-terminated omission procedure as compared to a fixed-trial procedure. This latter finding suggests that stimulus-change may influence omission responding in the rat, a point also noted by O'Connell (1979).

Locurto et al. (1978, unpublished data) also noted differences between omission and yoked subjects in the ratio of lever-presses/lever-contacts. Naive omission subjects evidenced ratios less than 1.0 throughout training; that is, more contacts than presses. Yoked subjects displayed the opposite pattern of responding with three of four subjects producing ratios greater than 1.0, that is, more presses than contacts, by the end of training. Reasonably, ratios greater than 1.0 reveal that after touching the lever during a trial, subjects typically remained in contact with it. The result would be a small number of contacts and a relatively large number of presses, perhaps as a by-product of biting or pawing the lever. This possibility was supported by periodic observation. A similar pattern was observed for subjects exposed to autoshaping prior to omission training. During the last five autoshaping sessions, seven of eight subjects produced ratios greater than 1.0. In the following phase of training the ratios of each of four omission subjects declined to a value less than 1.0. For yoked subjects, although local variability was evident, ratios remained above 1.0 throughout extended training. These results are consistent with the conclusion that the omission procedure engenders distinctive response topographies as compared to a procedure in which instrumental relations are possible. One might also infer from these data that the response topographies of omission subjects are more "tentative" than those of yoked subjects, a finding documented by Stiers and Silberberg (1974).

In species other than the rat it appears that the omission procedure produces diverse effects. Wasserman (1973; Wasserman, Hunter, Gutowski, & Bader, 1975) made an extensive study of a preparation involving 3-day-old chicks in which keypecking was autoshaped using the activation of a heat lamp as the reinforcer in a cold test chamber (15° F at the start of training). An omission procedure maintained responding on approximately .25–.55 of the trials over a 5-day period of training, although these levels were lower than those observed in a yoked treatment. In a later study by Woodruff and Starr (1978) newly hatched chicks were force-fed food and water from birth until the initiation of omission training. This procedure eliminated any prior experience with approach to and/or pecking of the reinforcer. Nevertheless, persistent responding was observed during five training sessions, averaging .50 using food as the reinforcer and .32 using water. In addition, the topography of autoshaped responses resembled consummatory behavior, that is, ballistic pecking in the case of food, or drink motions using water.

Little or no response maintenance under an omission contingency, however, has been observed in crows keypecking using a food reinforcer (Powell & Kelly, 1976) and in guinea pigs using a retractable lever-food preparation (Poling & Poling, 1978; cf. Bottjer, Scobie, & Wallace, 1978, for omission training in fish). In addition, Gamzu and Schwam (1974) report a series of studies with male squirrel monkeys in which keypressing using a food reinforcer was autoshaped by a response-terminated procedure. When an omission procedure was instituted, keypressing was eliminated within 5–10 sessions; omission training supported responding no better than extinction. It was also the case that the introduction of a fixed-trial autoshaping procedure resulted in significant reductions in the keypressing of two monkeys. It is difficult to resist the conclusion that autoshaped responding in the squirrel monkey is influenced decisively by the relation between responses and food (see also Schwam & Gamzu, 1975, for corroboration of these findings using different conditioned stimuli and response manipulanda).

In cases where omission training does not maintain responding, as in some of the preceding examples, it is not clear whether the conditioned stimulus has simply lost control over responding or whether it retains control and responding is best characterized as redirected. Barrera's (1974) data certainly support the latter alternative in the case of pigeons' keypecking using a food reinforcer. Similarly, Boakes (1977) noted that during autoshaping rats predominantly contacted either the signal (sign-tracking) or the site of food delivery (goal-tracking). An omission contingency was then applied to the predominant response or, in some cases, to both responses concurrently (i.e., a double-omission procedure). Boakes observed that the omission contingency reduced both sign-tracking and goal-tracking responses to similarly low levels, which averaged approximately .12. With a double-omission procedure both responses were reduced to low levels. In some, but not all cases, suppression of the target response resulted in increases in the other response (e.g., if sign-tracking defined the omission contingency, goal-tracking increased). For yoked subjects the distribution of responses was little affected during training (see also, Boakes, 1979; Holland, 1979, for extensions of this finding).

Response distribution during omission training was also studied by Locurto, Tierney, and Fitzgerald (1979) in rats using a positive-conditioned suppression procedure. Omission trials (the insertion of a retractable lever paired with food on trials without a contact) were superimposed over a baseline of instrumental lever-pressing. The rate of instrumental lever-pressing during omission trials as compared to nontrial periods was taken as an index of the strength of the conditioned stimulus. Contacts with the retractable lever occurred at low levels (.05–.20) after extended omission training. However, instrumental lever-pressing continued to be moderately suppressed during trials (Kamin suppression ratios of .25–.35). These data are consistent with the notion that although an organism exhibits sensitivity to an omission contingency, as indexed by reductions in contact with the conditioned stimulus, that signal persists to some degree in controlling conditioned behavior.

Discussion

This review of omission training indicates that:

1. The procedure supports intermediate levels of responding when applied to the pigeon's keypeck using a food reinforcer in a standard experimental arrangement. The mechanism underlying this response persistence is, however, not satisfactorily understood.

2. When other response systems are studied, a variety of results are observed. These outcomes do not readily suggest a classification rule to permit prediction of omission performance.

With respect to the first point, it has been uniformly assumed that omission training serves as a criterion test of Pavlovian control. This assumption depends on the theoretical characterization of maintained performance under an omission contingency. If the pigeon's keypeck during omission training is composed of a unique class of short-duration responses that are insensitive to instrumental relations, then the procedure may indeed serve to distinguish Pavlovian control. However, keypecking during omission training may be the result of the incomplete redirection of behavior, coupled with the adventitious reinforcement of components of that response sequence. If so, the level of maintained keypecking may not index the degree of Pavlovian control.

Unfortunately, it is not possible to distinguish between these accounts. Moreover, in some respects these positions are not mutually exclusive. The redirected pecks noted by Barrera may be long-duration pecks. Those keypecks that persist during omission training may not be glancing responses, but simply those Pavlovian pecks discussed by Schwartz and Williams. Barrera's data do not demonstrate that oblique-angled keypecks were of short duration, although the data are consistent with this possibility. One needs experimental evidence that long- and short-duration keypecks are distinguished by their angle of incidence to the key to pursue this point further. It is also possible that not all short-duration keypecks are equivalent; some may be Pavlovian key-directed pecks, while others are the result of pecking inaccuracy.

The issue is whether the behavior maintained during omission training should be viewed as a distinctive response class, or simply as weak, that is, low strength, behavior. At very least, the characteristics of signal-contact responding during omission training, that is, relatively low rate, long latency, and intermediate-response probability, are compatible with the view that this behavior is of low strength. Short-duration keypecks are also observed during the early portions of acquisition under an autoshaping procedure, and during the extinction of an autoshaped keypeck (Gibbon, Farrell, Locurto, Duncan, & Terrace, 1980). These instances are just those in which keypecking would be expected to be comparatively weak.

The second point has been addressed by noting that the greater stereotopy of an organism's consummatory pattern, the more persistent will be signal-contact responding under an omission contingency (Gamzu & Schwam, 1974; Powell & Kelly, 1976). More generally, perhaps an organism's ability to adopt response topographies incompatible with signal-contact responding during omission training serves as a predictor of omission performance. It looks very much as if some sort of *response substitution* principle is operative during omission training. The data offered by Barrera (1974), Boakes (1977), and Locurto et al. (1980) are compatible with this assumption. One might argue that, as compared to the pigeon, rats, guinea pigs, crows, and squirrel monkeys have available a greater range of alternative behaviors, many of which do not result in signal contacts (see also a description by Williams [Chapter 3] of an unpublished study by Morrison concerning response substitution in the pigeon).

Yet it cannot simply be species differences that are critical in determining omission responding. As exemplified by the Woodruff and Williams study, the pigeon displays pervasive sensitivity to an omission contingency when water is the reinforcer. It seems likely that prediction of omission performance depends on specification of the components of the *response system*. If so, then persistent omission responding, or the virtual elimination of behavior in any species, awaits only selection of the appropriate response system for study. Holland (1979), for example, noted wide variability in the susceptibility of different response systems in the rat to an omission procedure. If a visual conditioned stimulus was used, goal-tracking was eliminated and increases in rearing behavior were observed. Conversely, if rearing was the target behavior, that response was reduced (though not eliminated), and increases in goal-tracking followed reductions in rearing. However, using an auditory signal, goal-tracking was reduced but no increases in compensatory behavior were noted. A similar result occurred when head jerks defined the omission contingency.

It is also the case that the response system interacts with the experimental context to influence the distribution of behavior. Boakes (1979), for example, noted that relatively little goal-tracking is observed in the autoshaped responding of the pigeon as compared to the rat. However, this difference reflected not species differences per se, but the fact that in the standard pigeon test chamber the delivery of food is reliably predicted by the illumination of the food tray. When the predictiveness of food delivery was reduced, by constantly illuminating the food tray or using no illumination, significant increases in goal-tracking were noted in the pigeon. One might infer from this finding that under an omission contingency, if goal-tracking were induced in the pigeon in this manner, perhaps response substitution and hence lowered levels of keypecking would be observed. Conversely, if the typical pattern of goal-tracking in the rat were eliminated, perhaps more persistent sign-tracking during omission training would occur. These speculations are of theoretical import, for they question whether a characteristic level of performance associated with a particular response system under an omission contingency is an inherent property of that system. Alternately, that level may be more properly viewed as the product of interactions between a specified response system and situational variables.

The foregoing analysis makes it apparent that the interpretation of omission training is complex, whether responding is maintained or eliminated. In the latter case, the observation of redirected responding may be characterized in

Pavlovian terms or in instrumental terms. From a Pavlovian perspective, assume that the stimuli associated with approach and signal-contact responding come to predict nonreinforcement. As the subject's signal-contact responding wanes, other stimuli in the chamber become paired with reinforcement and come to control directed (i.e., autoshaped) responding. Thus, the elimination of signal-contact responding in omission training may be regarded as Pavlovian discrimination learning (Bindra, 1972; Dickinson & Mackintosh, 1978; Moore, 1973). Alternatively, one might assume that redirected behavior represents sensitivity to the negative response–reinforcer contingency coupled with the adventitious reinforcement of behaviors that are incompatible with signal-directed responding.

Given these difficulties, it is problematic to assume that omission training serves as an assay of Pavlovian control. To by-pass these difficulties, one strategy would combine omission training with other evaluative procedures to form a sort of test battery, much in the manner as has been suggested in the study of conditioned inhibition (e.g., Hearst, Besley, & Farthing, 1972).

ADDITIONAL EVALUATIVE PROCEDURES

Omission Analogs

Several procedures have been studies that are similar in intent to omission training in that signal-directed responding results in the loss, reduction, or delay in delivery of the reinforcer. Jenkins (cited in Hearst & Jenkins, 1974) used a "long box" test chamber in which the response key was located 91 cm from the site of food delivery. By this arrangement, if the pigeon approached the key during its 5-sec illumination, all or a portion of the reinforcer might be lost. This manipulation served as an indicator of Pavlovian control under the assumption that if behavior were influenced predominantly by response–reinforcer contingencies, the subject would distribute its behavior to produce minimal delay in receiving the reinforcer. Jenkins reported variable results, but most of the seven subjects apparently continued to approach the key, although they produced little keypecking during 10 sessions (see also Boakes, 1977, for a replication of this finding).

A different type of manipulation using pigeons was studied by Deich and Wasserman (1977), in which an omission contingency was in effect during either the first- or second half of an 8-sec trial for different groups of subjects. These conditions were compared to standard autoshaping and omission treatments. If adventitious response–reinforcer pairings are influential in maintaining autoshaped responding, then higher response levels should be supported by those treatments in which these relations are possible—in autoshaping and in the procedure wherein the omission contingency is in effect during only the first half of a trial. This was precisely the pattern of results observed.

Deich and Wasserman's (1977) study and studies comparing yoked and omission subjects are attempts to evaluate the role of instrumental factors in autoshaping. Traditionally, a strategy for specifying this influence has been delayed reinforcement (see Mackintosh, 1974, for a review). Locurto, Duncan, Terrace, and Gibbon (1980) arranged for each lever-contact response by rats to delay the termination of an autoshaping trial by t sec (either 2.5 or 10.0 sec for different groups). All trials were nominally defined by the 15-sec insertion of a lever that terminated with food delivery. Each subject exposed to this trial-offset-delay (TOD) procedure was paired with a yoked subject that experienced the same trial durations as did delay subjects. Responses of the yoked partner might occur in close temporal proximity to food delivery. This arrangement equated subjects in terms of Pavlovian relations but allowed the relations between lever-contacts and food to differ for master and yoked subjects.

The effects of this procedure in experimentally naive subjects are shown in Figure 4.4. Subjects exposed to the delay contingency responded at lower levels than did their yoked partners at both values of the delay interval. As might be expected, greater deficits in responding were generally noted for those delay subjects exposed to the larger t values. The response probabilities of five of the eight master subjects were no greater than their operant-levels throughout training, whereas seven of the eight yoked subjects produced uniformly high response probabilities.

Interestingly, Myerson, Myerson, and Parker (1979) studied the same procedure ($t = 7$ sec) as did Locurto et al. (1980) using pigeons' keypecking and a food reinforcer. They found no differences in the responding maintained by master and yoked subjects. The divergent outcomes of these two studies parallel those

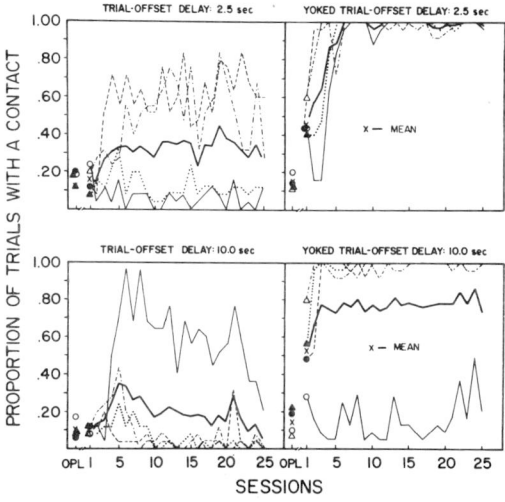

Figure 4.4. Probability of a lever-contact for naive rats (each represented by a different symbol) exposed to the trial-offset-delay procedure used by Locurto et al. (1980). Points to the left of session 1, OPL, indicate the average response probability during the last five operant-level sessions. The data for master subjects are given in the left panels; the performance of yoked subjects is shown in the right panels. (Copyright © 1980 by the Psychonomic Society. Reprinted with permission.)

found when the omission responding of pigeons and rats is studied under standard experimental arrangements. (See Williams, Chapter 3, for the results of a comparable procedure using pigeons; see also Moore & Gormezano, 1961, for a similar procedure in human eyelid conditioning).

Differential–Nondifferential Procedure

Gamzu and Williams (1971, 1973) studied an autoshaping procedure in which reinforcers were scheduled to occur with a probability of .03/sec during autoshaping trials (8.6 sec of key illumination) only or during both trials and intertrial intervals (average 30-sec duration). Substantial rates of responding were maintained only during the "differential" procedure in which reinforcer probability was higher during the conditioned stimulus than during the intertrial interval. When reinforcers were programmed "nondifferentially," with equal probability during the conditioned stimulus and the intertrial interval, near-zero rates were observed (cf. Rescorla, 1967; see also Boakes, 1977, for comparable results using rats).

These data have been viewed as providing support for a Pavlovian analysis of autoshaping. For although the nondifferential procedure eliminates the predictive relation between the conditioned stimulus and the reinforcer, it might be expected to have little effect upon any adventitious instrumental relations that occur during the conditioned stimulus. These relations are equally possible in both the differential and nondifferential procedure. Accordingly, if instrumental relations are important it is difficult to see why adding reinforcers to the intertrial interval should so drastically reduce autoshaped responding.

However, it is possible that response–reinforcer relations are influential in this procedure. Assume that in the nondifferential case behaviors incompatible with keypecking are established through adventitious reinforcement during the intertrial interval. These behaviors may continue to occur and be reinforced during conditioned stimulus presentations, thereby interfering with keypecking (see Deich & Wasserman, 1977, footnote 2; Jenkins, 1977). As a result, the transition from differential to nondifferential training may not only eliminate the signaling function of the conditioned stimulus, it may also engender competing responses with respect to keypecking.[5]

---

[5]The importance of response–reinforcer relations in this procedure was used by Schwartz and Gamzu (1977) to account for two unanticipated findings observed during differential training when the nondifferential procedure was administered first: (*a*) Low response rates were observed during subsequent differential training; and (*b*) peck durations were invariably short, whereas if differential training occurred first, peck durations were predominantly long. It was suggested that competing behaviors were developed during initial nondifferential training and that these behaviors continued to occur during the subsequent differential procedure, in effect blocking the development of long-duration keypecks. As a result, those keypecks engendered by the differential procedure were controlled solely by the Pavlovian relation (cf. Boakes, 1977).

Blocking Autoshaped and/or Consummatory Responses

A perennial question in the analysis of Pavlovian conditioning asks whether the occurrence of overt conditioned responses is necessary for acquisition. A common strategy has been to conduct conditioning in a situation wherein responding is blocked through either chemical or surgical means. Testing for the presence of conditioned responses takes place after removal of the blocking agent (see Solomon & Turner, 1962, for a review). Studies of this sort have been conducted to examine the role of adventitious response–reinforcer relations and, by implication, the nature of the association formed during Pavlovian conditioning. The evidence points to the fact that at least in some instances overt responses are unnecessary (Mackintosh, 1974). These data suggest that the association in Pavlovian procedures is between the conditioned stimulus and the reinforcer, and not between that stimulus and some overt response. (Second-order conditioning provides another means of studying this question; see Rashotte, Chapter 5).

Several studies have applied the strategy to autoshaping in the pigeon. Moore (1973) blocked directed skeletal responses following magazine training by placing a barrier in front of the conditioned stimulus during autoshaping. Eight of nine subjects keypecked on the first unreinforced test trial after removal of the barrier. Zentall and Hogan (1975) studied a procedure in which, after magazine training, a keylight was paired with inaccessible food. Six of ten subjects keypecked during this procedure although pecking was not sustained.

The most systematic observations using this strategy were made by Browne (1976). Following magazine training, food was made inaccessible for three sessions during which different groups received either positive, negative, or random correlations between the conditioned stimulus and reinforcer. Little keypecking was noted during this phase. In a later autoshaping transfer test with accessible food, subjects receiving positive correlations acquired keypecking faster and maintained higher rates than did the remaining groups. In a second experiment, a 75-cm-long test chamber was used with the response key located 35 cm from the site of food delivery. Approach responses to the conditioned stimulus were recorded for groups receiving either positive- or negative-contingency training with inaccessible food, as well as for subjects in a subsequent autoshaping transfer test with the barrier removed. No consistent approaches or withdrawals were noted for either treatment during the inaccessible-food phase. During autoshaping, subjects receiving positive correlations approached sooner and more often than did those in the negative group. However, neither group developed reliable keypecking during autoshaping, perhaps because of the nature of the chamber (see also footnote 4).

These studies have been interpreted as supporting a view of autoshaping that emphasizes the stimulus–reinforcer relation rather than the adventitious reinforcement of skeletal responses. Unfortunately, while these data support this conclusion, they would appear to be far less convincing than the traditional Pavlovian conditioning work cited earlier which differs from these autoshaping studies in two important respects: First, as is common in Pavlovian conditioning, no prior exposure to the reinforcer was necessary; and second, all skeletal movement was virtually blocked during conditioning (e.g., Solomon & Turner, 1962). The fact that neither of these conditions has been met in autoshaping experiments allows for the possibility that instrumental relations are involved.

In the procedure in which training is conducted with inaccessible food, although food consumption is blocked, the stimuli associated with food delivery have been previously established as conditioned reinforcers. As a result, the occurrence of these stimuli may reinforce any precursors of the keypeck in the forward-pairing procedure (cf., however, Browne, 1976, who observed no consistent approach behaviors during pretraining). In pretraining with negative or random pairings, behaviors incompatible with subsequent keypecking may be adventitiously reinforced.

Thus, these studies cannot be used to determine whether unprogrammed instrumental relations contribute to subsequent responding. This strategy can, however, be used to assess the characteristics of the minimal, necessary reinforcer. That is, if signal-contact responding emerges although access to the reinforcer is blocked, it reveals at least that the performance of the unconditioned response during training is unnecessary for conditioning. In this sense, the previously discussed work by Woodruff and Williams (1976) and Woodruff and Starr (1978) may also be characterized as attempts to block the usual consummatory pattern. They demonstrate that signal-contact responding emerges without the usual approach–consumption sequence.

In the procedure where access to the conditioned stimulus but not to the reinforcer is blocked during Pavlovian trials, it is possible that components of the keypeck sequence receive primary reinforcement. Indeed, Wasserman *et al.* (1975, Experiments 2, 3, and 5), who studied this procedure in chicks, used a heat reinforcer and noted frequent approaches to and pecking towards the key (see also Moore, 1973). Thus, the strategy may be used *only* to determine whether adventitious primary reinforcement of the terminal response of a sequence, that is, the signal-contact component, is necessary for the acquisition and/or maintenance of that response.

Similarity of Conditioned and Unconditioned Responses

The strategies used to specify the influence of Pavlovian and instrumental relations in Pavlovian conditioning procedures have included the study of the topographical similarity between conditioned and unconditioned responses. If implicit instrumental contingencies are important, then the form of the conditioned response might be expected to be relatively independent of the form of the unconditioned response, depending instead on which topography is adventitiously reinforced or best prepares the subject for the forthcoming reinforcer (cf. Gormezano & Coleman, 1973, with Prokasy, 1965, and Wahlsten & Cole, 1972). Conversely, from a Pavlovian perspective conditioning occurs because in some manner the conditioned stimulus comes to predict the reinforcer reliably. It follows that the form of the conditioned response might be expected to resemble closely that of the unconditioned response (see Jenkins & Moore, 1973, for a distinction between "substitution" and "surrogation" accounts of Pavlovian conditioning).

Previous research has produced inconsistent evidence as to conditioned–unconditioned response correspondence. In some preparations, notably, in dogs' conditioned salivation to food or acid and leg flexion to paw shock, close topographical similarity is evident (Mackintosh, 1974; cf. Terrace, 1973). In other instances the correspondence is less apparent, as may be the case in eyelid conditioning (cf. Kimble, 1961). There are, moreover, examples in which the forms of the two responses appear to differ, as in heart rate conditioning (see Mackintosh, 1974, pp. 98–104, for a review sympathetic to a Pavlovian interpretation).

Autoshaping studies reflect this diversity of results. In the case of the pigeon's keypeck to a visual stimulus for food or water, it is by now clear that the topographies of the conditioned and unconditioned responses are virtually identical (Jenkins & Moore, 1973). A more equivocal case may be found in assessing the chick's pecking to heat reinforcement (Wasserman, 1973, and Chapter 2; cf. Hogan, 1973; Woodruff and Starr, 1978). There is divergence in the forms of these responses in the squirrel monkey (Gamsu & Schwam, 1974; Schwam & Gamzu, 1975) and in the rat's autoshaped response to the presentation of another rat predicting food delivery (Timberlake & Grant 1975).

These data do not admit to a straightforward conclusion regarding response correspondence. Perhaps more important, topographical similarity does not invariably predict Pavlovian control, at least as assessed by the omission procedure. As noted earlier, the pigeon's autoshaped keypeck with both food and water as the reinforcer closely resembles the form of the unconditioned response. Yet, the keypeck appears to be far more sensitive to an omission contingency using water as compared to food as the reinforcer (cf. Woodruff & Williams, 1976, with Williams & Williams, 1969). These findings suggest that the existence of a topographical similarity between conditioned and unconditioned responses does not rule out the influence of instrumental relations on response probability.

As a corollary, if these response forms diverge one cannot conclude that stimulus–reinforcer relations are unimportant in controlling response probability. Mackintosh (1974) has argued that topographical differences between these responses may be a function of the extent to which conditioned responses are mediated by other response systems. Heart rate, for example, is affected by respiration which, in turn, may depend upon a host of situational variables. Moreover, response correspondence may also depend upon the capacity of a particular conditioned stimulus to elicit components of the unconditioned response (Hearst & Jenkins, 1974; Holland, 1977; Timberlake & Grant, 1975; Zener, 1937; see also Gormezano & Kehoe, 1975; Kimmel & Burns, 1975; and Woodruff & Williams, 1976, for arguments from an evolutionary perspective concerning the implications of response-form divergence for interpretations of Pavlovian conditioning).

Discussion

The results surveyed in this section may be summarized by the following points:

1. Omission-analog procedures (pp. 121-123) that have sought to manipulate the instrumental relation through the response-contingent delay, reduction, or cancellation of the reinforcer provide a complicated picture of the role played by that relation. Yet, there are clear instances in which instrumental relations disrupt Pavlovian control (e.g., Deich & Wasserman, 1977; Locurto et al., 1980). Unfortunately, these strategies all necessitate some alteration in the standard autoshaping procedure. As a result, they are susceptible to the same logical caveats as is omission training.

2. Other strategies such as the differential–nondifferential procedure (p. 123) or the various blocking studies (pp. 124-125) derive from the central question as to the conditions sufficient to engender and maintain autoshaped responding. The results of much of this work are compatible with an account that emphasizes either instrumental or Pavlovian relations. It must be recognized, however, that instrumental explanations often rely on the emergence of competing response through unprogrammed response–reinforcer relations. This form of explanation is a perennial one in psychological theory, but rarely has it received extensive experimental support (Staddon, 1977). Of course, as noted earlier, matters are further complicated when it is recognized that explanations of this sort may be recast entirely in terms of Pavlovian stimulus differentiation.

3. Studies of topographical similarity reveal that autoshaped responses need not bear structural correspondence to consummatory responses. The theoretical significance of these findings is, however, difficult to determine. Only the most narrowly based view of Pavlovian conditioning includes topographical similarity as a requisite construct.

It is difficult to survey the results of these efforts without questioning the ability of any combination of experimental procedures to distinguish Pavlovian from instrumental control (see Hearst, 1975; cf. Gray, 1975). This problem, as well as a unique strategy, was illustrated by Jenkins (1977) in determining whether a response acquired by Pavlovian relations would be less susceptible to instrumental control than one that had been instrumentally conditioned. Two response systems were established as discriminated operants. Pigeons' keypecking was autoshaped and placed under the discriminative control of a visual stimulus. Head positioning, defined by the intersection of photocell beams, was shaped through the method of successive approximations and placed under the discriminative control of an auditory stimulus. Jenkins then studied the effects of removing either the Pavlovian or instrumental relation from these response systems. The stimulus–reinforcer relation (i.e., the discriminative stimulus predictive of food) was eliminated by delivering reinforcers independently of responding during the intertrial interval at the same rate at which they were available on a response-contingent basis during trials. The response–reinforcer relation was removed by delivering reinforcers independently of responding during trials.

One might expect that by removing the instrumental relation, leaving only a Pavlovian contingency, keypecking would be maintained at relatively higher levels than head positioning. Yet, in practice the removal of the instrumental relation had similar effects on both response systems, inducing reductions but not the elimination of either response. Surprisingly, when the Pavlovian relation was removed, leaving only the instrumental contingency, keypecking was maintained at levels higher than those observed for head positioning. Thus, keypecking was supported by either Pavlovian or instrumental relations. Head positioning, however, appeared to require the unaltered discriminated operant contingency containing both Pavlovian and instrumental relations for its maintenance.

These results demonstrate in a novel manner the problem of attempting to infer those mechanisms that normally maintain a response using strategies such as the omission procedure. For if omission training had been used, head positioning would surely have been eliminated, whereas keypecking would have persisted at intermediate levels. Yet this pattern of findings could not be taken to mean that head positioning was supported sufficiently by instrumental relations prior to the introduction of the omission contingency. As a corollary, the persistence of keypecking would not reveal the fact that this response may be supported by instrumental relations alone. Thus, there is no necessary link between performance under an omission contingency and the potential influence of instrumental factors. More generally, the manner by which a response is educed (i.e., either through autoshaping or response-contingent shaping) fails to predict the conditions sufficient for response maintenance. Doubtless, these considerations apply to the other experimental strategies surveyed in this chapter as well.

Jenkins' (1977) study is a significant one, and it is likely to serve as the reference experiment for future work. It would appear that strategies of this type bypass the traditional question of the distinction between instrumental and Pavlovian conditioning in that no assumptions are made as to the nature of either process. Instead, both relations are viewed as independent variables that may affect conditioned behavior. This type of "interactive" position has recently been applied by Woodruff, Connor, Gamzu, and Williams (1977) in a study of pigeons' keypecking within a multiple variable-interval–extinction schedule. The instrumental relation was studied by manipulating the percentage of reinforcers delivered on a delayed basis within the variable-interval component. The Pavlovian relation was studied by altering the relative durations of the components. It was noted that alterations in both relations affected response rate. Most importantly, the influence of either relation depended upon the value of the other: One relation had maximum influence when the second was weak (see also Wessells, 1979).

This approach suggests that the apparent predominance of Pavlovian relations results primarily from the standard practice, in autoshaping studies, of programming this relation at near-maximal strength as compared to the instrumental relation. The complementary situation, wherein instrumental relations disrupt Pavlovian influence, should be equally possible to observe by appropriate manipulation of parameters. In the extreme, instrumental relations should be capable of blocking Pavlovian control (cf. Locurto et al, 1980). An example of this possibility may be found in the differential-reinforcement-of-other-behavior (DRO) schedule, a free-operant procedure in which each response delays the delivery of the reinforcer. In this omission-analog procedure there is no distinctive stimulus predictive of reinforcement. Thus, it may be conceptualized as one in which the Pavlovian relation is weak whereas the (negative) instrumental relation is relatively strong. From this perspective it should not be surprising that pigeons' keypecking for food is eliminated more quickly under DRO schedules than under an extinction procedure (e.g., Zeiler, 1971).

CONCLUSIONS

A *Fable*

In a college philosophy course, an instructor spent an entire class refuting the existence of God. At the end of class one student, visibly upset, demanded to know what the instructor had given his students to replace their now-shattered beliefs. The instructor replied that it was not asked even of Hercules that he do more than simply clean out the Aegean Stables.

The question raised by the discovery of any new phenomenon concerns the evaluation of the new data in view of existing theory. In pursuing that question, at least two choices, the extremes of a wider family of options, confront theorists. One may incorporate the novel findings within current theory, altering prevailing interpretations only when such changes appear warranted. Conversely, one might conclude that to retain current interpretations would be a stumbling block, and then one would adopt alternative approaches.

This chapter has centered on the more conservative of these options, the incorporation of autoshaping within a Pavlovian/instrumental framework. This framework relies on the presumed effectiveness of evaluative procedures to distinguish Pavlovian from instrumental control. From the findings surveyed here, three conclusions emerge

1. Omission training does not serve as a simple test of Pavlovian control.
2. The difficulties inherent in interpretating the outcomes of other evaluative procedures render it unprofitable, if not impossible, to construct a family of procedural tests to partition the respective influence of each conditioning paradigm.
3. The results of any evaluative procedure depend on the response system under study and the expression of that system in a particular experimental context.

These conclusions indicate that it is not possible to answer the types of questions typically posed for two-factor theory. There are, for example, no uniform answers to the questions, "What is autoshaping?", or, "Is the pigeon's autoshaped keypeck under Pavlovian control?" It is more efficacious to ask what the level of evocation of a particular response system will be under a specified experimental arrangement.

One might regard these conclusions as unfortunate, in that they seem to discourage the formulation of general laws (see also Seligman, 1970). Yet, this analysis does not preclude the development of principles that span different response systems or experimental arrangements. At the least, it is certain, however, that useful generalizations need not consist of attempts to label experimental outcomes as indicators of one sort of conditioning or another.

REFERENCES

Atnip, G. W. Stimulus- and response-reinforcer contingencies in autoshaping, operant, classical, and omission training procedures in rats. *Journal of the Experimental Analysis of Behavior*, 1977, 28, 59–69.

Balsam, P. D., Brownstein, A. J., & Shull, R. L. Effects of varying the duration of grain presentation on auto-maintenance. *Journal of the Experimental Analysis of Behavior*, 1978, 29, 27–36.

Barrera, F. J. Centrifugal selection of signal-directed pecking. *Jounal of the Experimental Analysis of Behavior*, 1974, 22, 341–355.

Bindra, A. A. Unified account of classical conditioning and operant training. In A. H. Black & W. F. Prokasy (Eds.), *Classical conditioning II: Current theory and research.* New York: Appleton-Century-Crofts, 1972.

Boakes, R. A. Performance on learning to associate a stimulus with positive reinforcement. In H. David & H. M. B. Hurwitz (Eds.), *Operant-Pavlovian interactions*. Hillsdale, N.J.: Erlbaum, 1977.

Boakes, R. A. Interactions between Type I and Type II processes involving positive reinforcement. In A. Dickinson & R. A. Boakes (Eds.), *Mechanisms of learning and motivation: A memorial volume to Jerzy Konorski*. Hillsdale, N.J.: Erlbaum, 1979.

Bottjer, S. W., Scobie, S. R., & Wallace, J. Positive behavioral contrast, autoshaping, and omission responding in the goldfish (Carassius auratus). *Animal Learning and Behavior*, 1977, *5*, 342–366.

Brown, P. L., & Jenkins, H. M. Autoshaping of the pigeon's key-peck. *Journal of the Experimental Analysis of Behavior*, 1968, *11*, 1–8.

Brown, M. P. The role of primary reinforcement and overt movements in autoshaping in the pigeon. *Animal Learning and Behavior*, 1976, *4*, 287–292.

Brownstein, A. J., & Balsam, P. D. A search for conditioned reinforcement effects in negative automaintenance of key pecking. *Bulletin of the Psychonomic Society*, 1975, *6*, 165–168.

Deich, J. D., & Wasserman, E. A. Rate and temporal pattern of key pecking under autoshaping and omission schedules of reinforcement. *Journal of the Experimental Analysis of Behavior*, 1977, *27*, 399–405.

Dickinson, A., & Mackintosh, N. J. Classical conditioning in animals. In M. R. Rosenzweig & L. W. Porter (Eds.), *Annual review of psychology*. Palo Alto, Calif.: Annual Review, 1978.

Dunham, P. J., Mariner, A., & Adams, H. Enhancement of off-key pecking by on-key punishment. *Journal of the Experimental Analysis of Behavior*, 1969, *12*, 789–797.

Gamzu, E., & Schwam, E. Autoshaping and auto-maintenance of a key-press response in squirrel monkeys. *Journal of the Experimental Analysis of Behavior*, 1974, *21*, 361–371.

Gamzu, E., & Williams, D. R. Classical conditioning of a complex skeletal response. *Science*, 1971, *171*, 923–925.

Gamzu, E., & Williams, D. R. Associative factors underlying the pigeon's keypecking in autoshaping procedures. *Journal of the Experimental Analysis of Behavior*, 1973, *19*, 225–232.

Gibbon, J., Baldock, M. D., Locurto, C., Gold, L., & Terrace, H. S. Trial and intertrial durations in autoshaping. *Journal of Experimental Psychology: Animal Behavior Processes*, 1977, *3*, 264–284.

Gibbon, J., Farrell, L., Locurto, C. M., Gold, L., & Terrace, H. S. Partial reinforcement in autoshaping with pigeons. *Journal of Experimental Psychology: Animal Behavior Processes*, 1980, *8*, 45–59.

Gormezano, I., & Coleman, S. R. The law of effect and CR-contingent modification of UCS. *Conditional Reflex*, 1973, *8*, 41–56.

Gormezano, I., & Kehoe, E. J. Classical conditioning: Some methodological–conceptual issues. In W. K. Estes (Ed.), *Handbook of learning and cognitive processes: Conditioning and behavior theory* (Vol. 2). Hillsdale, N.J.: Erlbaum, 1975.

Gormezano, I., & Moore, J. W. Classical conditioning. In M. H. Marx (Ed.), *Learning: Processes*. London: Macmillan, 1969.

Gray, J. A. *Elements of a two-process theory of learning*. London: Academic Press, 1975.

Griffin, R. W., & Rashotte, M. A note on the negative automaintenance procedure. *Bulletin of the Psychonomic Society*, 1973, *2*, 402–404.

Hearst, E. The classical–instrumental distinction: Reflexes, voluntary behavior, and categories of associative learning. In W. K. Estes (Ed.), *Handbook of learning and cognitive processes: Conditioning and behavior theory* (Vol. 2). Hillsdale, N.J.: Erlbaum, 1975.

Hearst, E., Besley, S., & Farthing, C. W. Inhibition and the stimulus control of operant behavior. *Journal of the Experimental Analysis of Behavior*, 1970, *14*, 373–409.

Hearst, E., & Jenkins, H. M. *Sign-tracking: The stimulus–reinforcer relation and directed action.* Austin, Tex.: The Psychonomic Society, 1974.

Herendeen, D. L., & Shapiro, M. M. Extinction and food-reinforced inhibition of conditioned salivation in dogs. *Animal Learning and Behavior,* 1975, 3, 103–106.

Herrnstein, R. J., & Loveland, D. H. Food avoidance in hungry pigeons and other perplexities. *Journal of the Experimental Analysis of Behavior,* 1972, 18, 369–383.

Hinde, R. A. *Animal behavior: A synthesis of ethology and comparative psychology.* (2nd ed.) New York: McGraw-Hill, 1970.

Hogan, J. A. How young chicks learn to recognize food. In R. A. Hinde & J. S. Hinde (Eds.), *Constraints on learning.* New York: Academic Press, 1973.

Holland, P. C. Conditioned stimulus as a determinant of the form of the Pavlovian conditioned response. *Journal of Experimental Psychology: Animal Behavior Precesses,* 1977, 3, 77–104.

Holland, P. C. Differential effects of omission contingencies on various components of Pavlovian appetitive conditioned responding in rats. *Journal of Experimental Psychology: Animal Behavior Processes,* 1979, 5, 178–193.

Hursh, S. R., Navarick, D. J., & Fantino, E. Automaintenance: The role of reinforcement. *Journal of the Experimental Analysis of Behavior,* 1974, 21, 112–124.

Jenkins, H. M. Sensitivity of different response systems to stimulus–reinforcer and response–reinforcer relations. In H. Davis & H. M. B. Hurwitz (Eds.), *Operant–Pavlovian interactions.* Hillsdale, N.J.: Erlbaum, 1977.

Jenkins, H. M., & Moore, B. R. The form of the autoshaped response with food or water reinforcers. *Journal of the Experimental Analysis of Behavior,* 1973, 20, 163–181.

Kimble, G. A. *Hilgard and Marquis' conditioning and learning* (2nd ed.) New York: Appleton-Century-Crofts, 1961.

Kimmel, H. D., & Burns, R. A. Adaptational aspects of conditioning. In W. K. Estes (Ed.), *Handbook of learning and cognitive processes: Conditioning and behavior theory* (Vol. 2). Hillsdale, N.J.: Erlbaum, 1975.

Lajoie, J., & Bindra, D. An interpretation of autoshaping and related phenomena in terms of stimulus-incentive contingencies alone. *Canadian Journal of Psychology,* 1976, 30, 157–173.

Locurto, C. M., Duncan, H., Terrace, H. S., & Gibbon, J. Autoshaping in the rat: Interposing delays between responses and food. *Animal Learning and Behavior,* 1980, 8, 37–44.

Locurto, C., Terrace, H. S., & Gibbon, J. Autoshaping, random control, and omission training in the rat. *Journal of the Experimental Analysis of Behavior,* 1976, 26, 451–462.

Locurto, C. M., Terrace, H. S., & Gibbon, J. Omission training (negative automaintenance) in the rat: Effects of trial offset. *Bulletin of the Psychonomic Society,* 1978, 12, 11–14.

Locurto, C. M., Tierney, J., & Fitzgerald, S. *Autoshaping and positive conditioned suppression: Effects of an omission contingency.* Paper presented at the meeting of the Eastern Psychological Association, Philadelphia, April, 1979.

Lucas, C. A. The control of keypecks during automaintenance by prekeypeck omission training. *Animal Learning and Behavior,* 1975, 3, 33–36.

Mackintosh, N. J. *The psychology of animal learning.* London: Academic Press, 1974.

Miller, N. Learning of visceral and glandular responses. *Science,* 1969, 163, 434–445.

Moore, B. R. The role of directed Pavlovian reactions in simple instrumental learning in the pigeon. In R. A. Hinde & J. Stevenson-Hinde (Eds.), *Constraints on learning.* New York: Academic Press, 1973.

Moore, J. W., & Gormezano, I. Yoked comparisons of instrumental and classical eyelid conditioning. *Journal of Experimental Psychology,* 1961, 62, 552–559.

Myerson, J., Myerson, W. A., & Parker, B. K. Automaintenance without stimulus-change reinforcement: Temporal control of keypecks. *Journal of the Experimental Analysis of Behavior,* 1979, 31, 395–403.

O'Connell, M. F. Temporal distribution of responding during discrete-trial omission training in rats. *Journal of the Experimental Analysis of Behavior*, 1979, 31, 31-40.

Pavlov, I. P. *Lectures on conditioned reflexes* (Vol. 2): *Conditioned reflexes and psychiatry* (W. H. Gantt, trans.). New York: International University Press, 1941.

Peden, B. F., Browne, M. P., & Hearst, E. Persistent approaches to a signal for food despite food omission for approaching. *Journal of Experimental Psychology: Animal Behavior Processes*, 1977, 3, 377-399.

Peterson, G. B., Ackil, J. E., Frommer, G. P., & Hearst, E. Conditioned approach and contact behavior toward signals for food or brain-stimulation reinforcement. *Science*, 1972, 177, 1009-1011.

Peterson, M. R., Lyon D. O., Stone, W., & Scott, W. The role of conditioned reinforcement in the acquisition and maintenance of omission responding. *Psychological Record*, 1977, 27, 235-254.

Poling, A., & Poling, T. Automaintenance in guinea pigs: Effects of feeding regimen and omission training. *Journal of the Experimental Analysis of Behavior*, 1978, 30, 37-46.

Powell, R. W., & Kelly, W. Responding under positive and negative response contingencies in pigeons and crows. *Journal of the Experimental Analysis of Behavior*, 1976, 25, 219-225.

Prokasy, W. F. Classical eyelid conditioning: Experimenter operations, task demands and response shaping. In W. F. Prokasy (Ed.), *Classical conditioning: A symposium*. New York: Appleton-Century-Crofts, 1965.

Rachlin, H. Autoshaping of key pecking in pigeons with negative reinforcement. *Journal of the Experimental Analysis of Behavior*, 1969, 12, 521-531.

Razran, G. *Mind in evolution: An East-West synthesis of learned behavior and cognition*. Boston: Houghton, 1971.

Rescorla, R. A. Pavlovian conditioning and its proper control procedures. *Psychological Review*, 1967, 74, 71-80.

Rescorla, R. A., & Solomon, R. S. Two-process learning theory: Relationships between Pavlovian conditioning and instrumental learning. *Psychological Review*, 1967, 74, 151-182.

Rosenthal, R. L., & Matthews, T. J. Effects of prefeeding in autoshaping and omission training. *Bulletin of the Psychonomic Society*, 1978, 11, 153-156.

Schlosberg, H. The relationship between success and the laws of conditioning. *Psychological Review*, 1937, 44, 379-394.

Schwam, E., & Gamzu, E. Constraints on autoshaping in the squirrel monkey: Stimulus dimension and response topography. *Bulletin of the Psychonomic Society*, 1975, 5, 369-372.

Schwartz, B. The role of positive conditioned reinforcement in the maintenance of key pecking which prevents delivery of primary reinforcements. *Psychonomic Science*, 1972, 28, 277-278.

Schwartz, B. Maintenance of key pecking in pigeons by a food avoidance but not by a shock avoidance contingency. *Animal Learning and Behavior*, 1973, 1, 164-166.

Schwartz, B. Studies of operant and reflexive key pecks in the pigeon. *Journal of the Experimental Analysis of Behavior*, 1977, 27, 301-314. (a)

Schwartz, B. Two types of pigeon key pecking: Suppression of long but not short-duration key pecks by duration-dependent shock. *Journal of the Experimental Analysis of Behavior*, 1977, 27, 393-398. (b)

Schwartz, B., & Gamzu, E. Pavlovian control of operant behavior: An analysis of autoshaping and its implications for operant conditioning. In W. K. Honig & J. E. R. Staddon (Eds.), *Handbook of operant behavior*. Englewood Cliffs, N.J.: Prentice-Hall, 1977.

Schwartz, R., & Willams, D. R. The role of the response reinforcer contingency in negative auto-maintenance. *Journal of the Experimental Analysis of Behavior*, 1972, 71, 351-357. (a)

Schwartz, B., & Williams, D. R. Two different kinds of key peck in the pigeon: Some properties of responses maintained by negative and positive response-reinforcer contingencies. *Journal of the Experimental Analysis of Behavior*, 1972, 18, 210-216. (b)

Seligman, M. E. P. On the generality of laws of learning. *Psychological Review*, 1970, *17*, 406–410.

Shapiro, M. M., & Herendeen, D. L. Food-reinforced inhibition of conditioned salivation in dogs. *Journal of Comparative and Physiological Psychology*, 1975, *88*, 628–632.

Sheffield, F. D. Relation between classical conditioning and instrumental learning. In W. F. Prokasy (Ed.), *Classical conditioning*. Englewood Cliffs, N.J.: Prentice-Hall, 1965.

Skinner, B. F. The phylogeny and ontogeny of behavior. *Science*, 1966, *153*, 1205–1213.

Solomon, R. L., & Turner, L. H. Discriminative classical conditioning in dogs paralyzed by curare can later control discriminative avoidance responses in the normal state. *Psychological Review*, 1962, *69*, 202–219.

Solomon, R. L., & Wynne, L. C. Traumatic avoidance learning: Acquisition in normal dogs. *Psychological Monographs*, 1953, *67*, (4, Whole No. 354).

Staddon, J. E. R. Schedule-induced behavior. In W. K. Honig & J. E. R. Staddon (Eds.), *Handbook of operant behavior*. New York: Appleton-Century-Crofts, 1977.

Staddon, J. E. R., & Simmelhag, V. L. The "superstition" experiment: A reexamination of its implications for the principles of adaptive behavior. *Psychological Review*, 1971, *78*, 3–43.

Stiers, M., & Silberberg, A. Lever-contact responses in rats: Automaintenance with and without a negative response–reinforcer dependency. *Journal of the Experimental Analysis of Behavior*, 1974, *22*, 497–506.

Terrace, H. S. Stimulus control. In W. K. Honig (Ed.), *Operant behavior: Areas of research and application*. Englewood Cliffs, N.J.: Prentice-Hall, 1966.

Terrace, H. S. Classical conditioning. In J. A. Nevin (Ed.), *The study of behavior*. New York: Scott, Foresman, 1973.

Timberlake, W., & Grant, D. L. Auto-shaping rats to the presentation of another rat predicting food. *Science*, 1975, *190*, 690–692.

Wahlsten, D. L., & Cole, M. Classical and avoidance training of leg flexion in the dog. In A. M. Black & W. F. Prokasy (Eds.), *Classical conditioning II: Current research and theory*. New York: Appleton-Century-Crofts, 1972.

Wasserman, E. A. Pavlovian conditioning with heat reinforcement produces stimulus-directed pecking in chicks. *Science*, 1973, *181*, 875–877.

Wasserman, E. A., Hunter, N. B., Gutowski, K. A., & Bader, S. A. Auto shaping chicks with heat reinforcement: The role of stimulus–reinforcer and response–reinforcer relations. *Journal of Experimental Psychology: Animal Behavior Processes*, 1975, *1*, 158–169.

Wessells, M. G. The effects of reinforcement upon the pre-pecking behaviors of pigeons in the autoshaping experiment. *Journal of the Experimental Analysis of Behavior*, 1974, *21*, 125–144.

Wessells, M. G. The effects of the stimulus–reinforcer correlation in a discrete-trials IRT $> t$ procedure. *Journal of the Experimental Analysis of Behavior*, 1979, *31*, 307–320.

Wiener, N. *The human use of human beings: Cybernetics and society*. Garden City, N.Y.: Anchor, 1954.

Wilkie, D. M. Keypecking under different intertrial intervals in negative automaintenance. *Bulletin of the Psychonomic Society*, 1976, *8*, 431–432.

Williams, D. R. Classical conditioning and incentive motivation. In W. F. Prokasy (Ed.), *Classical conditioning: A symposium*. New York: Appleton-Century-Crofts, 1965.

Williams, D. R., & Williams, H. Auto-maintenance in the pigeon: Sustained pecking despite contingent non-reinforcement. *Journal of the Experimental Analysis of Behavior*, 1969, *12*, 511–520.

Woodard, W. T., Ballinger, J. C., & Bitterman, M. E. Autoshaping: Further study of "negative automaintenance." *Journal of the Experimental Analysis of Behavior*, 1974, *22*, 47–52.

Woodruff, G., Connor, N., Gamzu, E., & Williams, D. R. Associative interaction: Joint control of key pecking by stimulus–reinforcer and response–reinforcer relationships. *Journal of the Experimental Analysis of Behavior*, 1977, *28*, 133–144.

Woodruff, G., & Starr, M. D. Autoshaping of initial feeding and drinking reactions in newly hatched chicks. *Animal Learning and Behavior*, 1978, *6*, 265-272.

Woodruff, G., & Williams, D. R. The associative relation underlying autoshaping in the pigeon. *Journal of the Experimental Analysis of Behavior*, 1976, *26*, 1-13.

Zeiler, M. Eliminating behavior with reinforcement. *Journal of the Experimental Analysis of Behavior*, 1971, *16*, 401-405.

Zener, K. The significance of behavior accompanying conditioned salivary secretion for theories of the conditioned response. *American Journal of Psychology*, 1937, *50*, 384-403.

Zentall, T. R., & Hogan, D. E. Key pecking in pigeons produced by pairing keylight with inaccessible grain. *Journal of the Experimental Analysis of Behavior*, 1975, *23*, 223-232.

Ziriax, J. M., & Silberberg, A. Discrimination and emission of different key-peck durations in the pigeon. *Journal of Experimental Psychology: Animal Behavior Processes*, 1978, *4*, 1-21.

II

Associative Factors

MICHAEL E. RASHOTTE | 5

Second-Order Autoshaping: Contributions to the Research and Theory of Pavlovian Reinforcement by Conditioned Stimuli[1]

INTRODUCTION

Much research in classical conditioning demonstrates that the ongoing responsiveness of an organism is influenced by presentation of a strongly conditioned stimulus (CS). CSs can also play a role in behavior change by functioning as Pavlovian reinforcers that modify the associative strength of other CSs. The reinforcing function of CSs was discovered by Pavlov about 1910 (Pavlov, 1928; Timofeeva, 1959) and is studied under the rubric *higher-order conditioning*. Higher-order conditioning is said to occur when all or part of the associative strength of a CS comes from the reinforcing action of another CS. In *second-order conditioning*, for example, a first-order CS (S1) that derives its associative strength from pairings with a biologically powerful unconditioned stimulus (US) serves as the reinforcer for conditioning another CS (S2). In *third-order conditioning*, S2 serves as the reinforcer for S3, and so on.

On the face of it, higher-order conditioning would seem to occur more commonly than first-order conditioning. In everyday experience, and in many conditioning procedures in the behavioral laboratory, there seem to be more opportunities for CSs to be paired with each other than for CSs to be paired with USs. Nevertheless, the importance of higher-order conditioning in behavioral control and its relation to other conditioning phemonena remains in doubt. The main reason for this state of affairs is that, early on, higher-order conditioning gained the reputation of being difficult to demonstrate, even under well controlled laboratory conditions (e.g., Pavlov, 1927, p. 69; Razran, 1955, p. 327, as com-

---

[1]The research conducted in my laboratory was supported in part by Grant BNS77-16844 from the National Science Foundation and Grant MH-11218 from the National Institutes of Health.

pared with Razran, 1961, p. 89; Skinner, 1938, p. 258), and experimental interest in it waned. Since the mid-1960s, however, the number of successful demonstrations of second-order conditioning in Western laboratories has accelerated sharply, and robust second-order conditioning has been reported in a variety of conditioning preparations and species, including fear conditioning in rats (e.g., Rescorla, 1973a), odor-aversion learning in neonatal rat pups (e.g., Cheatle & Rudy, 1978), eyelid conditioning in rabbits (Sears, Baker & Frey, 1979), appetitive conditioning in goldfish (Amiro & Bitterman, 1980), and autoshaped keypecking in pigeons (e.g., Rashotte, Griffin, & Sisk, 1977). The prospects now seem very good that variables influencing the Pavlovian reinforcing effectiveness of CSs will be researched intensively in some of these second-order conditioning preparations during the next few years.

This chapter summarizes published data on second-order conditioning of autoshaped keypecking in pigeons (cf. Brown & Jenkins, 1968), and presents new data on this topic from our laboratory. It also outlines a theoretical approach to the problem of understanding variations in the Pavlovian reinforcing effectiveness of CSs. This approach is cast within the general framework of the Rescorla–Wagner model (Rescorla & Wagner, 1972), and it is particularly concerned with the long-recognized but poorly understood relationship between higher-order conditioning and conditioned inhibition.

SOME BASIC FACTS ABOUT SECOND-ORDER AUTOSHAPING IN PIGEONS

Demonstration of Second-Order Autoshaping

The demonstration of second-order autoshaping by Rashotte *et al.* (1977, Experiment 1) employed 4 sec access to mixed grain as the US and different colored keylights as S2 and S1, each 6 sec in duration. Keypecks were recorded electronically, but they never influenced the timing of stimulus presentations. Trials were separated by 120-sec intervals during which the response key was dark. The experiment was conducted in two phases and included an experimental group and two control groups.

The experimental group (P–P) received 600 S1→US pairings (30/session) in the first phase of the experiment to ensure that S1 acquired asymptotic first-order associative strength. The Pavlovian reinforcing strength of S1 was tested in the second phase, which involved two kinds of training sessions: in second-order sessions the grain US was never presented and only 10 S2→S1 pairings were given; in first-order sessions S1→US pairings occurred on 30 trials exactly as in the first phase of the experiment. Throughout the second phase, the first-order and second-order sessions were given on alternate days. Also, at the outset S2 was presented alone on the 10 trials in each second-order session until generalized keypecking weakened, whereupon S2→S1 pairings began. Figure 5.1 presents data from the second-order sessions. The upper panel indicates that keypecking was weak when S2 was presented alone. However, in the four sessions in which S2 and S1 were paired for Group P–P, keypecking to S2 was acquired and maintained. The lower panel shows that S1 reliably evoked keypecking in Group P–P on the S2→S1 trials in second-order sessions.

In a valid case of second-order conditioning, S2 acquires conditioned strength because it is paired with S1 *and* because S1 has a conditioning history. Both these conditions were met in Group P–P but not in the control groups, each of which lacked one condition. Group P–R had the S1→US pairings necessary to establish S1 as a first-order excitatory CS, but in second-order sessions S2 and S1 were presented randomly with respect to each other rather than being paired. Group R–P had the necessary S2→S1 pairings in second-order sessions, but S1 was prevented from acquiring first-order excitatory strength by being presented randomly with respect to US in first-order sessions. The upper panel of Figure 5.1 shows that neither control group acquired keypecking to S2, and the bottom panel indicates that the level of pecking evoked by S1 on S2→S1 trials was appropriate for the "paired" and "random" first-order conditioning treatments each group received. The differences in responding to S2 between the experimental and control groups confirm that genuine second-order autoshaping was demonstrated in Group P–P.

The data presented in Figure 5.1 were obtained in a training situation where S2 and S1 were both visual stimuli projected on the same response key. Other experiments have successfully conditioned pecking to a keylight-S2 when S1 was a house light or a hopper light that signaled response-independent presentations of grain (Leyland, 1977, Experiment V; Zentall & Hogan, 1975), a keylight that

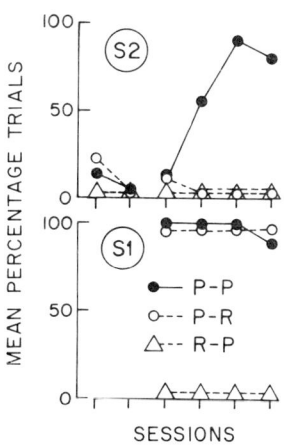

Figure 5.1. Demonstration of second-order autoshaping in pigeons. The measure plotted is the percent of trials on which S2 (upper panel) and S1 (lower panel) evoked at least one keypeck. Data are not presented for the first-order autoshaping sessions which alternated with the sessions shown here. In the first two sessions S2 was presented alone for all groups. In the remaining four sessions S2 and S1 were presented to each group in the manner described in the text. (After Rashotte *et al.*, 1977, Experiment 1.)

signaled response-independent grain but occurred on a different response key (Marshall, Gokey, Green, & Rashotte, 1979; Rescorla & Cunningham, 1979), and either a keylight or a tone that controlled keypecking for grain reinforcement on an operant fixed-ratio schedule (Rashotte et al., 1977, Experiment 3). There is also evidence that an auditory signal for response-independent grain presentations can act as an effective S1 to establish pecking to a keylight-S2 (Leyland, 1977, Experiment IV; Patterson & Winokur, 1973; Rashotte et al., 1977, Experiment 3). Taken together, these findings indicate that second-order autoshaping to a visual S2 projected on a response key can be convincingly demonstrated in pigeons when a range of stimulus conditions serves as the Pavlovian reinforcer.

Effect of Altering the Conditioned Status of S1 after Second-Order Autoshaping is Complete

Beginning with experiments in Pavlov's laboratory (Pavlov, 1932) and continuing through the present (e.g., Rescorla, 1973a; Timofeeva, 1959), there have been attempts to determine in a definitive way the nature of the association formed when the Pavlovian reinforcer is a CS. The general plan in these experiments has been to establish S2 as a second-order excitatory stimulus by pairing it with S1; then, to alter the conditioned status of S1 independently of any further second-order conditioning; and, finally, to determine whether S2 continues to evoke its original conditioned response when presented alone in a test.

According to the logic of these experiments, the nature of the association formed in second-order conditioning can be inferred from performance in the test. That is, if S2 continues to evoke the original second-order response in the test even though its Pavlovian reinforcer no longer does so, the implication would be either that an S–R association had formed between S2 and the response that had been evoked by S1 on second-order trials, or that an S–S association had formed between S2 and the neural representation of the US that was (presumably) evoked by S1 on second-order trials. In the event of this result, further tests would be necessary to separate the two possible interpretations. However, if the response evoked by S2 in the test were similar to the *new* response evoked by S1, an S–S association between the neural correlates of S2 and S1 would be implicated. The logic of these experiments is discussed in greater detail elsewhere (Holland & Straub, 1979; Rashotte et al., 1977; Rescorla, 1973a; Rozeboom, 1958).

The autoshaping preparation has been employed in several experiments of this sort to study the nature of the association formed in second-order conditioning (Leyland, 1977; Rashotte et al., 1977; Rescorla, 1979). The basic finding is illustrated in an experiment by Rashotte et al. (1977, Experiment 2). Three groups of pigeons were trained under conditions identical to those described for Group P–P in Figure 5.1. That is, a keylight-S1 was first paired with grain to establish it as a first-order CS for keypecking, and then S1 was used as a Pavlovian reinforcer to establish pecking to a keylight-S2 during alternate days of first-order and second-order conditioning. The data points to the left of the dashed vertical line in Figure 5.2 indicate that S2 strongly evoked keypecking in all three groups by the end of second-order conditioning, and that responding to S1 was strong on the S2→S1 trials.

Between the final second-order conditioning session and a subsequent test session, two experimental groups received first-order conditioning treatments designed to weaken the conditioned strength of S1. For Group P–P–E, S1 was repeatedly presented without grain in extinction sessions; for Group P–P–R, S1 and grain were presented randomly with respect to each other. Each pigeon was exposed to these treatments until its pecking reached a strict criterion of low responding (10% or fewer S1 presentations with a peck in each of two successive sessions). A control group, P–P–P continued to receive S1-grain pairings during this period instead of having responding to S1 weakened. Data for these first-order treatment sessions are not shown in Figure 5.2.

In the subsequent test session, S2 and S1 were each presented 10 times on separate trials, and grain was not presented. The final data points in each panel of Figure 5.2 represent performance in this test. Responding to S1 *and* to S2 was weaker in the experimental groups (P–P–E, P–P–R) than in the control group (P–P–P), a result that implies that an S2–S1 connection had formed in second-order conditioning. It may be noted that Figure 5.2 is definitive in showing that the first-order conditioning treatments weakened keypecking to S2 in the experimental groups. The measure plotted is the percent of trials on which two observers agreed that at least one pecking movement was directed toward the stimuli, *whether or not* those movements resulted in contact with the response key. Because this measure is not based solely on electronically recorded pecks

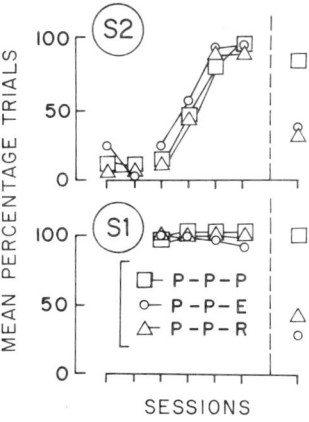

Figure 5.2. Effect of altering the conditioned status of S1 after second-order autoshaping is complete. The measure plotted is the percent of trials in each second-order session on which observers agreed that at least one peck was directed toward the stimuli, irrespective of whether it resulted in contact with the response key. Data points to the left of the dashed vertical line were obtained under conditions identical to those employed for Group P–P, as shown in Figure 5.1. The data to the right of the line show responding in the test session after the groups had received treatments described in the text. (After Rashotte et al., 1977, Experiment 2.)

that contacted the response key (as is the case in most autoshaping experiments), these test data avoid any charge that although S2 may actually have evoked strong pecking most pecks simply failed to contact the key.

Although the test data in Figure 5.2 imply that the effectiveness of S2 after second-order autoshaping is heavily dependent on the conditioned strength of S1, these data alone are open to alternative interpretations. The most important possibility is that extinction of pecking to any keylight similar to S2 will reduce responsiveness to S2 through stimulus generalization of extinction. However, several findings indicate that generalized extinction between visual stimuli is not a major factor in this result. For one thing, Rashotte et al. (1977, Experiment 4) reproduced the essential aspects of the original test data in a separate experiment in which S1 was an auditory stimulus. Also, Rashotte and Griffin (1974) found that whereas extinction of pecking to a keylight-S1 markedly reduced responsiveness to a keylight-S2 in the test session, the same number of extinction trials to S2 in a yoked-extinction group had little effect on responding to S1 in the subsequent test. Finally, experiments employing two S1s in first-order autoshaping have shown that extinction of pecking to the S1 that served as the Pavlovian reinforcer weakened responding to S2 whereas extinction of the other S1 had very little effect on S2 (Leyland, 1977, Experiment IV, V; Rescorla, 1979, Experiment 1).

Taken together, these findings indicate that the ability of S2 to evoke keypecking after second-order autoshaping is complete depends heavily on the retention by S1 of its original conditioned strength. According to the logic outlined above, that result implies that an S–S connection forms between the neural correlates of S2 and S1 in second-order autoshaping (e.g., Rescorla, 1973a). This implication is noteworthy because recent second-order conditioning experiments with other animals and other conditioning preparations all point to a different conclusion. In rats trained in fear (e.g., Rescorla, 1973a), activity (e.g., Holland & Rescorla, 1974), or odor-aversion learning (e.g., Cheatle & Rudy, 1978), and in goldfish trained in appetitive conditioning (Amiro & Bitterman, 1980), all the data obtained to date indicate that S2 continues to evoke its original response after the conditioned status of S1 is changed. That type of result, in conjunction with others, suggests that an S–R association forms between S2 and the response evoked by the Pavlovian reinforcer on second-order trials (e.g., Rescorla, 1973a). In fact, the possibility has been raised that second-order and first-order conditioning might be distinguished on grounds that an S–R association forms in the former case whereas an S–S association (between CS and US) forms in the latter case (Rescorla, 1973a, b). However, the autoshaping result indicates that the two "orders" of conditioning cannot be so neatly distinguished in this way.

The difference in outcomes between the pigeon-autoshaping experiments and experiments with other animals and preparations might arise from a variety of sources. For example, second-order autoshaping is characterized by highly stimulus-directed responding, and by a possible special relation between visual signals and food in the pigeon (Rashotte et al., 1977; Rescorla, 1979). An important factor is undoubtedly the thoroughness with which the conditioned effectiveness of S1 is changed prior to the test; even within the autoshaping preparation, it would be expected that S2 would retain some of its original conditioned effectiveness in the test if training to change the conditioned status of S1 were not sufficiently complete (Rashotte et al., 1977; cf.Rescorla, 1979). Because these and other possibilities have not been studied as yet, it is too early to conclude that second-order autoshaping is truly anomalous with respect to the other preparations. It is instructive, for example, to consider one case where varied outcomes seem to be obtained. Lindberg's unpublished experiment with dogs is frequently cited in support of the claim that S2 continues to evoke the second-order reflex after the conditioned status of its Pavlovian reinforcer has been altered (e.g., Konorski, 1948, p. 107; Pavlov, 1932; Rescorla, 1973a). In Lindberg's experiment, S2 continued to evoke salivation after S1 was transformed from a CS for salivation into a CS that evoked defensive leg flexion. However, other experiments of this sort with dogs indicate that whereas S2 sometimes evokes the second-order response in the test (as Lindberg found), in other cases it evokes either the new response established to S1 or both that response and the second-order response (Timofeeva, 1959). The reasons for these different outcomes are not clear. The possibility noted here is that a similar range of outcomes might be found in any single second-order conditioning preparation, depending on experimental conditions.

The results reviewed here concerning the effects of altering the conditioned status of S1 following second-order conditioning imply that a general conclusion about whether an S–S or S–R connection forms in second-order conditioning is premature, at best. Instead, the data seem more consistent with the possibility that multiple connections can form in any conditioning procedure, at least in animals with relatively complex nervous systems. The type of connection that actually forms, and/or the type of connection that predominates in testing, could be influenced by specific aspects of the experimental situation, such as CS modality, type of US, response-system studied, and the animal's prior history. While there is currently no firm evidence concerning this possibility in second-order conditioning, there is related evidence that inferences about the nature of the association formed in at least some *first*-order conditioning preparations will depend on the type of US employed (Holland & Straub, 1979). In fact, pigeons seem capable of learning about varied aspects of the Pavlovian reinforcer in second-order autoshaping (Rescorla, 1979), and other findings imply that a rich matrix of connections form in at least some procedures (e.g., Asratyan, 1965, 1976; Rudenko, 1974).

The Conditioned Status of S2 after Extended Training with US Absent on Second-Order Trials

Recent theoretical advances in understanding conditioned inhibition include the well-known case in which an initially neutral stimulus (i.e., S2) becomes a conditioned inhibitor as a consequence of being present *simultaneously* with an excitatory S1 on nonreinforced trials (e.g., Boakes & Halliday, 1972; LoLordo, 1979). However, there has been virtually no attempt to provide a theoretical account for the case where *sequential* presentation of S2 and an excitatory S1 on nonreinforced trials seems to result in S2 first becoming a second-order conditioned excitor and later a conditioned inhibitor (Herendeen & Anderson, 1968; Pavlov, 1928, p. 105 ff; Rescorla, 1973a, p. 141). In this section, some data are presented from the autoshaping preparation that document, in the most complete fashion yet reported, that S2 indeed becomes inhibitory when a large amount of second-order training is given in which US is absent on the second-order trials. These data are relevant to the theoretical formulation presented later in this chapter, which attempts to characterize the interaction between excitation and inhibition in the US-absent procedure for second-order conditioning.

According to current thinking, the inhibitory status of a CS is most thoroughly assayed by combining *summation* and *acquisition* tests of inhibition (e.g., Rescorla, 1969). In a summation test, an inhibitory S2 will reduce the strength of responding to an excitatory CS when the two stimuli are presented together. In an acquisition test, more reinforced trials will be required to establish an inhibitory S2 as a first-order excitatory CS than are required to condition a neutral stimulus. The inhibitory status of S2 might also be evident in two ways on second-order trials themselves if S2 leaves a residual inhibitory aftereffect that summates algebraically with the excitatory state evoked by S1. First, the strength of the response evoked by S1 should be reduced on S2→S1 trials relative to the trials on which S1 is presented alone and paired with US. Second, S2 should eventually lose its ability to evoke keypecking, at least in part because its inhibitory aftereffect should reduce the reinforcing effectiveness of S1 (Rescorla, 1973a).

In autoshaping experiments Gokey and Collins (1980) have obtained data that indicate that the inhibitory status of S2 is evident in all the ways described above. Their experiments were actually conducted to examine *feature-negative* discrimination learning (Jenkins & Sainsbury, 1969) as a function of the temporal arrangement of stimuli on nonreinforced S− trials. In a feature-negative discrimination, reinforced (S+) trials signaled by a given stimulus (here termed S1) are intermixed among nonreinforced (S−) trials signaled by another stimulus (here termed S2) presented in combination with S1. The feature-negative discrimination procedure is formally identical to Pavlov's (1927) second-order conditioning procedure when a) S2 precedes S1 on nonreinforced S− trials, and b) the reinforcer for S1 on S+ trials occurs independently of responding. Both conditions were met by some groups described in Gokey and Collins' (1980) paper. The implications of their findings for second-order conditioning were not discussed in the original paper, and they are elaborated here.

Figure 5.3 shows responding to S1 on S1→US trials, and responding to each of S2 and S1 when they occurred in the S2→S1 sequence on second-order trials (Gokey & Collins, 1980, Experiment 2). The data points are averaged keypeck rates for a group of 16 pigeons that received 20 S1→US trials and 20 S2→S1 trials in each session. Data are shown from the outset of training; S1 was not pretrained as in most other second-order autoshaping experiments discussed in this chapter.

Considering only the first few training sessions, there was a negatively accelerated increase in the rate of keypecking evoked by S1 when it was presented alone on reinforced first-order trials and when it occurred in the S2→S1 sequence on nonreinforced second-order trials. This finding indicates the expected acquisition of first-order excitatory strength by S1. There was also an initial acceleration in the rate of keypecking to S2, and Gokey (1977, 1979) has demonstrated that such acceleration depends on S2 being paired with S1 on second-order trials in this conditioning situation. We may conclude, therefore, that the increased responsiveness to S2 evident in the early sessions shown in Figure 5.3 represents second-order autoshaping.

Two aspects of the data for the later training sessions in Figure 5.3 suggest that

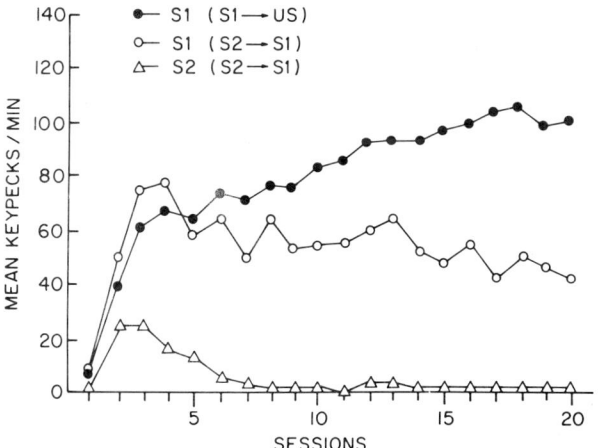

Figure 5.3. Effects of extended training on rate of keypecking to S1 on first-order trials (solid circles), and to S2 (triangles) and S1 (open circles) on second-order trials. The CSs were 6-sec red or white keylights counterbalanced across animals for S2 and S1; the US was 4 sec access to mixed grain. The intertrial interval averaged 60 sec. (After Gokey & Collins, 1980, Experiment 2.)

S2 eventually became inhibitory in this experiment. One is that, beginning in Session 5 and continuing until the end of training, responding to S1 was suppressed on S2→S1 trials relative to S1→US trials. The other is that there was virtually no keypecking to S2 after about the fifth session. These findings are consistent with the idea discussed earlier that an inhibitory aftereffect of S2 summated with the excitatory state evoked by S1.

More conclusive evidence that S2 became inhibitory was obtained in tests conducted following the last training session shown in Figure 5.3. When S2 was paired with grain in a first-order acquisition test for half the pigeons, over 30 S2→grain pairings were required to reach an acquisition criterion of maintained keypecking on S2 trials. In comparison, keypecking to a novel stimulus (S^N) reached criterion after fewer than 10 S^N→grain pairings. These acquisition test data are summarized in the left panel of Figure 5.4. The data from a summation test conducted with the remaining pigeons provided additional evidence that S2 had become inhibitory. In preparation for this test, a novel stimulus (S^N) was established as a first-order excitatory CS following the last training session shown in Figure 5.3. Then, in a test session, the excitatory S^N was presented alone or in combination with S2. The summation panel of Figure 5.4 shows that when S^N was presented alone on nonreinforced test trials the pigeons keypecked about 75 times per min. When S2 preceded S^N ($S2→S^N$) or when S2 and S^N were presented simultaneously on different response keys ($S2 + S^N$), however, keypecking to S^N was reduced to about 50 pecks per min.

Gokey and Collins' (1980) data clearly demonstrate that S2 initially became a conditioned excitor that evoked keypecking but subsequently became a con-

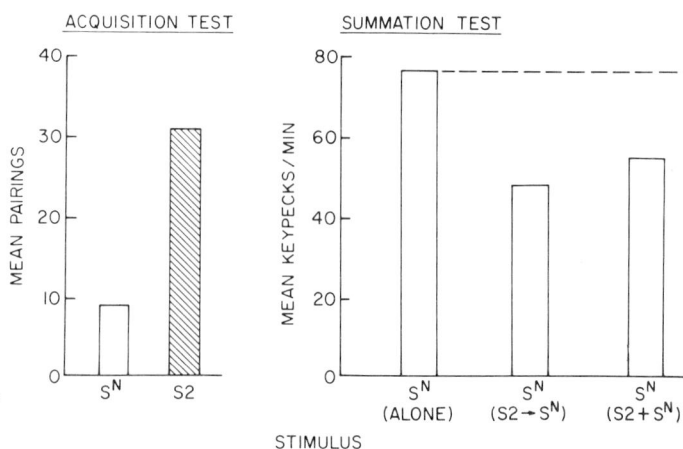

Figure 5.4. Two tests of the inhibitory status of S2 after extended training. S^N was a 6-sec green keylight; S2 was a 6-sec red or white keylight counterbalanced across animals. (After Gokey & Collins, 1980, Experiment 2.)

ditioned inhibitor that suppressed keypecking. These results confirm and extend others which indicate that second-order excitatory conditioning represents only a transient phase in the transformation of S2 from a neutral CS into a conditioned inhibitor in the US-absent procedure (Herendeen & Anderson, 1968; Pavlov, 1928, p. 105 ff; Rescorla, 1973a, p. 141).

The influence of the temporal relationship between S2 and S1 on second-order trials in Gokey & Collins's experiment deserves special comment. The pattern of results shown in Figure 5.3 was obtained whether S2-offset coincided with S1-onset (as it did in the experiment discussed above) or whether S2 preceded *and overlapped* S1 (Collins, 1976). However, a very different result was obtained when S2 and S1 were presented strictly simultaneously on different response keys (Collins, 1976; Gokey & Collins, 1980). In Gokey and Collins (1980, Experiment 2), for example, one group was given training identical to that given the group shown in Figure 5.3 except that the S2 and S1 keylights occurred simultaneously on different response keys on nonreinforced trials. In this case, S2 failed to show a second-order excitatory phase and also failed to become a conditioned inhibitor, as evidenced both in summation and acquisition tests and in the failure of S2 to suppress responding to S1 on the nonreinforced trials. A probable reason for these failures is that the stimulus arrangement may have severely limited the animals' exposure to S2 on nonreinforced trials, making it difficult for S2 to acquire conditioned excitatory or inhibitory strength (Gokey & Collins, 1980; cf. Nye, 1973). In the sequential case, in contrast, the likelihood is great that the animals experienced S2 for at least several seconds on each trial before S1 was presented and that S2 (or its sensory trace) could enter into a conditioning arrangement with S1. Hearst (1978) has discussed other factors that influence the ability of S2 to suppress responding to S1 in similar training procedures.

On the basis of Gokey & Collins's (1980) data it may be concluded that during extended second-order autoshaping in the pigeon the conditioned status of S2 changes from neutral, to excitatory, to inhibitory, as previously demonstrated in extended second-order salivary conditioning in dogs (Pavlov, 1928, p. 105 ff) and fear conditioning in rats (Herendeen & Anderson, 1968; Rescorla, 1973a, p. 141). Taken together, these findings encourage further analysis of the relationship between second-order excitatory conditioning and conditioned inhibition in the US-absent procedure. That relationship is the focus of discussion in the third major section of this chapter.

Conditioned Effectiveness of S2 during Extended Training with US Present on Second-Order Trials

Demonstrations such as that reported in the previous section in which S2 only temporarily becomes a second-order excitor and ultimately becomes a conditioned inhibitor should not be construed as evidence that second-order conditioning is inherently short-lived and unstable. That result is obtained in the US-absent procedure where S1→US pairings are intermixed among S2→S1 trials on which S2 explicitly signals the omission of US. The fact that S2 signals US-omission undoubtedly contributes to the eventual establishment of S2 as a conditioned inhibitor in this case. The second-order excitatory strength of S2 should be far more durable in procedures where this signaling relationship is weak or absent.

One such procedure is first-order successive-compound conditioning in which a *sequence* of short CSs precedes US presentation on all trials (e.g., Baker, 1968; Wickens, 1965). For example, on two-stimulus successive-compound trials (i.e., S2→S1→US), S2 and S1 would both be expected to acquire first-order excitatory strength in accordance with their individual temporal relationships with US. However, once it acquires conditioned strength, S1 might also act as a Pavlovian reinforcer to add second-order excitatory strength to S2, and second-order conditioning should not be impeded by inhibition in this case because every trial ends with a US.

The addition of second-order strength to S2 should be evident when the conditioned effectiveness of S2 in the successive compound is compared to a comparable S2 in trace conditioning. In this comparison, the first-order temporal relationship between S2 and US would be preserved in both groups, but S1 would never be presented in the interval between S2-offset and US onset in the trace group. Providing that certain alternative interpretations are ruled out, stronger responding to S2 in the successive-compound group would imply that S1 acted as a Pavlovian reinforcer to add associative strength to S2 in that case.

Marshall (1979) has obtained data in our laboratory that imply that second-order autoshaping is highly durable in the successive-compound procedure. In her experiment, one group of pigeons ($N = 11$) received successive-compound training in which S2 and S1 were two different colored keylights, each 6-sec in duration, presented successively on the same response key. The US was five 45-mg food pellets presented immediately after each S2→S1 sequence. A trace-conditioning group ($N = 5$) received exactly the same treatment except that the response key was always dark (the intertrial interval stimulus condition) during the 6-sec period between S2 offset and US presentation. Thirty trials were given in each daily session, with an intertrial interval averaging 90 sec.

Figure 5.5 presents rates of keypecking to the stimuli during 20 training sessions. Strong first-order autoshaping is evident in the high rate of keypecking to S1 by the successive-compound group. The amount of keypecking to S2 that can be attributed to *first*-order conditioning is defined by the performance of the trace-conditioning group. The significantly higher level of keypecking to S2 by the successive-compound group than by the trace group is the result that implies that second-order autoshaping provided added response strength to S2 in the

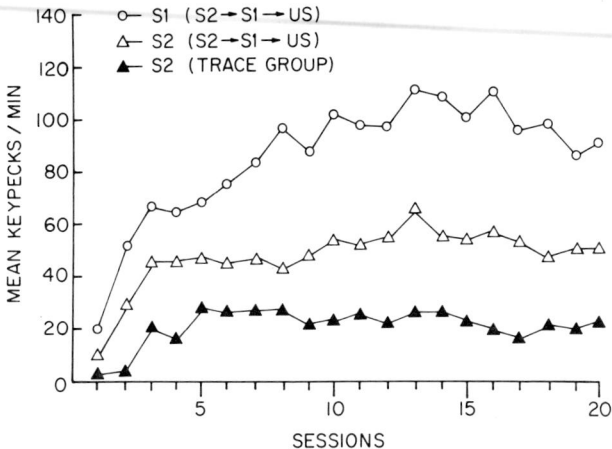

Figure 5.5. Effect of extended training on rate of keypecking to S2 and S1 when US is presented on all second-order trials. Responding to S2 (open triangles) and to S1 (circles) by the successive-compound group is plotted, along with responding to S2 (closed triangles) by the trace-conditioning group. (After Marshall, 1979.)

successive compound. It is of particular interest here that the size of this difference in responding to S2 by the two groups remained essentially unchanged late in training. This finding implies sustained second-order autoshaping, as expected when the procedure prevents the development of inhibition.

A possible alternative interpretation of this result is that generalization of high keypeck rates from S1 to S2 accounts for the relatively high level of responding to S2 in the successive-compound group; the trace group would not have a comparable source of generalization. However, Marshall (1979) trained another trace group and successive-compound group for which US occurred on only a random 50% of the trials, and the result was identical to that shown in Figure 5.5 except that rate of responding to S1 was approximately twice as high in the 50% successive-compound group. A generalization account predicts that such a high rate of responding to S1 would enhance responding to S2 in the 50% successive-compound group, but that result was not found. Instead, both the original and the 50% successive-compound groups responded at the same level to S2, and both responded significantly more strongly than their trace-conditioning comparison groups. We have shown in other experiments that although a 50% reinforcement schedule enhances response rate to a first-order CS in autoshaping, it does not seem to alter the ability of that CS to act as a Pavlovian reinforcer in second-order autoshaping (see pp. 168–171). Consequently, we propose that, relative to trace-conditioning groups, responding to S2 in our successive-compound groups is enhanced by the second-order reinforcing action of S1.

Marshall's latter finding also seems contrary to the possibility that responding to S2 in the successive compound is mediated solely by an S2–S1 connection formed through "sensory conditioning" (e.g., Wickens, 1965). In that case, too, the strength of responding to S2 should have been correlated with the strength of responding to S1. Finally, responding to S2 may have been stronger in the successive-compound than in the trace group because S1 acted as an instrumental (conditioned) reinforcer to strengthen responses made to S2. It is difficult to eliminate instrumental reinforcement by the Pavlovian reinforcer in many conditioning preparations (e.g., Gormezano & Kehoe, 1975; Jenkins, 1977; Terrace, 1973). However, we have noted elsewhere that many behavioral effects attributed to instrumental conditioned reinforcement might result from skeletal responses being directed toward higher-order Pavlovian CSs in the instrumental training situation (Marshall *et al.*, 1979; Rashotte *et al.*, 1977). On the whole, then, the data shown in Figure 5.5 seem reasonably interpreted as a demonstration of sustained second-order autoshaping when US is present on second-order trials.

It is worth noting that second-order conditioning will not necessarily occur free from inhibition in all successive-compound procedures. In particular, when S2 is sufficiently long in duration, inhibition of delay would be expected to develop to S2 and to interact with second-order excitation. Such cases should produce a transient second-order excitatory effect, perhaps similar to that observed in the procedure where US is omitted on second-order trials.

SOURCES OF VARIATION IN THE REINFORCING EFFECTIVENESS OF CONDITIONED STIMULI

A Theoretical Formulation

A theoretical treatment of the Pavlovian reinforcing effectiveness of CSs is described here as a step toward achieving a deeper understanding of higher-order conditioning. The choice of a theoretical framework was influenced by two main considerations. First, because the reinforcement process is likely to be similar whether a US or a CS serves as the reinforcer, it seemed reasonable to turn to a successful account of the reinforcing effectiveness of USs to provide the framework for constructing such an account for CSs. Second, the close relationship between excitation and inhibition that characterizes second-order conditioning when the US-absent procedure is employed made it imperative that the theoretical framework readily deal with inhibitory phenomena. The present theoretical treatment is cast in the general format of the Rescorla–Wagner model (Rescorla & Wagner, 1972; Wagner & Rescorla, 1972), which has dealt successfully with a range of excitatory and inhibitory phenomena in first-order conditioning (e.g., LoLordo, 1979).

The basic Rescorla–Wagner equation for computing the change in associative strength of a CS resulting from any single CS–US pairing is,

$$\Delta V_{S1} = \alpha_{S1} \beta (\lambda - V_{S1+Sn}), \tag{1}$$

where ΔV_{S1} represents the size of the change in associative strength of a first-order CS (S1); α_{S1} and β are learning-rate parameters whose values, respectively, are related to the properties of the specific CS and US employed; λ represents the maximum associative strength the US is capable of supporting; and, V_{S1+Sn} represents the algebraic summation of the pretrial associative strengths of S1 and all other stimuli present when S1 occurs (e.g., background stimuli).

The equation specifies as a necessary condition for associative change that there must be a discrepancy between the maximum associative strength the US can support and the *combined* pretrial associative strengths of all the stimuli present on the trial (i.e., the expression $\lambda - V_{S1+Sn}$ must not equal zero). Furthermore, the *size* of the change resulting from any trial will be determined jointly by the absolute size of the discrepancy between λ and V_{S1+Sn} and by the values of the learning rate parameters. And, the *direction* of the change will be determined by the algebraic sign of the difference between λ and V_{S1+Sn}: when $\lambda > V_{S1+Sn}$ there will be an associative increment to S1; when $\lambda < V_{S1+Sn}$ S1 will suffer a loss in associative strength. In the model's lexicon, S1 is said to be excitatory or inhibitory according to whether the *net* value of V_{S1} is positive or negative, respectively. Two additional assumptions are made that are not included in equation (1). One is that temporal contiguity between S1 (or its sensory trace) and US is assumed on conditioning trials. The other is that the associative strength of S1 is only one determinant of performance in the presence of S1; provided the other determinants are held constant, ordinal relations among different associative strengths represented as different values of V_{S1} are assumed to be preserved in performance.

The reinforcing effectiveness of CSs can be conceptualized by application of the Rescorla–Wagner model. The application is illustrated here for the US-absent procedure and for the type of second-order trial summarized in the schematic diagram at the top of Figure 5.6. On these trials, S2 and S1 are assumed to occur in strict sequence such that S2-offset coincides with S1-onset, and US is never presented. A key assumption in the theory to be outlined is also illustrated in the trial schematic; a decaying sensory trace of S2 (i.e., S2′) is shown to overlap, at least partly, the presentation of S1. The parameters of S2′ (e.g., its intensity and duration) are assumed to depend on the physical characteristics of S2. For simplicity, the schematic omits two features of the procedure that deserve note. One feature is that the S2→S1 sequence occurs in the context of background stimuli. Consequently, the sequence of stimulus events on the second-order trial is more properly viewed as a sequence of two simultaneous stimulus compounds; "S2 + background cues" followed by "S2′ + S1 + back-

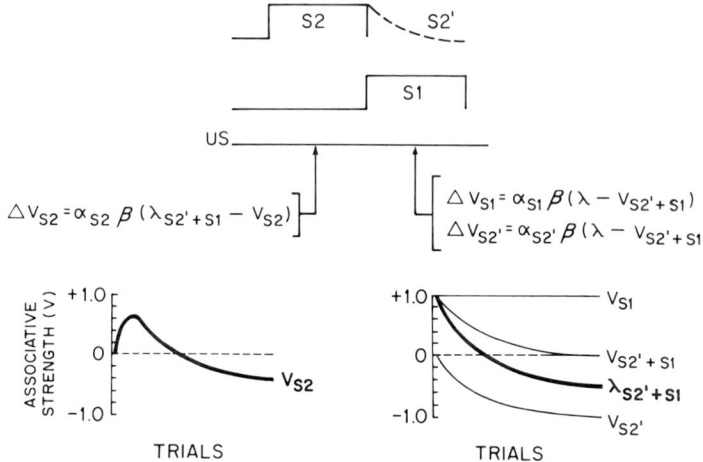

Figure 5.6. Theoretical account of associative processes when US is absent on second-order trials.

ground cues." Background cues are ignored in presenting the key ideas of the theory below, but their role is discussed in a later section. The other feature is that the second-order trials are assumed to be intermixed among first-order S1→US trials. These first-order trials help to preserve the associative strength of S1, which is presumably reduced by the nonreinforced occurrences of S1 on second-order trials.

The theory attempts to formalize two intuitions. One is that on the type of second-order trial shown schematically in Figure 5.6, the functional reinforcer for S2 is not solely S1 but, rather, is a simultaneous stimulus compound comprised of the trace of S2 (S2′) and S1. The other intuition is that the reinforcing effectiveness of this compound-stimulus reinforcer, itself, undergoes associative change as a result of training with US absent on second-order trials. In the simplest terms, the theory maintains that it is the changing strength of the Pavlovian reinforcer during extended second-order training that is primarily responsible for the acquisition and loss of excitatory strength by S2 and for the ultimate conversion of S2 into a conditioned inhibitor. It is proposed that the associative changes in both S2 and its reinforcer can be understood in the framework of the Rescorla–Wagner model.

Consider, first, the associative changes that the stimulus elements in the simultaneous S2′ + S1 compound are expected to undergo as a consequence of S2→S1 trials. Except for subscripts specific to this example, the two equations shown on the right-hand side of Figure 5.6 are identical to equation (1) and represent only a simple application of Rescorla and Wagner's treatment of conditioned inhibition in simultaneous compounds (Wagner & Rescorla, 1972). At the beginning of second-order training, the associative strength of S1 is assumed to be asymptotic because of its prior conditioning history (i.e., $V_{S1} = 1.0$) and S2' is assumed to be neutral (i.e., $V_{S2'} = 0$). The value of λ for the simultaneous compound is assumed to be zero throughout training because no Pavlovian reinforcer is ever presented following the compound. The equations specify that S2' and S1 will suffer associative losses on second-order trials. However, at least some of the loss to S1 can be recovered on the intermixed S1→US trials, and to simplify the following presentation, V_{S1} is assumed to maintain a value of 1.0 throughout training (see Gibbon, Farrell, Locurto, Duncan, & Terrace, 1980, footnote 7, for the correct formula to estimate the asymptote for a partially reinforced CS; cf. Rescorla & Wagner, 1972). The assumption of maintained associative strength by S1 on second-order trials is reflected in the curve labeled V_{S1} in the lower right panel of Figure 5.6.

The equation for $\Delta V_{S2'}$ in Figure 5.6 was employed to simulate the associative changes in S2' over 55 second-order trials. In the simulation, $V_{S1} = 1.0$, $\lambda = 0$, and each of the learning rate parameters ($\alpha_{S2'}$ and β) were set at values of .25. The value of $V_{S2'}$ was set at zero on the first second-order trial since S2 and its trace were assumed to have no associative strength at the beginning of training. The outcome of the simulation is shown as the curve labeled $V_{S2'}$ in the lower right panel of Figure 5.6. It indicates that the trace of S2 assumes increasingly negative values as training proceeds because the associative losses it suffers on each second-order trial are not offset by associative gains from reinforced trials, as is the case with S1. According to the Rescorla–Wagner treatment of conditioned inhibition, S2' will continue to suffer associative decrements until $V_{S2'} = -1.0$, which perfectly balances the positive value of V_{S1}.

The curve labeled $V_{S2'+S1}$ in the figure shows change in the net associative strength of the S2' + S1 compound across second-order trials. The values of this curve were obtained by applying the Rescorla–Wagner assumption that the associative strengths of simultaneously occurring stimuli summate algebraically to yield a net associative strength of the compound (e.g., Wagner & Rescorla, 1972). It is evident from this curve that the net associative strength of the S2' + S1 compound must decrease from 1.0 to 0 in a negatively accelerated fashion across these trials, entirely as a consequence of the fact that S2' becomes inhibitory.

The fourth curve plotted in the lower right panel of Figure 5.6 is labeled $\lambda_{S2'+S1}$ and it represents an assumption not found in the Rescorla–Wagner treatment of conditioned inhibition. This curve depicts the changing *reinforcement potential* of the S2' + S1 compound across second-order trials. The present theory assumes that the reinforcing potential of a simultaneous compound comprised of excitatory and inhibitory stimulus elements is best represented by a weighted sum of the associative strengths of the individual stimulus elements. The inhibitory tendency is always weighted more heavily than the excitatory tendency. The values plotted for $\lambda_{S2'+S1}$ in Figure 5.6 were arrived at by arbitrarily weighting the negative values of $V_{S2'}$ by a factor of 1.5 when summated with the values of V_{S1}. The distinction made here between the net associative strength and the reinforcing potential of a simultaneous compound comprised of excitatory and inhibitory elements has some empirical support that is discussed later. For the present, it should be noted that the strategy of weighting the inhibitory member of the compound more heavily when reinforcing potential is computed allows the Pavlovian reinforcer for S2 to assume a negative value. In fact, the reinforcer can become negative before S2' is sufficiently negative to offset the excitatory strength of S1. Thus, it should be possible for S2 to acquire inhibitory strength from the S2' + S1 reinforcer even though S2' does not yet completely suppress responding to S1 on second-order trials.

Associative changes in S2 resulting from pairings of S2 and S1 on second-order trials are given by the equation,

$$\Delta V_{S2} = \alpha_{S2}\ \beta(\lambda_{S2'+S1} - V_{S2+Sn}), \qquad (2)$$

where α_{S2} and β are learning rate parameters whose values are determined by the characteristics of S2 and the Pavlovian reinforcer for S2, respectively; $\lambda_{S2'+S1}$ represents the maximum associative strength the Pavlovian reinforcer for S2 can support, its value is specified by the weighted sum of $V_{S2'}$ and V_{S1} computed on each trial, as described earlier; and V_{S2+Sn} represents an algebraic summation of the pre-trial associative strengths of S2 and of all other stimuli simultaneously present on the trial for which ΔV_{S2} is to be computed. Although equation (2) has the familiar form of the Rescorla–Wagner equation, it incorporates the new assumption that the value of the Pavlovian reinforcer declines across trials in the US-absent procedure for second-order conditioning rather than remaining fixed, as is assumed in first-order conditioning.

The implications of equation (2) are illustrated by a 55-trial simulation of second-order conditioning in the US-absent procedure. Values for $\lambda_{S2'+S1}$ on each trial were determined from the simulation described earlier (right-hand panel of Figure 5.6). The learning rate parameters, α_{S2} and β, were each fixed at .5 for the simulation; the value of V_{S2} on the first trial was zero. The outcome of the simulation, which is plotted in the lower left panel of Figure 5.6, shows that initially S2 should grow in excitatory strength. Eventually, however, the associative strength of S2 will exceed the declining strength of the Pavlovian reinforcer, causing S2 to suffer associative decrements. With continued training, the value of $\lambda_{S2'+S1}$ must eventually become negative, reaching an asymptotic value determined by the weighting factor. In the present simulation, the value of the weighting factor was 1.5, so that the asymptotic value of $\lambda_{S2'+S1}$ must be $-.50$. Accordingly, V_{S2} will continue to suffer associative losses on each trial until it, too, reaches a value of $-.50$, whereupon the conditioning process will stop. The eventual result, as shown in the lower-left panel of Figure 5.6, is that S2 will be an inhibitory stimulus after extended training. Thus, equation (2) predicts associative changes in $S2$ that parallel behavioral indicants of the changing associative strength of $S2$ during extended training with the US-absent procedure (Gokey & Collins, 1980; Herendeen & Anderson, 1968; Rescorla, 1973a, p. 141). The reasoning summarized in Figure 5.6 provides a rationale for those changes in terms of the changing reinforcing effectiveness of the reinforcer for $S2$.

Four aspects of the theoretical account described here deserve further comment.

Emphasis on the Stimulus Trace of S2

Many theories have appealed to stimulus traces in their accounts of conditioning phenomena (e.g., Hull, 1943; Pavlov, 1927; Smith, Coleman, & Gormezano, 1969), and the present theory is not unique in that respect. However, this theory assumes that the growth of inhibition to $S2'$ occurs independently of associative changes to $S2$, so it requires that $S2$ and its trace be highly discriminable. In fact, there is little direct evidence about the discriminability of stimulus traces and the stimuli that generate them, and generalization between $S2$ and $S2'$ remains a clear possibility. Furthermore, all stimuli must be assumed to leave sensory traces, not just $S2$. For example, a trace of $S1$ ($S1'$) is assumed to follow the offset of $S1$ on $S2 \rightarrow S1$ trials. Some implications of generalization between $S2$ and $S2'$, and of the occurrence of a trace of $S1$, are discussed on pages 158–159.

The Weighted-Sum Rule for Estimating Reinforcing Potential of a Compound Stimulus

Perhaps the most novel aspect of the present theory is its distinction between the reinforcing potential and the net associative strength of the $S2' + S1$ compound. This distinction rests on the more general assumption, stated in this chapter for the first time, that the reinforcing potential of any simultaneous compound composed of excitatory *and* inhibitory stimulus elements is best estimated by a weighted sum of the associative strengths of the individual stimuli, in which inhibitory strength is always weighted more heavily than excitatory strength. The weighted-sum rule is used by the theory to estimate the ability of the $S2' + S1$ compound to act as a reinforcer for $S2$. The ability of that same compound stimulus to evoke a response on $S2 \rightarrow S1$ trials is estimated by the simple algebraic-sum rule employed by Rescorla & Wagner (1972).

Only limited empirical evidence bears on the weighted-sum rule, but none of it is contradictory. Experiments on second-order conditioned inhibition provide one line of support (Pavlov, 1927, p. 107 ff; Rescorla, 1976, Experiment 1). In those experiments, an initially neutral $S2$ was paired with a simultaneous stimulus compound comprised of two CSs, one excitatory and one inhibitory. According to the simple algebraic summation rule, the net associative strength of that compound should have been zero, or a very low positive value, at the beginning of training. Yet the outcome reported in those experiments indicated that the compound was capable of acting as a reinforcer that readily established S2 as a second-order inhibitor. The weighted-sum rule provides one way of conceptualizing the apparent inhibitory reinforcing potential of the stimulus compounds in experiments such as these.

The other line of evidence concerning the weighted-sum rule is provided by Gokey & Collins's (1980) experiment described on pages 146–149. In that experiment, S2 became inhibitory even though the reinforcing $S2' + S1$ compound remained capable of evoking a reasonable level of keypecking on $S2 \rightarrow S1$ trials. That result, too, is consistent with the weighted-sum rule since $S2' + S1$ should be able to establish S2 as an inhibitory stimulus through a reinforcement process, even though $S2'$ has not yet become sufficiently inhibitory to completely suppress responding to S1 on second-order trials.

Sources of Associative Change for S2 and S2'

In the present theory, the reinforcing potential of the $S2' + S1$ compound is assigned the major responsibility for altering the associative strength of S2. In the long run, this assertion is likely to prove too conservative, but it seems a reasonable starting point for further analysis. In fact, the associative strength of S2 and of $S2'$ might be subject to change from a variety of sources. For example, because S2 and $S2'$ are likely to be similar, as discussed above, inhibition might generalize from $S2'$ to S2, and excitation (early in training) or inhibition (late) might generalize from S2 to $S2'$. Furthermore, it is possible that in cases where $S2'$ terminates before S1 (or even its trace, $S1'$) ceases, $S2'$ may gain (second-order) excitatory strength from the reinforcing effects of that part of S1 (or $S1'$) which follows $S2'$.

Another potential complication is posed by Pavlov's (1927, p. 71 ff; 1928, p. 104 ff) finding that *simultaneous* presentation of a neutral stimulus and an excitatory S1 can result in second-order excitatory conditioning of the neutral stimulus. Accordingly, $S2'$ might gain *excitatory* strength from its simultaneous occurrence with the excitatory S1 on $S2 \rightarrow S1$ trials. In that case, at least some of the excitatory strength displayed by S2 might result from a generalization process involving the (presumably) similar and excitatory $S2'$. Also, the conversion of $S2'$ into a conditioned inhibitor would proceed in a more complex way than is assumed by the present theory. Consideration of simultaneous conditioning of $S2'$ in this situation is encouraged by recent findings. For example, there is good evidence that *first-order* excitatory conditioning can result from simultaneous CS–US presentation (e.g., Burkhardt & Ayers, 1978), and "within-compound" associations between simultaneously presented flavor stimuli have been demonstrated (Rescorla & Cunningham, 1978).

Finally, a possible role for background stimuli in the second-order conditioning situation deserves note. The Rescorla–Wagner treatment of first-order conditioning often appeals to the fact that experimentally presented CSs occur in a context of background stimulation. For example, the fact that a CS becomes inhibitory as a consequence of being explicitly unpaired with US is accounted for by the fact that CS occurs along with excitatory background cues in a simultaneous compound that is not reinforced (Wagner & Rescorla, 1972). In the second-order conditioning procedure under discussion here, background cues would occur in combination both with $S2$ *and* with the reinforcing $S2' + S1$ compound on the nonreinforced $S2 \rightarrow S1$ trials. It is possible that these cues would contribute to the eventual inhibitory status of $S2$ and of $S2'$ much in the way that they are assumed to contribute to an explicitly unpaired CS's inhibitory status in first-order conditioning. Some experimental evidence about the influence of contextual cues on second-order conditioning is discussed on pp. 173–174. Parenthetically, the possibility of *second-order* conditioning of background cues should be recognized by theories in which background cues play an important role. The evidence now available that second-order conditioning is robust raises the possibility that every CS presentation constitutes the occurrence of a Pavlovian reinforcer that may alter the associative strength of temporally contiguous background stimuli.

Application of the Theory to Other Higher Order Conditioning Procedures

In this chapter the theoretical account of variations in the reinforcing effectiveness of CSs has been elaborated for a US-absent procedure in which $S2$ and $S1$ occur in strict sequence on nonreinforced trials intermixed among $S1 \rightarrow US$ trials. The same theoretical approach can apply to other cases as well. For example, the theory can be readily applied to the US-present procedure in which the $S2 \rightarrow S1$ sequence is followed by US. In fact, that procedure is theoretically much simpler than the US-absent case because $S2'$ should not become inhibitory and it should acquire little or no excitatory strength from its pairings with US because the highly conditioned $S1$ should "block" first-order conditioning of $S2'$ (Kamin, 1968; see this chapter, pp. 173–174). Accordingly, this theory requires that the $S2' + S1$ compound will maintain its excitatory reinforcing potential throughout training. Therefore, it correctly anticipates the sustained higher order conditioning to $S2$ that is obtained in the US-present procedure (see pages 149–152).

The present theory can also be applied to orders of conditioning higher than the second order. In third-order conditioning, for example, the ability of $S3 \rightarrow S2$ pairings to establish $S3$ as a third-order conditioned excitor could be predicted by using the general logic outlined in Figure 5.6. Of course, the Pavlovian reinforcer in this case would be the $S3' + S2$ compound.

Finally, the theory can be applied to the case where $S1$ is a well established conditioned inhibitor at the outset of training and second-order conditioned inhibition is studied. Here, the theory will require that S2 become inhibitory because the S2′ + S1 compound would be calculated to have inhibitory reinforcing potential from the outset. In this respect it is consistent with the available data (e.g., Lindberg, 1933; Pavlov, 1927, p. 107 ff; Rescorla, 1976). Predictions about associative changes in S2 during extended second-order conditioned inhibition training are made by the theory, but it is not practical to elaborate them here.

Experimental Studies

The theoretical formulation outlined above implicates several variables as important determinants of the reinforcing effectiveness of CSs in second-order conditioning. Studies carried out with the second-order autoshaping preparation have attempted to manipulate some of those variables experimentally. The outcomes of those studies are summarized here, along with pertinent evidence from other preparations. The experiments are concerned with manipulations of the inhibitory strength of S2′, the excitatory strength of S1, and the excitatory strength of contextual cues presented along with S2.

Manipulation of the Inhibitory Strength of S2′

In the present theory, it is principally the inhibitory strength of S2′ that alters the reinforcing potential of the S2′ + S1 compound in the US-absent procedure. Accordingly, experimental manipulations designed to influence the associative strength of S2′ should be informative about the theory's soundness. In particular, a procedure successful in weakening the inhibitory strength of S2′ would be expected to have two effects. One is that the net associative strength of the S2′ + S1 compound should remain relatively high for an extended period of training; performance measures should show that responding to S1 remains relatively strong on S2→S1 trials. The other is that the reinforcing potential of the S2′ + S1 compound should maintain a relatively positive value for a large number of trials; other things being equal, performance measures should show relatively durable second-order excitatory conditioning of S1.

The logic of the Rescorla–Wagner model that is adopted by the present theory predicts that inhibition accumulated to S2′ would be lessened if that stimulus were presented alone (i.e., without the excitatory S1) on a nonreinforced trial. Such a trial should yield an associative increment to S2′ because the value of the expression $\lambda - V_{S2'}$ in the equation used to compute $\Delta V_{S2'}$ (see Figure 5.6) must be positive (i.e., λ would equal zero, and $V_{S2'}$ would have a negative value). In fact, if a sufficiently large number of nonreinforced S2′ presentations were given, and if the background stimuli were associatively neutral, associative increments should accumulate to S2′ until $V_{S2'}$ approximates a value of zero (cf. Zimmer-Hart & Rescorla, 1974). Of course S2' can occur in an experimental setting only if S2 has been presented. Consequently, in order that the inhibitory strength of S2' be weakened on a nonreinforced trial, it is necessary for S2 to occur on that trial as well, and this poses additional complications. For example, if it is assumed that S2 has already acquired some excitatory strength from S2→S1 pairings, the theory requires that S2 suffer a loss in excitatory strength on the nonreinforced trial (this point is elaborated in a discussion of the theory at the end of this section).

In summary, although an S2-alone trial should enhance the future reinforcing potential of the S2' + S1 compound, it should also weaken the current excitatory strength of S2. A difficulty is posed here by the fact that the excitatory strength of S2 indexes the reinforcing potential of the S2' + S1 compound. That is, experimental attempts to evaluate whether S2-alone trials enhance the reinforcing potential of S2' + S1 may be made difficult because S2-alone trials should also cause S2 to lose excitatory strength. One procedure in which it is successfully demonstrated that S2-alone trials cause the expected enhancement of the reinforcing potential of S2' + S1 is described in the following paragraphs.

In virtually all second-order conditioning experiments the probability that S1 will follow S2 on second-order trials has been set at a value of 1.0. The theory described in this chapter asserts that it is on those trials that S2' suffers the associative decrements that make it inhibitory in the US-absent procedure. As described earlier, however, the present theory implies that the level of inhibition associated with S2' should be reduced by introducing S2-alone trials in second-order conditioning. A procedure in which S2-alone trials are randomly intermixed among S2→S1 trials would constitute second-order conditioning in which the probability of S1 is set at less than its usual value of 1.0. No experiments that employ this procedure have been reported in the literature as yet, and it is not difficult to understand why this should be the case. It was noted earlier in this chapter that, until recently, higher order conditioning carried the reputation of being difficult to demonstrate, even under the best of laboratory conditions. From a number of perspectives, it might appear that a reduction in the probability of S1 following S2 would constitute far less than optimal conditions for second-order conditioning. For example, it might be anticipated that a low probability of S1 would greatly retard, or even prevent, second-order conditioning because the animal could learn more easily that S2 is never followed by US.

In preliminary work in my laboratory, Marshall (1976; Marshall & Rashotte, 1977) arranged for S1 to follow S2 in second-order autoshaping (US-absent procedure) with a probability of 1.0, .5, or .25 in different groups of pigeons. The most striking feature of her data was that the .25 probability group required more second-order sessions to acquire keypecking to S2, but persisted in responding to S2 at a higher level for more sessions than did the 1.0 probability group. The latter finding provided one indication that S2-alone trials might reduce the inhibitory strength of S2'. However, Marshall's experiment was not sufficiently complete to provide conclusive data on this possibility. We have now completed a more extensive study of the effects of 1.0 and .25 probabilities of S1 during extended second-order autoshaping with the US-absent procedure (Rashotte, Marshall, & O'Connell, 1980). That work is summarized here.

In the experiment, all pigeons initially received 750 first-order autoshaping trials (30/session, 90-sec intertrial interval) on which a 6-sec S1 (key color) was followed immediately by five 45-mg food pellets. In a second phase, it was first demonstrated that S2 (a 6-sec key color) did not evoke high rates of keypecking, and only then were S2→S1 trials introduced to begin the second-order conditioning process. The intertrial interval continued to average 90 sec in this phase of the experiment. Only four first-order S1→US trials occurred in each session, irregularly mixed among the remaining trials on which the food US was never presented. The properties of these trials are described separately for each group.

To reproduce Marshall's original result, Group 100%-12 (N = 15) received 12 S2→S1 pairings in each session and Group 25% (N = 13) received three S2→S1 pairings which occurred in an irregular sequence intermixed among nine S2-alone trials in each session. Each group continued training until it had experienced 168 S2→S1 pairings (14 sessions for Group 100%-12; 56 sessions for Group 25%). In second-order autoshaping experiments some pigeons usually fail to reach a criterion that assures acquisition of responding to S2. The criterion in the present experiment demanded pecking on at least four of five successive S2 presentations. Two of the 15 pigeons in Group 100%-12 and four of the 13 pigeons in Group 25% failed to meet criterion. Their data are excluded from consideration, leaving Groups 100%-12 and 25% with Ns of 13 and 9, respectively.

The data plotted in Figure 5.7 indicate that Marshall's original finding was replicated in the present experiment. Group 25% required more sessions to acquire keypecking to S2 and continued to respond to S2 at a high rate for many more sessions than Group 100%-12. More precisely, Group 25% required a median of 91 trials (range: 21-204) to reach the acquisition criterion whereas Group 100%-12 required only 13 trials (range: 2-58). When training was terminated after 672 trials on which S2 had been presented, Group 25% was still responding at about 20 keypecks per min, whereas when training for Group 100%-12 ceased after only 168 second-order trials, responding had decreased precipitously to about 5 keypecks per min (cf. Gokey & Collins, 1980). These differences in performance early and late in training were statistically significant.

Of course, from the present theoretical viewpoint, the important question about the result shown in Figure 5.7 concerns the role of S2-alone trials in the 25% group. To help provide a conclusive answer to this question, the experiment included two additional groups that received the same number and temporal distribution of S2→S1 pairings as did Group 25%, but that never experienced

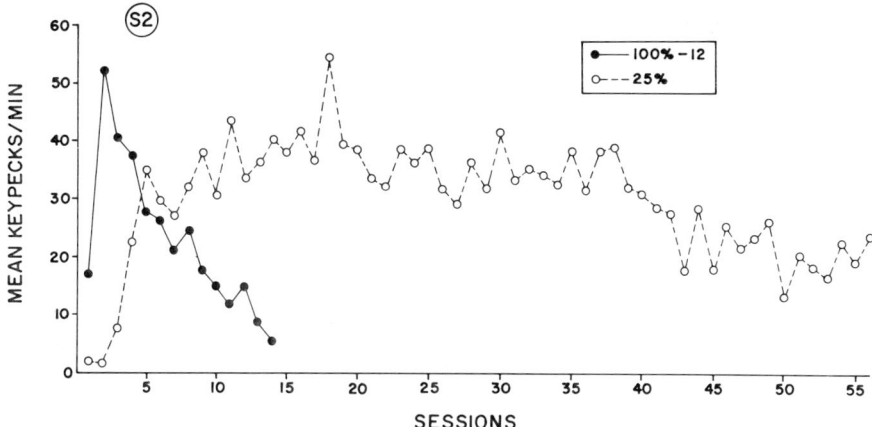

Figure 5.7. Second-order autoshaping when the probability of S1 on second-order trials is 1.0 (Group 100%-12) or .25 (Group 25%). Mean rate of keypecking computed across all 12 S2 trials in each session is plotted for each of the 14 sessions given to Group 100%-12, and for the 56 sessions given to Group 25%.

S2 alone. One Group ($N = 8$) received 56 second-order sessions exactly like those given to Group 25% except that the nine S2-alone trials in each session were omitted. The other group ($N = 7$) also received training identical to Group 25% except that a novel keylight (S3) was presented in place of S2 on trials when S2 would have occurred alone. In each of these additional groups the probability that S1 followed S2 was 1.0 but, unlike Group 100%-12, they received only three S2→S1 pairings per session (instead of 12) at relatively long interpairing intervals. There are three preliminary points of note concerning the performance of the two additional groups. First, one pigeon in the group with $N = 8$, and two pigeons in the group with $N = 7$, failed to reach criterion for acquisition of keypecking to S2. Data from these pigeons are excluded from consideration here. Second, the group that received a novel keylight in place of S2-alone trials pecked that keylight very little. Finally, analyses of variance indicated that these groups did not differ in any performance measure and, therefore, their data were combined to form a single group comprised of 12 pigeons, Group 100%-3.

Comparisons among Groups 100%-12, 100%-3 and 25% provided information about the role of S2-alone trials in second-order autoshaping. There are three major findings. The first is that the occurrence of S2-alone trials at the beginning of training did not significantly increase the number of S2→S1 pairings necessary to reach the acquisition criterion. The median number of pairings was 13 (range: 2–58), 7.5 (range: 4–15) and 23 (range: 6–51) for Groups 100%–12, 100%–3 and 25%, respectively. Differences among the groups in this measure did not reach statistical significance (Mann–Whitney tests, $ps > .05$). The implication of this result is that the S2-alone trials seem to play no role prior to acquisition of responding to S2. Rather, S2→S1 pairings seem entirely responsible for the establishment of keypecking to S2 in second-order autoshaping as indexed by a "pairings to criterion" measure. This finding is in agreement with acquisition data from studies of partial reinforcement in first-order autoshaping (Gibbon et al., 1980).

The second major finding is based on a comparison of responding to S2 by the three groups during extended training. This comparison indicates that S2-alone trials decrease the strength of responding in the early second-order sessions but enhance the strength of responding in later sessions. The left-hand panel in Figure 5.8 summarizes the comparison by presenting rate of responding to S2 for the three groups in successive blocks of trials. Each block included 12 S2→S1 pairings (i.e., 12 S2 presentations for the 100% groups, 48 S2 presentations for Group 25%) so that every data point reflects the reinforcing effects of 12 trials. Of course, Groups 100%-12 and 100%-3 differed in the temporal distribution of those trials (i.e., 12 per session *versus* 3 per session), and the 25% group is distinguished from the other two in having S2-alone trials. Statistical analyses indicated that the two 100% groups did not differ from each other but, in a

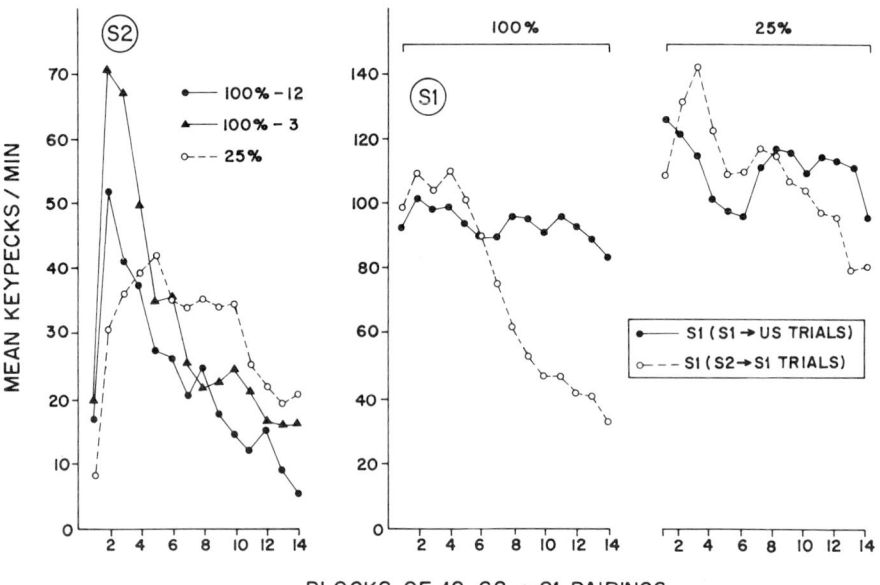

Figure 5.8. Responding to S2 (left panel) and to S1 (right panel) by groups receiving S2→S1 pairings on 100% or 25% of the trials. The data are presented in blocks of 12 S2→S1 pairings for each group, and include the entire 168 pairings given in the experiment. In the right-hand panel, the 100% groups are combined. That panel presents responding to S1 on the first-order trials in each block (closed circles) and on the 12 S2→S1 trials in each block (open circles).

comparison with the 25% group, there was a significant Groups-by-Blocks interaction that obviously is attributable to the fact that the 100% groups showed more rapid acceleration of responding to S2 early in training but more rapid loss of response strength later in training than did the 25% group.

Some additional information about the effects of S2-alone trials is provided by a molecular analysis of responding to S2. In other experiments, analysis of the distribution of keypecks across the CS period has revealed distinctively shaped distributions that seem differentially related to the reinforcement condition. For example, in first-order autoshaping the asymptotic distribution of keypecks approximates a linear increasing gradient when the reinforcer occurs with a relatively low frequency or has a relatively low magnitude; when the reinforcement conditions are more favorable, however, keypecking increases across the early portions of a CS but remains steady (or even is suppressed) later in the CS when reinforcer presentation is most imminent (Gibbon et al., 1980; Marshall, 1979; O'Connell & Rashotte, 1980). From this perspective, the distributions of keypecking shown for the 100% and 25% groups in Figure 5.9 have two interesting features. One is that, from Block 2 until the end of training, the 25% group displayed the increasing gradient of keypecks that seems characteristic of weak reinforcement conditions. The other is that, in the early sessions (Blocks 2 and 3), the 100% group's distributions resembled those for a stronger reinforcement condition but, as training progressed, those distributions assumed a more linear increasing shape, which is characteristic of weaker reinforcement. These features of the data are in general agreement with the theoretical account described here.

The last major finding in the experiment concerns the rate at which respond-

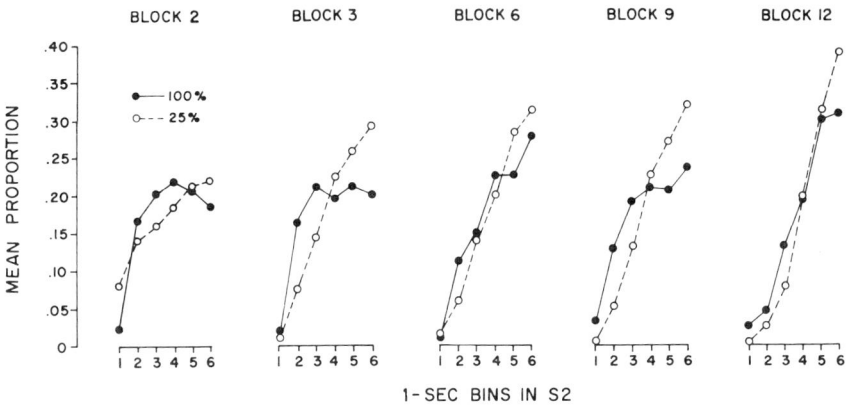

Figure 5.9. Distributions of keypecking during S2 presentations in the combined 100%–12 and 100%–3 groups (closed circles) and in the 25% group (open circles). The proportion of keypecks in each of the six 1-sec intervals of S2 is plotted for representative blocks of 12 S2→S1 pairings throughout training. Bin 1 represents the first second S2 was present on the key, Bin 6 represents the final second.

ing to S1 was suppressed on S2→S1 trials in the 100% and 25% groups. Figure 5.8 plots the strength of keypecking evoked by S1 when it occurred on S1→US trials and when it occurred in the S2' + S1 compound on S2→S1 trials. The earlier and more profound suppression of responding to S1 in the 100% group shown in Figure 5.8 was confirmed in an analysis of variance. This finding too, is consistent with the present theory's implications. That is, maintained reinforcement potential by the S2' + S1 compound late in training is attributed by the theory to the relatively weak inhibitory strength of S2'. Accordingly, it could be expected that the 25% group would show both relatively maintained response strength to S2 *and* relatively strong response strength to the S2' + S1 compound. Both results were obtained in this experiment.

In summary, the present experiment indicates that in second-order autoshaping, S2-alone trials seem to play no functional role at the very outset of training; instead, it appears that the number of S2→S1 pairings control the initial establishment of keypecking to S2. However, S2-alone trials subsequently become functional. In the early sessions, when S2 should be acquiring excitatory strength most rapidly, S2-alone trials seem to slow the growth of excitation. In later sessions, when S2 should be losing excitatory strength most rapidly, S2-alone trials seem to retard the loss of excitation.

The pattern of results obtained in this experiment can be conceptualized in terms of the present theoretical approach. In fact, it is possible to simulate the effects of a low probability of S1 in second-order conditioning by making certain additions to the theoretical framework summarized in Figure 5.6. Instead of working through such a simulation here, however, a more general account of the application will be briefly described.

First, it is assumed that associative changes in S2, S2' and S1 that result from the S2→S1 trials would be handled in the manner prescribed for that type of trial on pages 154–157.

Second, on the intermixed S2-alone trials, associative changes would be expected for both S2 and S2'. With respect to S2', the discussion earlier in the present section described why the equation for $\Delta_{S2'}$ (Figure 5.6) would require than any inhibitory strength S2' had acquired would be reduced by an S2-alone trial. The situation with respect to S2 is slightly more complex. It would be expected that an S2-alone trial would reduce the excitatory strength of S2 in either of two ways. On the early S2-alone trials, excitatory strength would be lost simply because S2 occurs without US (i.e., for these trials, the value of λ in equation [2] would be zero). Should S2' become inhibitory after further training, however, it could function as a reinforcing event for S2 on S2-alone trials (where S2' must be assumed to follow S2 immediately). In this case, S2 could suffer an associative loss as a consequence of the inhibitory reinforcing potential of S2' (i.e., for these trials, λ in equation [2] would assume a negative value). In both cases, it is assumed that the learning rate parameter associated with the reinforcer (i.e., β) in equation (2) is lower on S2-alone trials than on S2→S1 trials. The implication of this assumption is that associative change in S2 resulting from S2-alone trials will be small relative to the change occasioned by S2→S1 trials.

The data presented in this section encourage the view that the inhibitory strength of S2′ plays a central role in altering the potential of the reinforcer when second-order conditioning is conducted with the US-absent procedure. Of course, that view is endorsed by the theory outlined in this chapter. It will be important to evaluate this position more completely by employing other experimental manipulations designed to alter the contribution of S2′ to the S2′ + S1 compound, and by employing conditioning preparations other than autoshaping. With respect to the latter point, it must be noted that partial reinforcement seems to have a unique effect in first-order autoshaping that is not found in other classical conditioning preparations; it results in enhanced asymptotic keypeck rates relative to a 100% reinforcement schedule (see next section). The possibility exists, therefore, that the present effects of partial reinforcement in second-order autoshaping may be unique to this preparation.

Manipulations of the Excitatory Strength of S1

According to the present theoretical formulation, first-order conditioning manipulations that set the associative strength of S1 at different values before second-order conditioning begins should have several important consequences. For example, in the US-absent procedure a stronger S1 should allow V_{S2} to reach a criterion level of excitatory strength after relatively few S2→S1 pairings at the beginning of training. V_{S2} should also achieve a relatively high value before it begins to suffer decrements mid-way through training. These predictions follow because in equation (2) the value of $\lambda_{S2' + S1}$ will be determined primarily by the value of V_{S1} in the early part of training. The theory also requires that the asymptotic inhibitory strength of S2′ balance the maintained excitatory strength of S1 after extended training. Consequently, through its contribution to the reinforcing potential of the S2′ + S1 compound, S2′ should be capable of imparting more inhibitory strength to S2 when the excitatory strength of S1 is strong.

We have attempted to vary the associative strength of S1 in second-order autoshaping experiments by manipulating either the probability or the magnitude of US paired with S1 in first-order training. The data we have collected to date bear principally on whether those manipulations alter the ability of S1 to establish keypecking to S2, and whether they influence the excitatory strength of S2 in subsequent training.

We chose to manipulate probability and magnitude of US in our initial experiments because these variables are generally viewed as determinants of associative strength (e.g., Mackintosh, 1974) *and* because they appear to have unorthodox effects on performance in first-order autoshaping. Accordingly, these experiments have twin goals. First, by evaluating how these variables influence the reinforcing effectiveness of a first-order CS, we hoped to provide information relevant to the present theoretical position. Second, we expected this information to shed some light on the nature of the associative effects these variables have in first-order autoshaping. Several experiments encouraged the latter expectation. For example, Holland (1977) has shown that tests of the reinforcing effectiveness of a CS can reveal associative strength that is not expressed well in first-order conditioned performance.

Probability of US. In most classical conditioning preparations, presentation of US following only a random subset of CS presentations results in lower (or, at best, equivalent) asymptotic responding to CS than when CS–US pairings occur on every trial (e.g., Mackintosh, 1974). The implication of this finding is that partial reinforcement yields a CS with weaker (at best, equivalent) associative strength than does continuous reinforcement. In first-order autoshaping, however, partial reinforcement has the unique effect of producing a *higher* asymptotic rate of keypecking than does continuous reinforcement (e.g., Gibbon et al., 1980). The reasons for this exceptional effect of partial reinforcement are not understood, but theories of conditioning would lead us to suspect that it reflects the influence of performance variables specific to autoshaping, rather than greater excitatory strength established to S1 by the partial reinforcement schedule (Gibbon *et al.*, 1980; Marshall & Rashotte, 1979).

Other conditioning preparations have yielded only fragmentary data on how partial reinforcement influences the reinforcing strength of S1 in second-order conditioning. Shapiro, Sadler, and Mugg (1971) reported poor second-order salivary conditioning in dogs when S1 was partially reinforced, but second-order conditioning was weak even when S1 was continuously reinforced in their experiment. Kamil (1969, Experiment 2), using rats, reported very little difference in second-order fear conditioning as a function of whether S1 had been paired with shock on a 50% or a 100% reinforcement schedule. The result obtained by Rashotte, O'Connell, and Marshall (1980) in an autoshaping experiment is described below.

Different groups of pigeons initially received first-order autoshaping with either a 100% ($N = 7$) or a 50% ($N = 8$) reinforcement schedule. Both groups were given 650 first-order trials (30 trials/session) but, of course, S1 was followed by US on only 375 of those trials in the 50% group. S1 was a 6-sec keylight, the US was five 45-mg food pellets, and the intertrial interval averaged 90 sec. By the end of first-order conditioning, the 100% group's rate of keypecking to S1 was about 60 per min, and the 50% group's rate was about 120 per min. This finding replicates others in the first-order autoshaping literature (e.g., Gibbon *et al.*, 1980).

In the next phase of the experiment, it was demonstrated that S2 (a 6-sec keylight) did not strongly evoke keypecking before the second-order S2→S1 pairings began. In subsequent second-order conditioning sessions there were twelve S2→S1 trials intermixed among four first-order trials on which S1 and US were paired on the appropriate reinforcement schedule for the two groups. Training continued for 25 sessions (300 S2→S1 trials).

The results of the experiment showed that the reinforcement schedule associated with S1 in first-order autoshaping had no statistically reliable effects on performance to S2. In particular, at the outset of training, the number of S2→S1 trials required to meet the criterion for established keypecking to S2 was 17.5 and 16.0 trials for the 100% and the 50% groups, respectively. Also, during the entire 25 sessions of second-order training, the rate of keypecking to S2 was not reliably influenced by the reinforcement schedule associated with S1, according to an analysis of variance. Figure 5.10a provides a summary of data on which the analysis was performed. In Figure 5.10b, response rate to S1 on first-order and second-order trials is plotted for each group. The apparent earlier and more profound suppression of keypecking to S1 on second-order trials in the 100% group was confirmed by an analysis of variance.

This experiment provides mixed indications about how partial reinforcement in first-order autoshaping influenced the reinforcing potential of the S2' + S1 compound. On the one hand, the S2 data imply that the compound was equally reinforcing in the 100% and 50% groups because they did not differ in strength of responding to S2. From the present theory's viewpoint, a further implication is that S1 had the same associative strength in the 100% and 50% groups. On the other hand, the S1 data suggest that S2' became more inhibitory in the 100% group where it more completely suppressed responding to S1. According to the present theory, this latter finding implies that S1 was more excitatory in the 100% group because the inhibitory strength of S2' should be inversely related to the excitatory strength of S1. Taken at face value, this pattern of results suggests that the theory may be incorrect with respect to its reliance on the inhibitory strength of S2' as the principal source of decrement in the excitatory strength of S2 during extended training. That is, since the S1 data appear to indicate different levels of inhibition associated with S2', that difference should have been reflected in responding to S2 which indexes the reinforcing potential of the S2' + S1 compound. It is worth noting that the implication of the S1 data for the inhibitory status of S2' are not entirely clear-cut in this case. For example, the partial reinforcement manipulation produced sizeable between-group differences in the absolute rate of responding to S1 that may be related to the ease with which an inhibitory S2' can suppress responding to S1. Possibilities such as this need to be evaluated in independent tests of the inhibitory status of S2' (cf. Gokey & Collins, 1980).

The present experiment provides preliminary information about how the reinforcing effectiveness of a CS is influenced by the probability of US in first-order autoshaping. A more complete experimental approach to the problem will include a variety of manipulations. For example, only one level of partial rein-

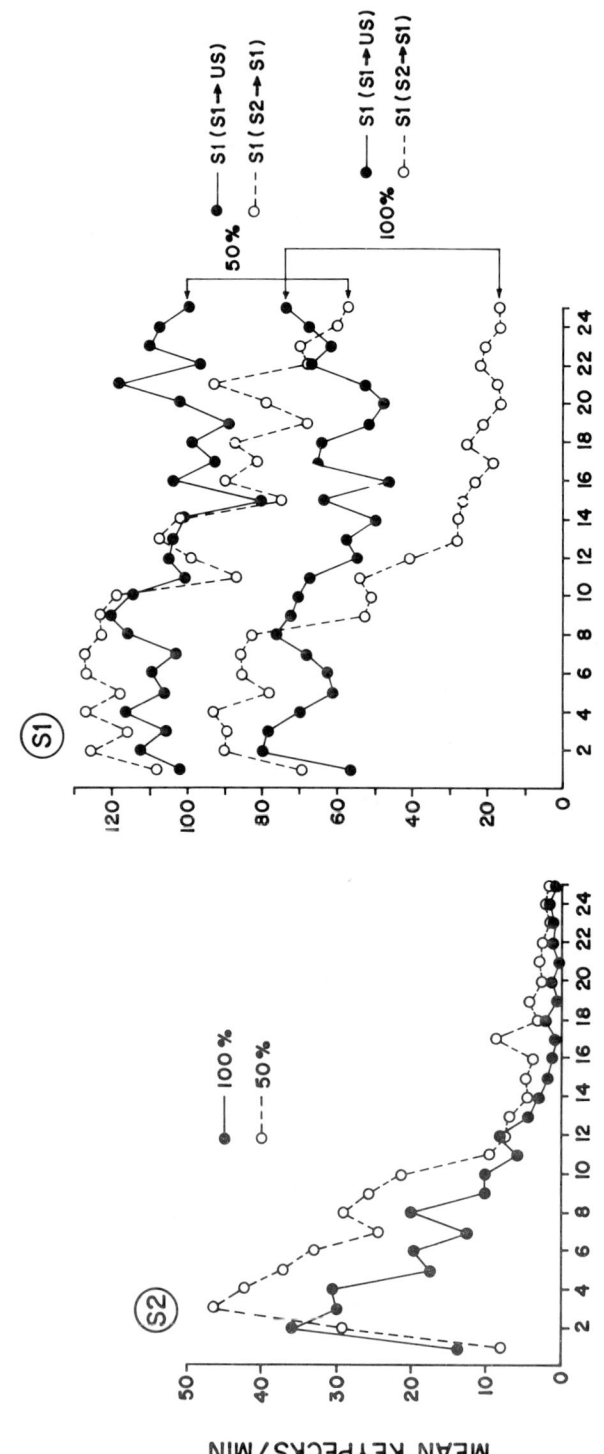

Figure 5.10. Responding to S2 (left panel) and to S1 (right panel) by groups receiving S1→US pairings on 100% or 50% of the trials in first-order autoshaping. Data are presented for all 25 second-order sessions in the experiment. There were 12 S2→S1 pairings in each session. The right-hand panel shows, for each group, responding to S1 on first-order trials (closed circles) and on second-order trials (open circles).

forcement was employed here; additional levels, particularly lower ones, should be studied. Also, the reinforcing effectiveness of diffuse first-order CSs (e.g., tones, houselights) associated with different US probabilities should be examined. Diffuse CSs do not evoke keypecking, thereby eliminating any possible contribution to second-order responding of differential keypeck rates evoked by partially or continuously reinforced keylight S1s. Additional experiments along these lines should benefit both the development of the present theoretical approach and the understanding of the relationship between associative and performance factors in first-order autoshaping.

Magnitude of US. Several experiments have reported that the strength of keypecking evoked by S1 in first-order autoshaping bears little or no relationship to the magnitude of reinforcement (defined by the duration of access to grain) signaled by S1 (Balsam, Brownstein, & Shull, 1978; Perkins, Beavers, Hancock, Hemmindinger, Hemmindinger, & Ricci, 1975). This result contrasts with findings from many other preparations in which the strength of the conditioned response evoked by S1 is positively related to US magnitude (e.g., Mackintosh, 1974, p. 70 ff). O'Connell and Rashotte (1979) have examined whether US magnitude determines the ability of S1 to act as a reinforcer in second-order autoshaping.

We varied reinforcement magnitude by controlling the number of 45-mg food pellets presented following S1 on first-order trials. This manipulation provides excellent control over both the volume of food ingested on each trial and the number of consummatory pecks made following each presentation of S1 (i.e., approximately one peck per pellet). For our high and low magnitudes we chose 10 and 2 pellets, respectively (cf. Gonzalez & Champlin, 1974), and in one comparison we included an intermediate case in which 5 pellets were used.

In the first phase of the experiment, four groups (Ns = 8) received 20 sessions of first-order autoshaping in which S1 was a red keylight on half the trials in each session and a blue keylight on the remaining trials. The key colors were 6 sec in duration and occurred in an irregular order across the 40 trials in each session. Every trial ended in food presentation. One group received within-subject training in which the different colored keylights signaled 2 or 10 pellets (counterbalanced across stimuli). Both colors signaled the same number of pellets in the other three groups (2, 5, or 10 pellets, depending on the group). The first-order autoshaping data indicated that number of food pellets had little effect on either speed of acquisition or asymptotic rate of pecking to S1. These findings essentially duplicate the results of earlier first-order autoshaping experiments (Balsam et al., 1978; Perkins et al., 1975).

In the second phase of the experiment, each of the two S1 stimuli was paired with its appropriate US magnitude on two trials in each session. Two new 6-sec keylight stimuli were introduced as different S2s for second-order conditioning.

These stimuli were horizontal or vertical black-line grids on a white background, and each was presented on six trials in every session. In the within-subject condition, one S2 was immediately followed by the 2-pellet S1, and the other S2 was followed by the 10-pellet S1. The identical sequences of key stimuli occurred on second-order trials in the between-group condition but, of course, for any one group both S1s had been paired with the same US magnitude in first-order conditioning.

The distinctive feature of the second-order conditioning data was that reinforcement magnitude had the clearest effect in the within-subject condition. In fact, seven of the eight pigeons in that condition met the criterion for established responding to S2, and six of those reached criterion after fewer S2→S1 pairings with the 10-pellet S1 than with the 2-pellet S1 (the seventh pigeon reached criterion on both S2s after an identical number of pairings). Furthermore, all seven of these pigeons responded more strongly at asymptote to the S2 paired with the 10-pellet S1 than to the S2 paired with the 2-pellet S1. These two aspects of the within-subject data conform rather closely to the theory's implications for different associative strengths of S1 in the early sessions of second-order conditioning. The between-group data, however, provided no indication that responding to S2 was systematically related to the US magnitude associated with S1. Figure 5.11 presents responding to S2 in individual sessions during the second phase of the experiment. The data points for the first two sessions in each panel indicate that generalized responding to the S2s had declined to a low level when these stimuli were presented alone before second-order conditioning began.

Although it is not unusual that between-group designs are less sensitive than within-subject designs in classical conditioning (e.g., Grice & Hunter, 1964), it remains of interest to determine why the different US magnitudes associated with S1 had such little effect on responding to S2 in the between-group condition. One possibility that deserves further examination is that the within-subject data are influenced by simultaneous negative contrast effects resulting from the pigeons' exposure to different reinforcer magnitudes in each session (cf. Gonzalez & Champlin, 1974; Rashotte, 1979). For example, contrast between the first-order US magnitudes might have reduced the perceived value of the 2-pellet US so that it functioned as a weaker reinforcer for S1 in the within-subject condition than in the between-group condition. And, exposure to two S2s associated with different S1 magnitudes in the within-subject case may have contributed to differential responsiveness through a contrast process in second-order conditioning.

Finally, it should be noted that in the number of second-order sessions reported here it was too early to gauge whether the suppression of responding to S1 on S2→S1 trials was related to US magnitude. Consequently, it is not possible to draw at least preliminary inferences from the S1 data about the inhibitory strength of S2'.

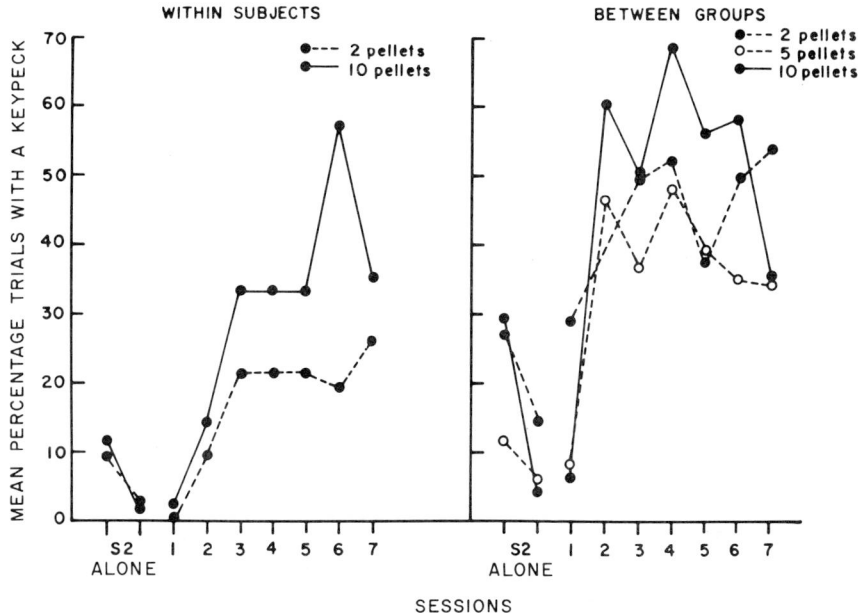

Figure 5.11. Percent of trials with a keypeck to S2 in each session as a function of the number of 45-mg food pellets associated with S1. Data are not available for session 2 in the 2-pellet group of the between-groups comparison. The intertrial interval averaged 60 sec.

In summary, our preliminary attempts to manipulate the excitatory strength of S1 by varying the probability or magnitude of US in first-order autoshaping were only moderately helpful in providing information concerning the present theory. On the whole, the data indicate that these manipulations involve a number of subtleties that must be examined in more detail before the implications of the data for the theory can be assessed.

Manipulation of the Associative Strength of Contextual Cues

Kamin (1968, 1969) made the important discovery that the effectiveness of a Pavlovian reinforcer in first-order conditioning is greatly influenced by the associative strength of contextual stimuli that occur along with the US on conditioning trials. For example, several pairings of a light with electric shock will normally establish the light as a CS for conditioned fear. However, fear conditioning to the light can be greatly retarded by presenting the light in combination with a well-conditioned CS for fear on each conditioning trial. The presence of the well-conditioned stimulus "blocks" the US from acting as a reinforcer for the neutral light–CS.

The Rescorla–Wagner model provides an account of blocking (Rescorla & Wagner, 1972), and the present application of that model to second-order conditioning implies that blocking by contextual cues should be operative there as well. A second-order autoshaping experiment by Leyland and Mackintosh (1978, Experiment 2) provides the evidence. Their experiment employed a compound second-order CS comprised of a keylight-S2 and a diffuse stimulus (a specific color of a houselight or the sound of a clicker). On each trial, the CS was followed by a keylight-S1 which served as the nominal Pavlovian reinforcer. The experiment demonstrated that the keylight-S2 was established as a second-order CS for keypecking in a group for which the diffuse stimulus had no conditioning history. However, conditioning to S2 was blocked in a second group for which the diffuse stimulus itself had been paired previously with S1 in a second-order conditioning procedure.

Leyland and Mackintosh's result demonstrates that a second-order excitatory CS can block the reinforcing function of S1, just as a first-order excitatory CS can block the reinforcing function of US. A theoretical account of this result is achieved in the present theory by direct extrapolation from the Rescorla–Wagner account of blocking in first-order conditioning. While the latter account is not without flaws (e.g., LoLordo, 1979), the demonstration of blocking in second-order conditioning encourages exploration of other contextual effects in that setting which are suggested by the Rescorla–Wagner logic.

CONCLUSION

The research summarized in this chapter provides ample evidence that autoshaping makes a valuable addition to the more traditional conditioning methods used in the study of higher-order conditioning. The ease with which robust second-order autoshaping in pigeons can be produced in apparatus that already exists in a large number of conditioning laboratories recommends it highly as a method for future study of theoretical questions, such as those posed here. At the present time, however, second-order autoshaping has been demonstrated only in pigeons, and in the heat-reinforcement autoshaping procedure in chicks (see Wasserman, Chapter 2 of this volume). It remains to be seen how readily second-order autoshaping can be demonstrated in the large number of other species-response combinations that yield good evidence of first-order autoshaping. There are some suggestions that the comparative study of higher-order conditioning may be informative about species differences (and individual differences) in susceptibility to inhibition (Teplov, 1964, p. 102 ff).

The present chapter has outlined a theoretical approach to the reinforcing effectiveness of CSs that is based on the Rescorla–Wagner model's treatment of the reinforcing effectiveness of USs in first-order conditioning. The theory is particularly intended to provide a detailed account of the acquisition and loss of excitatory strength by S2, and to account for the ultimate establishment of S2 as a conditioned inhibitory stimulus, when the US-absent procedure is employed. Perhaps most important, the theory points in a reasonably direct way to certain experimental operations that should influence the associative changes that are presumed to occur in this training procedure. The limited evidence available is in some agreement with the theory. However a much broader range of experimental manipulations, employed in a variety of conditioning preparations, must be used to evaluate its adequacy. The theory currently rests on a number of key assumptions that deserve careful experimental scrutiny. A prime example is the assumption that an inhibitory stimulus is more heavily weighted than an excitatory stimulus when the reinforcement potential of a simultaneous compound of these stimuli is calculated.

Two additional comments should be made about this theory. One is that it undoubtedly could be amended to include various changes proposed to bring the Rescorla–Wagner logic into closer conformity with certain experimental results (e.g., Mackintosh, 1975).

The other is that some aspects of the theory are similar to ideas discussed by Rescorla (1972, 1973a) in considering changes in the associative strength of S2 during extended training with the US-absent procedure. Rescorla proposed that those changes might come about because S2 *simultaneously* acquires independent excitatory and inhibitory tendencies on each trial. According to this account, the excitatory tendency grows because S2 is paired with S1, and the inhibitory tendency grows because S2 (or its trace) is present along with S1 when US is omitted. Because it is assumed that excitation grows faster than inhibition, S2 will be primarily excitatory early in training. However, once the inhibitory tendency becomes sufficiently strong, it is portrayed as suppressing the excitatory strength of S1, thereby reducing S1's reinforcing effectiveness. This, in turn, should initiate a process of extinction of the second-order excitatory tendency already acquired by S2 so that, eventually, S2 will be left only with its inhibitory tendency.

Rescorla's approach specifies that S2 simultaneously acquires excitatory and inhibitory tendencies that do not summate but independently influence responding to S2 (the excitatory tendency) and responding to S1 (the inhibitory tendency). While there is empirical evidence that a single CS can simultaneously evoke opposing conditioned responses (e.g., "binary reflexes", Asratyan, 1965, p. 175 ff), many theories assume that an individual CS is excitatory *or* inhibitory according to the algebraic sign of a *single* associative process (e.g., Rescorla & Wagner, 1972), and that excitatory and inhibitory tendencies (associated with different stimuli) summate algebraically to yield a net associative strength for any stimulus condition (e.g., Rescorla & Wagner, 1972; Spence, 1937). The present theory also appeals to excitatory and inhibitory processes but they are assigned to discriminably different sensory events (i.e., S2 and S2'). It may be noted that if S2 were to precede *and* overlap S1 on second-order trials, the present theory would assume that excitation and inhibition are associated with the initial and terminal portions of S2, which are assumed to be discriminable.

There is a large body of experimental work on the *instrumental* reinforcing effectiveness of CSs (e.g., Gollub, 1977; Hendry, 1969; Wike, 1966). This work is concerned with cases in which the experimentally programmed consequence of performing some response is the presentation of an arbitrary stimulus which, itself, has been paired previously with a US. It is a well-demonstrated fact that such stimuli have a reinforcing effect on responses they follow, and it is widely assumed that they acquire this effectiveness through a process of Pavlovian conditioning. In a complete treatment of the reinforcing effectiveness of CSs, both the *instrumental* and the *Pavlovian* reinforcing functions of these stimuli would be considered. It is not possible to undertake such a task here, but we might expect that a given variable would have similar effects on reinforcing effectiveness in both cases and, possibly, that a single theoretical treatment would be applicable in both. In this regard, we have suggested elsewhere that the apparent instrumental reinforcing function of a CS may at least partly be attributed to the Pavlovian second-order conditioning of stimuli in the instrumental training situation (Marshall *et al.*, 1979; Rashotte *et al.*, 1977). To the extent that this proposal is correct, there would be even more reason to expect communality between the instrumental and Pavlovian reinforcing function of CSs.

The robust second-order conditioning we and others have demonstrated in recent years in several conditioning preparations provides a substantive reason for reevaluating the role of higher order conditioning in a variety of laboratory and natural settings. Early attempts to explore these possibilities (e.g., Hull, 1943, Chapter 7) were open to the criticism that higher order conditioning is a weak and transient phenomenon that could not possibly carry the explanatory load that some assigned to it (e.g., Razran, 1955). However, we have shown in this chapter that, even in the US-absent procedure, second-order conditioning can be sustained for hundreds of trials in the autoshaping situation by the simple expedient of reducing the probability of S1 following S2 to a value below its usual value of 1.0. This single result emphasizes that very little is known as yet about the determinants of second-order conditioned reactions, even in well-controlled laboratory settings. It also enhances the possibility that second-order conditioning is an important influence in natural settings where stimulus–reinforcer pairings are likely to be intermittent.

ACKNOWLEDGMENT

I am grateful to Robert L. Collins and Daniel S. Gokey for permission to adapt data from a series of experiments conducted in Collins's laboratory at Florida State University. I also thank Herbert D. Kimmel for providing a translation of the "Wednesday" meeting cited here as Pavlov (1932). Dianne L. Beidler, David F. Foster, Daniel S. Gokey, Patricia L. Green, Robert W. Griffin, Beverly S.

Marshall, Jeffrey M. O'Connell, Cheryl L. Sisk, Donna L. Venezky, and Eileen M. Welson made perceptive comments on an earlier draft of this chapter and helped conduct some of the experiments reported here. I thank them for their help. I am particularly indebted to Beverly Marshall and Jeffrey O'Connell for many contributions to the research and ideas presented here, to David Foster for discussions of the theory proposed in this chapter, and to John Gibbon for comments on an earlier version of the chapter.

REFERENCES

Amiro, T. W., & Bitterman, M. E. Second-order appetitive conditioning in goldfish. *Journal of Experimental Psychology: Animal Behavior Processes*, 1980, 6, 41–48.

Asratyan, E. A. *Compensatory adaptations, reflex activity, and the brain*. Oxford: Pergamon, 1965.

Asratyan, E. A. Some aspects of the problem of motivation in the light of Pavlovian teaching. *Acta Physiologia Academiae Scientiarum Hungaricae*, 1976, 48, 323–334.

Baker, T. W. Properties of compound stimuli and their conditioned components. *Psychological Bulletin*, 1968, 70, 611–625.

Balsam, P. D., Brownstein, A. J., & Shull, R. L. Effects of varying the duration of grain presentation on automaintenance. *Journal of the Experimental Analysis of Behavior*, 1978, 29, 27–36.

Boakes, R. A., & Halliday, M. S. (Eds.). *Inhibition and learning*. New York: Academic Press, 1972.

Brown, P. L., & Jenkins, H. M. Autoshaping of the pigeon's keypeck. *Journal of the Experimental Analysis of Behavior*, 1968, 11, 1–8.

Burkhardt, P. E., & Ayres, J. J. B. CS and US duration effects in one-trial simultaneous fear conditioning as assessed by conditioned suppression of licking in rats. *Animal Learning and Behavior*, 1978, 6, 225–230.

Cheatle, M. D., & Rudy, J. W. Analysis of second-order odor-aversion conditioning in neonatal rats: Implications for Kamin's blocking effect. *Journal of Experimental Psychology: Animal Behavior Processes*, 1978, 4, 237–249.

Collins, R. L. *Successive discrimination between a single element and a successive compound stimulus*. Paper presented at the annual meeting of the Southeastern Psychological Association, New Orleans, March 1976.

Gibbon, J., Farrell, L., Locurto, C. M., Duncan, H. J., & Terrace, H. S. Partial reinforcement in autoshaping with pigeons. *Animal Learning and Behavior*, 1980, 8, 45–59.

Gokey, D. S. *The role of conditioned inhibition in feature negative discrimination learning*. Unpublished master's thesis, Florida State University, 1977.

Gokey, D. S. Personal communication, May 15, 1979.

Gokey, D. S., & Collins, R. L. Conditioned inhibition in feature negative discrimination learning with pigeons. *Animal Learning and Behavior*, 1980, 8, 231–236.

Gollub, L. R. Conditioned reinforcement: Schedule effects. In W. K. Honig & J. E. R. Staddon (Eds.), *Handbook of operant behavior*. Englewood Cliffs, N. J.: Prentice-Hall, 1977.

Gonzalez, R. C., & Champlin, G. Positive behavioral contrast, negative simultaneous contrast, and their relation to frustration in pigeons. *Journal of Comparative and Physiological Psychology*, 1974, 87, 173–187.

Gormezano, I., & Kehoe, E. J. Classical conditioning: Some methodological-conceptual issues. In W. K. Estes (Ed.), *Handbook of learning and cognitive processes* (Vol. 2): *Conditioning and behavior theory*. Hillsdale, N.J.: Erlbaum, 1975.

Grice, G. R., & Hunter, J. J. Stimulus intensity effects depend upon the type of experimental design. *Psychological Review*, 1964, 71, 247–256.

Hearst, E. Stimulus relationships and feature selection in learning and behavior. In S. H. Hulse, H.

Fowler, & W. K. Honig (Eds.), *Cognitive processes in animal behavior*. Hillsdale, N. J.: Erlbaum 1978.

Hendry, D. P. *Conditioned reinforcement*. Homewood, Ill.: Dorsey, 1969.

Herendeen, D., & Anderson, D. C. Dual effects of a second-order conditioned stimulus: Excitation and inhibition. *Psychonomic Science*, 1968, *13*, 15–16.

Holland, P. C. Conditioned stimulus as a determinant of the form of the Pavlovian conditioned response. *Journal of Experimental Psychology: Animal Behavior Processes*, 1977, *3*, 77–104.

Holland, P. C., & Rescorla, R. A. Second-order conditioning with food unconditioned stimulus. *Journal of Comparative and Physiological Psychology*, 1975, *88*, 459–467.

Holland, P. C., & Straub, J. J. Differential effects of two ways of devaluing the unconditioned stimulus in Pavlovian appetitive conditioning. *Journal of Experimental Psychology: Animal Behavior Processes*, 1979, *5*, 65–78.

Hull, C. L. *Principles of behavior: An introduction to behavior theory*. New York: Appleton-Century-Crofts, 1943.

Jenkins, H. M. Sensitivity of different response systems to stimulus–reinforcer and response–reinforcer relations. In H. Davis & H. M. B. Hurwitz (Eds.), *Operant–Pavlovian interactions*. Hillsdale, N. J.: Erlbaum, 1977.

Jenkins, H. M., & Sainsbury, R. S. The development of stimulus control through differential reinforcement. In N. J. Mackintosh & W. K. Honig (Eds.), *Fundamental issues in associative learning*. Halifax, Canada: Dalhousie Univ. Press, 1969.

Kamil, A. C. Some parameters of second-order conditioning of fear in rats. *Journal of Comparative and Physiological Psychology*, 1969, *67*, 364–369.

Kamin, L. J. "Attention-like" processes in classical conditioning. In M. R. Jones (Ed.), *Miami symposium on the prediction of behavior 1967: Aversive stimulation*. Coral Gables, Fla.: Univ. of Miami Press, 1968.

Kamin, L. J. Predictability, surprise, attention, and conditioning. In B. A. Campbell & R. M. Church (Eds.), *Punishment and aversive behavior*. New York: Appleton-Century-Crofts, 1969.

Konorski, J. *Condioned reflexes and neuron organization*. London and New York: Cambridge Univ. Press, 1948.

Leyland, C. M. Higher order autoshaping. *Quarterly Journal of Experimental Psychology*, 1977, *29*, 607–619.

Leyland, C. M., & Mackintosh, J. J. Blocking of first- and second-order autoshaping in pigeons. *Animal Learning and Behavior*, 1978, *6*, 391–394.

Lindberg, A. A. The formation of negative conditioned reflexes by coincidence in time with the process of differential inhibition. *Journal of General Psychology*, 1933, *8*, 392–419.

LoLordo, V. M. Classical conditioning: Compound CSs and the Rescorla–Wagner model. In M. E. Bitterman, V. M. LoLordo, J. B. Overmier, & M. E. Rashotte, *Animal learning: Survey and analysis*. New York: Plenum, 1979.

Mackintosh, N. J. *The psychology of animal learning*. London: Academic Press, 1974.

Mackintosh, N. J. A theory of attention: Variation in the associability of stimuli with reinforcement. *Psychological Review*, 1975, *82*, 276–298.

Marshall, B. S. *Factors influencing acquisition and maintenance in second-order conditioning of the pigeon's key peck: Partial reinforcement*. Unpublished master's thesis, Florida State Univ., 1976.

Marshall, B. S. *Reinforcement schedule effects in successive-compound conditioning: The pigeon autoshaping preparation*. Unpublished doctoral dissertation, Florida State Univ., 1979.

Marshall, B. S., Gokey, D. S., Green, P. L., & Rashotte, M. E. Spatial location of first- and second-order visual conditioned stimuli in second-order conditioning of the pigeon's keypeck. *Bulletin of the Psychonomic Society*, 1979, *13*, 133–136.

Marshall, B. S., & Rashotte, M. E. *Partial reinforcement during second-order conditioning of the pigeon's keypeck*. Paper presented at the annual meeting of the Midwestern Psychological Association, Chicago, May 1977.

Marshall, B. S., & Rashotte, M. E. *Partial reinforcement in autoshaping: Conditioning theory and species-typical feeding behavior.* Poster presentation at the annual meeting of the Eastern Psychological Association, Philadelphia, April 1979.

Nye, P. W. On the functional differences between frontal and lateral visual fields of the pigeon. *Vision Research,* 1973, *13,* 559-574.

O'Connell, J. M., & Rashotte, M. E. *Reinforcement magnitude effects in first- and second-order autoshaping.* Paper presented at the annual meeting of the Psychonomic Society, Phoenix, November 1979.

Patterson, D. D., & Winokur, S. Autoshaping pigeons' keypecking with a conditioned reinforcer. *Bulletin of the Psychonomic Society,* 1973, *1,* 247-249.

Pavlov, I. P. *Conditioned reflexes: An investigation of the cerebral cortex.* London and New York: Oxford Univ. Press, 1927.

Pavlov, I. P. *Lectures on conditioned reflexes: Twenty-five years of objective study of the higher nervous activity (behavior) of animals.* New York: Livewright, 1928.

Pavlov, I. P. "The report of Wednesday meeting of 2 November, 1932." (H. D. Kimmel, trans.)

Perkins, C. C., Jr., Beavers, W. O., Hancock, R. A., Jr., Hemmendinger, P. C., Hemmendinger, D., & Ricci, J. A. Some variables affecting rate of key pecking during response-independent procedures (autoshaping). *Journal of the Experimental Analysis of Behavior,* 1975, *24,* 59-72.

Rashotte, M. E. Reward training: Contrast effects. In M. E. Bitterman, V. M. LoLordo, J. B. Overmier, & M. E. Rashotte, *Animal learning: Survey and analysis.* New York: Plenum, 1979.

Rashotte, M. E., & Griffin, R. W. *Second-order appetitive conditioning in the pigeon.* Paper presented at the annual meeting of the Psychonomic Society, Boston, November 1974.

Rashotte, M. E., Griffin, R. W., & Sisk, C. L. Second-order conditioning of the pigeon's keypeck. *Animal Learning and Behavior,* 1977, *5,* 25-38.

Rashotte, M. E., Marshall, B. S., & O'Connell, J. M. *Signaling functions of the second-order CS: Partial reinforcement during second-order conditioning of the pigeon's keypeck.* Manuscript in preparation, 1980.

Rashotte, M. E., O'Connell, J. M., & Marshall, B. S. *Associative and performance effects of partial reinforcement in classical conditioning of directed motor action.* Manuscript in preparation, 1980.

Razran, G. A note on second-order conditioning—and secondary reinforcement. *Psychological Review,* 1955, *62,* 327-332.

Razran, G. The observable unconscious and the inferable conscious in current Soviet psychophysiology: Interoceptive conditioning, semantic conditioning and the orienting reflex. *Psychological Review,* 1961, *68,* 81-147.

Rescorla, R. A. Pavlovian conditioned inhibition. *Psychological Bulletin,* 1969, *72,* 77-94.

Rescorla, R. A. Informational variables in Pavlovian conditioning. In G. H. Bower (Ed.), *The psychology of learning and motivation* (Vol. 6). New York: Academic Press, 1972.

Rescorla, R. A. Second-order conditioning: Implications for theories of learning. In F. J. McGuigan & D. B. Lumsden (Eds.), *Contemporary approaches to conditioning and learning.* New York: Wiley, 1973. (a)

Rescorla, R. A. Effect of US habituation following conditioning. *Journal of Comparative and Physiological Psychology,* 1973, *82,* 137-143. (b)

Rescorla, R. A. Second-order conditioning of Pavlovian conditioned inhibition. *Learning and Motivation,* 1976, *7,* 161-172.

Rescorla, R. A. Aspects of the reinforcer learned in second-order Pavlovian conditioning. *Journal of Experimental Psychology: Animal Behavior Processes,* 1979, *5,* 79-95.

Rescorla, R. A., & Cunningham, C. L. Within-compound flavor associations. *Journal of Experimental Psychology: Animal Behavior Processes,* 1978, *4,* 267-275.

Rescorla, R. A., & Cunningham, C. L. Spatial contiguity facilitates Pavlovian second-order conditioning. *Journal of Experimental Psychology: Animal Behavior Processes,* 1979, *5,* 152-161.

Rescorla, R. A., & Wagner, A. R. A theory of Pavlovian conditioning: Variations in the effectiveness of reinforcement and nonreinforcement. In A. H. Black & W. F. Prokasy (Eds.), *Classical conditioning II*. New York: Appleton-Century-Crofts, 1972.

Rozeboom, W. W. "What is learned."—An empirical enigma. *Psychological Bulletin*, 1958, 65, 22–33.

Rudenko, L. P. On the functional structure of conditioned reflexes to serial stimuli in dogs. *Acta Neurobiologicae Experimentalis*, 1974, 34, 69–79.

Sears, R. J., Baker, J. S., & Frey, P. W. The eye blink as a time-locked response: Implications for serial and second-order conditioning. *Journal of Experimental Psychology: Animal Behavior Processes*, 1979, 5, 43-64.

Shapiro, M. M., Sadler, E. W., & Mugg, G. J. Compound stimulus effects during higher order salivary conditioning in dogs. *Journal of Comparative and Physiological Psychology*, 1971, 74, 222–226.

Skinner, B. F. *The behavior of organisms: An experimental analysis*. New York: Appleton-Century, 1938.

Smith, M. C., Coleman, S. R., & Gormezano, I. Classical conditioning of the rabbit's nictitating membrane response at backward, simultaneous, and forward CS–UCS intervals. *Journal of Comparative and Physiological Psychology*, 1969, 69, 226–231.

Spence, K. W. The differential response in animals to stimuli varying within a single dimension. *Psychological Review*, 1937, 44, 430–440.

Terrace, H. S. Classical conditioning. In J. A. Nevin (Ed.), *The study of behavior*. Glenview, Ill.: Scott, Foresman, 1973.

Timofeeva, E. A. The nerve mechanism of the conditioned reflex of the second order. *Pavlov Journal of Higher Nervous Activity*, 1959, 9, 231–238.

Teplov, B. M. Problems in the study of general types of higher nervous activity in man and animals. In J. A. Gray (Ed.), *Pavlov's typology*. New York: Macmillan, 1964.

Wagner, A. R., & Rescorla, R. A. Inhibition in Pavlovian conditioning: Application of a theory. In R. A. Boakes & M. S. Halliday (Eds.), *Inhibition and learning*. London: Academic Press, 1972.

Wickens, D. D. Compound conditioning in humans and cats. In W. F. Prokasy (Ed.), *Classical conditioning*. New York: Appleton-Century-Crofts, 1965.

Wike, E. L. *Secondary reinforcement*. New York: Harper, 1966.

Zentall, T. R., & Hogan, D. E. Key pecking in pigeons produced by pairing keylight with inaccessible grain. *Journal of the Experimental Analysis of Behavior*, 1975, 23, 199–206.

Zimmer-Hart, C. L., & Rescorla, R. A. Extinction of Pavlovian conditioned inhibition. *Journal of Comparative and Physiological Psychology*, 1974, 88, 837–845.

ARTHUR TOMIE | 6

Effect of Unpredictable Food on the Subsequent Acquisition of Autoshaping: Analysis of the Context-Blocking Hypothesis[1]

INTRODUCTION

Simple associative learning, or conditioning, has often been organized by learning theorists into two discrete types differentiated on the basis of the class of events that are to become associated (Miller & Konorski, 1928; Mowrer, 1947; Rescorla & Solomon, 1967; Schlosberg, 1937; Skinner, 1935; Solomon & Wynne, 1954). The two associative learning paradigms set forth by two-factor theorists are Pavlovian conditioning and instrumental conditioning. The derivation of conditioning in both of these associative learning paradigms is often characterized as dependent on the contingency, or the conditional probabilities, that exists between the two discrete events that are to become associated (Bloomfield, 1972; Gibbon, Berryman, & Thompson, 1974; Rescorla, 1967).

In instrumental conditioning, the events that are to become associated are the instrumental response and the intrumental reinforcer, and, to the degree that the presentation of the reinforcing event is made contingent on the instrumental response, instrumental conditioning will proceed. In Pavlovian conditioning, the events that are to become associated are the conditioned stimulus (CS) and the unconditioned stimulus (US), and, to the degree that the presentation of the US is made contingent upon the presentation of the CS, Pavlovian conditioning will proceed. Pavlovian conditioning, therefore, can be viewed as procedurally analogous to instrumental conditioning, insofar as the Pavlovian relationship

---

[1] The preparation of this chapter and the research reported therein were supported by National Institute of Mental Health predoctoral fellowship MH-35181, National Institute of Mental Health postdoctoral fellowship MH-05182, National Institute of Mental Health Grant MH-29425, National Science Foundation Grant 77-20564, Biomedical Sciences Support Grants administered by Rutgers University, and Rutgers Research Council Grants awarded to the author.

between the CS and the US is analogous to the instrumental relationship between the response and the reinforcer.

Recently, much theoretical interest has been focused upon the question of whether or not conditioning occurs in the special case where no contingency is arranged between the two associative events in question. That is, investigators have sought to determine what would happen, in the instrumental case, if the reinforcing event were presented independently of the subject's instrumental behavior, or, alternatively, in the Pavlovian case, if the US were presented randomly with respect to the CS. Congingency notions of conditioning would predict that no conditioning should occur under such an arrangement. That is, there should be no strengthening of an instrumental response when the reinforcing stimulus is presented without regard to that instrumental response. Similarly, there should be no acquisition of the conditioned response (CR) by the CS when the US is presented randomly with respect to the CS.

While one must acknowledge that "superstitious" responding may occur in the absence of an explicit contingency between a response and reinforcer (cf. Skinner, 1948), the conditioning literature is, nonetheless, largely sympathetic to the notion that arbitrary instrumental behaviors neither develop nor benefit from such an arrangement (Appel & Hiss, 1962; Boakes, 1973; Edwards, Peek, & Wolfe, 1970; Edwards, West, & Jackson, 1968; Halliday & Boakes, 1971, 1972; Harrnstein, 1966; Herrnstein & Morse, 1957; Huff, Sherman, & Cohn, 1975; Lachter, 1971, Lattal, 1972, 1973, 1974; Lattal & Maxey, 1971; Rescorla & Skucy, 1969; Sherman & Spitzner, 1975; Weisman & Ramsden, 1973; Wilkie, 1972; Zeiler, 1968). Similarly, Pavlovian conditioning fails to occur when the CS and the US are unrelated (Ayres & Quinsey, 1971; Benedict & Ayres, 1972, Experiment 2; Bilbrey & Winokur, 1973; Bull & Overmier, 1968; Davis & McIntyre, 1969; Gamzu & Schwartz, 1973; Gamzu & Williams, 1971, 1973; Mackintosh, 1973; Rescorla, 1967, 1968, 1969; Wasserman, 1973; Wasserman, Franklin, & Hearst, 1974; Wasserman, Hunter, Gutowski, & Bader, 1975).

NEGATIVE TRANSFER EFFECTS FOLLOWING UNCORRELATED PRETRAINING

Instrumental Conditioning

Although it seems to be the case that arranging no relationship between the critical events produces no acquisition, it is not clear that such a preparation produces no associative by-products. For it appears that prior experience with a situation where events are unrelated to one another subsequently retards the learning of a relationship between those events. In the instrumental realm several investigators have shown that prior experience with response-independent reinforcement has a severe retardation effect upon subsequent instrumental conditioning. That is, subjects previously exposed to a situation where reinforcement was delivered without regard to their instrumental behavior are subsequently retarded in acquiring an instrumental response maintained by the reinforcer. For example, Maier, Seligman, and Solomon (1969) have shown that dogs placed in a Pavlovian restraining harness and intermittently shocked independently of their behavior, are subsequently severely retarded in acquiring a hurdle-jump response to escape shock in a standard shuttle-box apparatus. In interpreting their results they propose that animals are capable of learning about the independence of events. In the harness situation, where shock termination is programmed independently of the subject's instrumental behavior, the subject learns that there is nothing that can be done to affect the termination of shock. The dog learns that with respect to shock termination he is helpless. This expectation of helplessness produces a cognitive, associative deficit that transfers to the test task where shock termination is now contingent on the dog's instrumental behavior and proactively interferes with the learning of the instrumental escape contingency.

It is important to note that the retardation, or helplessness, effect is partly associative in nature (cf. Maier & Jackson, 1979; Maier & Seligman, 1976; Maier & Testa, 1975). That is, it is not the case that the subject fails to respond altogether and thereby fails to experience the instrumental escape contingency. Such animals on occasion do respond and thereby terminate shock. However, they seem to be unable to profit from such an experience. They seem to be unable to perceive the relationship between their behavior and the termination of shock.

The retardation of instrumental conditioning has come to be called *learned helplessness* and has been replicated in the appetitive realm where it has been called *learned laziness* (cf., Engberg, Hansen, Welker, & Thomas, 1972; Russell & Glow, 1976; Welker, 1976). Both learned helplessness and learned laziness can be described as the retardation of instrumental conditioning following exposure to a situation where reinforcement was presented without regard to the subject's behavior.

Pavlovian Conditioning

Insofar as Pavlovian relationships between CSs and USs are analogous to instrumental relationships between responses and reinforcers, it seems reasonable to speculate as to whether there is a Pavlovian analogue to the instrumental retardation effect. That is, will experience with a situation in which the US is presented randomly with respect to the CS retard subsequent Pavlovian conditioning?

Data reported by Kremer (1971, Experiment 2; also Baker & Mackintosh, 1979) who used a conditioned emotional response (CER) procedure with rats, suggests that prior experience with random presentations of a CS and a US proactively interferes with the acquisition of conditioning wherein the CS and the US are paired. Similar retardation of acquisition following random-pretraining has been noted with the nictitating membrane CR in rabbits (Siegel & Domjan, 1971).

Retarded acquisition of Pavlovian conditioning to a CS does not appear to be dependent on prior uncorrelated pretraining with that particular CS. Seligman (1968), using a conditioned suppression paradigm, compared the acquisition of fear conditioning in two groups of rats. He found that rats that had experienced the random presentation of a tone CS with respect to shock were subsequently slower than original-learning control subjects (subjects with no previous experimental history) in fear conditioning to a visual CS. Seligman interpreted his results as evidence for nonspecific Pavlovian associative interference. That is, he suggests that pretraining with randomly related CS and US presentations teaches the subjects that the US is unpredictable. This learning produces a cognitive, associative deficit that transfers to the test task and proactively interferes with the learning of the relationship between the tone CS and the US.

Learning that the US is unpredictable should not require the services of a randomly presented CS. Extensive pre-exposure to intermittent, unsignaled US presentation should be an effective preparation for generating Pavlovian associative interference and retarded acquisition of conditioning. This appears to be the case. Mis and Moore (1973) observed that unsignaled US presentations subsequently interfere with the acquisition of the nictitating membrane CR in rabbits. Chambers and Szakmary (1979) Randich and LoLordo (1979) and Baker and Mackintosh (1979) have reported a similar effect using a CER procedure with rats.

Autoshaping

Recently these types of retardation effects have been reported in studies that utilize the Brown and Jenkins (1968) autoshaping procedure. For example, Gamzu and Williams (1971, 1973) exposed two groups of pigeons to correlated and uncorrelated presentations of a lighted-key CS and food US within the context of a response-independent multiple schedule of reinforcement. Autoshaping was observed in the correlated group but not in the uncorrelated group. When the subjects in the uncorrelated condition were subsequently transferred to the correlated condition, they were observed to exhibit markedly suppressed asymptotic rates of keypecking, relative to those subjects who had experienced only the correlated condition. Thus, it appears that uncorrelated pretraining has an effect upon subsequent autoshaping and that the nature of the effect is similar to that observed in other Pavlovian procedures (cf. Kremer, 1971).

A similar type of interference with autoshaping has been reported by Mackintosh (1973). Mackintosh has noted that pigeons exposed to random presentations of a green-key CS and food US were subsequently profoundly retarded in the acquisition of autoshaping, requiring many more pairings of the green key and the food to establish reliable keypecking. Mackintosh's observations have been replicated by Wasserman et al. (1974) and are consistent with the observations of other investigators (cf. Bilbrey and Winokur, 1973). These experiments indicate that prior exposure to random presentations of a CS and a US retards the subsequent acquisition of autoshaping to that CS.

Hall and Honig (1974) have reported a similar type of retardation effect using a somewhat different procedure. In their experiment, pigeons were administered response-independent food reinforcement in the presence of diffuse green and red houselights. For one group of subjects, the presentation of food was correlated with the color of the houselight such that reinforcers were presented in only one component of a two-component multiple schedule, while, for the other group, the reinforcers were presented in an uncorrelated manner (i.e., food was presented in both components equally often). The subjects were subsequently tested for the acquisition of autoshaping in the presence of a neutral white houselight. These investigators observed that the acquisition of keypecking to the autoshaping CS was substantially retarded following the prolonged experience with uncorrelated houselight-CS–food-US presentations.

The pattern of results reported by Hall and Honig (1974) is important, for it indicates that the interference engendered by uncorrelated CS–US pretraining is *not specific* to the pretraining CS. That is, where Gamzu and Williams (1971, 1973), Mackintosh (1973), and Wasserman et al. (1974) reported that uncorrelated or random CS–US presentations proactively interfere with the acquisition of autoshaping to the pretraining CS, Hall and Honig's (1974) results indicate that such interference does not depend specifically on prior experience with the autoshaping CS.

The observation that the retardation effect in autoshaping is general and nonspecific was replicated by Tomie (1976a), who reported that the type of relationship between a given CS and the US during pretraining has a profound impact upon the subsequent acquisition of autoshaping to an alternative CS. In that study, a group of pigeons having extensive prior experience with randomly related tone-CS–food-US presentations, were observed to be retarded in the development of keypecking to a green-key autoshaping CS. Retardation effects were evaluated by means of control groups that received either no pretraining (original learning controls) or pretraining with forward pairings of the tone CS and the food US in a Pavlovian delay-conditioning procedure.

Tomie (1975) has replicated this pattern of results in a number of different experiments and has accumulated evidence that indicates that the physical characteristics of the randomly presented pretraining CS have no systematic effect on the magnitude of the subsequently observed retardation. That is, whether the randomly presented pretraining CS is a diffuse auditory stimulus (e.g., tone) or a localized visual stimulus (e.g., red light projected onto the response key), the subsequent effects of such pretraining upon the acquisition of autoshaping are identical. Thus, while nonspecific retardation effects are observed in autoshaping, they seem to be unrelated to the nature of the randomly presented pretraining CS.

Finally, to fully develop the parallel between the Pavlovian and autoshaping literatures in this matter, it appears that the debilitating effects on autoshaping of unpredictable US presentations during pretraining is not dependent on the use of a random pretraining CS. Engberg et al. (1972), Downing and Neuringer (1976), and Schwartz and Balsam (1979) have observed that the acquisition of autoshaping was retarded following extensive pretraining with intermittent, unsignaled US presentations.

In summary, the autoshaping literature indicates that the following pretraining manipulations involving unpredictable food proactively interfere with the acquisition of keypecking.

1. Uncorrelated relationship (nondifferential multiple VT–VT schedule) between the autoshaping CS and the US (Gamzu & Williams, 1971, 1973)
2. Random relationship between the autoshaping CS and the US (Mackintosh, 1973; Wasserman et al., 1974)
3. Uncorrelated relationship between a stimulus other than the autoshaping CS and the US (Hall & Honig, 1974)
4. Random relationship between a stimulus other than the autoshaping CS and the US (Tomie, 1975, 1976a, 1976b)
5. Intermittent, unsignaled US presentations (Downing & Neuringer, 1976; Engberg et al., 1972; Schwartz & Balsam, 1979).

THEORETICAL INTERPRETATIONS OF THE NEGATIVE TRANSFER EFFECT IN AUTOSHAPING

General Transfer of Training Interpretations

Several of these investigators have appealed to "general transfer of training" mechanisms to explain their data. For example, Mackintosh (1973) suggested that *learned irrelevance* may account for the retardation of autoshaping following exposure to a situation wherein the autoshaping CS is randomly related to the US. Hall and Honig (1974) suggested that a concept of *general inattentiveness* was demanded by the observation of retardation of autoshaping following uncorrelated houselight-food presentations. The concept of *learned laziness*, as an appetitive analogue to the instrumental aversive learned helplessness phenomenon (cf. Maier *et al.*, 1969) has been advocated by Engberg *et al.* (1972) in order to account for the deleterious effects of unsignaled response-independent reinforcement upon subsequent autoshaping.

Although each of these general transfer of training mechanisms can provide a reasonable account of the data to which they are addressed, each fails to provide a unified, integrated account of the alternative types of retardation that have been observed. For example, a learned irrelevance hypothesis suggests that during pretraining the subject learns that a *particular* CS bears no relationship to the US. This learning transfers to the autoshaping situation where it interferes with the learning of the CS–US association. This learned irrelevance hypothesis cannot explain the retardation of autoshaping following exposure to randomly related stimulus events when the pretraining CS and the test CS are *different* from one another. Furthermore, the learned irrelevance account offers no explanation of the retardation of autoshaping following extended US pre-exposure, where no CS is presented during pretraining.

The general inattentiveness position advocated by Hall and Honig (1974) states that uncorrelated CS–US relationships teach the subjects that stimuli are insignificant. The subjects consequently become generally less attentive to all stimuli, and this attentional deficit interferes with the acquisition of autoshaping. The general inattentiveness hypothesis does not predict the results obtained by Engberg *et al.* (1972), in which retardation is observed in the absence of prior experience with stimulus events other than the US. The learned laziness account is equally deficient. This hypothesis suggests that response-independent US pre-exposure teaches the subject that reinforcement is independent of the subject's behavior. This learning presumably produces a general associative deficit that transfers to the test situation and interferes with the acquisition of autoshaping. The learned laziness hypothesis fails to account for the fact that response-independent US pre-exposure per se is not sufficient to engender retardation of subsequent autoshaping. Hall and Honig (1974) and Tomie (1976a) have shown that training involving correlated CS–US presentations or forward CS–US pairings does not engender interference with subsequent autoshaping; yet, in each study subjects had extensive experience with response-independent US pre-exposure.

In summary, each of the different types of retardation effect that have been observed in autoshaping has prompted a somewhat different type of theoretical explanation. While the particulars of these accounts differ, they share the premise that the retarded acquisition of autoshaping is a general transfer of training effect and a by-product of the associative impairment engendered by pretraining wherein the US is unpredictable or uncontrollable. Although each of these explanations is consistent with the data from which it arose, no one of them can to provide an integrated, unified account of the alternative observations of retardation.

Context-Blocking Interpretation

Unfortunately, the transfer of training interpretations have not been extensively examined. Recent theoretical and empirical developments indicate that a more rigorous examination is warranted, for, alternative mechanisms of associative retardation have been identified. For example, using a conditioned suppression paradigm, Kamin (1969) demonstrated that conditioning to a novel CS is retarded if that novel CS is compounded with another CS_x that has been previously conditioned to the US. The phenomenon is called *blocking*, and related work has indicated that the magnitude of the blocking effect is directly related to the amount of CS_x conditioning that has preceded the introduction of the novel CS. Therefore, a blocking interpretation can account for differences in the acquisition of keypecking to the autoshaping CS if the key CS is compounded with a previously conditioned CS that is more highly conditioned in the groups that are retarded than in the groups that are not.

The blocking interpretation requires the identification of the blocking stimulus. A blocking stimulus must be (*a*) present during pretraining; (*b*) conditioned during pretraining; and (*c*) compounded with the lighted-key CS during autoshaping. The static, background, contextual stimuli of the conditioned environment fulfill these physical requirements. Furthermore, a growing body of literature indicates that the static, situational, contextual stimuli are conditioned as a function of being paired with the US (Chambers & Szakmary, 1979; Dweck & Wagner, 1970; Kremer, 1974; Olding-Smee, 1975a, 1975b, 1978; Schwartz & Balsam, 1979; Sheafor, 1975; Siegel, 1976; Tomie, 1975, 1976a, 1976b; Welker, Tomie, Davitt, & Thomas, 1974). Furthermore, Welker *et al.* (1974) have established that contextual stimuli can block the acquisition of control by a localized visual (lighted-key) CS, and Olding-Smee (1975a) has presented evidence that indicates that the degree to which the context is conditioned is inversely related to the correlation between a discrete CS and the US. That is, the context is conditioned as a function of its being paired with the US unless its effect is overshadowed by more reliable predictors of the US (cf. Wagner, 1969). Finally, recent theoretical formulations of Pavlovian conditioning suggest that the procedures that produce the retardation of autoshaping are precisely those procedures that favor the development of relatively strong context conditioning (Rescorla & Wagner, 1972).

Recent experiments on autoshaping (Blanchard & Honig, 1976; Tomie, 1976a, 1976b) lend support to a context-blocking analysis of the retardation phenomenon. Blanchard and Honig (1976) demonstrated that the speed of acquisition of autoshaping was inversely related to the degree to which the background stimuli present during autoshaping were previously associated with the US. That is, autoshaping was retarded when administered in the presence of a form CS+ for food, relative to when administered in the presence of either a former CS− or a novel CS. Their results indicate that autoshaping may be blocked by embedding the CS used in autoshaping within a nonlocalized, background CS that has been paired extensively with the US. Their experiment provides support for a context-blocking analysis in that it demonstrates that the background stimuli present during the administration of autoshaping can function as effective blocking stimuli in an autoshaping procedure.

Further support for a context-blocking analysis is provided by Tomie (1976a), who found that the retardation of autoshaping following pretraining with unpredicatable US presentations is a context-specific phenomenon. Tomie (1976a) replicated the observation that the acquisition of autoshaping is retarded following experience with uncorrelated or random CS–US presentations (Hall & Honig, 1974). A context-blocking interpretation of these results was suggested by the observation that the retardation effect was eliminated when pretraining and testing were administered in the presence of different contextual stimuli. That is, changing the context between pretraining and testing alleviated the retardation effect.

The contextual specificity of the retardation effect has been observed in a number of different experiments utilizing a wide range of pretraining CS values (Tomie, 1975, 1976b). Additional support for a context-blocking analysis of this pattern of result is provided by the observation that the contextual influence can be extinguished by nonreinforced presentations of the context (Tomie, 1976b, Experiment 2), and that contextual stimuli can block the acquisition of autoshaping when redundantly paired with the visual key CS during the test for the acquisition of autoshaping (Tomie, 1976b, Experiment 3).

In summary, two different types of hypotheses have been put forth to account for the retardation of autoshaping following a number of different types of pretraining. General transfer of training accounts argue that some aspect of the pretraining procedure teaches the subject that the US is "unpredictable." This learning transfers to the autoshaping task and proactively interferes with the development of the CS–US association, which is reflected in the retardation of autoshaping. The context-blocking hypothesis also assumes that the retardation of the learning of the CS–US relationship is responsible for the observed retardation; however, the context-blocking hypothesis ascribes the locus of that retardation to the prior conditioning of contextual CSs with which the autoshaping CS is compounded during the test.

EXPERIMENTAL ANALYSIS OF THE CONTEXT-BLOCKING HYPOTHESIS

Effects of a Context Change on the Negative Transfer Effect

The context-blocking hypothesis predicts that exposure during pretraining to unpredictable US presentations will retard the acquisition of subsequent autoshaping and that the retardation will be alleviated to the degree that a context change is implemented between pretraining and testing. The following experiments investigate the effects of a context change upon autoshaping following different pretraining regimes that expose the subject to unpredictable US presentations.

In all experiments groups of pigeons ($N = 8$ or 12) were tested for the acquisition of autoshaping using standard Pavlovian delay-conditioning trials. The CS consisted of the illumination of the response key by a light of 555 nm for 6.0 or 7.5 sec; the US consisted of presentation of pigeon grain for 3.0 or 4.0 seconds. The interstimulus interval was equal to the CS duration. The test was administered in an illuminated, unlined chamber (see Tomie, 1976b for a description of the apparatus). Subjects in the context change conditions were pretrained in an unilluminated, cardboard or masonite liner built to fit the full inside dimensions of the chamber. Apertures were cut in the liners to accommodate the pecking key, grain hopper, and speaker grill. Masking noise was provided either by the use of a Grason–Stadler model 1724 Noise Generator or by the running of exhaust fans. White noise was used only in conjunction with the unlined chambers.

General Inattentiveness Effect

The context specificity of the general inattentiveness effect was assessed by comparing autoshaping acquisition in two groups of subjects receiving 10 days of pretraining involving random presentations of a vertical-line CS and a food US, (vertical-line truly random control group, or ϕ TRC). The CS consisted of a vertical white line which bisected an otherwise dark response key. The US consisted of 4.0 sec of access to a tray of mixed pigeon grain. In each of 30 daily sessions, 60 US presentations and a comparable number of CS presentations were administered. Stimulus events were presented in accordance with a VT 45-sec schedule in both pretraining and in testing. An original-learning control group (OLC) was trained to approach and eat from the hopper (approximately 50 feedings) on the day immediately preceding the first day of testing for autoshaping.

Figure 6.1 presents the mean acquisition functions for each of the four groups of subjects. The figure reveals that subjects in the ϕ TRC–no context change condition were retarded in the acquisition of autoshaping relative to both the OLC–no context change and the ϕ TRC–context change groups. These observations are confirmed by two-group mixed-design analysis of variance (alpha = .05). These findings indicate that pretraining involving random presentations of CS1 and the US subsequently retards the acquisition of conditioning when CS2 and the US are paired. The deleterious effects of such pretraining, however, are alleviated when a context change is introduced with the initiation of the autoshaping test.

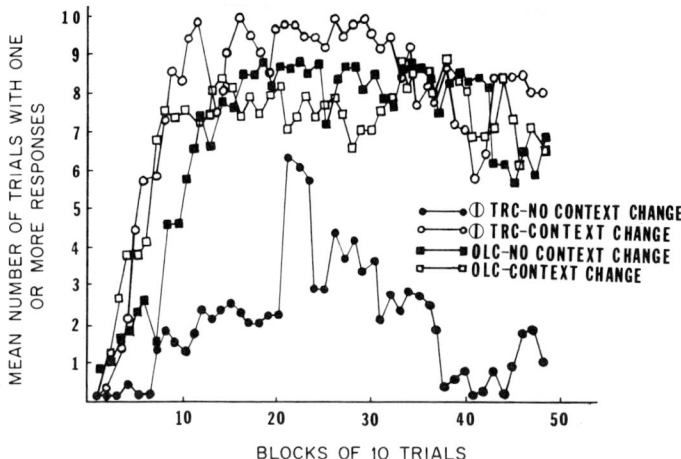

Figure 6.1. Mean number of trials with one or more responses as a function of 10 trial blocks for φ TRC–no context change, φ TRC–context change, OLC–no context change, and OLC–context change groups.

A second experiment was performed that utilized 30 rather than 10 days of φ truly random control pretraining. The expectation that increasing the duration of pretraining would enhance the magnitude of the retardation effect was not confirmed. As can be seen from Figure 6.2, the φ TRC–no context change group is not retarded in the acquisition of autoshaping. Analysis of variance revealed a significant three-way interaction between type of pretraining, context treatment, and trials; however, this effect is undoubtedly attributable to the breakdown in automaintenance by subjects in the φ TRC–no context change group, since no differences in rate of acquisition are discernible.

In summary, it appears that the acquisition of autoshaping is retarded following 10 days of general inattentiveness pretraining but that the effect is virtually eliminated when the pretraining is extended to 30 days. This result is unexpected and equally embarassing to both theoretical formulations. The breakdown in automaintenance by subjects in the φ TRC–no context change group is also unexpected but perhaps more easily reconciled. Suppressed levels of automaintenance following pretraining with unpredictable food has been reported by Gamzu and Williams (1971, 1973); however, in this case subjects who have previously acquired the response are observed to cease responding temporarily, for large numbers of trials. The experiment was run in three successive replications of four subjects each; therefore, the disruption in asymptotic performance is not reaily attributable to extra-experimental factors.

One possible interpretation relies on the premise that instrumental factors are more intrusive in automaintenance than autoshaping (cf. Schwartz, Reisberg, &

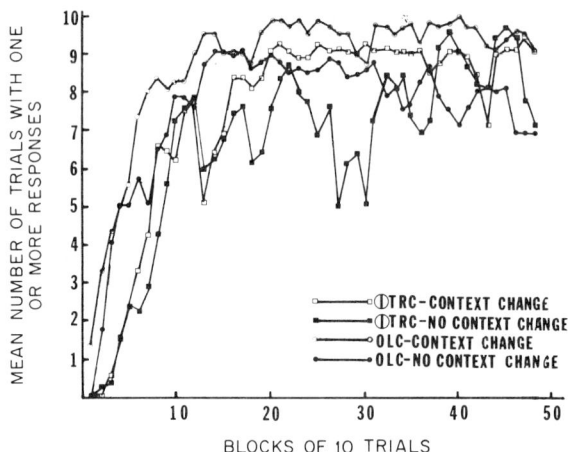

Figure 6.2. Mean number of trials with one or more responses as a function of 10 trial blocks for ϕ TRC change, ϕ TRC–no context change, OLC–context change, and OLC–no context change groups.

Vollmecke, 1974; Williams & Williams, 1969). It is conceivable that the temporal contiguity between the keypeck response and food establishes the behavior as an instrumental response, and that this instrumental acquisition process is hindered by extended pretraining with unpredictable food. Such pretraining might be expected to generate superstitious patterns of behavior that are more well-established following 30 as compared to 10 days of pretraining (cf. Staddon & Simmelhag, 1971). The superstitiously maintained competing response may influence automaintenance but not autoshaping. There are data that indicate that competing instrumental responses do not interfere appreciably with the acquisition of autoshaping (cf. Engberg et al., 1972; LoLordo, McMillan, & Riley, 1974; Schwartz et al., 1974; moreover, their deleterious effects on the maintenance of the keypeck response seem to be more impressive (Schwartz et al., 1974; Schwartz & Williams, 1972).

Learned Laziness Effect

The US only pretraining manipulation has been shown to retard the acquisition of autoshaping (Downing & Neuringer, 1976; Engberg et al. 1972; Schwartz & Balsam, 1979; Tomie, 1976b, Experiment 2). In order to ascertain whether this retardation effect is alleviated by a change in the context, a 2 × 2 factorial experiment was executed with two levels of pretraining (US only versus OLC) and two levels of context treatment (context change versus no context change). Subjects in the US only groups received 30 daily sessions of pretraining (30 USs/session) with unsignaled US presentations administered according to a VT 30-sec schedule.

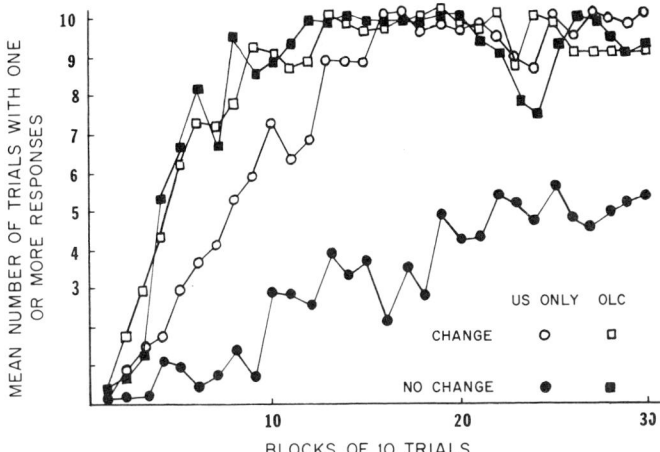

Figure 6.3. Mean number of trials with one or more responses as a function of 10 trial blocks for US only–no context change, US only–context change, OLC–no context change, and OLC–context change groups.

The mean acquisition functions for each of the four groups of subjects are presented in Figure 6.3. The figure reveals that subjects in the US only–no context change condition are retarded in the acquisition of autoshaping relative to the remaining three groups. This observation is confirmed by a three-way mixed-design analysis of variance that reveals a reliable three-way interaction, indicating that the effect of pretraining on acquisition varies with context treatment. There is a small context effect in the original learning control condition, indicating that perhaps some context conditioning is established by the 50 US presentations administered during hopper training; however, the effect is not statistically reliable.

Figure 6.4 presents mean acquisition functions for a similar experiment which differs from the previous experiment in the following ways: (*a*) Trials during pretraining and testing were presented in accordance with a VT 45-sec schedule, (*b*) US only subjects were administered 60 trials per session for 30 sessions, and (*c*) OLC subjects were tested for autoshaping immediately following successful hopper training (defined as five consecutive US presentations during which the pigeon feeds from the hopper). The figure and the statistical analyses support the same conclusions as those of the previous experiment. Retarded acquisition is observed in the US only–no context change group but not in the US only–context change group.

Insofar as between-experiment comparisons may be useful, it should be noted that acquisition by the original learning control groups is faster under the VT 45-sec schedule than under the VT 30-sec schedule. This difference is maintained in the US only conditions and is expected based on data from parametric

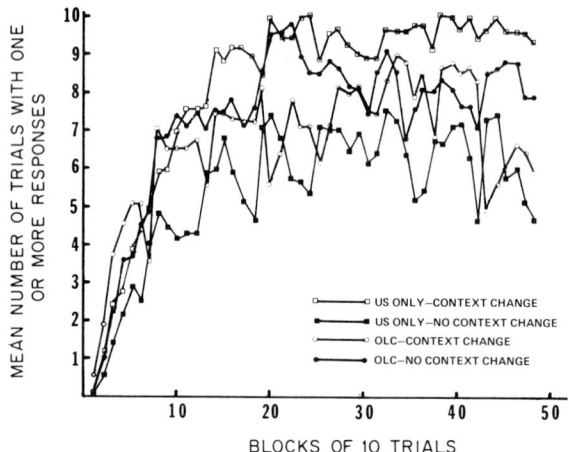

Figure 6.4. Mean number of trials with one or more responses as a function of 10 trial blocks for US only–context change, US only–no context change, OLC–context change, and OLC–no context change groups.

investigations of intertrial interval effects in autoshaping (Terrace, Gibbon, Farrell, & Baldock, 1975). Furthermore, one might expect the context to be more highly conditioned during pretraining by a VT 30-sec schedule and thus to exercise a larger blocking effect. It should also be noted that the nonsignificant context effect in the original learning control condition observed in Figure 6.3 is absent in Figure 6.4 and that perhaps this discrepancy may be attributable to the difference in the number of US presentations administered following successful hopper training.

Learned Irrelevance Effect

Pretraining involving random presentations of a CS and US subsequently retards the acquisition of autoshaping to that CS (Bilbrey & Winokur, 1973; Mackintosh, 1973; Wasserman *et al.*, 1974. In order to determine whether this stimulus-specific retardation effect is constrained by the context manipulation, the acquisition functions of four groups of subjects arranged in a pretraining-by-context 2 × 2 factorial design were compared (see Figure 6.5). Subjects in the G TRC group received 30 days of learned irrelevance pretraining. Each daily session consisted of 60 US presentations and a comparable number of CS presentations programmed according to independent VT 45-sec schedules. The OLC groups are those presented in Figure 6.4.

The figure reveals that both G TRC groups are retarded in the acquisition of autoshaping relative to the OLC groups and that the effect is more impressive in the no context change condition. Three-way mixed-design analysis of variance

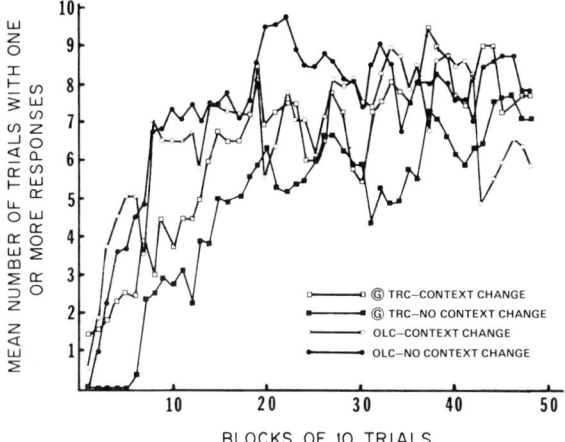

Figure 6.5. Mean number of trials with one or more responses as a function of 10 trial blocks for G TRC–context change, G TRC–no context change, OLC–context change, OLC–no context change groups.

revealed significant main effects of pretreatment and context but neither a reliable pretreatment-by-context interaction or three-way interaction.

The data confirm the observation that learned irrelevance pretraining retards the acquisition of subsequent autoshaping; however, the alleviation of the retardation effect by changing the context seems to be less complete than in the other experiments, indicating that stimulus-specific retardation effects are, perhaps, not entirely attributable to contextual considerations. On the other hand, the residual retardation that survives the context change is not particularly impressive and is not statistically reliable (i.e., groups G TRC–context change and OLC–context change do not differ reliably).

To summarize to this point, it appears that three different types of pretraining procedures that expose the subject to unpredictable food generally retard the acquisition of subsequent autoshaping. Furthermore, the retardation effects are either entirely or partially alleviated by changing the context between pretraining and testing. These results are predicted directly from a context-blocking analysis, and, at the very least, they question the generality of the applicability of the general transfer notion. It is important to note that the context-conditioning analysis does not argue that cognitive, general transfer effects do not exist but only that previous demonstrations of such effects confound considerations based on context conditioning and that future experiments should include appropriate manipulations to control for possible contextual influences. One might ask how general transfer of training interpretations would account for the context effect. The accommodation may be relatively simple and straightforward. It is conceivable that the contextual stimuli may act as retrieval cues for the memory of what was learned during pretraining. That is, learning that food is unpredictable may have occurred, but the influence of such learning is not observed owing to the absence of appropriate retrieval cues. The cognition may be present but inoperative because it is unretrievable. The effectiveness of contextual stimuli as retrieval cues in conditioning–memory experiments has been impressively documented (Hickis, Robles, and Thomas, 1977; Miller, 1972; Spear, 1971, 1973); however, the accommodation is post hoc and depends on the attachment of contextual retrieval cues to the memory of higher-order cognitions rather than on simple response tendencies.

The following experiment may indicate that the general inattentiveness effect is also capable of surviving a context shift. A group of pigeons ($N = 8$) was given 18 days of pretraining involving random presentations of six different CS values and the US (MULT CS TRC group). The six different CSs were a red keylight, a vertical white line on the response key, tones of 200 Hz, 1000 Hz, 9500 Hz, and white noise. Only one CS was used per session, and each of the six CSs was utilized three times in a randomized sequence. Pretraining was administered in the lined chambers, and testing for autoshaping to a green-key CS was conducted in the unlined chambers.

The mean acquisition functions for the MULT CS TRC group and three control groups (US only, CS only, OLC) are presented in Figure 6.6. The figure reveals that the MULT CS TRC group is retarded in the acquisition of autoshaping relative to the other groups, despite the implementation of a context change. The data suggest that perhaps subjects are capable of learning that CSs are

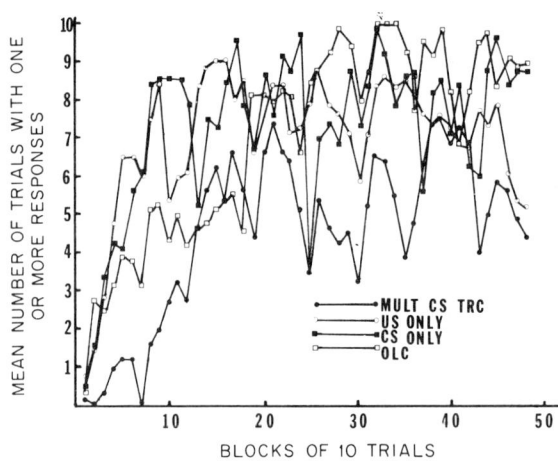

Figure 6.6. Mean number of trials with one or more responses as a function of 10 trial blocks for MULT CS TRC, US only, CS only, and OLC groups.

unrelated to USs, but that such a cognitive set is engendered only after repeated experience with a number of different pretraining CS values.

Effects of Nonreinforced Pre-exposure to the Context

The context-conditioning interpretation of the retardation effect specifies that the contextual influence is derived from straight-forward conditioning considerations. The preceding experiments provide considerable data that are consistent with the notion that the context is conditioned as a function of being paired with the US. If the contextual influence is a by-product of conditioning, one ought to be able to attenuate the contextual influence by extinguishing the context either before (latent inhibition procedure) or after (extinction procedure) the pretraining phase. Tomie (1976b, Experiment 2) has reported that the retardation effect is alleviated by inserting two sessions of context extinction between pretraining and testing, and preliminary data indicate that autoshaping is facilitated when 10 sessions of nonreinforced pre-exposure to the context is administered prior to US only pretraining (see Figure 6.7).

Effects of US on Response Elimination and Reacquisition

Additional support for a context-conditioning analysis comes from data collected on the elimination of autoshaping. Twenty-four pigeons received 12 days of autoshaping with a green-key CS. The subjects were divided into three groups matched for acquisition rate and frequency of asymptotic responding. On Day

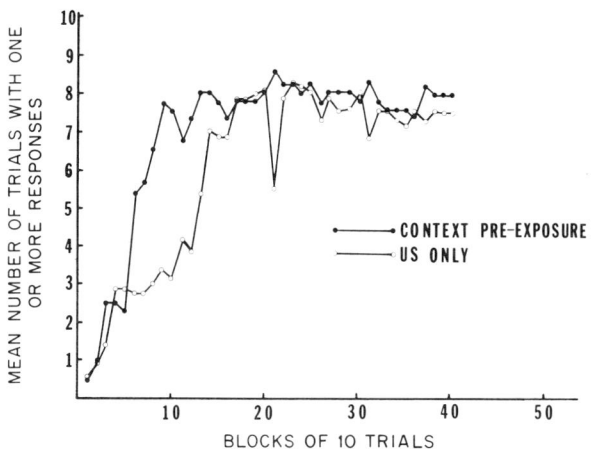

Figure 6.7. Mean number of trials with one or more responses as a function of 10 trial blocks for context pre-exposure and US only groups.

11, subjects in the CS extinction group received the first of five sessions of training wherein the CS was presented and nonreinforced. Subjects in the backward conditioning group received backward conditioning trials, while subjects in the TRC group received randomly related presentations of the CS and the US. Following five sessions of training all subjects were given a test for the reacquisition of autoshaping in which the CS was a vertical white line projected onto the response key.

The mean number of trials to attain a response elimination criterion of nonresponding for five consecutive presentations of the CS is presented in Figure 6.8a. As can be seen from the panel, the CS extinction group required approximately twice as many trials to attain the response elimination criterion as did the other two groups.

One might argue that the more rapid elimination of responding in the backward conditioning group is attributable to the antagonistic influence of inhibitory strength accrued to the backward CS. The argument seems persuasive. There is considerable experimental evidence in the Pavlovian conditioning literature that backward conditioning produces associative inhibition as assessed in retardation (cf. Siegel & Domjan, 1971) and summation (cf. Moscovitch & LoLordo, 1968) test procedures. The retardation test of inhibition is predicated on the assumption that inhibition may be assessed by the retardation of excitation. It seems reasonable to suggest that the accrual of inhibition during exposure to a suspected inhibitory preparation (i.e., backward conditioning) may be assessed by the dissipation of excitation (indexed by the elimination of the CR). That is, the more rapid elimination of responding in the backward conditioning group may be a function of inhibition produced by that procedure. The supposition that the interaction between excitation and inhibition would be algebraically symmetrical is reasonable and would account for the backward versus CS extinction dif-

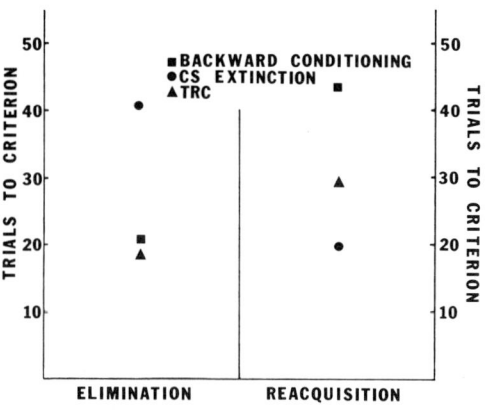

Figure 6.8. (Left panel) Mean number of trials to attain a response-elimination criterion of nonresponding for five consecutive trials. (Right panel) Mean number of trials to attain a criterion of responding on five consecutive trials.

ference; however, the TRC versus CS extinction difference cannot be explained by reference to differences in inhibition.

A more parsimonious interpretation relies on the assumption that the context is conditioned when paired with the US in the response elimination phase. Both the truly random control and backward conditioning groups cease responding at approximately the same rate and faster than the CS extinction group, and both groups experience unsignaled US presentations at that time. If the unsignaled US presentations condition the context, then the CS is compounded with the excitatory context and nonreinforced. It has been demonstrated that the decrement in excitatory associative strength suffered by a CS is proportional to the excitatory value of alternative CSs with which the CS is compounded and nonreinforced (Wagner, 1969). Therefore, one may attribute the resistance to response elimination exhibited by the CS extinction group to the fact that the CS is compounded with a weakly excitatory context (a context that is not paired with an unsignaled US).

The reacquisition data are presented in Figure 6.8b. The figure reveals that the CS extinction group reqcquires the response the most rapidly, followed by the truly random control and backward conditioning groups. These differences may be taken to reflect differences in the excitatory strength of the context at the end of the response elimination phase of the experiment. That is, the groups that experience unsignaled US presentations during response elimination (i.e., backward conditioning and TRC groups) may be retarded in reacquiring the autoshaping response due to the blocking influence of the context. The CS extinction group does not experience context–US pairings during response elimination; therefore, the context should become extinguished and less capable of exerting a blocking influence in the reacquisition test.

The reacquisition data are certainly consistent with the notion that unsignaled US presentations promote excitatory conditioning of the context that subsequently blocks conditioning to a novel CS within that context. Moreover, the replication of the retardation effect in a reacquisition test is difficult to reconcile with cognitive positions. All subjects have a common history of previous autoshaping during initial acquisition that, ostensibly, not only should provide all subjects with common cognitions (i.e., key illumination predicts food) but also might be expected to provide "immunization" against the deleterious effects of cognitive associative interference.

The reacquisition effect is important in still another regard. The reacquisition data are, not surprisingly, less subject to the variability (often extreme) observed in the initial acquisition of autoshaping. It seems reasonable to surmise that perhaps the reacquisition data provide a cleaner assessment of the accrual of associative strength by the autoshaping CS than do the initial acquisition data, which are subject to greater contamination by performance factors. That is, for the subject who has acquired the response previously, reacquisition is more likely to reflect the learning of the CS–US relationship independently of the learning of the mechanistic performance attributes of the consummatory keypeck CR. There is considerable experimental evidence (cf. Wasserman et al., 1974) that the initial acquisition of autoshaping does not accurately reflect the learning of the CS–US association in that the acquisition of approach behavior is not necessarily correlated with the acquisition of keypecking.

Context-Induced Facilitation of Conditioning

So far I have limited my evaluation of the contextual influence to the analysis of its retarding properties. The notion that the contextual influence is associative suggests several alternative modes of inquiry that might successfully divorce the context from its retarding tendencies. For example, one might assess the effects of unpredictable US pre-exposure on the acquisition of inhibition rather than excitation. The context-conditioning hypothesis would predict facilitation in an inhibitory transfer test. Unfortunately, neither the Pavlovian literature (cf. Baker & Mackintosh, 1977) nor the results of a pilot experiment conducted in my laboratory are sympathetic or supportive of this prediction.

Other tactics employed to provoke context-induced facilitation have yielded equally unencouraging results. For example, one might expect to facilitate the acquisition of autoshaping by establishing the context as an inhibitor during pretraining prior to the autoshaping test. Presumably the context can be made inhibitory by nonreinforcing the context when it is compounded with a previously established signal for food (1000-Hz tone reliably paired with food in a different apparatus); however, facilitation of subsequent autoshaping in the "inhibitory" context was not observed. It appears that context-induced facilitation of acquisition is an elusive and as yet undocumented phenomenon. Whether the difficulties encountered in this regard are attributable to a genuine asymmetry in the nature of contextual influence or to alternative considerations (such as the asymmetrical involvement of perhaps tenuous or ephemeral inhibitory mediators) remains to be determined.

Auditory Stimuli and Distribution of Trials as Context CSs

Auditory Stimuli

The context-conditioning analysis of the retardation effect specifies that the contextual influence is expressed through a Pavlovian blocking mechanism. It is important to note that not all interpretations of the retardation effect attribute the locus of the interference effect to Pavlovian factors. An alternative type of interpretation proposes that subjects exposed to unpredictable US occurrences do not autoshape readily because the prolonged intermittent US pre-exposure has instrumentally reinforced superstitious patterns of motor behavior that are topographically incompatible with the keypeck response (cf. Gamzu, 1971; Gamzu, Williams, & Schwartz, 1973; Schwartz et al., 1974; Wasserman, 1972). To determine whether the retardation effect is attributable to blocking by contextual stimuli or interference by competing responses, it is necessary to implement an independent variable that would differentiate among the two mechanisms.

The straightforward manipulation of the context itself, as performed in previously discussed experiments, provides relatively ineffective leverage. This is because the consistent administration of the test for autoshaping in the unlined chambers has resulted in the uniform confounding of the context change with the locus of pretraining. Thus, context change groups were uniformly pretrained in the lined chambers and no context change groups were uniformly pretrained in the unlined chambers. Since the pigeons are observed to remain relatively stationary in the unilluminated liners, they are less likely to develop active operants that are topographically incompatible with the performance of keypecking when pretrained in those liners.

Experimental attempts to counterbalance this design by testing for autoshaping in the lined chambers have been unsuccessful (see Tomie, 1976b), owing to the failure of the majority of the subjects to autoshape under such conditions. Wasserman (1973) has suggested that the absence of illumination (as in the lined environment) reduces the *localized* signal characteristics of the key CS, an effect that is important in autoshaping.

If the absence of illumination in the lined environment is responsible for the failure to observe autoshaping within that environment, one may properly counterbalance the experimental design by manipulating only the auditory (or other nonvisual) aspects of the context. That is, one can separate the effects of pretraining locus from the effects of a context change by factorially combining tone and no-tone context conditions with pretraining and testing conditions.

Four groups of pigeons were administered 30 days of US only pretraining and tested for autoshaping to a green-key CS. The groups were arranged in a 2 × 2 factorial design with two levels of pretraining context (tone versus no tone) and two levels of test context (tone versus no tone). The entire experiment was conducted in the unlined chambers without masking noise.

The mean acquisition functions for each of the four groups of subjects are presented in Figure 6.9. The figure reveals that a retardation effect is established by the tone in pretraining but that the retardation is alleviated by testing in the absence of the tone (a tone–context effect); however, no retardation effect is produced by the no tone pretraining conditioning. The failure to obtain retardation when subjects are trained and tested in the absence of the tone is surprising in one sense and not surprising in another. Previously published experiments have shown that maintaining contextual conditions between pretraining and testing retards the acquisition of autoshaping. Those contextual conditions have

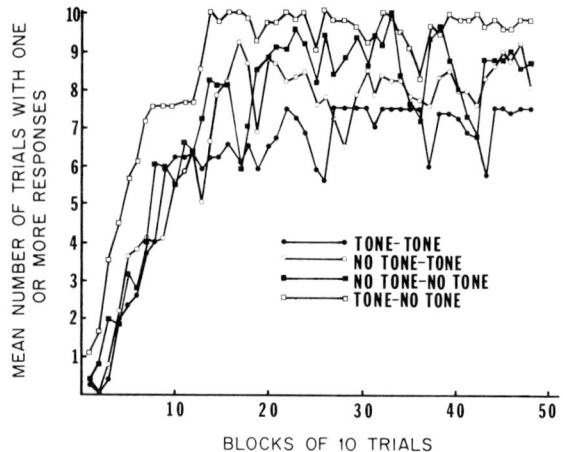

Figure 6.9. Mean number of trials with one or more responses as a function of 10 trial blocks for tone–tone, no tone–tone, no tone–no tone, and tone–no tone groups.

always included a distinct auditory component (i.e., presence of masking noise) whose presence has covaried with the presence of the liners. In the present experiment the retardation effect is observed only when a distinct auditory component is present in both pretraining and testing, indicating that the absence of tone does not function as an effective contextual stimulus. It is worth noting that the tone is a distinctive stimulus unique to the conditioning environment, whereas on the other hand, the absence of tone is experienced by the subjects outside the experimental setting, and it is therefore less strictly correlated with food. The inability of the visual, tactile, olfactory, etc., context to maintain the retardation effect without auditory support is perhaps indicative of the dominant role of auditory stimulation in context conditioning. It is also surprising. The observation that the retardation effect is dependent upon a distinctive auditory context has been replicated in my laboratory in an independent experiment and implies that auditory-food associations are important sources of control over the behavior of the pigeon. This implication, incidentally, is contrary to the spirit of the literature, which tends to suggest that auditory stimuli are difficult to establish as signals for food (Foree & LoLordo, 1973; Powell, 1973).

The attenuation of the retardation effect in the tone–no tone group indicates that the absence of illumination in the context change pretraining locus is not a necessary condition for the alleviation effect. This is particularly important since it eliminates a point of accommodation for the competing response interpretation. That is, it now seems unlikely that the systematic failures to observe retardation despite exposure to unpredictable food (as in the context change groups) can be attributed to the inactivity of birds pretrained in unilluminated liners. These data thereby encumber the competing response interpretation with the considerable task of providing an explanation of the context effect without recourse to this notion. I prefer this mode of challenge, rather than to go about manipulating culprit responses since competing-response interpretations have proliferated for decades and have a convincing history of resiliency predicated on ubiquity and ambiguity.

Distribution of Trials

The identification of the contextual stimuli that are responsible for the retardation effect was further pursued in the following experiment. Four groups of pigeons were tested for autoshaping to a green-key CS following 30 days of US only pretraining. The groups were arranged in a 2 × 2 factorial design with two levels of test schedule (VT 30-sec versus VT 90-sec) and two levels of test schedule (VT 30-sec versus VT 90-sec). The entire experiment was run in the unlined chambers. The distribution of trials generated by the schedule parameter is a contextual stimulus that has been invariant in previous experiments. There is considerable experimental evidence (cf. Sheffield, 1949) that trial distribution is an effectively conditioned stimulus event when control is assessed in transfer designs, and such an effect would presumably be manifested as a criss-cross interaction (comparing groups that maintain the same schedule across pretraining and testing with groups that receive different schedules) in the 2 × 2 factorial.

The mean number of trials to attain a criterion of responding on five consecutive trials for each of the four groups of subjects is presented in Figure 6.10. The figure reveals a main effect of test schedule parameter such that subjects tested under the VT 90-sec schedule autoshape faster than subjects tested under the VT 30-sec schedule. This observation is consistent with previous parametric investigations of intertrial interval effects in autoshaping (Terrace *et al.*, 1975) and follows from recent theoretical formulations of Pavlovian conditioning (Gibbon,

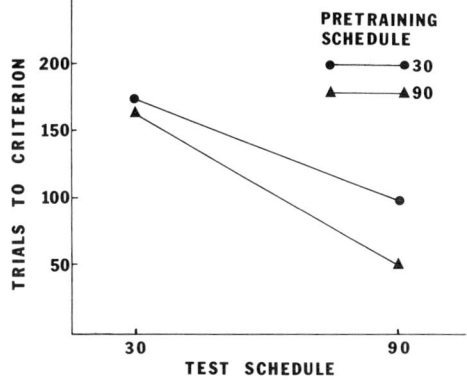

Figure 6.10. Mean number of trials to attain a criterion of responding on five consecutive trials for VT 30–VT 30, VT 30–VT 90, VT 90–VT 30, and VT 90–VT 90 groups.

1977; Rescorla & Wagner, 1972). There is very little indication of a main effect of pretraining schedule parameter or of a criss-cross interaction between the two variables. The groups that receive the same schedule parameter in both pretraining and testing are observed to autoshape at least as fast as those that receive a change in the distribution of trials between pretraining and testing. It, therefore, appears to be the case that the trial distribution variable does not function as a potent contextual stimulus since retardation is not alleviated by altering the distribution of trials between pretraining and testing.

Effects of Blocking Manipulations in Autoshaping

Unblocking

The context-blocking analysis specifies that the retardation effect is attributable to a Pavlovian blocking mechanism. It therefore follows that procedures known to influence blocking should modulate the magnitude of the retardation effect. Kamin (1969) has reported that blocking may be alleviated by increasing the magnitude of the US between pretraining and compound conditioning. The unblocking of the retardation effect has been unsuccessfully pursued in my laboratory. That is, increasing the duration of the hopper presentation from 3.0 to 7.5 sec between US only pretraining and testing for autoshaping has impressively failed to alleviate retardation. In fact, such subjects are at least as retarded in the acquisition of autoshaping as subjects who received 3.0 sec of hopper availability throughout the experiment. Moreover, a modification of this procedure employing two consecutive 3.0-sec hopper presentations with the initiation of testing for autoshaping has also failed to provide any evidence of an unblocking effect.

Blocking by Compounded Visual-Key Stimuli

As a further embarassment to the blocking aspect of the context-blocking analysis, demonstrations of blocking in autoshaping have uniformly utilized nonlocalized, off-key stimuli (cf. Blanchard & Honig, 1976; Schwartz and Balsam, 1979; Straub & Gibbon, 1977; Tomie, 1976b, Experiment 3), and demonstrations of blocking using visual stimuli compounded on the response key are conspicuously absent from the autoshaping literature. No evidence for blocking by compounded visual key stimuli has been observed in any of four separately conducted experiments in my laboratory.

In the initial experiment, subjects were autoshaped to a green CS for 10 days and then administered five sessions of compound conditioning (compound consisted of a green CS with a superimposed vertical-white-line CS). Reinforced presentations of the vertical-line CS generally yielded high rates of response on the very first test trials. Even subjects who exhibited disruption of responding generally showed full recovery of responding by the third test trial, and there were no indications of differences between subjects in the blocking group and control subjects who were not run in the initial phase of the experiment.

A similar experiment that differed only in that testing for control by the vertical-white-line CS was conducted in extinction revealed both high rates of responding on the first test trial and no between groups differences in resistance to extinction. Efforts to suppress control by the simple onset of key illumination were implemented by administering discriminative Pavlovian conditioning procedures prior to testing; however, this tactic was unsuccessful in either eliminating responding on the early test trials or producing group differences in resistance to extinction.

Reducing the number of compound conditioning trials to 10 (minimum number of trials required to recover asymptotic levels of responding in the majority of subjects) was also ineffective in reducing responding on the first test trial. The inescapable conclusion seems to be that blocking of a visual CS projected onto the response key by another previously conditioned visual CS projected onto the response key is not readily observed. Whether this difficulty is attributable to the selection of inappropriate parameters, the "preparedness" of the autoshaping response, or the intrusion of instrumental factors that mask blocking in autoshaping is left to conjecture.

IMPLICATIONS

The data reported here are consistent with the autoshaping literature and largely sympathetic to predictions forthcoming from a context-blocking interpretation of the retardation effect. The alleviation of retardation by both the context-change manipulation and the context pre-exposure manipulation is neither easily reconciled nor directly predicted by either general transfer of training or competing response interpretations. The effects of unsignaled US presentations on the elimination and reacquisition of autoshaping is also readily understood in terms of context conditioning, consistent with the Pavlovian literature (cf. Frey & Butler, 1977) and not readily reconciled with alternative formulations of the retardation effect.

The data presented here also reveal certain weaknesses of the context analysis. The incomplete alleviation of retardation in context change groups presents problems of interpretation. Is residual retardation to be taken to indicate the presence of another operative (e.g., cognitions or competing responses), or is it due to the incompleteness of the context manipulation itself? One cannot possibly change everything, and, to the degree that one fails to do so, residual context blocking may be expected.

There are other problems as well. The associative nature of the contextual influence is challenged by the asymmetry of its effectiveness in supporting both retardation and facilitation effects. This observation, in turn, provokes the conjecture that, perhaps, "sameness" or lack of change can only retard autoshaping. The disquieting extrapolation toward a primitive, nonassociative, arousal mechanism is obvious. The most perplexing problem, however, resides in the conspicuous lack of congruence between the known properties of the Pavlovian blocking phenomenon and the dynamics of "blocking" in autoshaping. The failure to observe unblocking combined with the elusiveness of on-key blocking in autoshaping make it impossible to profile the contextual influence adequately in a blocking framework and difficult to maintain that it is reasonable to attempt to do so.

Despite these considerations, the support provided by these data for the contest-blocking interpretation of retardation in autoshaping is considerable and raises the question of whether the context blocking analysis has application outside the realm of autoshaping. The possibilities and implications are numerous, for transfer designs are commonly used in learning research and context manipulations are rarely included. Obviously, retarded acquisition of Pavlovian conditioning (cf. Chambers & Szakmary, 1979; Kremer, 1971; Mis & Moore, 1973; Seligman, 1968) following exposure to unpredictable US presentations is subject to reinterpretation as context blocking. It is interesting that Seligman (1968) reported great difficulty in reestablishing baseline rates of free-operant lever-pressing following exposure to unpredictable shock in an on-the-baseline CER procedure. He interpreted this disruption as evidence for chronic fear due to the absence of a reliable predictor of shock. The context-blocking analysis suggests that chronic fear is not produced by the absence of a predictive CS, but by the presence of an excitatory one. The negative transfer effect that Seligman subsequently observed may be attributable to the blocking influence of previously conditioned contextual CSs in the subsequent on-the-baseline conditioned emotional response acquisition test.

The context-blocking analysis may also be extended to negative transfer effects documented in the realm of free-operant discrimination learning. Consider, for example, the following experiment performed by Eck, Noel, and Thomas (1969). In that experiment, groups of pigeons were tested for the acquisition of a successive discrimination involving two wavelengths in a free-operant keypeck situation. The groups were differentiated only on the basis of the nature of the training they received prior to the test for discrimination acquisition. One group was given pretraining on an orthogonal successive discrimination involving two different line angles (differential or correlated condition), while a second group was given a similar amount of training with the same line angle except that reinforcers were delivered equally often in the presence of S1 and S2 (nondifferential or uncorrelated condition). The latter group was found to be retarded in the acquisition of the wavelength discrimination transfer task. These investigators attributed this difference to the development of a general set to either attend to or ignore stimulus differences. A set of general attentiveness or of general inattentiveness is presumably engendered by pretraining wherein the discriminative stimuli and the reinforcer are correlated or uncorrelated, respectively. Similar types of retardation effects have been reported in the free-operant transfer literature (cf. Eck & Thomas, 1970; Thomas, Miller, & Svinicki, 1971) where they have been uniformly interpreted as evidence for the existence of a general attentional or general transfer of training effect.

In each of these experiments, pretraining and testing were conducted in the same context; therefore, the results are subject to reinterpretation as instances of context blocking. A context-blocking interpretation of this type of result is particularly attractive in view of the recently reported observation that the negative transfer effect is context-specific (i.e., changing the context alleviates the retardation) (Deeds, 1978).

Effects of differential and nondifferential pretraining on performance in a generalization transfer test have also been extensively documented in the free-operant literature (Bresnahan, 1970; Honig, 1969; Switalski, Lyons, & Thomas, 1966; Thomas, Freeman, Svinicki, Burr, & Lyons, 1970; Turner & Macintosh, 1972). These investigators have shown that discrimination, or differential, training produces sharp generalization gradients, whereas nondifferential training produces flat gradients. Thomas and his associates view these differences in generalization slope as a bi-directional attentional effect, and they suggest a mechanism of general attentiveness to account for the diffrences. According to the general attention position, in discrimination training subjects learn that stimulus differences are significant and, as a consequence, become more attentive to all stimulus differences, exhibiting sharp generalization gradients. Conversely, in nondifferential training subjects learn that stimulus differences are insignificant. These subjects consequently become less attentive to all stimulus differences and show flat generalization gradients.

Although the preceding interpretation is clearly consistent with the data, it should be noted that in all of these experiments training and testing were conducted in the same environment and, therefore, flattening of generalization slope by nondifferential training may reflect enhanced control over test responding by contextual CSs for subjects previously exposed to unsignaled pairings of context and food. The context is present throughout the generalization test, and, to the degree that context acts as a discriminative stimulus for free-operant keypecking, one would expect subjects to respond to stimuli other than the S^d in the generalization test (cf. Mackintosh, 1977).

Such an interpretation is particularly worthy of consideration in view of the observations made by Welker *et al.* (1974) that contextual stimuli exercise substantial control over free-operant responding and that previously conditioned contextual stimuli can block the acquisition of control by more traditional types of on-key discriminative stimuli. Furthermore, the manner in which flattening of generalization slope is achieved is consistent with the context analysis. That is, examination of absolute generalization gradients reveals that the flattening of generalization slope by nondifferential pretraining is largely attributable to enhancement of responding to test stimuli furthest removed (i.e., most dissimilar) from S^d. The "masking" of dimensional stimulus control by the presence of a salient discriminative stimulus has been documented in the free-operant generalization literature (cf. Thomas, Svinicki, & Svinicki, 1970), and a context-masking interpretation of these contingency transfer effects in generalization is supported by the recent observation that such effects are dependent upon pretraining and testing in the same context (Jackson and Hickis, 1980).

Blocking by previously conditioned contextual stimuli can also conceivably account for a number of related findings attributed to nonspecific transfer of training that have been reported in the instrumental discrimination learning literature. For example, Maier and Feldman (1948) have shown that rats reinforced randomly for jumping to one of two stimulus displays are subsequently profoundly retarded in the acquisition of a simultaneous discrimination based on an orthogonal set of stimulus values. Since training and testing were conducted in the same environment, a context-conditioning analysis may apply.

Transfer designs are also commonly used in free-operant experiments investigating behavioral contrast. In the typical behavioral contrast experiment, pigeons are exposed to nondifferential training (e.g., MULT VI 1-min–VI 1-min) until stable baseline rates of keypecking are established to both discriminative stimuli. The schedule of reinforcement in effect in the S2 component of the multiple schedule is then changed (e.g., MULT VI 1-min–EXT). Behavioral contrast is observed when the response rate in the unaltered S1 component increases over its previous baseline.

The similarity between the procedures utilized in the behavioral contrast and the previously discussed autoshaping literature is striking, and recent evidence that behavioral contrast in the pigeon is attributable to autoshaping (cf. Gamzu & Schwartz, 1973; Keller, 1974) makes the parallels even more compelling. The obvious implication is that the development of contrast is attributable to the acquisition of autoshaping and should be influenced by contextual factors in a similar fashion.

Behavioral contrast experiments are uniformly executed without a context change; consequently, the context-blocking analysis might help to explain the differential effects of correction and noncorrection procedures on behavioral contrast. Bloomfield (1966) has demonstrated enhancement of behavioral contrast when component changeover during differential training is contingent upon the meeting of a nonresponse criterion (correction procedure). The use of such correction procedure markedly increases the duration of the S2 component, which, in turn, has two effects that would be expected to facilitate autoshaping: It increases the correlation between the S1 stimulus and food, and it increases the duration of nonreinforced exposure to the context (i.e., context extinction). It has already been documented that autoshaping is facilitated by extinguishing the context between the types of pretraining and testing utilized in behavioral contrast designs; therefore, the effects of the correction procedure on behavioral contrast may be viewed as analogous to the effects of context extinction on autoshaping.

The context-blocking analysis may also provide an alternative interpretation of the instrumental learned helplessness effect. That is, one can argue that the emotional state engendered by shock termination (i.e., "relief") is conditionable to cues that are present at the time of shock termination. Subjects who can control shock termination are analogous to subjects in the correlated US condition in the Pavlovian situation; their yoked partners, who cannot control shock termination, are analogous to subjects in the uncorrelated US condition. That is, proprioceptive cues arising from the escape response provide a reliable predictor of shock termination that is unavailable to subjects in the yoked group. Therefore, the subjects in the yoked group are administered precisely those conditions that are known to generate strong context conditioning. If the context is highly conditioned in the yoked group, one would expect that the context would block the learning of the association between the proprioceptive cues arising from the test escape response and the termination of shock.

The helplessness effect has been documented in a number of experiments that utilize different experimental environments during pretraining as compared to during testing (i.e., a context change); therefore, an interpretation of the retardation effect in terms of context blocking seems less tenable (cf. Maier & Testa, 1975; Testa, Juraska, & Maier, 1974). It should be noted, however, that much of the experimental evidence that supports the learned helplessness interpretation of the retardation effect is derived from experiments that do not incorporate a context change. Nevertheless, experiments that include a context change are not altogether exempt from a context analysis since salient contextual elements are common to the two environments (e.g., contact with the shock electrodes).

The failure to consider contextual factors has serious theoretical implications beyond the application of the analysis to the negative transfer effect itself. Consider, for example, the implications of the context-blocking analysis for the contemporary issue of biological constraints on learning. Recently the general process assumptions of associative learning theory have become the focus of intensive experimental scrutiny. More specifically, it has been argued that all events are not equally associable and that such constraints on associability are mediated by evolutionary considerations. Organisms exposed to an aspect of their environmental structure (such as the correlation between taste and gastrointestinal illness) are subject to natural selection based on the facility with which they learn to associate the two. The selective advantage conferred to rapid learners is presumed to be responsible for the double-dissociation interaction typically observed in taste-aversion experiments.

While the taste-aversion effect is consistent with the biological constraints on learning position, alternative interpretations of that effect based on principles of associative learning have been advocated. For example, Mackintosh (1973) has pointed out that the double-dissociation interaction does not necessarily indicate that the impact of environmental structure on learning is mediated through genetic predispositions. Because that same environmental structure is also present during pre-experimental ontogeny, the constraints effect may reflect prior learning about the presence and absence of correlations between events that is subsequently transferred to the experimental setting. Mackintosh's learned irrelevance hypothesis suggests that organisms are capable of learning about the absence of a relationship between the occurrence of two events. The learning that A is unrelated to the occurrence of B should proactively interfere with the subsequent learning of an association between A and B. Hence the failure to associate audiovisual stimuli with gastrointestinal consequences may reflect learning during ontogeny of the independence of these events.

Empirical support for the learned irrelevance hypothesis is derived from experiments that demonstrate retarded acquisition of conditioning following pretraining wherein the CS and US are presented randomly with respect to one another (cf. Mackintosh, 1973). However, it has been observed that the retardation effect is severely attenuated by changing the context between pretraining and testing. This observation suggests that the learned irrelevance effect may be an artifact of context blocking and questions the pertinence of the hypothesis to the double-dissociation interaction.

The application of the context-blocking analysis to retardation phenomena observed in transfer designs requires only the absence of a context change and the presence of between-group differences in context conditioning with the initiation of testing. Numerous learning experiments provide these circumstances and are therefore susceptible to interpretation along those lines. The validity of the conjecture is an empirical matter that is certainly worthy of additional analysis.

ACKNOWLEDGMENT

The author wishes to thank Charles Hickis, Raymond Jackson, Stephen Fath, Stan Zebrowski, John Kruse, Susan DellAglio, Arthur Murphy, Diane Abbondandolo, Mark Hayden, Debi Biehl, Stacy Furstein, and Nick DeFabrizio for their contributions to this research.

REFERENCES

Appel, J. B., & Hiss, R. H. The discrimination of contingent from non-contingent reinforcement. *Journal of Comparative and Physiological Psychology*, 1962, 55, 37–39.

Ayres, J. J. B., & Quinsey, V. L. Between groups incentive effects on conditioned suppression. *Psychonomic Science*, 1971, 24, 31–33.

Baker, A. G., & Mackintosh, N. J. Excitatory and inhibitory conditioning following uncorrelated presentations of CS and UCS. *Animal Learning and Behavior*, 1977, 5, 315–319.

Baker, A. G., & Mackintosh, N. J. Preexposure to the CS alone, US alone, or CS and US uncorrelated: Latent inhibition, blocking by context or learned irrelevance? *Learning and Motivation*, 1979, 10, 278–294.

Benedict, J. O., & Ayres, J. J. B. Factors affecting conditioning in the truly random control procedure in the rat. *Journal of Comparative and Physiological Psychology*, 1972, 78, 323–330.

Bilbrey, J., & Winokur, S. Controls for and constraints on autoshaping. *Journal of the Experimental Analysis of Behavior*, 1973, 29, 323–332.

Blanchard, R., & Honig, W. K. Surprise value of food determines its effectiveness as a reinforcer. *Journal of Experimental Psychology: Animal Behavior Processes*, 1976, 2, 67–74.

Bloomfield, T. M. Two types of behavioral contrast in discrimination learning. *Journal of the Experimental Analysis of Behavior*, 1966, 9, 155–161.

Bloomfield, T. M. Reinforcement schedules: Contingency or contiguity? In R. M. Gilbert & J. R. Millenson (Eds.), *Reinforcement: Behavioral analyses*. New York: Academic Press, 1972.

Boakes, R. A. Response-decrements produced by extinction and response-independent reinforcement. *Journal of the Experimental Analysis of Behavior*, 1973, 19, 293–302.

Bresnahan, E. L. Effects of extradimensional pseudodiscrimination and discrimination training upon stimulus control. *Journal of Experimental Psychology*, 1970, 85, 155–156.

Brown, P. L., & Jenkins, H. M. Autoshaping of the pigeon's keypeck. *Journal of the Experimental Analysis of Behavior*, 1968, 11, 1–8.

Bull, J. A., III, & Overmier, J. B. Additive and subtractive properties of excitation and inhibition. *Journal of Comparative and Physiological Psychology*, 1968, 66, 511–514.

Chambers, B., & Szakmary, G. A. *Effects of US-preexposure on the acquisition of the CER*. Paper presented at the meeting of the Eastern Psychological Association, Philadelphia, April 1979.

Davis, H., & McIntyre, R. W. Conditioned suppression under positive, negative, and no contingency between conditioned and unconditioned stimuli. *Journal of the Experimental Analysis of Behavior*, 1969, 12, 633–640.

Deeds, W. C. *Effects of contextual cues on transfer of training*. Paper presented at the Midwestern Psychological Association Meetings, Chicago, May 1978.

Downing, K., & Neuringer, A. Autoshaping as a function of prior food presentations. *Journal of the Experimental Analysis of Behavior*, 1976, 26, 463–469.

Dweck, C. S., & Wagner, A. R. Situational cues and correlation between CS and US as determinants of the conditioned emotional response. *Psychonomic Science*, 1970, 18, 145–147.

Eck, K. O., Noel, R. C., & Thomas, D. R. Discrimination learning as a function of prior discrimination and non-differential training. *Journal of Experimental Psychology*, 1969, 82, 156–162.

Eck, K. O., & Thomas, D. R. Discrimination learning as a function of prior discrimination and nondifferential training: A replication. *Journal of Experimental Psychology*, 1970, 83, 511–513.

Edwards, D. D., West, J. R., & Jackson, V. The role of contingencies in the control of behavior. *Psychonomic Science*, 1968, 10, 39–40.

Edwards, D. D., Peek, V., & Wolfe, F. Independently delivered food decelerates fixed-ratio rates. *Journal of the Experimental Analysis of Behavior*, 1970, 14, 301–307.

Engberg, L. A., Hansen, G., Welker, R. L., & Thomas, D. R. Acquisition of key-pecking via auto-shaping as a function of prior experience: "Learned laziness?" *Science*, 1972, 178, 1002–1004.

Foree, D. D., & LoLordo, V. M. Attention in the pigeon: Differential effects of food-getting vs shock-avoidance procedures. *Journal of Comparative and Physiological Psychology*, 1973, 85, 555–558.

Frey, P. W., & Butler, C. S. Extinction after aversive conditioning: An associative or nonassociative process? *Learning and Motivation*, 1977, 8, 1–17.

Gamzu, E. *Associative and instrumental factors underlying the performance of a complex skeletal response.* Unpublished doctoral dissertation, University of Pennsylvania, 1971.

Gamzu, E., & Schwartz, B. The maintenance of key-pecking by stimulus contingent and response independent food presentation. *Journal of the Experimental Analysis of Behavior*, 1973, *19*, 65-72.

Gamzu, E., & Williams, D. R. Classical conditioning of a complex skeletal response. *Science*, 1971, *171*, 923-925.

Gamzu, E., & Williams, D. R. Associative factors underlying the pigeon's key pecking in autoshaping procedures. *Journal of the Experimental Analysis of Behavior*, 1973, *19*, 225-232.

Gamzu, E., Williams, D. R., & Schwartz, B. Pitfalls of organismic concepts: "Learned laziness?" *Science*, 1973, *181*, 367-368.

Gibbon, J. Scalar expectancy theory and Weber's Law in animal timing. *Psychological Review*, 1977, *84*, 279-325.

Gibbon, J., Berryman, R., & Thompson, R. L. Contingency spaces and measures in classical and instrumental conditioning. *Journal of the Experimental Analysis of Behavior*, 1974, *21*, 585-605.

Hall, G., & Honig, W. K. Stimulus control after extradimensional training in pigeons: A comparison of response contingent and noncontingent training procedures. *Journal of Comparative and Physiological Psychology*, 1974, *87*, 945-952.

Halliday, M. S., & Boakes, R. A. Behavioral contrast and response-independent reinforcement. *Journal of the Experimental Analysis of Behavior*, 1971, *16*, 429-434.

Halliday, M. S., & Boakes, R. A. Discrimination involving response-independent reinforcement: Implications for behavioral contrast. In R. A. Boakes & M. S. Halliday (Eds.), *Inhibition and learning*. London: Academic Press, 1972.

Herrnstein, R. J. Superstition: A corollary of the principles of operant conditioning. In W. K. Honig (Ed.), *Operant behavior: Areas of research and application*. New York: Appleton-Century-Crofts, 1966.

Herrnstein, R. J., & Morse, W. H. Some effects of response-independent positive reinforcement on maintained operant behavior. *Journal of Comparative and Physiological Psychology*, 1957, *50*, 461-467.

Hickis, C. F., Robles, L., & Thomas, D. R. Contextual stimuli and memory retrieval in pigeons. *Animal Learning and Behavior*, 1977, *5*, 161-168.

Honig, W. K. Attentional factors governing the slope of the generalization gradient. In N. S. Sutherland & R. M. Gilbert (Eds.), *Animal discrimination learning*. London: Academic Press, 1969.

Huff, R. C., Sherman, J. E., & Cohn, M. Some effects of response-independent reinforcement on auditory generalization gradients. *Journal of the Experimental Analysis of Behavior*, 1975, *23*, 81-86.

Jackson, R. L., & Hickis, C. F. *Contextual stimuli modulate the effects of prior discrimination and non-differential training on stimulus generalization in pigeons.* (In preparation, 1980).

Kamin, L. J. Predictability, surprise, attention and conditioning. In B. A. Campbell & R. M. Church (Eds.), *Punishment and aversive behavior*. New York: Appleton-Century-Crofts, 1969.

Keller, K. The role of elicited responding in behavioral contrast. *Journal of the Experimental Analysis of Behavior*, 1974, *21*, 249-257.

Kremer, E. F. Truly random and traditional control procedures in CER conditioning in the rat. *Journal of Comparative and Physiological Psychology*, 1971, *76*, 441-448.

Kremer, E. F. The truly random control procedure: Conditioning to the static cues. *Journal of Comparative and Physiological Psychology*, 1974, *86*, 700-707.

Lachter, G. C. Some temporal parameters of non-contingent reinforcement. *Journal of the Experimental Analysis of Behavior*, 1971, *16*, 207-217.

Lattal, K. A. Response-reinforcer independence and conventional extinction after fixed-interval and

variable-interval schedules. *Journal of the Experimental Analysis of Behavior*, 1972, *18*, 133–140.
Lattal, K. A. Response-reinforcer dependence and independence in multiple and mixed schedules. *Journal of the Experimental Analysis of Behavior*, 1973, *20*, 265–271.
Lattal, K. A. Combinations of response-reinforcer dependence and independence. *Journal of the Experimental Analysis of Behavior*, 1974, *22*, 357.
Lattal, K. A., & Maxey, G. C. Some effects of response independent reinforcers in multiple schedules. *Journal of the Experimental Analysis of Behavior*, 1971, *16*, 225–231.
LoLordo, V. M., McMillan, J. C., & Riley, A. L. The effects upon food-reinforced pecking and treadle-pressure of auditory and visual signals for response-independent food. *Learning and Motivation*, 1974, *5*, 24–41.
Macintosh, N. J. Stimulus selection: Learning to ignore stimuli that predict no change in reinforcement. In R. A. Hinde & J. Stevenson-Hinde (Eds.), *Constraints on learning*. New York: Academic Press, 1973.
Mackintosh, N. J. Stimulus control: Attentional factors. In W. K. Honig & J. E. R. Staddon (Eds.), *Handbook of operant behavior*, Englewood Cliffs, N.J.: Century Psychology Series, 1977.
Maier, N. R. F., & Feldman, R. S. Studies of abnormal behavior in the rat: Strength of fixation and duration of frustration. *Journal of Comparative and Physiological Psychology*, 1948, *41*, 348–363.
Maier, S. F., & Jackson, R. L. Learned helplessness: All of us were right (and wrong): Inescapable shock has multiple effects. In G. H. Bower (Ed.), *The psychology of learning and motivation*. New York: Academic Press, 1979.
Maier, S. F., Seligman, M. E. P., & Solomon, R. L. Pavlovian fear conditioning and learned helplessness. In B. A. Campbell & R. M. Church (Eds.), *Punishment and aversive behavior*. New York: Appleton-Century-Crofts, 1969.
Maier, S. F., & Seligman, M. E. P. Learned helplessness: Theory and evidence. *Journal of Experimental Psychology: General*, 1976, *105*, 3–46.
Maier, S. F., & Testa, T. J. Failure to learn to escape by rats previously exposed to inescapable shock is partly produced by associative interference. *Journal of Comparative and Physiological Psychology*, 1975, *88*, 554–564.
Miller, J. T. *The effect of contextual cue change during reversal training on postdiscrimination generalization gradients*. Unpublished doctoral dissertation, University of Colorado, 1972.
Miller, S., & Konorski, J. Sur une forme particulière des réflexes conditionnels. *Compte Rendu Hebdomadiare des Séances et Memoires de la Societé de Biologie*, 1928, *99*, 1151–1157.
Mis, F. W., & Moore, J. W. Effect of preacquisition UCS exposure on classical conditioning of the rabbit's nictitating membrane response. *Learning and Motivation*, 1973, *4*, 108–114.
Moscovitch, A., & LoLordo, V. M. Role of safety in Pavlovian backward fear conditioning. *Journal of Comparative and Physiological Psychology*, 1968, *66*, 673–678.
Mowrer, O. H. On the dual nature of learning: A re-interpretation of "conditioning" and "problem solving." *Harvard Educational Review*, 1947, *17*, 102–148.
Olding-Smee, F. J. The role of background stimuli during Pavlovian conditioning. *Quarterly Journal of Experimental Psychology*, 1975, *27*, 201–209. (a)
Olding-Smee, F. J. Background stimuli and the inter-stimulus interval during Pavlovian conditioning. *Quarterly Journal of Experimental Psychology*, 1975, *27*, 387–392. (b)
Olding-Smee, F. J. The overshadowing of background stimuli by an informative CS in aversive Pavlovian conditioning with rats. *Animal Learning and Behavior*, 1978, *6*, 43–51.
Powell, R. W. Effects of stimulus control and deprivation upon discriminative responding. *Journal of the Experimental Analysis of Behavior*, 1973, *19*, 351–360.
Randich, A., & LoLordo, V. M. Preconditioning exposure to the unconditioned stimulus affects the acquisition of a conditioned emotional response. *Learning and Motivation*, 1979, *10*, 245–277.
Rescorla, R. A. Pavlovian conditioning and its proper control procedures. *Psychological Review*, 1967, *74*, 71–80.

Rescorla, R. A. Probability of shock in the presence and absence of CS in fear conditioning. *Journal of Comparative and Physiological Psychology*, 1968, 66, 1-5.

Rescorla, R. A. Conditioned inhibition of fear. In N. J. Mackintosh & W. K. Honig (Eds.), *Fundamental issues in associative learning*. Halifax, Canada: Dalhousie Univ. Press, 1969.

Rescorla, R. A., & Skucy, J. C. Effect of response-independent reinforcer during extinction. *Journal of Comparative and Physiological Psychology*, 1969, 67, 381-389.

Rescorla, R. A., & Solomon, R. L. Two-process learning theory: Relationships between Pavlovian conditioning and instrumental learning. *Psychological Review*, 1967, 74, 151-182.

Rescorla, R. A., & Wagner, A. R. A theory of Pavlovian conditioning: Variations in the effectiveness of reinforcement and nonreinforcement. In A. H. Black & W. F. Prokasy (Eds.), *Classical conditioning II: Current theory and research*. New York: Appleton-Century-Crofts, 1972.

Russell, A., & Glow, P. H. Exposure to non-contingent light change in separate sessions prior to light-contingent bar pressing. *Quarterly Journal of Experimental Psychology*, 1976, 28, 403-408.

Schwartz, A. L., & Balsam, P. D. *Retardation of autoshaping following US-only pretraining*. Paper presented at the meeting of the Eastern Psychological Association, Philadelphia, April 1979.

Schwartz, B., Reisberg, D., & Vollmecke. T. Effects of treadle training on autoshaped key pecking: Learned laziness and learned industriousness or response competition? *Bulletin of the Psychonomic Society*, 1974, 3, 369-372.

Schlosberg, H. The relationship between success and the laws of conditioning. *Psychological Review*, 1937, 44, 379-394.

Schwartz, B., & Williams, D. R. The role of the response-reinforcer contingency in negative automaintenance. *Journal of the Experimental Analysis of Behavior*, 1972, 17, 351-357.

Seligman, M. E. P. Chronic fear produced by unpredictable electric shock. *Journal of comparative and Physiological Psychology*, 1968, 66, 402-411.

Sheafor, P. J. "Pseudoconditioned" jaw movements of the rabbit reflect association conditioned to contextual background cues. *Journal of Experimental Psychology: Animal Behavior Processes*, 1975, 104, 245-260.

Sheffield, V. F. Extinction as a function of partial reinforcement and distribution of practice. *Journal of Experimental Psychology*, 1949, 39, 511-526.

Sherman, J. E., & Spitzner, J. H. Some factors controlling the interaction between response-dependent and response-independent schedules of reinforcement. *Bulletin of the Psychonomic Society*, 1975, 6, 625-628.

Siegel, S. Morphine analgesic tolerance: Its situation specificity supports a Pavlovian conditioning model. *Science*, 1976, 193, 323-325.

Siegel, S., & Domjan, M. Backward conditioning as an inhibitory procedure. *Learning and Motivation*, 1971, 2, 1-16.

Skinner, B. F. Two types of conditioned reflex and a pseudo type. *Journal of Genetic Psychology*, 1935, 12, 66-77.

Skinner, B. F. "Superstition" in the pigeon. *Journal of Experimental Psychology*, 1948, 38, 168-172.

Solomon, R. L., & Wynne, L. C. Traumatic avoidance learning: The principles of anxiety conservation and partial irreversibility. *Psychological Review*, 1954, 61, 353-385.

Spear, N. E. Forgetting as retrieval failure. In W. K. Honig & P. James (Eds.), *Animal memory*. New York: Academic Press, 1971.

Spear, N. E. Retrieval of memory in animals. *Psychological Review*, 1973, 80, 163-194.

Staddon, J. E. R., & Simmelhag, V. L. The "Superstition experiment": A reexamination of its implications for the principles of adaptive behavior. *Psychological Review*, 1971, 78, 3-43.

Straub, R., & Gibbon, J. *Contextual blocking with a diffuse temporal stimulus*. Paper presented at the meeting of the Eastern Psychological Association, Boston, April 1977.

Switalski, R. W., Lyons, J., & Thomas, D. R. Effects of interdimensional training on stimulus generalization. *Journal of Experimental Psychology*, 1966, 72, 661-666.

Terrace, H. S., Gibbon, J., Farrell, L., & Baldock, M. D. Temporal factors influencing the acquisition and maintenance of an autoshaped keypeck. *Animal Learning and Behavior*, 1975, *3*, 53-62.
Testa, T. J., Juraska, J. M., & Maier, S. F. Prior exposure to inescapable electric shock in rats affects extinction behavior after the successful acquisition of an escape response. *Learning and Motivation*, 1974, *5*, 380-392.
Thomas, D. R., Freeman, F., Svinicki, J. G., Burr, D. E. S., & Lyons, J. The effect of extradimensional training on stimulus generalization. *Journal of Experimental Psychology*, 1970, *83* (1, pt 2).
Thomas, D. R., Svinicki, M. D., & Svinicki, J. G. Masking of stimulus control during generalization testing. *Journal of Experimental Psychology*, 1970, *84*, 479-482.
Thomas, D. R., Miller, J. T., & Svinicki, J. G. Nonspecific transfer effects of discrimination training in the rat. *Journal of Comparative and Physiological Psychology*, 1971, *74*, 96-101.
Tomie, A. *Mechanisms of retardation of Pavlovian conditioning.* Unpublished doctoral dissertation, University of Colorado, 1975.
Tomie, A. Retardation of autoshaping: Control by contextual stimuli. *Science*, 1976, *192*, 1244-1246. (a)
Tomie, A. Interference with autoshaping by prior context conditioning. *Journal of Experimental Psychology: Animal Behavior Processes*, 1976, *2*, 323-334. (b)
Wagner, A. R. Stimulus selection and a "modified continuity theory." In G. H. Bower & J. T. Spence (Eds.), *The psychology of learning and motivation* (Vol. 3). New York: Academic Press, 1969.
Wasserman, E. A. *Autoshaping: The selection and direction of behavior by predictive stimuli.* Unpublished doctoral dissertation, Indiana University, 1972.
Wasserman, E. A. The effect of redundant contextual stimuli on autoshaping the pigeon's keypeck. *Animal Learning and Behavior*, 1973, *1*, 198-206.
Wasserman, E. A. Pavlovian conditioning with heat reinforcement produces stimulus directed pecking in chicks. *Science*, 1973, *181*, 875-877.
Wasserman, E. A., Franklin, S. R., & Hearst, E. Pavlovian appetitive contingencies and approach vs withdrawal to conditioned stimuli in pigeons. *Journal of Comparative and Physiological Psychology*, 1974, *86*, 616-627.
Wasserman, E. A., Hunter, N. B., Gutowski, K. A., & Bader, S. A. Autoshaping chicks with heat reinforcement: The role of stimulus-reinforcer and response-reinforcer relations. *Journal of Experimental Psychology: Animal Behavior Processes*, 1975, *104*, 158-169.
Weisman, R. G., & Ramsden, M. Discrimination of a response-independent component of a multiple schedule. *Journal of the Experimental Analysis of Behavior*, 1973, *19*, 55-64.
Welker, R. L. Acquisition of a free-operant appetitive response in pigeons as a function of prior experience with response-independent food. *Learning and Motivation*, 1976, *7*, 394-405.
Welker, R. L., Tomie, A., Davitt, G. A., & Thomas, D. R. Contextual stimulus control over operant responding in pigeons. *Journal of Comparative and Physiological Psychology*, 1974, *86*, 549-562.
Wilkie, D. M. Variable time reinforcement in multiple and concurrent schedules. *Journal of the Experimental Analysis of Behavior*, 1972, *17*, 59-66.
Williams, D. R., & Williams, H. Automaintenance in the pigeon: Sustained pecking despite contingent non-reinforcement. *Journal of the Experimental Analysis of Behavior*, 1969, *12*, 511-520.
Zeiler, M. D. Fixed and variable schedules of response-independent reinforcement. *Journal of the Experimental Analysis of Behavior*, 1968, *11*, 405-414.

III

Temporal Factors

JOHN GIBBON
PETER BALSAM

7

Spreading Association in Time[1]

INTRODUCTION

Learning and timing are related intimately. In classical conditioning, responding in the presence of a cue reliably paired with a biologically important event is observed in advance of the actual occurrence of that event. Excitatory conditioning is inferred precisely to the extent that responding occurs in anticipation of, rather than following, reinforcement. Consider a prototypical classical conditioning situation in which a trial stimulus (T) is paired in a forward manner with a reinforcing stimulus (S^*) in a repetitive series of trials. The two lines of the diagram below depict traditional conditioning procedures in which the "consequence" follows the cue in a reliable manner. They differ only in the temporal spacing of trials. A time sense that did not contain quantitative information but

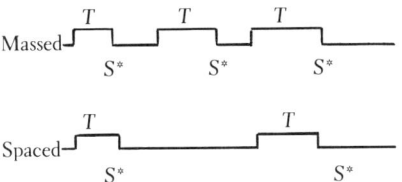

simply associated contiguous events would not differentiate the two procedures. Yet, one produces slow conditioning (massed training), and the other rapid conditioning (spaced training). A critical aspect of excitatory conditioning is

---

[1]This work was supported by National Science Foundation Grants BNS76-01229 and BNS78-23616 (John Gibbon, Principal Investigator) and National Institute Mental Health Grant MH33383-01 (Peter Balsam, Principal Investigator).

therefore a quantitative appreciation of the temporal parameters of training. The two pairing procedures shown in the diagram differ greatly in their effectiveness, although the signal is an equally reliable precursor of food when trials are massed as when they are spaced.

This chapter examines in some detail the way in which the temporal placement of trial signals and food presentations modulate the speed with which birds learn an association between these two events in the autoshaping paradigm (Brown & Jenkins, 1968). The question of whether the responding that emerges after a period of training is indeed associative rather than due to other processes will not be treated in much depth here (but see Gibbon, Chapter 9; Jenkins, Chapter 8, this volume) except to note that traditional as well as noncontingent control procedures (Brown & Jenkins, 1968; Rescorla, 1967) have been effective in preventing or eliminating autoshaped responding (Gamzu & Williams, 1973; Gibbon, Locurto, & Terrace, 1975). Rather, the associative nature of the signal–food relationship will be assumed.

Our purpose here is to relate findings from several sources on the control by temporal factors over the rapidity of acquisition. The data will be seen to place important constraints on the time sense involved in the psychological process of association formation. Then, these constraints will be examined in the light of Scalar Expectancy Theory elaborated recently to apply to a broad range of findings on asymptotic temporal control in learning (Gibbon, 1977).

TRIAL SPACING

In a typical autoshaping procedure, widely spaced trials consisting of a few seconds of illumination of a response key are followed by access to a hopper tray filled with grain. Under appropriate conditions, after a number of such pairings, birds come to peck the visual cue that reliably signals a brief time to reinforcement. Several studies from our laboratory (Gibbon, Baldock, Locurto, Gold, & Terrace, 1977; Terrace, Gibbon, Farrell, & Baldock, 1975) have examined the control over acquisition speed exerted by the traditional intertrial interval (ITI) variable, known to produce strong effects in other classical conditioning paradigms (e.g., Gormezano & Moore, 1969). The results confirmed the strong control by trial spacing. Autoshaped keypecking emerged much more rapidly when trials were widely spaced in time. The traditional conception of this effect is exemplified in the terms *spaced* versus *massed*, which implicitly assume a trial structure with an intertrial interval as a common denominator of the way animal subjects (and their experimenters) appreciate associative training procedures.

We will argue that this conception is wrong in a fundamental way: The learning that occurs here does not involve "trials" and "intertrial intervals" in the usual sense. Rather, excitation engendered by food presentations is "spread" in a continuous fashion over both the trial signals, and independently and concurrently over contextual stimuli present during training. Conditioned responding reflects the emergence of greater excitation levels associated with the trial signal embedded in this background. The intertrial interval does not play an explicit role in this conception, and in some sense is irrelevant to learning about the trial signal.

We begin with some evidence that intertrial stimuli, when they are explicitly programmed, are not appreciated as such by subjects, at least not until later in training after the associative connection between the trial signal and food has been established.

Intertrial Interval

In our first approach to the intertrial interval problem (Terrace et al., 1975) we studied the traditional autoshaping paradigm. Brief key illuminations followed immediately by food were separated by different intertrial periods, for different groups, in which the key was dark. As expected, long intertrial periods facilitated acquisition. The functional relation between speed of acquisition and the duration of the ITI in this experiment was compared with speed of acquisition in a second experiment in which the intertrial period was "filled" with explicit stimuli. A 10-sec green key was the positive signal followed by food on every occasion, as in Experiment 1. Throughout the interval between the green key presentations, 10-sec periods of red-key illumination separated by .5 sec dark-key periods were programmed.

In Figure 7.1, the number of reinforcers required before birds pecked the green key on three out of four consecutive trials is shown as a function of the mean time between green key trials on double log coordinates.[2] The open circles are from Experiment 1 with a dark-key intertrial period, and the filled circles are from Experiment 2, with explicit negative signals intervening between positive trials. The two procedures produced a very similar functional relation between speed of acquisition and time between positive trials. The two filled squares represent acquisition scores from two groups in a study by Gibbon et al. (1975) that also experienced negative signals between positive green-key trials. The negative (red) signals in this procedure, however, were separated by brief (1.5-sec) periods in which the key was illuminated by a third color (yellow). Acquisition to the positive signal does not appear to differ in these three procedures.

Now in the explicit negative signal procedures, what is the ITI? From the experimenter's point of view, one might think of these procedures as discrimination paradigms, with green key positive and red key negative and with each trial

---

[2]We originally reported the number of reinforcers to the first response. The three-out-of-four acquisition criterion, we have found subsequently, is a somewhat less variable measure of acquisition speed (Gibbon et al., 1977).

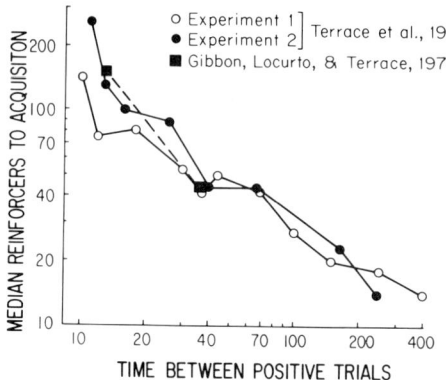

Figure 7.1. Number of reinforced trials required before subjects respond on three out of four consecutive trials. Open circles are from an experiment in which the response key was dark during the intertrial interval; filled circles are from an experiment in which the key was illuminated with explicit negative signals; filled squares are from a comparable experiment with explicit negative signals during the intertrial interval.

separated by a brief ITI. However, the data show that subjects acquire to the positive signal in the same manner, irrespective of whether the intervening time contains explicit lit-key trials. It is important to note that in the "filled" ITI procedures most subjects responded at low rates to the red and yellow stimuli, at least early in training, so that these stimuli were not "ignored" in the usual sense. On the other hand, negative signals must in some sense remain irrelevant to the associative mechanism generating responding to the positive signal, since they result in the comparable acquisition speeds evident in Figure 7.1.

On the basis of these considerations we might think of the *functional* ITI as periods inclusive of all events or stimuli other than the positive trial. However, there are ambiguities in this conception as well. While unreinforced signals appear to make little difference to the acquisition of associative responding to the positive signal, *reinforced* alternative signals, or indeed any reinforcements delivered in the absence of the positive signal, have a profound effect on acquisition speed. When "free" reinforcers are available at some rate in the nominal intertrial interval, associative responding to the signal is dramatically retarded (e.g., Gamzu & Williams, 1971, 1973; Gibbon et al., 1975). This is perhaps clearest in Barnes and Jenkins's (1976) and Jenkins's (Chapter 8, this volume) procedures in which added reinforcers were programmed to occur either close in time to the reinforced positive signal or spaced far from positive trials.

When additional reinforcers are programmed between reinforced trial signals, what is the ITI? Is it the period between positive signals? If so, it has not changed with added reinforcers, yet learning is greatly retarded. Alternatively, one might construe the intertrial interval as the period between the last reinforcer delivery and the next subsequent positive trial. Barnes and Jenkins's data argue against this construction. As long as overall mean reinforcement rate is constant, acquisition is retarded by about the same amount whether free reinforcers are grouped closely with the positive trial, or placed more remotely.

Trial Duration

Another line of evidence further obfuscates the intertrial interval conception. This evidence comes from an examination of the interaction between the trial and intertrial duration. Gibbon et al. (1977) studied acquisition in independent groups spanning a broad range of trial and intertrial values. The results of this study replicated the strong facilitating effect of increasing the intertrial interval but showed in addition that this facilitation was dependent on the trial signal remaining constant. If, as in several of the groups studied in that experiment, both trial and intertrial are increased in the same ratio (e.g., 48-sec ITI, 8-sec trial; 96-sec ITI, 16-sec trial, etc.), the speed of learning remains roughly constant. In terms of an intertrial interval analysis, the enhanced conditioning rate produced, say, by doubling the ITI must be exactly counterbalanced by a retardation produced by doubling the trial-signal duration.

To clarify these ambiguities, we propose that the associative connections actually formed bear only a very primitive relation to the trial structure that experimenters have used to study it. The core of the proposal is that in associative learning a comparison is made between the time that the positive trial is present (T) between reinforcement occasions, and the overall cycle time (C) between reinforcement occasions. The manner in which this comparison is made is a direct function of the ratio of these two times.

Evidence bearing on the ratio conception is shown in Figure 7.2. The data are taken from published work by the contributors to this volume. The ordinate, which is logged, represents the median number of reinforced trials before acquisition occurs and the abscissa, also on a log scale, represents the ratio of interreinforcement, or cycle, duration to trial duration (C/T). The ratio effect means that the number of reinforcements before keypecking emerges is approximately constant at constant ratios of the cycle to trial duration. This is, of course, implied by the constancy reported by Gibbon et al. (1977) with respect to the ratio of intertrial-to-trial time. In the figure, this means that acquisition scores corresponding to a given C/T ratio should superimpose. There is a great deal of scatter in these data, but it is not systematically related to absolute C and T values.

The power of trial spacing to modulate acquisition speed is now referred to the ratio variable and can be seen as the approximately linear decline in the (log) number of trials before acquisition, as a function of increases in the (log) C/T ratio. Increasing the ratio over a range of about one order of magnitude decreases acquisition scores by about one order of magnitude also. The heavy line through these data is a least-squares regression and shows that the relationship between the two is approximately a power function.[3] The lighter dashed curves represent the 95% confidence band on the regression.

---

[3]The regression is highly significant ($F(1/95) = 281.7$, $p < .001$) and the best fit function is $n = 260.6\,(C/T)^{-.8294}$ where n is the number of cycles before acquisition.

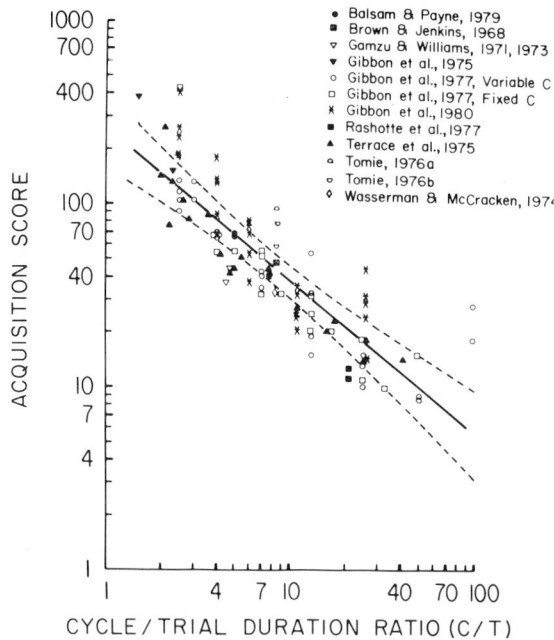

Figure 7.2. Reinforcers to acquisition (n) versus cycle to trial ratios (C/T) on double log coordinates. Data are from the studies indicated in the legend. The heavy line is the least squares regression, $n = 260.6 \, (C/T)^{-.8294}$. The dashed lines represent the 95% confidence limits around the regression.

Figure 7.2 demonstrates what might be thought of as both strong and weak sensitivity to time in this paradigm. The relationship is a strong one in that the C/T ratio changes acquisition speeds over an order of magnitude, from approximately 10, to approximately 100 trials before acquisition. On the other hand, the control by the ratio is weak in the sense that variability around the regression line is very substantial. The regression accounts for 70% of the data variance (75% if the deviant points at the largest C/T ratio are excluded). Thus, whatever mechanism is proposed to account for these data, it must possess both features: It must be able to predict large changes in the speed of learning and, at the same time, large variability in that speed. We present below an account that handles the first requirement and suggests reasons for the second.

SCALAR EXPECTANCY

The account we propose is adapted from Scalar Expectancy Theory (SET) (Gibbon, 1977) which has been developed in some detail as applied to temporal control of operant behavior studied to asymptote. A central feature of that account is that the relevant time values are estimated by animal subjects and compared by a "ratio comparator" that may be thought of as a mechanism indexing the relative excitatory strength associated with two alternative delays to reinforcement. In the application to autoshaping, subjects are regarded as developing an expectancy of when reinforcement is due, both in the trial signal and in the background, or overall. The background expectancy mechanism is a rudimentary one that is sensitive to the average time between reinforcements but insensitive to finer distinctions within interreinforcement intervals. The background, or context, gains associative value or expectancy in inverse proportion to the average time between reinforcement occasions (the average cycle time, C). In the application of SET to asymptotic temporal control in periodic reinforcement schedules (Gibbon, 1977, Section I) the conception of background expectancy has just this undifferentiated character. It is an index of average overall rate of reinforcement, to be contrasted with temporally differentiated expectancy that develops over the course of extended training.

Expectancy of food in the trial signal develops independently of the context and is similarly inversely related to the time it is present (T) between reinforcement deliveries. On this view, the strength of associative responding evoked by the signal is directly related to the degree to which expectancy in the signal exceeds the overall or background reinforcement expectancy.

Primitive Timing

In the autoshaping paradigm, associative responding emerges too rapidly for fine temporal discriminations to play a role. There are two pieces of evidence for this. First, acquisition speed does not depend on whether the intertrial interval is fixed or variable. In the Gibbon et al. (1977) study, two experiments were reported, one of which used a variable cycle (or ITI) procedure, and the other a fixed cycle with values comparable to the arithmetic means of the variable schedule. The resulting relationship between acquisition score and C/T was virtually identical (Gibbon et al., 1977, Figure 9, replotted in terms of C/T in Figure 7.2 as circles and squares, for the variable-cycle and fixed-cycle procedures, respectively). If the association mechanism that compares trial strength to background strength were sensitive to variation in the background depending on what *point* in the cycle the comparison was made, then background strength might be expected to be higher toward the end of a fixed cycle than at the beginning, but more uniform under the variable-cycle case. Since trial signals in the fixed cycle procedure always occur at a predictable point—the end of the cycle—one might expect retarded acquisition relative to the variable case. Retardation was not observed, and so it seems likely to us that the primitive time sense involved here contains no finer information than the average time between reinforcements.

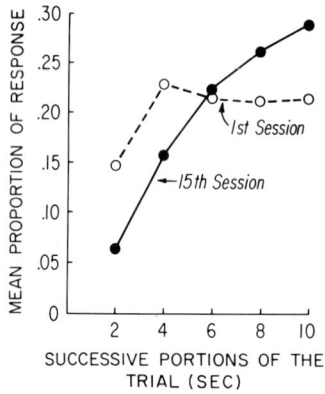

Figure 7.3. Average proportion of total responses in successive 2-sec portions of the 10-sec trial. Open circles are taken from the first day with at least 25 responses and filled circles from the fifteenth day of maintenance training.

A second line of evidence on what might be thought of as "mean or average timing" as opposed to point estimation, stems from an observation by Gibbon, Farrell, Locurto, Duncan, and Terrace (1980) in which the development of accelerated responding over the trial duration was observed in a partial-reinforcement-of-autoshaping study. This experiment, described in more detail below, found that under partial reinforcement schedules, responding over the duration of the trial signal early in training was roughly uniform except for the very beginning of the trial, when responding was low. However, when subjects were studied for an additional fifteen sessions after the session in which responding began, accelerated responding over the trial was evident. In Figure 7.3, average responding of subjects exposed to intermittent reinforcement of the trial signal is shown. The experiment studied a variety of probability values and intertrial interval values, and data have been averaged over all groups with probability of reinforcement less than .75.[4] The ordinate represents the mean proportion of total responses emitted during the trial as a function of successive 2-sec periods of the 10-sec trial signal. The open circles represent the first day containing at least 25 responses, and the filled circles represent the fifteenth day of training. The responding is roughly uniform early in training but shows a smooth acceleration to a high rate at the end of the trial after extended training. We have not observed acceleration of responding over the trial signal until about the fifth or sixth session of maintenance training. These data imply then, that timing successive temporal positions within the trial signal is quite imprecise

---

[4]Consistent reinforcement ($P = 1.0$) groups were also studied under these conditions, and keypecking reflected timing less powerfully when reinforcement occurred on every trial. Gibbon *et al.* (1980) produce evidence to show that this probably does not reflect a failure of timing in the consistently reinforced birds, but rather the emergence of anticipatory behavior incompatible with keypecking toward the end of the trial.

when responding first emerges during acquisition and becomes differeniated slowly over the course of extended training.

Taken together, these two pieces of evidence lead us to believe that fine temporal discriminations are not made until some time after responding emerges in the autoshaping paradigm. Thus, the appreciation of time required to produce the strong effects of the C/T variable on acquisition must remain primitive at this stage in training. Subjects are sensitive to overall cycle time and trial time values but insensitive to different times within the cycle and trial intervals, as these intervals elapse.

Expectancy

The central features of our primitive expectancy account are illustrated in Figure 7.4. Expectancy is shown on the ordinate, and the time between two reinforcements is indicated as one cycle (C) on the abscissa. Each reinforcer is thought of as supporting a given amount of expectancy (H), which is spread back over the interreinforcement and trial intervals uniformly. This spread, or averaging, of different points within the interval is to be distinguished from the differentiation of elapsing time observable later in training (Figure 7.3) and from no timing whatever, in which expectations could not depend upon the average interreinforcement interval. The uniform spread labeled h_C is the background, or cycle expectancy, and is indicated by diagonal hatching. The height of this function is simply the total expectancy that reinforcement will support, spread evenly over the cycle, $h_C = H/C$. Expectancy of reinforcement in the signal, h_T, is shown by the vertical hatching and is just the scale transform of expectancy appropriate to the shorter interval, $h_T = H/T$. The areas under both functions are therefore the same.

The figure depicts expectancy levels after some training. As these levels accrue to the background and the trial stimuli, subjects make a comparison between them by taking their ratio, $r = h_T/h_C$. This is the ratio comparator assumed in SET, and represents the same kind of mechanism for these primitive discriminations as for the finer temporal discriminations observed at asymptote. When the

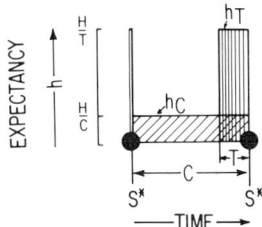

Figure 7.4. Expectancy diagram for the standard autoshaping procedure. The trial expectancy, spread over T units of time, is indicated by vertical hatching. The background expectancy spread over the cycle time, C, between reinforcement occasions (circles) is indicated by diagonal hatching.

ratio exceeds a criterion or threshold value, b, autoshaped responding emerges. We will defer for a moment specification of the manner in which these levels are approached with successive reinforcement experiences, except to note that large ratios may be expected to reach criterion more rapidly than small ratios. That is, a big difference between the final expectancy levels (illustrated in Figure 7.4) means a more rapid approach to a difference between them sufficient to engender responding.

Qualitatively, the trial spacing effect is straightforward, since increasing the cycle time without changing the trial time results in lower background expectancy levels and thus a more rapid approach to the ratio criterion. The ratio effect is also immediate, since if the trial and intertrial durations are both increased by the same factor, their ratio remains unchanged. Constant acquisition speed with constant C/T is therefore a consequence of the ratio comparator assumption ($r = h_T/h_C = C/T$).

On this construction it is also clear that explicit negative signals intervening between positive trials (Figure 7.1) may be expected to have no effect on acquisition. Since associative learning about the positive signal reflects a comparison with *overall* reinforcement rate, it is not surprising that the presence or absence of other signals is irrelevant.[5]

Motivation

The expectancy account holds that a ratio comparison is made between excitation levels engendered by the signal and those engendered by the overall reinforcement rate. In the quantitative construction of these values (Figure 7.4) the motivational parameter, H, plays no role since the same incentive value perforce engenders both trial expectancy and background expectancy. It therefore cancels in the ratio and variations in parameters such as duration, intensity or quality of the reinforcer are predicted to have no effect. This is a fairly radical view and one not shared by other theoretical accounts.

In the autoshaping literature, few experiments relate directly to motivational differences, but those that do are in accord with the no-effect prediction. For example, Jenkins and Moore (1973) exposed birds to either grain or water using identical temporal and stimulus parameters and found approximately the same speed of acquisition with these two reinforcers. Balsam, Brownstein, and Shull (1978) studied the effect of different feeder durations on maintained levels of keypecking in the autoshaping paradigm. They found no effect on maintained responding as long as a single feeder duration was studied within a given experi-

---

[5]The negative relationship with reinforcement is a valid one for learning inhibitory properties, and may be demonstrated in the autoshaping paradigm (Wasserman & Molina, 1975). We believe, however, that the time course for learning inhibitory associations is slower than that for excitatory associations (Rescorla, 1975). Essentially, appreciation of an explicit negative relationship requires prior establishment of an excitatory context.

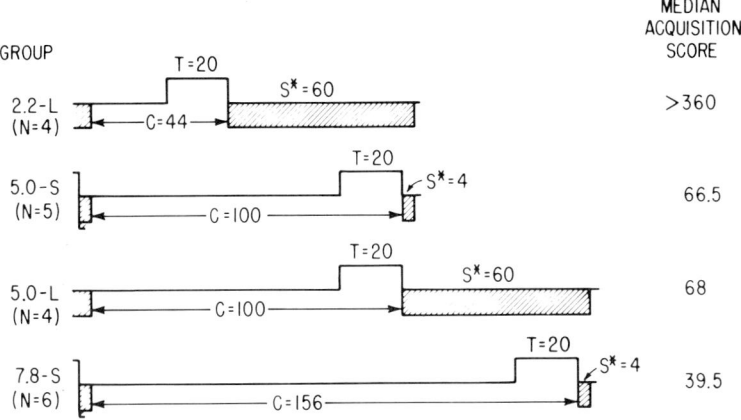

Figure 7.5. Design (on the left) and acquisition score (on the right) for four groups studied by Balsam and Payne (1979). Reinforcement durations indicated by hatching were either short (4 sec) or long (60 sec). Groups are labeled by C/T ratio (left column).

mental session. Perkins, Beavers, Hancock, Hemmendinger, Hemmendinger, and Ricci (1975) also failed to find a consistent effect of feeder duration on maintained responding.[6]

In our construction thus far (Figure 7.4), we have proceeded as though the reinforcement occasion was essentially instantaneous, or equivalently, as though the relevant cycle and trial periods were calculated excluding reinforcement duration. That is, the effective cycle time is regarded as the time from the offset of one reinforcer to the onset of the next, with the reinforcement duration excluded from the excitation level calculation. Balsam and Payne (1979) have studied this issue directly. The experimental design is presented in Figure 7.5. After brief hopper training, four groups of subjects were exposed to an autoshaping paradigm with 20-sec signals. For two of these groups (2.2-L and 5-L) the reinforcer access time (diagonal hatching) was 60 sec. For the other two (5-S and 7.8-S) the reinforcer duration was 4 sec. The long- and short-reinforcer duration groups were exposed to different cycle times. The groups represented by the top two lines in the figure received cycle durations of 44 sec and 100 sec ($C/T = 2.2$ and 5.0) excluding the reinforcer duration. If reinforcer duration is added to these times, the overall time between hopper offsets is equal (104 sec). For the two groups represented by the bottom two lines, the cycle durations were 100 sec and 56 sec ($C/T = 5.0$ and 7.8) so that the offset-to-offset times were equal for these two groups also (160 sec).

---

[6]Subjects exposed to a 1-sec feeder duration responded at somewhat lower rates than those exposed to longer feeder durations. However, if subjects did not eat within a few seconds after feeder presentation, the hopper was lowered until the next trial. It may be that the 1-sec duration resulted in some frequency of omission of reinforcement.

The design allows several implications. If long reinforcer duration enhances acquisition speed, groups 2.2-L and 5.0-L should be superior to groups 5.0-S and 7.8-S. In particular, if we take cycle time into account, group 5.0-L should be superior to group 5.0-S since these groups did not differ in C/T ratio but did differ in reinforcer duration. If however, the overall cycle time is calculated *including* reinforcer access, groups represented by the top two lines should acquire at about the same speed and groups represented by the bottom two lines should acquire at about the same speed.

On the right of the figure the median trials to satisfy the acquisition criterion are indicated. The group with the 2.2 C/T ratio did not acquire in 360 reinforcer presentations. This is to be contrasted with group 5.0-S which acquired in 66 cycles. Similarly, group 5.0-L was retarded relative to group 7.8-S. These comparisons indicate that reinforcement time is not included in the functional cycle and trial durations. The two middle groups with identical C/T ratios acquired at virtually the same number of food presentations, even though group 5.0-L experienced reinforcer durations 15 times longer than group 5.0-S.

In the literature on other infrahuman classical conditioning preparations, between-group comparisons have generally failed to find an effect of reinforcer duration. In GSR conditioning with cool air reinforcement (Furedy, 1967) and with electric shock (Coppock & Chambers, 1959; Salz, Kitai, & Asdourian, 1963), the duration of the reinforcer was not systematically related to the strength of the conditioned response. In some cases, maintained responding varies with reinforcer duration (Frey & Butler, 1973; eyeblink conditioning in rabbits) while in others no effect is seen (Mowrer & Solomon, 1954: secondary punishment associated with different electric shock durations; Wegner & Zeaman, 1958: heart-rate conditioning with different electric shock durations).

Insensitivity of birds to reinforcer duration in autoshaping is in sharp contrast to robust effects of reinforcer duration in choice procedures (Catania, 1963; Moffit & Shimp, 1971; Shimp, 1968). Moreover, an inverse relation between amount and delay of reinforcement has been demonstrated by Rachlin and Green (1972) and Ainslie (1974) in the provocative "self-control" paradigm. In choosing between incentives, birds are quite sensitive to reinforcer durations as well as delays, while in forming an association between a signal and food, they appear to be sensitive only to delays. In Scalar Expectancy Theory, this results from changes by the same factor in both background and signal expectancy values. This is quite a different prediction from one of no effect whatever. That is, reinforcer magnitude effects do not appear in acquisition measures because the ratio comparator equates them—not because they are absent.

There is some evidence that reinforcer magnitude effects may be observed in the autoshaping paradigm when different magnitudes are experienced within the same session. In one procedure (Balsam et al., 1978) two reinforcer durations were cued by different key colors, and maintained asymptotic responding was more vigorous in the cue that predicted the longer feeder duration. Such an effect would be expected were background values averaged, as we will argue later, so that the cue associated with the long feeder duration was relatively more excitatory. A similar result in maintained responding has been observed by Perkins et al. (1975). It is not clear at present, however, whether contextual effects with different reinforcer magnitudes experienced within the same session may be observed in acquisition.

INTEGRATION

Averaging across Cycles

We have argued that background expectancy levels are undifferentiated. The excitation levels appropriate to the single reinforcer at the end of the cycle are spread uniformly across all time points within the cycle. This primitive integration we believe applies across cycles as well.

The evidence comes again from the experiment on trial and intertrial durations (Gibbon et al., 1977). With variable cycle lengths, birds acquired at about the same rate as their counterparts in the fixed cycle-length procedure when the fixed cycle length was set at the arithmetic mean of the variable cycles. Asssuming that conditioning reflects a comparison of signal to background, this implies that subjects average across cycles to obtain comparable background expectation levels. The implication depends on a comparison of variability in acquisition scores within groups. That is, if little averaging occurred, one might expect that in the variable cycle-length procedure, some birds experiencing a few long cycles early in training would acquire rapidly, while others experiencing a few short cycle lengths early in training would acquire slowly. Variability across subjects would be large for the variable-cycle procedure. The data on standard deviation of acquisition scores rule out this possibility. Variance was, if anything, slightly larger for the fixed as opposed to the variable case. This means that the relation between mean C/T and acquisition score in Figure 7.2 is not the result of central tendency established by more divergent individual performances in the variable cycle case.

Moreover, the averaging implied here must be arithmetic rather than geometric or harmonic. Comparability was found between the fixed and the arithmetic mean of the variable cycle procedure. The geometric mean of the variable cycle lengths is smaller by about a factor of 2 than the arithmetic mean for these schedules. Thus, were birds averaging logarithmically rather than linearly, their background expectancy levels would have been elevated by a factor of 2, resulting in retarded acquisition to the trial signal. A similar argument for the harmonic mean predicts more rapid acquisition in the variable case, and so these two kinds of averaging appear to be ruled out.

The above conclusions would be more compelling were there not such sizeable variance in acquisition under both procedures. We will argue later that most of this variability comes from nontemporal sources, which thus obscure the relative contribution of timing to variation in acquisition speed.

The linear average of background expectancy levels here is paralleled quite precisely by the analysis of backgrounds in periodic temporal discrimination paradigms at asymptote (Gibbon, 1977). The parallel suggests to us that in both signaled and unsignaled reinforcement procedures the context expectancy mechanism involved remains undifferentiated with respect to time points within a cycle as the cycle elapses. Temporal discrimination effects, even after long training, appear to require an undifferentiated appreciation of overall reinforcement rate against which to compare local, temporally distinct expectancies.

Integration within Cycles: Partial Reinforcement

The complementary experiment to the variable- versus fixed-cycle procedures would be one in which trials were programmed with variable or fixed durations. This experiment remains to be done. However, we would expect the results to show the same finding; that integration over the trial would require an averaging mechanism that is insensitive to local changes in duration as long as average trial durations were maintained constant. Certainly, temporal discriminations of the elapsing trial interval are not apparent early in training when responding first begins. It is only after considerable experience with a constant trial duration that birds show an appreciation of how much time has elapsed in the trial signal (Figure 7.3).

In this context, the partial reinforcement experiment in which only some of the nominal trial signals are reinforced, takes on added significance. For if integration occurs within cycles, then the effect of a partial reinforcement schedule may parallel the effect of increasing the total trial and total cycle time.

Gibbon et al. (1980) studied the partial reinforcement variable at a variety of cycle values (C) and partial reinforcement (P) values. The results of principal interest are shown in Figure 7.6. The ordinate represents reinforcers (not trials) before subjects satisfied our three-out-of-four criterion as a function of the probability with which the nominal trial signal was followed by food. The duration was the same (10 sec) for all groups.

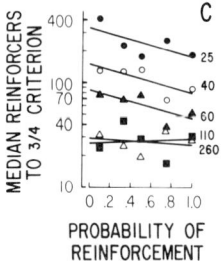

Figure 7.6. Median reinforcers to acquisition as a function of probability of reinforcement per (nominal) trial signal. Groups were studied at five different cycle values (C), identified to the right of each regression line.

The regression lines shown in the figure were fit to the logged medians of the groups from each cycle value. They are displaced downward with increasing C, thus confirming the strong effect of trial spacing on speed of acquisition. However, these data do not represent a reliable effect for partial reinforcement. A two-way analysis of variance was performed on the logged acquisition scores from all subjects. There was a large effect of cycle ($F[4/87] = 27.64$, $p < .001$) but no effect for probability of reinforcement or interaction. Evidently, intermittency does not retard the speed with which keypecking emerges when the measure of acquisition speed is the number of reinforcements or cycles required before the criterion is met.

The considerable variability in individual subjects' data, however, may have obscured a small partial reinforcement effect. When only the medians of Figure 7.6 were tested for a departure from a combined slope of zero, a (marginal) difference was obtained ($F[1/15] = 4.77$, $.025 < p < .05$).

The number of reinforcers before acquisition is not commonly reported in the classical conditioning partial reinforcement literature. Quite generally, reports of Pavlovian partial reinforcement procedures assess acquisition speed by the number of trials rather than cycles before responding emerges. Gibbon et al. (1980, Table 2) surveyed this literature and found that there were surprisingly few cases of retarded acquisition when the data were reanalyzed in terms of the number of reinforcement cycles rather than the number of trials before acquisition occurs. In fact, the frequency with which retardation was found was very close to traditional Type I error levels.

In light of the integration within and across cycles implied for the background excitation levels, the per-cycle perspective for trial episodes is the appropriate one for SET. It says that the entire cycle between reinforcement occasions is treated as a unit containing both a background, the complete cycle, and a "trial," the total time the signal is present within the cycle.

Expectancy

The expectancy analysis for partial reinforcement is diagrammed in Figure 7.7. A 50% partial reinforcement schedule is shown in which reinforcement is not delivered at the end of the first trial but is delivered at the end of the second. The dashed lines indicate the expectancy levels appropriate to regular reinforcement. That is, the dashed lines correspond to h_C and h_T as in Figure 7.4. When

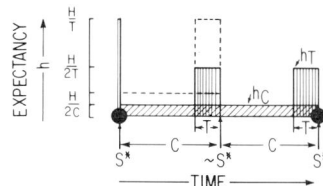

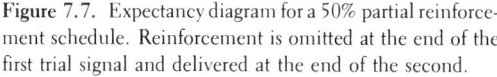

Figure 7.7. Expectancy diagram for a 50% partial reinforcement schedule. Reinforcement is omitted at the end of the first trial signal and delivered at the end of the second.

reinforcement is omitted at the end of the first trial and delivered at the end of the second, the result from the expectancy perspective is that the *functional* cycle length has now been doubled (2C) and the functional trial length has also been doubled (2T). The primitive integration process cumulates total signal time between reinforcers and compares the resulting expectancy level to that appropriate to the total cycle time between reinforcers. Functionally, this is equivalent to a continuous reinforcement procedure with double the trial value and double the cycle value. In the figure, the expectancy levels appropriate to 2T and 2C are shown as the vertical and diagonally hatched areas. A ratio comparison between these two levels faces the same degree of difficulty as the continuous schedule. That is, the ratio of total trial time to total cycle time remains invariant with changing probability. In a sense, the lack of a probability of reinforcement effect is entailed by the presence of the ratio effect. An intermittent reinforcement schedule in which food is delivered with probability, P, at the end of the nominal trial signal results in total trial and cycle times that are multiplied by 1/P. The ratio of these values then remains the same independent of P.

It is important to recognize that integration of trial signals requires contiguity of at least some "portions" of the signal with reinforcement. For example, if the second trial in Figure 7.7 was moved back into the middle of the interreinforcement interval, a trace (or inhibitory) procedure would be in effect. Trace procedures profoundly retard acquisition (Balsam, 1975; Newlin & LoLordo, 1976).

Split Trials

The realization of intermittent reinforcement studied above is one in which the nominal trial and intertrial durations were held constant and reinforcement frequency was decreased by omitting reinforcers. The expectancy diagram (Figure 7.7), however, may be interpreted in just the reverse fashion: When cycle time is kept constant but early portions of the trial signal are displaced from the end into the middle of the cycle period, the ratio of total trial time to cycle time remains the same. It is important to demonstrate, then, that this latter arrangement, in which a portion of the trial occurs before the end of the cycle, produces the same equivalence as when the cycle times are lengthened.

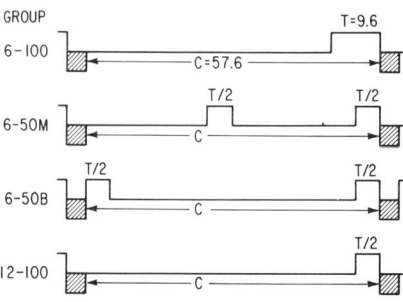

Figure 7.8. Design diagrams for groups in the split trial experiment. Groups identified by the top three lines have the same total signal time between reinforcers. The two split groups have the first half of the signal displaced either to the beginning or to the middle of the cycle. The group on the bottom has the same signal duration contiguous with reinforcement, but the displaced half-signal is omitted.

An unpublished study from our laboratory employed the design in Figure 7.8. Four groups corresponding to the four diagrams experienced the same cycle duration, C = 57.6 sec. The groups represented by the top three lines experienced a total signal duration of 9.6 sec, and therefore a $C/T = 6$ ratio. The 6-100 group (top line) received the conventional procedure, with a single trial signal just preceding reinforcement delivery. The next two lines present two 50% reinforcement groups, with two trial signals per cycle, each half the duration (4.8 sec) of the 6-100 group trial. For group 6-50M, the unreinforced signal occurs in the middle of the cycle, followed by the reinforced signal at the end of the cycle. For group 6-50B, the unreinforced signal occurs at the beginning of the cycle directly following reinforcement. Thus, both of these groups have the same total signal time per cycle, but one-half of the signal duration is displaced either to the middle (6-50M) or the beginning (6-50B) of the cycle. The final group (12-100) received only the short trial signal depicted in the bottom line. This short delay group experienced a 100% schedule but with the signal duration 1/2 that of the other three groups, so that for this group $C/T = 12$. The primitive integration assumed in SET predicts that the three groups with the same total signal duration (6-100, 6-50M, 6-50B) have the same signal expectancy, and should acquire at about the same speed. But the half-signal short-delay group (12-100) has double the signal expectancy, and should acquire substantially faster.

The number of reinforcers required before birds responded to three out of four consecutive trials is displayed in Figure 7.9. The height of the histogram bars represents the mean of the logged acquisition scores, and the vertical brackets indicate plus and minus one standard deviation. The median for each group is shown as a dashed horizontal line. The mean was taken over subjects that acquired within our observation period (360 cycles). The numbers that acquired out of total group sizes were 14/15, 15/15, 14/18, and 15/15 for groups 6-100, 6-50M, 6-50B and 12-100, respectively.

Both measures show the most rapid acquisition in the short-delay group

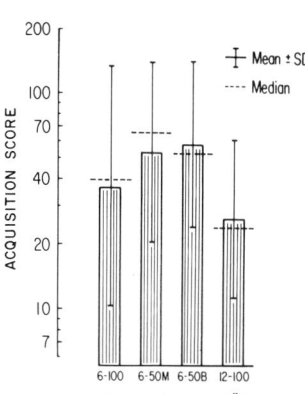

Figure 7.9. Acquisition scores for the split trial experiment. Bar heights are means, and brackets indicate plus or minus 1 SD (not standard error of the mean). Dashed horizontal lines indicate corresponding medians for each group.

12-100, as expected from the more favorable C/T ratio. The partial reinforcement groups appear somewhat retarded in the mean (though perhaps not in the median) relative to group 6-100; however, the variance in all groups is large.

The data were analyzed by three orthogonal planned comparisons. The first comparison between the two 50% groups showed that placement of the first half of the trial, either in the beginning or the middle of the cycle, did not reliably alter acquisition scores. A comparison between the combined 50% groups and the 6-100 long-delay group also was not reliable. The final contrast was between the short-delay group, 12-100, and the combined 6-100, 6-50M and 6-50B groups. The comparison just reached significance ($t[55] = 2.01$, $p < .05$). While the size of this effect is not as large as one might wish, it is in the appropriate direction: Early portions of the trial signal are in some manner cumulated with later reinforced portions, retarding acquisition relative to the short-delay group. The early trial signals are not "ignored" in the usual sense, since when the unreinforced trial signals are omitted, the association is learned more rapidly. A caveat must be registered with respect to these results. The Ns were chosen large to give the no-effect finding some status. However, the considerable variability in acquisition scores from both partial reinforcement experiments may have obscured some retardation in the intermittent groups relative to the 100% long-delay group. What these results do demonstrate is that temporal variables control more powerfully than the probability of reinforcement variable. The acquisition socres from the Gibbon et al. (1980) partial reinforcement experiment have been included at the appropriate C/T values in Figure 7.2. They are indicated there by asterisks and it is clear that they fit the general relationship about as well as do those from the other studies with continuous reinforcement. The data from Gibbon et al. (1975) shown in Figure 7.1 were also obtained using a partial reinforcement schedule ($P[S^*] = .25$). These data also fit with the C/T analysis (inverted filled triangles in Figure 7.2).

In summary then, time controls strongly and probability of reinforcement controls weakly if at all in the autoshaping paradigm. We believe this results from integration of total signal time and total interreinforcement time. The excitation levels engendered by these two periods are compared by a ratio comparator. The comparability of intermittent and continuous reinforcement data implies that the association mechanism is insensitive to the *position* of portions of the trial within the cycle, provided the last (nominal) signal is followed by food.

LEARNING SPEED

The account thus far has argued for a primitive appreciation of the average delay to reinforcement in the signal and the average delay between reinforcements. The speed with which these average values are learned has not been addressed, except in the sense that large C/T ratios may be expected to result in more rapid emergence of associative responding, since the difference between trial and cycle times should be easier to discriminate. We now wish to propose a form for the speed with which the association is learned. Responding reflects a discrimination between expectancy in the signal and the background. Accordingly, there are potentially two associations to understand. We believe that the acquisition of expectancy in the background proceeds quite rapidly relative to the formation of expectancy in the signal, and this asymmetry is important for the temporal properties of the associative mechanism.

Rapid Background Learning

Most of the data reported above have been from "naive" subjects. Strictly speaking, this nomenclature is incorrect. Subjects in the autoshaping paradigm must learn to eat from the feeder before signal training is begun. This hopper training constitutes a pretreatment in which birds may be expected to begin forming background or context expectancy levels appropriate to the food cycles employed. For most of the data from the Columbia University laboratory, an eating criterion was employed in hopper training that resulted in 50–80 reinforcement episodes before testing for acquisition to the key light was begun. The hopper training procedures employed in the other studies reviewed here varied somewhat from experiment to experiment, but in all cases, "naive" means brief hopper training with a mean cycle time that is generally short relative to most of the cycle values employed in autoshaping training.

Consider the implications of this for the ratio effect in Figure 7.2. If learning the background value proceeded relatively slowly, then the adjustment to a new cycle time that is either longer or shorter than the hopper training cycle might produce effects in opposite directions. When subjects are shifted from a short hopper-trining cycle to a long autoshaping cycle, background levels begin relatively high and must drop to a new low value associated with the long cycle. However, a shift to shorter cycle durations requires an increase in background levels above those obtained during hopper training. If the autoshaping test is conducted at the same C/T ratio but with different absolute values, acquisition speeds would not in general remain constant at constant ratios independent of the absolute values.

This implication is shown schematically in Figure 7.10. The ordinate represents expectancy levels on a log scale as a function of successive cycles on the abscissa. To the left of the vertical dashed line, the solid function represents a rather slow growth of background expectancy appropriate to a hopper training cycle of 20 sec ($h_C = H/C$ at asymptote) for 80 hopper presentations. To the right of the dashed vertical line, autoshaping testing is begun. The two curves rising from zero represent the growth expectancy appropriate to a trial value of

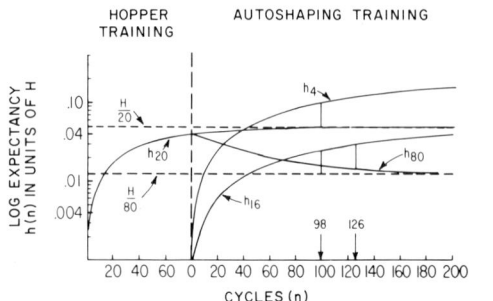

Figure 7.10. Hypothesized growth functions for background and trial expectancy on a log scale as a function of successive reinforced cycles. To the left of the dashed vertical line, hopper training is conducted for 80 reinforcers at a cycle length of 20 sec. The solid curve represents growth of background expectancy during this training. To the right of the dashed line, autoshaping training is depicted for two groups. The dropping function represents a slow approach to a new cycle value of 80 sec, and the two rising functions (h_4 and h_{16}) represent the growth of expectancy for a 4-sec and a 16-sec trial signal. The vertical arrows show the points at which the expectancy ratio reaches 2.0 for comparison of trial to background for the two groups.

4 sec and 16 sec. Consider a group tested with a 4-sec trial and a 20-sec cycle. The background may be expected to continue to rise to the asymptote of $H/20$ (solid curve, h_{20}). When a sufficient differential is achieved, keypecking emerges. A ratio comparison between expectancy in the 4-sec signal and the 20-sec background is shown as reaching a criterion value (set at $b = 2$) at the left vertical arrow. in this case, after 98 cycles.

Now consider a group trained with a 16-sec signal and an 80-sec cycle after the same hopper training experience. Such a group has the same C/T ratio ($C/T = 5$) but the speed with which the background adjusts to the longer cycle length will affect the point at which the same differential between trial and background is achieved. The background expectancy levels are shown by the falling curve asymptoting at $H/80$. In this case, the point at which the same threshold is reached is indicated by the right vertical arrow at 126 cycles. The example shows that if background learning is relatively slow, the ratio effect does not hold because long *absolute* cycle durations result in retarded acquisition relative to a cycle duration equal to the hopper training cycle value.[7]

Consider now what would happen if context learning were quite rapid. Then the achievement of the two background levels, $H/20$ and $H/80$ would occur long before the expectancy in the signals had reached substantial levels. The result is the ratio effect. Variations in absolute C values would produce negligible differences in the speed with which the asymptotes (indicated by dashed lines in the

[7]In the representation in Figure 7.10 it is moot whether expectancy is best represented on a logarithmic or linear scale. The logarithmic representation is convenient to show visually that a ratio comparison between trial and background achieves threshold at the same absolute distance between the growth function for the trial and that for the background.

figure) were approached. In this case criterion would be reached at the same number of cycles for a 16-sec signal against an 80-sec background as for the 4-sec signal against a 20-sec background.

We have examined the data in Figure 7.2 for the presence of an effect of the absolute size of C on acquisition speed. While there is considerable scatter in the data, it is not systematically related to absolute C values. An experiment addressed explicitly to this point would examine acquisition speed as a function of both hopper training cycle duration and autoshaping cycle duration at several C/T values. We have not conducted such an experiment, but data from several groups reported in Figure 7.2 and from some unpublished work in the Columbia laboratory are relevant. In the split trial experiment described earlier, and in another unpublished experiment (Balsam and Gibbon, 1978), hopper training was conducted at the same cycle value as birds experienced later in autoshaping training. Data from these groups may be contrasted with selected groups from the Gibbon *et al.* (1977) study which experienced approximately the same C/T ratio but after a constant 20-sec hopper training cycle.

In Table 7.1 the median number of cycles in autoshaping training required

TABLE 7.1
Acquisition Scores from Selected Studies in Which the Pretraining Cycle was the Same as the Training Cycle (Left Four Cells) or in Which the Pretraining Cycle Was 20 Sec (Right Four Cells)[a]

Ratio of cycle to trial (C/T)	Pretraining cycle = training cycle		Pretraining cycle = 20 sec	
	Short	Long	Short	Long
Small (6,7)	Gibbon & Balsam (split trial, unpublished) 40	Balsam & Gibbon (1978) 60[b]	Gibbon *et al.* (1977) 48	Gibbon *et al.* (1977) 35
	Balsam *et al.* (in press) 41			Balsam (1975) 36.5
	N = 23[a]	N = 5	N = 12	N = 12
Large (12,13)	Gibbon & Balsam (split trial, unpublished) 24	Balsam & Gibbon (1978) 20[b]	Gibbon *et al.* (1977) 18.5	Gibbon *et al.* (1977) 21
	Balsam *et al.* (in press) 18			Balsam (1975) 27.5
	N = 23	N = 5	N = 8	N = 12

[a] All N's are pooled across studies and conditions within studies.
[b] These scores are the median 5th trial with at least one response. All other acquisition scores are the median number of cycles to satisfy a criterion of responses on three out of four consecutive trials.

before our acquisition criterion was met is presented along with the Ns from these studies. The groups from Gibbon et al. were selected to have approximately the same C/T ratio, either small ($C/T = 6$ or 7) or large ($C/T = 12$ or 13). The absolute cycle time values were selected to be either short ($C = 52$–57.6) or long ($C = 96$–112). On the left of the table the four cells represent cases in which the hopper training cycle equaled the autoshaping cycle, and on the right cases in which the hopper training cycle was fixed at 20 sec. While these groups are taken from different experiments, and as a consequence the N's and other procedural details differ from cell to cell, they do provide some evidence on the size of effects to be attributed to hopper training cycle, absolute C, and C/T ratio.

An analysis of variance performed on the logged acquisition scores for all subjects showed no effect for hopper training cycle fixed or equal to C, no effect for C short or long, and a large effect for C/T small or large ($F[1/91] = 15.75$, $p < .001$). All two-way interactions were not reliable, and the three-way interaction just met significance ($F[1/91] = 4.17$, $.025 < p < .05$). This three-way interaction reflects a rather high acquisition score for the Balsam and Gibbon small N group ($C = 96$, $C/T = 6$). Therefore, within the variance that is typical of autoshaping acquisition, the absolute size of C and whether it is equal to or different from the hopper training cycle, makes little difference to autoshaping acquisition. What counts is the ratio of cycle time to trial time. Tomie (Chapter 6, this volume) comes to a similar conclusion regarding different hopper training cycle lengths.

Some indirect evidence on rapid adjustment to different background cycle lengths is contained in a recent report by Killeen, Hanson, and Osborne (1978). These authors studied general activity, which they regard as an index of arousal under different schedules of periodic reinforcement. Their data show quite rapid adjustments of activity levels that are inversely related to the cycle duration. Killeen et al. argue that arousal as indexed by activity levels is a generic property of reinforcement schedules and that the asymptotes they observe depend directly on incentive presentations and are not necessarily tied to contextual background stimuli. From the present perspective however, one might as easily argue that activity levels are conditioned to background stimuli, and the adjustment to new timing cycles which is very rapid in their data (within about 10 cycle presentations) corresponds to the rapid adjustment which we have argued occurs to background contexts in the autoshaping procedure.

Form of the Learning Function

Finally, we wish to suggest a form for the learning of trial and background expectancy values. Our assumptions are speculative but capture the core of the ideas proposed above. We assume that learning about the background cycle length is virtually immediate so that the course of acquisition to the signal is described by the manner in which expectancy levels appropriate to the trial duration are achieved and compared with the background.

We have adopted the simple and time-honored linear operator assumption. Trial signals increment with each reinforcer some proportion (α_T) of the remaining distance between the asymptotic expectancy level appropriate to T ($h_T [\infty] = H/T$) and the current level. These assumptions were used to generate the learning curves in Figure 7.10. The exponential growth functions for the two trial durations were produced assuming a slow growth rate parameter ($\alpha_T = .005$). Since the ordinate is logarithmic a constant ratio criterion translates to a constant vertical distance between the appropriate trial and background expectancy functions.

Formally, assuming that background learning is immediate, the number of cycles, n, in autoshaping training required to reach threshold, b, is given by

$$n = \frac{\ln\left(1 - \frac{bT}{C}\right)}{\ln(1 - \alpha_T)}, \tag{1}$$

where α_T is the learning rate parameter for the speed with which the trial signal approaches its asymptote, H/T. In Appendix A, we derive the more general case in which background is not immediate but proceeds at a rate, α_C. There also, we show that a discernible effect of absolute cycle duration may be expected when $\alpha_C = \alpha_T$. For the present application, we have used the relation in equation 1 and subjected the data from Figure 7.2 (omitting the two deviant points at $C/T = 97$) to a minimum variance fit with b and α_T as free parameters. The result is the smooth curve in Figure 7.11. This fit, which accounts for 75% of the variance requires $b = 1.5$ and $\alpha_T = .005$.

The fit represented here is to be compared with the linear regression fit from Figure 7.2 reproduced here as the dashed line. It is clear that some upward curvature in the data at short C/T values is not accommodated by the linear regression and is accommodated here. In fact, in this deterministic form, C/T ratios that are less than b are never learned—hence, the rise toward infinity in the theoretical function as C/T approaches b.[8]

It is equally clear that for large C/T values, the linear regression does better than the theoretical account, since there appears to be a minimum in the data that is not reflected in the theoretical curve. In the theory, given a sufficiently large C/T value, learning may be virtually immediate. Although the variance of the data in Figure 7.11 precludes a realistic assessment of the approach to this minimum, it seems to be in the neighborhood of 5–10 trials. This is about the number of trials Killeen et al. (1978) find required for adjustment of activity to periodic feedings.

[8]Data from the $C/T = 1.5$ ratio ($C/T \leq b$) was excluded from the fit.

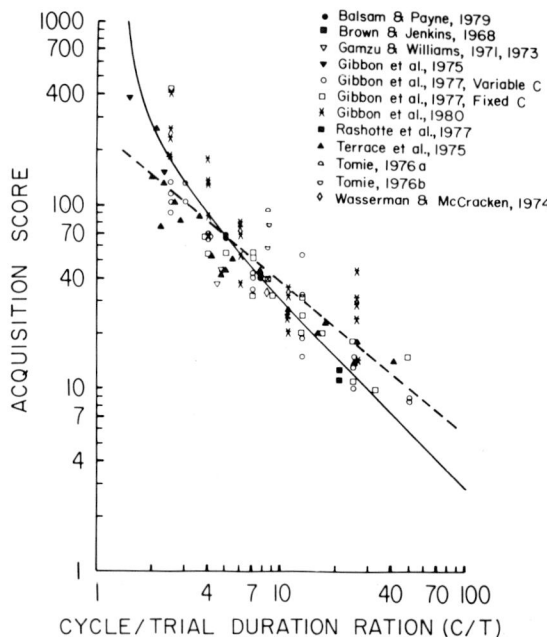

Figure 7.11. Log acquisition scores versus log C/T ratio. The smooth curve is a minimum variance fit to the deterministic scalar expectancy acquisition function. The dashed line is the minimum variance regression line.

VARIANCE

The expectancy ratio account embodied in equation (1) is deterministic. It regards each subject as learning about the background immediately, learning about the trial signal at a rate α_T and responding when the expectancy ratio exceeds b. In fact, the data are remarkable both for the strength of control by C/T and for the variability around any descriptive function. There are several ways in which such variability might arise. For example, the rate at which learning progresses may be expected to vary across a population of subjects. We have not analyzed this source of variance in much detail. One reason is that we do not wish to put too much weight on the linear operator assumption. We regard it as a convenient shorthand that captures the conception that learning about the signal is gradual and more rapid early in training than late. More direct evidence on continuous versus discrete state learning is not available for the autoshaping situation. Data from other classical conditioning preparations (e.g., Pfautz & Wagner, 1976; Prokasy, 1972; Theios & Brelsford, 1977) appear to favor multiple-state models, though the contribution of variable learning parameters has not been studied in depth.

Variability in the threshold, b, is similarly difficult to analyze. Again, a population of subjects may be expected to vary in this parameter, with a consequent variability in acquisition scores. In the account of Scalar Expectancy Theory applied to asymptotic temporal discrimination (Gibbon, 1977) this parameter reflects the response–nonresponse dimension. In the autoshaping application, b indexes the ease with which the keypeck is released by the signal for increased food expectancy.

Thus, while the speed of learning and the propensity to peck may be expected to vary across birds, we have little to contribute on how these sources add to the variance in our acquisition data.

Timing Precision

A feature of the association mechanism that has received considerable study in the asymptotic temporal discrimination context, however, is variability in the subjective assessment of the time values being compared. In the earlier account the coefficient of variation, $\gamma = \sigma/\mu$, is an index of the sensitivity of subjects to temporal variables. Gamma is the ratio of the standard deviation to the mean for the "unit timer" under the scalar timing assumption. The scalar rule requires that the coefficient of variation remain constant for estimates of any absolute time value.

A stochastic version of the expectancy ratio account that allows variability in the estimates of T and C is derived in Appendix B, and we will sketch the form of that analysis here. Imagine that upon each trial presentation following the first, an estimate of T and C is made by subjects and an expectancy value computed on the basis of the learning curves shown in Figure 7.10. The estimates of the trial and cycle time are then both variable. In this stochastic version of the model, learned changes in associative strength are restricted to learning how "predictive" the signal is, or how "expectant" to be after a reinforced trial and cycle episode. The trial and cycle times themselves, however, are estimated with as much precision early as late in training. The sensitivity of the system (γ) remains constant throughout training and what changes is the associative value attached to the signals. On this assumption, after each reinforced trial episode, the expectancy level is increased by the appropriate proportion of the distance to asymptote, and upon each subsequent trial, new estimates are obtained of T and C for a comparison of the corresponding expectancy levels. In Appendix B, it is shown that the probability that a subject will require more than n comparisons ($i > n$ where i is the trial at which the expectancy ratio exceeds threshold) is

$$P(i>n) = \prod_{k=1}^{n} \Phi[z(w_k)], \qquad (2)$$

where

$$z(W_k) = \frac{w_k - 1}{\gamma\sqrt{1 + w_k^2}} \quad (3)$$

is the Geary z-variate (cf. Gibbon, 1977) for the kth trial time estimate ratio and

$$w_k = \frac{bT}{C(1-\beta^n)} \quad (4)$$

is the appropriate scale transform of the threshold, with $\beta = 1 - \alpha_T$.

Equation (2) is the probability that acquisition has not occurred on trials 1, 2, ..., n, and assumes independence of successive comparisons. The terms in the product are cumulative normal probabilities associated with the (approximately) normal variate defined by equation (3). This variate changes with trial number (k) as defined by equation (4), to reflect the increments in expectancy in the trial signal as training progresses. Variability in the time estimates is contained in the random variables $z(w_k)$. If there were no variance here, $w_k = 1$ and equation (4) implies equation (1) for the deterministic model.

The point of this analysis is to determine the extent to which variability in acquisition scores may be attributed to variance in time estimation (γ). Accordingly, a computer program was written that computed the median of the decumulative distribution function (equation [2]). That is, the program calculated the value of n such that the right side of equation (2) was .5, given values of C/T and b, γ, and α_T. The program then fit the median acquisition score data allowing b, γ, and α_T as free parameters.

The fit is displayed in Figure 7.12. The solid curve is the best fitting median function $\omega^2 = .78$ with $C/T = 97$ excluded). The values for the learning rate and the threshold obtained are quite close to those for the deterministic model, $\alpha_T = .006$ and $b = 2.05$. The result of importance here, however, is the variance prediction entailed by γ, the sensitivity index. The dashed curves bracketing the median are the 25 and 75 percentile functions for the best fitting parameters. Fifty percent of all *individual* bird's acquisition scores should lie between these functions if the only source of variance was imprecision in timing. In fact, the data points are group *medians*, and somewhat less than 50% of these lie in the semi-interquartile range. Clearly, other sources of variance are present in these data.

A second feature of importance in the variance prediction is the absolute value of the best fitting sensitivity parameter, $\gamma = .22$. This value is quite close to those obtained for good discriminations by birds in asymptotic temporal discrimination situations (Gibbon, 1977, Figures 20–22).

This correspondence fits well the power of the C/T variable to modulate acquisition speed. It suggests that the sensitivity to temporal parameters is about as sharp early in the acquisition of an association as it is after long training in temporal discrimination. Moreover, intersubject variability in sensitivity to time

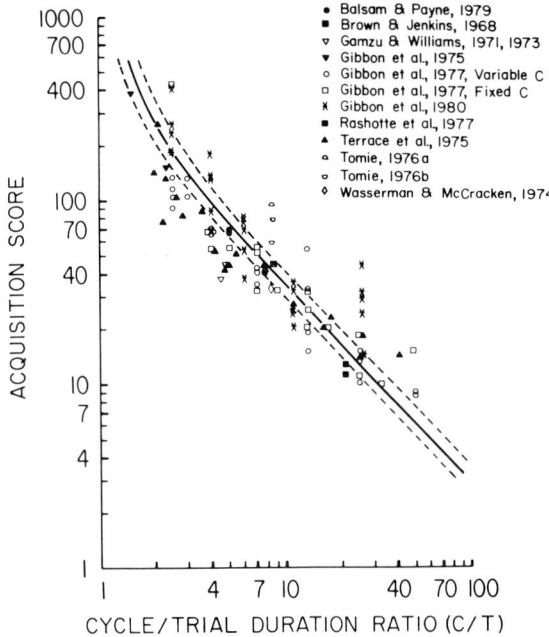

Figure 7.12. Log acquisition score versus C/T fit with the stochastic acquisition function for Scaler expectancy theory. The dashed functions represent the predicted semi-interquartile range.

is not an important contributor to variance here. The reason is that variability at small and large C/T ratios is comparable on the log scale in Figure 7.12. This property of the data is consonant with variance in trial-by-trial estimation of C and T, with a given sensitivity. This is illustrated by the constant spread in the semi-interquartile range functions.

It is *not* consonant with broad variation across subjects in individual γ values. Consider a slow learner exposed to a difficult C/T ratio. Such a subject might be retarded in acquisition because of poor temporal discrimination of T from C (high γ). But then a comparably poor discriminator would be even more retarded relative to the median subject at a more favorable C/T ratio. That is, for subjects that are relatively insensitive to time, changes in temporal predictiveness (C/T) make less of a difference in acquisition speed.

This idea is illustrated in a different way in Figure 7.13. The data points represent the proportion of subjects at two C/T ratios (taken from groups in Gibbon *et al.*, 1977) that did not acquire by n reinforced trials. The data are thus potential instantiations of the decumulative distribution form of equation (2). In the left panel, the solid curves are the predictions for this form from the fit to the medians in Figure 7.12. They intersect the distributions at about the median, but are clearly too steep to describe the more deviant performances. In the right panel, the solid curve through the data for $C/T = 4$ is a fit to these data that

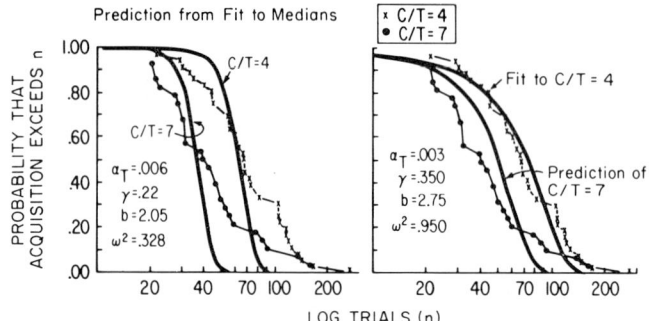

Figure 7.13. Proportion of subjects requiring more than n trials before acquisition. X's represent $C/T = 4$; open circles represent $C/T = 7$. In the panel on the left the smooth curves are the predictions of these data for the parameter values obtained from the fit to the medians in Figure 7.12. In the right panel, the two smooth curves are the predictions of the stochastic acquisition functions based on the data for $C/T = 4$.

allowed γ to vary. The result was a relatively close description ($\omega^2 = .95$) with a high coefficient of variation ($\gamma = .35$). The second curve displaced toward lower n is the prediction for the $C/T = 7$ data entailed by the same γ value. The prediction is clearly in error in the direction of too little sensitivity to the new C/T ratio. Real subjects acquire faster at $C/T = 7$ than the spread of performance at $C/T = 4$ predicts. Thus sources of variance other than temporal uncertainty, both within and between subjects, are present in autoshaping acquisition. Variation in the criterion for responding, b, seems to us a likely candidate for a major contribution. It is likely that such variability might be present within, as well as between, subjects.

Relatively good sensitivity to time is also consonant with the evidence presented above for rapid adjustment of background expectancy to different cycle lengths. While rapid background learning obviously requires a high learning rate parameter, it also perforce requires that subjects experience a discriminable difference between hopper training and autoshaping cycle lengths. In fact, we would like to speculate that the minimum of 5–10 trials before conditioning was observed, even at the most favorable C/T ratios, may reflect temporal adjustment to the C and T values. Above this minimum, graded acquisition performance reflects the gradual accumulation of expectancy in the signal above the background level. On this view, variability in acquisition scores, which is ubiquitous in the autoshaping preparation, contains only a moderate temporal component.

Limitations of the Theory

The account proposed above is tentative and will surely require modification in several important respects. For one thing, extinction is not accommodated on this view. There is no provision in the present version for an adjustment of expectancy levels in the absence of a feeding episode. Rather, expectancies were assumed to be updated only when reinforcement occurred, thus allowing for integration over unreinforced trial episodes in partial reinforcement schedules. In fact, of course, a sufficiently long wait without food must force an adjustment in food expectation; else expectancy values would remain indefinitely at their training levels and extinction would not occur. Gibbon et al. (1980) show that extinction rates are comparable when computed on a per-expected-reinforcer basis. This suggests that when an expected reward is omitted, this event forces an appropriate adjustment of expectancy levels. Such a view would provide a basis for the evidence Jenkins presents (Chapter 8, this volume) on the importance of the first long wait after hopper training in acquisition. When food expectancy during the hopper training regime has established a high background expectancy level and autoshaping training is begun at a substantially longer cycle length, several occasions in which expected reinforcement is omitted occur within the first long-cycle presentation. This may result in a lowered overall food expectation from which the improvement associated with the signal can emerge more readily.

A second important limitation of the theory that is less readily accommodated stems from the observations of Tomie (Chapter 6, this volume) and others that prior training within a given context may retard subsequent acquisition of autoshaping in the same context. In the proposal above, we have assumed that learning about the signal and about the background proceeded independently of each other. The expectancy levels in the diagrams depended only on the respective time periods, T and C and did not reflect interactions between them. While this may be appropriate to the asymptotes eventually achieved, the independence assumption is unlikely to be true of the speed with which these levels are approached. Rather, the rapid learning of a high context expectancy may act to overshadow later learning to expect food in the signal. Although it appears difficult to establish clear evidence for blocking of autoshaped responding in standard blocking paradigms (e.g., Jenkins, Chapter 8, this volume) there is accumulating evidence of overshadowing by prior context training (e.g., Straub & Gibbon, 1977; Tomie, 1976a, 1976b). This evidence argues for the kind of competition between the background and the signal that has been well documented in other classical conditioning preparations (Rescorla, 1975; Rescorla & Wagner, 1972). Whatever modifications are required to accommodate integration in the absence of food delivery (extinction) and competition in the acquisition of food expectation in the signal (blocking), they must preserve the central role of time elaborated here.

CONCLUDING REMARKS

The evidence we have summarized establishes, we believe, the primacy of temporal arrangements in the formation of the association between signal and food in the autoshaping preparation. It makes little difference to birds whether alternative signals negatively correlated with food are present or not, or whether the times between food presentations are variable or not, or whether the signals predicting food are consistent or inconsistent, provided at least a few signals are contiguous with food presentations.

The scalar expectancy theory account of these effects is speculative in several details but difficult to fault at its core. The central idea espoused is that the association between the signal and food depends on an appreciation of the improvement in the average delay to reinforcement in the signal compared with the average delay overall or in the background. This tenet of the theory receives additional support from its power in addressing quite distantly related temporal discrimination data (Gibbon, 1977). The commonalities between asymptotic temporal discrimination and the acquisition of association analyzed here are more impressive to us than the differences. In particular, both asymptotic temporal discriminations and the acquisition of autoshaped behavior require a temporally undifferentiated appreciation of the average wait between food deliveries, independently of whatever stimulus events may be experimentally programmed. This constant background modulates the degree to which associations between signals and food in autoshaping, and associations between elapsing time intervals and food in asymptotic temporal discriminations, are expressed.

A second commonality is that this discrimination is mediated by a ratio of the relevant time values. The ratio discrimination observed here appears to be a common property of the temporal structure of learned associations and bears an intimate relation to Weber's Law for animal time discrimination (Gibbon, 1977). There is a strong correspondence between the obtained values for temporal sensitivity (γ) and the threshold for associative improvement (b) in both acquisition and asymptotic performance. It means to us that the temporal control responsible is mediated by the same mechanism.

ACKNOWLEDGMENT

We thank Stephen Fairhurst for computer analysis. We would also like to thank Mary Ellen Natale and Ellen Mascoli for help in conducting some of the unpublished experiments reported here.

APPENDIX A: TRIALS TO CRITERION— DETERMINISTIC VERSION

Background Immediate: $h_c = H/C$

The change in expectancy, Δh on each trial is

$$\Delta h(n) = \alpha(L - h(n)),$$

where L is the asymptotic expectancy level, $L = H/T$. This difference equation is well known to have the solution

$$h(n) = L - (L - S)(1 - \alpha)^n, \quad (A1)$$

where $h(0) = S$ is the starting level. Therefore, assuming $h_T(0) = 0$, the expectancy ratio, $r(n) = h_T(n)/h_C$, will reach threshold, b, when

$$\frac{C}{T}[1 - (1 - \alpha)^n] = b,$$

or

$$n = \frac{\ln\left(1 - \frac{bT}{C}\right)}{\ln(1 - \alpha)}, \quad (A2)$$

which is equation (1).

Background Gradual

After m-many hopper training trials at a K-sec cycle with background salience, α_C,

$$h_K(m) = \frac{H}{K}[1 - (1 - \alpha_C)^m], \quad (A3)$$

assuming $h_K(0) = 0$. But then letting $h_K(m) = S$ in A1, the background after n additional autoshaping trials at cycle length, C, is

$$h_C(n) = \frac{H}{C}[1 - (1 - Ch_K(m))(1 - \alpha_C)^n],$$

while the trial expectancy is

$$h_T(n) = \frac{H}{T}[1 - (1 - \alpha_T)^n].$$

The expectancy ratio may be written

$$r(n) \equiv \frac{h_T(n)}{h_C(n)} = \frac{\frac{C}{T}(1 - \beta_T^n)}{1 - \beta_C^n[1 - \frac{C}{K}(1 - \beta_C^m)]}, \quad (A4)$$

where $\beta_J = 1 - \alpha_J$, $J = T, C$. The form (A4) does not provide an analytic solution for n at the threshold crossing, $r = b$, as long as $\alpha_T \neq \alpha_C$. However, when $\alpha_T = \alpha_C$, $r = b$ implies

$$\beta^n = \left[1 + \frac{1 - \beta^m}{\frac{K}{bT} - \frac{1}{C}} \right]^{-1}. \tag{A5}$$

In this form it is clear that n is a function of the absolute value of C. Increasing C increases n (cf. Figure 7.10).

APPENDIX B: TRIALS TO CRITERION; STOCHASTIC VERSION—BACKGROUND IMMEDIATE

Assume variance only in estimates of C and T, (x_C, x_T). Then P(no R on trial #k) = $P(r(k) < b)$, where

$$r(k) \equiv \frac{h_T(k)}{h_C} = \frac{\frac{H}{x_T}(1 - \beta_T^n)}{\frac{H}{x_C}} \tag{B1}$$

$r(k) < b$ then implies

$$\frac{x_C}{x_T} < \frac{b}{1 - \beta_T^n}. \tag{B2}$$

But assuming the scalar property for x_J, x_J is normal (J, γJ) so that the rule (B2) may be written

$$\frac{u}{v} < \frac{bT}{C(1 - \beta_T^n)}, \tag{B3}$$

where u,v are normal (1, γ). In Gibbon (1977) the probability of the event (B3) is shown to be (approximately) the normal integral, Φ, given by

$$P\left(\frac{u}{v} < w_k\right) \simeq \Phi[z(w_k)], \tag{B4a}$$

where

$$w_k = \frac{bT}{C(1 - \beta_T^n)}, \tag{B4b}$$

and

$$z(w_k) = \frac{w_k - 1}{\gamma\sqrt{1 + w_k^2}} \tag{B4c}$$

is the Geary z-variate for the transformed criterion (B3) on the kth trial. Therefore, assuming trial independence, the probability of no response by trial n is

$$P(\text{no R on trials } 1, 2, \cdots, n) = \prod_{k=1}^{n} \Phi[z(w_k)]. \qquad (B5)$$

REFERENCES

Ainslie, G. W. Impulse control in pigeons. *Journal of the Experimental Analysis of Behavior*, 1974, 21, 485–489.

Balsam, P. D. *The effects of varying the trace interval, CS duration, and the interreinforcement interval on key-pecking in the pigeon.* Unpublished doctoral dissertation, University of North Carolina, 1975.

Balsam, P. D., & Gibbon, J. Associative factors underlying the trace decrement in autoshaping. *Proceedings of the 49th Annual Convention of the Eastern Psychological Association*, 1978, 200.

Balsam, P. D., Brownstein, A. J., & Shull, R. L. The effects of duration of grain presentation on automaintenance. *Journal of the Experimental Analysis of Behavior*, 1978, 29, 27–36.

Balsam, P. D., Locurto, C. M., Terrace, H. S., Gibbon, J. A search for pretraining effects in autoshaping. *Psychological Record*, in press.

Balsam, P. D., & Payne, D. Intertrial interval and unconditioned stimulus durations in autoshaping. *Animal Learning and Behavior*, 1979, 7, 477–482.

Barnes, R. A., & Jenkins, H. M. Analysis of the trial-spacing effect in autoshaping. *Proceedings of the 47th Annual Convention of the Eastern Psychological Association*, 1976, 71.

Brown, P. L., & Jenkins, H. M. Autoshaping of the pigeon's keypeck. *Journal of the Experimental Analysis of Behavior*, 1968, 11, 1–8.

Catania, A. C. Concurrent performances: A baseline for the study of reinforcement magnitude. *Journal of the Experimental Analysis of Behavior*, 1963, 6, 253–263.

Coppock, H. W., & Chambers, R. M. GSR conditioning: An illustration of useless distinctions between "type" of conditioning. *Psychological Reports*, 1959, 5, 171–177.

Frey, P. W., & Butler, C. S. Rabbit eyelid conditioning as a function of unconditioned stimulus duration. *Journal of Comparative and Physiological Psychology*, 1973, 85, 289–294.

Furedy, J. J. Classical appetitive conditioning of the GSR with cool air as the UCS and the roles of UCS onset and offset as reinforcers of the CR. *Journal of Experimental Psychology*, 1967, 75, 73–80.

Gamzu, E., & Williams, D. R. Classical conditioning of a complex skeletal response. *Science*, 1971, 171, 923–925.

Gamzu, E., & Williams, D. R. Associative factors underlying the pigeon's keypecking in autoshaping procedures. *Journal of the Experimental Analysis of Behavior*, 1973, 19, 225–232.

Gibbon, J. Scalar expectancy theory and Weber's Law in animal timing. *Psychological Review*, 1977, 84, 279–325.

Gibbon, J., Baldock, M. D., Locurto, C. M., Gold, L., & Terrace, H. S. Trial and intertrial durations in autoshaping. *Journal of Experimental Psychology: Animal Behavior Processes*, 1977, 3, 264–284.

Gibbon, J., & Balsam, P. D. Temporal integration of trials under partial reinforcement. (In preparation.)

Gibbon, J., Farrell, L., Locurto, C. M., Duncan, H. J., & Terrace, H. S. Partial reinforcement in autoshaping with pigeons. *Animal Learning and Behavior.* 1980, 8, 45–59.

Gibbon, J., Locurto, C. M., & Terrace, H. S. Signal-food contingency and signal frequency in a continuous trials auto-shaping paradigm. *Animal Learning and Behavior*, 1975, 3, 317–324.

Gormezano, I., & Moore, J. W. Classical conditioning. In M. H. Marx (Ed.), *Learning: Processes.* Toronto: Macmillan, 1969.

Jenkins, H. M., & Moore, B. R. The form of the autoshaped response with food or water reinforcers. *Journal of the Experimental Analysis of Behavior*, 1973, 20, 163–181.

Killeen, P., Hanson, S. J., & Osborne, S. R. Arousal: Its genesis and manifestation as response rate. *Psychological Review*, 1978, 85, 571–581.

Moffit, M., & Shimp, C. P. Two-key concurrent paced variable-interval schedules of reinforcement. *Journal of the Experimental Analysis of Behavior*, 1971, 16, 39–49.

Mowrer, O. H., & Solomon, L. N. Contiguity vs. drive-reduction in conditioned and unconditioned stimulus. *American Journal of Psychology*, 1954, 67, 26–38.

Newlin, R., & LoLordo, V. A comparison of pecking generated by serial, delay and trace autoshaping procedures. *Journal of the Experimental Analysis of Behavior*, 1976, 25, 227–241.

Perkins, C. C., Jr., Beavers, W. O., Hancock, R. A., Jr., Hemmendinger, P. C., Hemmendinger, D., & Ricci, J. A. Some variables affecting rate of key pecking during response-independent procedures (autoshaping). *Journal of the Experimental Analysis of Behavior*, 1975, 24, 59–72.

Pfautz, P. L., & Wagner, A. R. Transient variations in responding to Pavlovian conditioned stimuli have implications for the mechanisms of "priming". *Animal Learning and Behavior*, 1976, 4, 107–112.

Prokasy, W. F. Developments with the two-phase model applied to human eyelid conditioning. In A. H. Black & W. F. Prokasy (Eds.), *Classical conditioning II: Current research and theory.* New York: Appleton-Century-Crofts, 1972.

Rachlin, H., & Green, L. Commitment, choice and self-control. *Journal of the Experimental Analysis of Behavior*, 1972, 17, 15–22.

Rashotte, M. E., Griffin, R. W., & Sisk, C. L. Second-order conditioning of pigeon's keypeck. *Animal Learning and Behavior*, 1977, 5, 25–38.

Rescorla, R. A. Pavlovian conditioning and its proper control procedures. *Psychological Review*, 1967, 74, 71–80.

Rescorla, R. A. Pavlovian excitatory and inhibitory conditioning. In W. K. Estes (Ed.), *Handbook of Learning and cognitive processes* (Vol. 2). Hillsdale, N.J.: Erlbaum, 1975.

Rescorla, M. E., & Wagner, A. R. A theory of Pavlovian conditioning: Variations in the effectiveness of reinforcement and non-reinforcement. In A. Black & W. Prokasy (Eds.), *Classical conditioning II: Current research and theory.* New York: Appleton-Century-Crofts, 1972.

Salz, E., Kitai, S., & Asdourian, D. Two-factor theory: Preliminary study of relationship between drive reduction and UCS duration. *Psychological Reports*, 1963, 12, 757–758.

Shimp, C. P. Magnitude and frequency of reinforcement and frequencies of interresponse times. *Journal of the Experimental Analysis of Behavior*, 1968, 11, 525–535.

Straub, R., & Gibbon, J. Contextual blocking with a diffuse temporal stimulus. *Proceedings of the 48th Annual Convention of the Eastern Psychological Association*, 1977, 147.

Terrace, H. S., Gibbon, J., Farrell, L., & Baldock, M. D. Temporal factors influencing the acquisition and maintenance of an autoshaped keypeck. *Animal Learning and Behavior*, 1975, 3, 53–62.

Theios, J., & Brelsford, J. W. A Markov model for classical conditioning: Application to eye-blink conditioning in rabbits. *Psychological Review*, 1966, 73, 393–408.

Tomie, A. Interference with autoshaping by prior context conditioning. *Journal of Experimental Psychology: Animal Behavior Processes*, 1976, 2, 323–334. (a)

Tomie, A. Retardation of autoshaping: Control by contextual stimuli. *Science*, 1976, 192, 1244–1246. (b)

Wasserman, E. A., & McCracken, S. B. The disruption of autoshaped keypecking in the pigeon by food-tray illumination. *Journal of the Experimental Analysis of Behavior*, 1974, 22, 39–45.

Wasserman, E. A., & Molina, E. J. Explicitly unpaired keylight and food presentations: Interference with subsequent autoshaped keypecking in pigeons. *Journal of Experimental Psychology: Animal Behavior Processes*, 1975, 104, 30–38.

Wegner, N., & Zeaman, D. Strength of cardiac conditioned response with varying unconditioned stimulus duration. *Psychological Review*, 1958, 65, 238–241.

H. M. JENKINS
R. A. BARNES
F. J. BARRERA

Why Autoshaping Depends on Trial Spacing

It is now well known through the work of several laboratories that the temporal spacing of trials has a major effect on autoshaping of the pigeon's keypeck (Gibbon, Baldock, Locurto, Gold, & Terrace, 1977; Gibbon, Locurto, & Terrace, 1975; Perkins, Beavers, Hancock, Hemmendinger, Hemmendinger, & Ricci, 1975; Terrace, Gibbon, Farrell, & Baldock, 1975). When the time between trials (pairing of a localized visual stimulus with the presentation of food) is too short, autoshaped keypecking does not develop reliably despite extensive exposure. In strong contrast, reliable acquisition can be obtained with less than a half-dozen trials with sufficiently long waiting times between trials. The effect of trial spacing is so large that no theory of autoshaping can be considered adequate unless it provides an account of how spacing exerts its effect.

The purposes of the present chapter are to report a series of experiments that attempts to isolate the cause of the trial-spacing effect and to relate the findings to current ideas about the role of contingency and predictability in the acquisition of signal value in classical conditioning.

DEMONSTRATION OF TRIAL SPACING EFFECT: EXPERIMENT 1

It will be useful to begin with a demonstration of the typical effect of trial spacing as it appears with the general procedures used in the present experiments. In Experiment 1, as in most of the experiments reported here, the procedure was conventional. King pigeons at 75% of free-feeding weight were first trained to approach quickly and to eat from a tray containing Purina pigeon checkers. Availability of food was signaled by lighting the tray opening (white bulb) whenever the tray was raised into position for eating. After the pigeons had experienced relatively long tray-up times, an automatically programmed schedule of food delivery was introduced; the tray was up for 2.5-sec intervals after variable waits averaging 75 sec (range of 12–132 sec). There were about 16 sessions of training with 40 food deliveries per session before trials were introduced. This was unusually extensive tray-training, and in other experiments far fewer preliminary sessions were used.[1]

The autoshaping stimulus was a backlighted red dot, 6 mm in diameter, presented at the center of a square pecking key 3.2 cm on a side. The dot appeared for a fixed duration of 8 sec. At its offset, the food tray operated. A constant intertrial interval was used. The intertrial interval is given as the time between trial onsets. In Experiment 1, data were obtained from 60 pigeons; half assigned at random to an intertrial period of 300 sec (Group 300); the remainder to an intertrial period of 30 sec (Group 30).[2] There were 12 daily sessions of autoshaping with 20 trials per session.

In Figure 8.1, acquisition is shown by two measures; percentage of birds that reach a criterion of acquisition and percentage of birds making at least one peck on a trial. The criterion is five consecutive trials with at least one peck, and it is plotted as though it was met on the first trial of the criterion run.

On average, about 20% of birds pecked at the first presentation of the stimulus, before the stimulus could acquire signal value. This rather high percentage is probably due in large part to the use of a small red dot as an autoshaping stimulus rather than the more usual stimulus of lighting the entire pecking disc. (A typical pecking disc would measure 2.5 cm in diameter.) It is of interest that there was, however, no correlation between the occurrence of a peck on the first trial and the number of trials required to reach criterion (Barnes, 1976, p. 31). The percentage of birds pecking increased sharply from the first trial in Group 300, whereas in Group 30 the curve actually dropped after the first trial. It then showed a far slower and more uncertain increase than in Group 300.

The number of trials to criterion showed a similar effect. Considering only subjects that reached criterion, the median number of trials to criterion was 9.5 in Group 300 and 55.0 in Group 30. Trial spacing also had some effect on the percentage of birds that eventually met the criterion within 12 sessions of training. In Group 300 only 7% failed to reach criterion; in Group 30, 30% failed. On the other hand, the rate of pecking was similar at the end of training (sessions 10–12) for those birds that reached criterion: 1.57 pecks per sec in Group 300,

---

[1] No obvious effects due to differences in the amount of preliminary tray training were found in the present series of experiments. For a review of systematic experiments on this variable see Tomie, Chapter 6, this volume.

[2] The numbering of experiments in this chapter does not correspond to their numbering in Barnes' thesis. The results reported here for Experiment 1 are based on pooled data from several experiments in which groups were run with the same intertrial intervals.

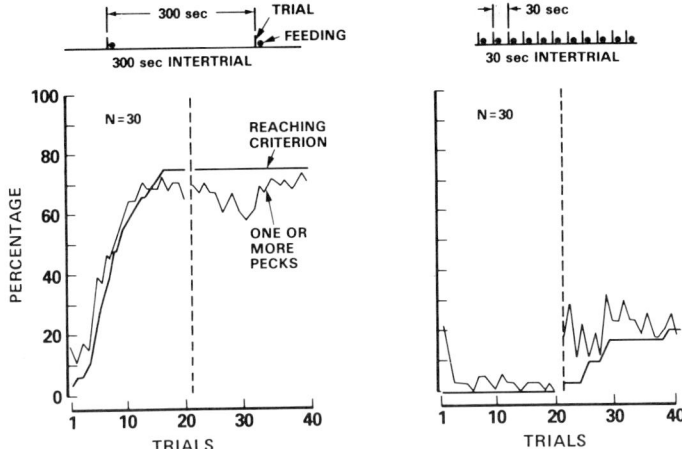

Figure 8.1. Acquisition of autoshaping measured by percentage of subjects reaching criterion, or percentage of subjects making one or more pecks on a trial, for an intertrial interval of 300 sec (left panel) or 30 sec (right panel).

and 1.50 in Group 30. The major effect of trial spacing was on the speed and reliability of acquisition.

EFFECT NOT DUE TO LOCAL INTERFERENCE

When trials are closely spaced, each one, except for the first and last, is both preceded and followed closely in time by another trial stimulus and by another feeding. This fact suggests the possibility that the events immediately surrounding any given trial interfere with the effectiveness of that trial in bringing about autoshaped key pecking. It is not hard to find theoretical arguments to support the idea that local interference lies behind the trial-spacing effect.

If local interference were the sole cause of the trial-spacing effect, performance under widely spaced trials would be reduced to the level found under closely spaced trials by injecting one, or a few, extra feedings or extra stimulus presentations in close temporal proximity to the otherwise widely spaced trials.

Location of Extra Feedings: Experiment 2

In this experiment the effect of delivering unsignaled food at different times in relation to the autoshaping trials was examined. To a greater extent than our other experiments on local interference, it was guided by a specific hypothesis. The hypothesis was as follows. One food delivery can serve as a signal for the next food delivery and can therefore compete with the autoshaping stimulus as a signal for food. In theory, the autoshaping stimulus would be subject to a greater degree of overshadowing (see Kamin, 1969) from a prior delivery when trials are closely spaced, and this could account for slower acquisition of autoshaped keypecking. Although the assumptions are somewhat different, the same prediction follows from an extension of the Wagner–Rescorla theory of classical conditioning. The application of that theory to spacing effects is taken up later (see p. 279).

In each group in Experiment 2, autoshaping was carried out under the same conditions as for Group 300 (300-sec intertrial intervals) except that four unsignaled food deliveries were placed in every intertrial interval. Group Before ($N = 18$) had extra feedings at 30, 60, 90, and 120 sec prior to the feeding on the trial; Group After ($N = 12$) had its four extra feedings at corresponding intervals following the trial feeding; Group Before–After ($N = 12$) had two extra feedings before, and two after, the trial feeding (30 and 60 sec before and 30 and 60 sec after the feeding). There were 12 20-trial sessions.

Summary data on acquisition for these groups are given in Table 8.1 along with the previously presented results from Group 300 and Group 30 (Experiment 1). The median number of trials to criterion in Table 8.1 is exclusive of birds that did not reach criterion within the 240 trials. On the overshadowing hypothesis, Group Before would be expected to perform more poorly than Group After, but the results show them to be quite comparable to each other and to Group Before–After. Median trials to acquisition was somewhat larger in each of the groups with extra feedings than in Group 300. (Group 300 versus pooled results for Group Before, Group After, and Group Before–After: $U = 437$, $p < .027$).[3] Acquisition in Group 30 was, however, significantly slower than acquisition in these groups (Group 30 versus pooled results; $U = 331$, $p < .006$).

The conclusion to be drawn from these results is that the trial-spacing effect cannot be reduced to the overshadowing of the autoshaping stimulus by prior food delivery as a competing signal of food. Nor can the spacing effect be reduced to possible local posttrial effects of food delivery or to the combination of local pretrial and posttrial effects. The results suggest that the retardation caused by the introduction of unsignaled food presentations was independent of their location with respect to the trial. That conclusion was further supported by two other groups (not shown in Table 8.1); one run with four extra feedings introduced at random times in each intertrial interval and one run with the four feedings regularly spaced, 60 sec apart. Acquisition results in these groups were not

---

[3]Whereas the median trial to acquisition, as reported in Table 8.1 and elsewhere in this chapter, is based only on subjects that reached the acquisition criterion, statistical tests are based on all subjects; those not reaching criterion are assigned the total number trials presented (e.g., 240 in Experiments 1 and 2). All U-tests are two-tailed.

TABLE 8.1
Effect of Unsignaled Feedings at Different Times with Respect to Trials, Experiment 2

	Median trials to criterion	Percentage reaching criterion
Group 300 (Experiment 1)	9.5	93
Group 30 (Experiment 1)	55.0	70
Group Before	28.0	94
Group After	16.0	83
Group Before–After	24.0	83

statistically distinguishable from the results obtained with the extra feedings close to the trial.

Extra Feeding Immediately before the Trial: Experiment 3

The maximum overshadowing effect would be expected from food delivered immediately before the onset of the autoshaping stimulus. Experiment 3 compared acquisition when there was a delivery immediately prior to acquisition, with no unsignaled feedings. The experiment was run with a single trial per daily session. Sessions were 15 min long. The trial was presented at the midpoint of the session. It consisted of an 8-sec illumination of the red dot on the pecking key followed at its offset by a 4-sec food delivery. In Group F ($N = 12$) the onset of the autoshaping stimulus was coincident with the end of a 4-sec feeding. In Group No F ($N = 12$) the extra food delivery was omitted; only the food delivery at the offset of the autoshaping stimulus was presented. Acquisition results are shown in Figure 8.2. The one-trial-per-session procedure produced very rapid

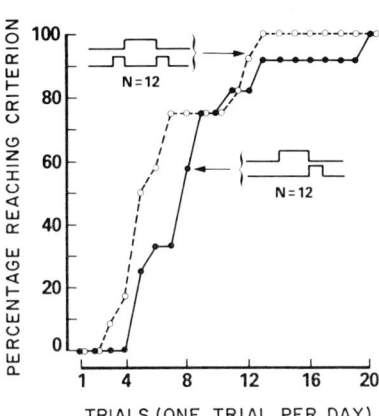

Figure 8.2. Acquisition of autoshaping with (Group F) and without (Group No F) a feeding immediately prior to trial onset.

acquisition in both groups. There was no retardation owing to the pretrial feeding. This surprising result is strong evidence against the hypothesis that the trial-spacing effect is due to local interference from prior food delivery.

Location of Extra Stimulus Presentations: Experiment 4

Another possible source of local interference is exposure to the autoshaping stimulus itself. It is conceivable that each exposure results in a depressed state of reactivity that recovers in time. Experiment 4 explored the effect of placing three unreinforced autoshaping trials at different times in relation to the reinforced autoshaping trials.

The procedure for this experiment was similar to the one used in Experiment 2 on the effects of unsignaled feedings. There were 20 reinforced autoshaping trials per session (red dot stimulus followed by 2.5-sec feeding) separated by 300-sec intertrial intervals. In Group Before ($N = 6$), unreinforced presentations were introduced at 30, 60, and 90 sec prior to the reinforced trial (times are intervals between onsets). In Group After ($N = 6$), the unreinforced trials followed the reinforced trial at the same intervals. Group Random ($N = 6$) received three unreinforced presentations at irregular times within the intertrial interval.

Acquisition results, shown in Table 8.2, showed no statistically detectable effect of the location of the nonreinforced stimulus presentations. In comparison with Group 300 (Experiment 1), which received no extra nonreinforced presentations, acquisition in these groups was somewhat slower (recall that median trials to acquisition in Group 300 was 9.5). The difference proved to be significant (Group 300 versus pooled results for groups with extra stimulus presentations; $U = 140$, $p \leq 0.005$).

Conclusion on Local Interference

Results from Experiments 2, 3, and 4 rule out an explanation of the trial-spacing effect in terms of local interference from events (feedings or stimulus presentations) that closely precede or follow each trial. Although introducing

TABLE 8.2
Effect of Unreinforced Stimulus Presentations at Different Times with Respect to Reinforced Trials, Experiment 4

	Median trials to criterion	Percentage reaching criterion
Group Before	38.0	100
Group After	29.0	83
Group Random	29.0	83

unsignaled food or unreinforced stimulus presentations caused some retardation in acquisition, there was no evidence that the temporal location of these events in relation to trials had any effect. It is necessary to look beyond the local context of trials for the cause of the trial-spacing effect.

EFFECT OF LONG WAITS

Of the conditions so far explored, the only one that resulted in very slow and uncertain acquisition of the keypeck was one in which the bird never experienced a long wait within the experimental chamber between trials. Perhaps the way to understand the trial-spacing effect is to learn how long waits between trials enhance acquisition.

Length of Wait before the First Trial: Experiment 5

Although implausible, we consider first the possibility that a single long wait in the experimental chamber before the first trial is presented might be sufficient to produce rapid acquisition even though all subsequent trials are closely spaced. Four groups were run. Group 30 ($N = 12$) and Group 300 ($N = 12$) were replications of the corresponding groups of Experiment 1 except for the use of 4-sec feedings (against 2.5 sec), 30 trials per session (against 20), and 8 sessions (against 12). In these groups the first trial began 30 sec after the bird was put in the chamber. Group W30 ($N = 6$) and Group W300 ($N = 6$) differed from Group 30 and Group 300 only by having a wait of 100 min prior to the presentation of the first autoshaping trial. The chamber was illuminated as usual during the long waits.

Acquisition data for these groups is given in Table 8.3. Acquisition appeared to be somewhat more rapid on the average in Group 30 and in Group 300 than in the corresponding groups of Experiment 2, but the fact of principal interest is that the long initial wait did not improve acquisition in the closely spaced trial condition; the advantage of the widely spaced trials persisted. It is of interest to

TABLE 8.3
Effect of Long Wait Prior to First Trial on Acquisition, Experiment 5

	Median trials to criterion	Percentage reaching criterion
Group 30	31.0	100
Group W30	32.0	83
Group 300	5.5	100
Group W300	2.0	100

note that all six subjects in Group W300 initiated a five-trial criterion run by the second trial.

Long Waits between Trial Clusters: Experiment 6

From the preceding experiment it is apparent that some interspersion of waits and trials is necessary for rapid acquisition. Experiment 6 was run in order to get some idea about how much interspersion of long waits is necessary for rapid acquisition. A group ($N = 6$) was run in which each session consisted of six clusters of five closely spaced trials (30 sec between onsets as in Group 30) with each cluster separated by a 21.5-min wait. This gave the same overall session duration as in Group 300.

Despite the fact that 80% of the trials were preceded closely by another trial, acquisition proved to be very rapid. The median number of trials to criterion was 7.5 and all birds met criterion; a performance quite comparable to that of Group 300, Experiment 5, where the median trials to acquisition was 5.5. It is apparent that even the first long wait interspersed between closely spaced trials was sufficient to have a substantial effect since without a long wait (Group 30, Experiment 5) the median number of trials to acquisition was 31.0 ($U = 2$, $p < .001$).

Stimulus Condition during the Wait: Experiment 7

In the experiments so far considered, the wait between trials was in the background stimulus condition that was also in effect when the autoshaping trial itself was presented. Is the effectiveness of a long wait in bringing about rapid acquisition dependent on having the same stimulus conditions throughout?

Dweck and Wagner (1970) have shown that nonreinforced exposure to the situational cues of the conditioning environment can facilitate acquisition in aversive fear conditioning. Their interpretation implies that the maximum effectiveness of a long wait (nonreinforced exposure to situational cues) would be found when the background stimulus conditions of the wait are the same as those in which the trial appears.

The design of Experiment 7 is shown in Figure 8.3. Daily sessions were 15 min long. A single trial was presented at the midpoint of the session. Six birds were assigned to each of four groups. In Group L/L the chamber remained lighted throughout the waiting period (as well as during the trial itself), whereas in Group BO/BO the chamber was darkened except for 30 sec before and after the onset of the trial. Group BO/L and Group L/BO differed in terms of the location of the lighted and darkened portion of the wait. These two groups provide important information on the possibility that a change in light level prior to the trial serves as an overshadowing signal for food delivery, as well as information on the possibility that unconditioned effects of a blackout persist over a 30-sec period and

8. WHY AUTOSHAPING DEPENDS ON TRIAL SPACING | 263

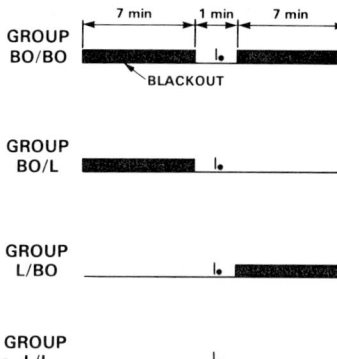

Figure 8.3. Experimental conditions and group designations in Experiment 7.

thereby interfere with acquisition. Group BO/L could be subject to both effects whereas Group L/BO is subject to neither.

In order to adapt subjects to light-level changes, all birds received two pre-experimental sessions in which a 7-min blackout was followed by a 1-min light-on period and then another 7-min blackout. Thirty-eight seconds into the light-on period a 4-sec feeding occurred. Thirty sessions of autoshaping were run with the usual 8-sec red-dot stimulus followed at offset by a 4-sec feeding. A white masking noise was on during the light-on periods but not during the blacked-out periods.

Acquisition data, presented in Table 8.4, show that an extended wait in the lighted chamber before and after the trial, only before the trial, or only after the trial, resulted in very rapid acquisition whereas when the extended wait was entirely in a darkened chamber, acquisition was substantially slower. Group L/L was significantly superior to Group BO/BO by U test ($U = O$, $p < .01$) but it was not significantly superior to Group L/BO or to Group BO/L. These results suggest the generalization that maximum effectiveness of long waits is found when they take place in the background conditions that are also present when the trial occurs.

TABLE 8.4
Effect of Stimulus Conditions during Long Waits on Acquisition, Experiment 7

	Median trials to acquisition	Percentage reaching criterion
Group BO/BO	18.0	83
Group L/L	3.5	100
Group L/BO	2.0	83
Group BO/L	5.0	100

The location of the wait (pretrial or posttrial) appears to have little or no bearing on its effectiveness.

Waits between Feedings: Experiment 8

When the contingency between the autoshaping stimulus and feeding is perfect (feedings occur if, and only if the stimulus is present) variations in the spacing of trials result in concomitant variations in the spacing of feedings. Perhaps the trial spacing effect is due to feeding rate rather than to the trial rate per se. In Experiment 8 the trial rate was held constant at one trial per daily session while the rate of unsignaled feedings was either low or high. In Group Lo F ($N = 5$) the unsignaled feedings occurred once every 300 sec, whereas in Group Hi F ($N = 5$) they occurred once every 30 sec. Both groups received a total of 30 4-sec feedings per session. Only the sixteenth feeding, at the midpoint of the session, was preceded by the autoshaping stimulus; an 8-sec presentation of the red dot. A control group with no unsignaled feedings, Group No F ($N = 6$), was included. In this case, the single trial was presented at the midpoint of a 15-min session (same session length as in Group Hi F). Thirty sessions were run.

Acquisition results are shown in Table 8.5. The rate of unsignaled feedings had a clear effect on acquisition. In the high-rate group only one of five birds met the criterion of acquisition, whereas in the low-rate group all birds met the criterion on or before trial 19($U = 1$, $p < .02$). An interesting finding was that acquisition with widely spaced unsignaled feedings (Group Lo F) was similar to acquisition with no unsignaled feedings despite the fact that in the former case only one of 30 feedings was signaled by the autoshaping stimulus. Moreover, the results for Group Lo F and Group Hi F are well within the bounds of the results obtained for the same feeding rates when all feedings were signaled; that is, for Group 300 and Group 30. Later we examine in more detail the possibility that signaled and unsignaled feedings interfere equally with the effectiveness of any given autoshaping trial.

The principal conclusion from Experiment 8 is that the time between feedings is a major cause of the trial spacing effect. With the trial rate constant at one trial

TABLE 8.5
Effect of Rate of Unsignaled Feedings on Acquisition, Experiment 8

	Median trials to acquisition	Percentage reaching criterion
Group No F	2.5	100
Group Lo F	6.0	100
Group Hi F	8.0	20

per session, variation in the feeding rate affected acquisition much the same way as did the comparable variation in the spacing of trials. One cannot, of course, conclude that there is no effect of the spacing of stimulus presentations as such, but it is correct to say that feeding rate alone is sufficient to produce the major effects of trial spacing on acquisition.

Conclusion on the Role of Long Waits

Some degree of interspersion of long waits with trials is required for rapid acquisition of autoshaped responding. Beyond that, the location of the wait with respect to trials is not critical. The stimulus condition during long waits is important. It is likely that the maximum effectiveness of long waits is obtained when the stimulus condition is the same as the condition that obtains when trials are presented. The trial-spacing effect may be largely, perhaps entirely, due to the waits between feedings; not to the waits between trials.

SPACING AND PREDICTIVE VALUE

The present experiments, and those reported by Gibbon and Balsam (Chapter 7, this volume) show that acquisition is insensitive to local, or short term predictabilities in the pattern of food delivery. In particular, we must reject the hypothesis that the events of an immediately preceding trial serve to predict the very next feeding and thereby overshadow the trial stimulus as a predictive signal for feedings. The absence of local effects does not, however, rule out a broader alternative; namely, that the effect of spacing on acquisition can be understood by relating the *average*, or long-term, spacing of food delivery to the predictive value of the trial stimulus. We now wish to consider whether this alternative can provide an explanatory framework for the effects of spacing.

The connection between spacing and predictive value of the autoshaping stimulus is quite direct. Suppose that as a result of exposure to the autoshaping regime the pigeon develops an expectation for food delivery in the next moment. The level of expectation is presumed to reflect the average waiting time between deliveries; longer average waiting times resulting in a lower level of expectation. The lower the prevailing food expectation at the time the autoshaping stimulus appears, the greater would be the predictive value of that stimulus (other things being equal). In the language of information theory, there is a greater degree of uncertainty to be reduced by the stimulus.

Dating from Kamin's very influential research on blocking and overshadowing (Kamin, 1969) there has been an accumulation of evidence that a predictable reinforcer is less effective for the acquisition of a new association than is an unpredictable reinforcer (for a review, see Mackintosh, 1974). Gibbon's scalar expectancy theory, which has been applied to many autoshaping phenomena by Gibbon and Balsam (Chapter 7, this volume) was developed with a closely related rationale in mind. The rationale is that the effectiveness of the autoshaping stimulus depends on how much it increases the expectation of food over the prevailing expectation. Later, we shall take a closer look at the application of scalar expectancy theory to the effects of spacing in autoshaping. For the present we are concerned only with the general hypothesis that the effects of spacing can be explained through the relation of spacing to predictive value.

For the hypothesis to succeed it is necessary, although not sufficient, for the acquisition of autoshaping to be inversely related to the expectation of food based on sources of prediction other than the trial stimulus itself. The blocking experiment provides the most direct experimental manipulation of the prior expectation of food delivery. In blocking, the to-be-conditioned stimulus is presented together with a stimulus that has been pretrained to serve as a signal for food delivery. The pretrained signal, according to the hypothesis, increases the expectation of food delivery and thereby robs the to-be-conditioned stimulus of predictive value. The procedure should, on the present hypothesis, severely retard the acquisition of autoshaping pecking.

Evidence on the blocking of autoshaping is patchy; positive results have been reported, but failures to block have also been noted. On the positive side, Blanchard and Honig (1976) showed that acquisition of autoshaped pecking was slower in the presence of a diffuse visual stimulus that had been pretrained as a signal of free feedings (S^+) than in the presence of another stimulus pretrained as a signal for the absence of feedings (S^-). Acquisition in the presence of S^- was, in fact, somewhat more rapid than in the presence of a novel stimulus. The authors suggested that feedings in the presence of S^- are especially surprising (unexpected) and are therefore especially effective in bringing about autoshaping whereas feedings in the presence of S^+ have less surprise value. Tomie (1976, Experiment 3), found that an auditory stimulus that was constantly present during ten sessions of free feeding virtually prevented the acquisition of autoshaped pecking when, in a later phase of the experiment, it was presented at the same time as the keylight stimulus. An appropriate control group showed that the pretraining of the auditory stimulus contributed to the lack of autoshaped responding. Tomie's results showed that strong blocking of acquisition to a visual stimulus by an auditory stimulus is possible. Leyland and Mackintosh (1978) obtained significant blocking of autoshaping by either an overhead visual stimulus or a clicker stimulus although acquisition was not very strong in the unblocked control group.

On the negative side, Tomie (Chapter 6, this volume) failed to find blocking using visual stimuli presented concurrently on the response key. Moreover, unreported experiments from my own laboratory in which a dot of one color was used as the blocking stimulus and a dot of another color as the stimulus to be blocked also failed to provide evidence of blocking when pecking to the later added dot was tested in extinction. Failures to block with a localized visual stimulus are especially difficult to understand because such stimuli are readily established as food signals; a fact amply testified to by autoshaping itself.

There are also hints in the literature that blocking by auditory stimuli may fail. The first report of blocking in autoshaping (Allaway, 1971) used an auditory blocking stimulus. Blocking was found in one experiment but not in another although there was no apparent reason for the discrepancy. In an unpublished experiment by LoLordo, Jacobs, and Foree (cited by LoLordo, 1978, p. 392 ff.) a pretrained auditory signal failed to block acquisition of discriminative control by a diffuse visual stimulus. The response in this case was treadle pressing for food reinforcement in pigeons, not autoshaping. Nevertheless this failure to block acquisition gives further reason to question the generality of blocking where food-getting responses in the pigeon are involved.

I wish to report briefly some further experiments on the blocking of autoshaping. The results of these experiments are not favorable to the general hypothesis that the acquisition of autoshaping is a reliable function of the extent to which the autoshaping stimulus increases the expectation of food delivery; consequently, they do not support the idea that the effects of spacing can be explained by the relation of spacing to the predictive value of the trial stimulus.

Effect of Trial Location in the Interval between Periodic Feedings: Experiment 9

The first experiment to be reported examined the possibility that food expectation could be controlled by extensive pretraining with a periodic schedule of food delivery and that the level of food expectation at different times within the fixed interfeeding interval would affect the acquisition of autoshaped pecking to a trial stimulus. Specifically, the hypothesis was that pretraining produces an increasing expectation of food delivery as the time of the next feeding approaches. Therefore, a trial stimulus introduced late in the interval is less able to increase food expectation than is one introduced early in the interval. If the effectiveness of a trial stimulus for autoshaping is dependent on the extent to which it increases food expectation, acquisition should be more rapid for an early than for a late trial stimulus. The experiment used extensive training on a periodic schedule prior to the introduction of the autoshaping stimulus in order to allow for the development of food expectation that would reflect the interfeeding interval.

The first phase of the experiment consisted of 35 sessions, each with 30 unsignaled 3-sec feedings delivered at a fixed interval of 65 sec. These periodic feedings continued throughout the second phase, which consisted of 28 sessions. In each second-phase session there was a single presentation of a 10-sec autoshaping stimulus followed at offset by a 3-sec feeding. The trial was presented between the fifteenth and sixteenth unsignaled feeding. Each of five groups received this trial at a different time within the interval. The earliest position was 62 sec prior to the next periodic feeding; the latest was only 10 sec prior to the next periodic feeding. In the last group the actual waiting time to the next feeding was not shortened at all by the appearance of the trial stimulus. There were four subjects in each of four groups and three subjects in the remaining group.

By the twenty-eighth trial, 12 of the 19 subjects met a criterion of five consecutive trials with at least one peck. The procedure produced a moderate level of acquisition; the overall median number of pecks per trial was 1.96 for subjects meeting criterion. However, the temporal location of the trial within the interval produced no hint of the hypothesized trend. In fact the rate of pecking in groups with the later trial positions was higher, not lower, than the rate in groups with the earlier trial positions (trend not significant). This experiment provided no support for the hypothesis that the lower the food expectation at the time the trial stimulus appears the greater the effectiveness of the trial for the acquisition of autoshaped pecking.

Attempt to Block Autoshaping by an Auditory Signal: Experiment 10

We consider now a blocking experiment of more conventional design in which an explicit, external blocking stimulus (auditory) was used. All subjects received the same first phase of training. In each of 21 sessions there were 40 10-sec presentations of an 80 dB white noise (scale B, General Radio Meter, Model 1551-C) followed at its offset by a 3-sec feeding. Intertrial intervals were equally often 26 or 39 sec in an irregular sequence. This training was designed to establish the noise as a signal for food. In the second phase of training there were 10 sessions. Each session contained 10 10-sec presentations of the autoshaping stimulus, of which 4 were followed at stimulus offset by a 3-sec feeding. The intertrial intervals were variable, with a mean of 130 sec. In Group Block, the 10-sec noise accompanied the 10-sec autoshaping stimulus. In Group Control, the noise was not presented. Eight subjects were assigned to each group.

Observation of the birds near the end of the first phase of training gave clear evidence that the noise had acquired signal value in all cases. At noise onset, some subjects oriented to the feeder opening, some toward the speaker (located to the left of the key), and others began rapid side-to-side head movements while orienting to the front panel at the level of the unlighted key.

Acquisition data are shown for Group Block and Group Control in Figure 8.4. The curve of performance rose more steeply in Group Control than in Group Block but the difference was small and did not reach significance even when the comparison was based on just the first five sessions of training, where the largest difference was found in mean percentage of trials with a peck ($U = 22$, $p < .2$). The same conclusion is reached when the rate of pecking is used as the measure.

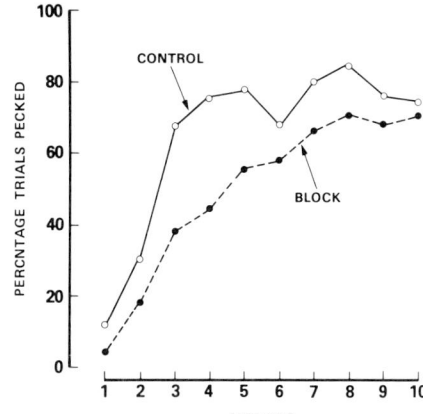

Figure 8.4. Acquisition in Group Block, in which a pretrained auditory signal accompanied the visual trial stimulus, and in Group Control, in which only the visual trial stimulus was presented.

If the effectiveness of an autoshaping trial were critically dependent on the predictive value of the autoshaping stimulus (or its ability to increase food expectation), one would expect to find little or no acquisition in Group Block. Therefore the present results provide another reason to doubt the generality of the concept of predictive value in the acquisition of autoshaped pecking.

Using the terms of the present hypothesis, the failure to block could be assigned to either of two causes: a failure of pretraining to control food expectation at the point where the autoshaping stimulus was introduced, or a failure of food expectation to control the effectiveness of the trial for autoshaping. It seems rather unlikely that food expectation would not be controlled by the extensive exposure to periodic feedings in Experiment 9; patterns of responding in the pigeon are known to be very sensitive to temporal regularities in schedules of reinforcement (see Zeiler, 1977, for a review). It seems even more unlikely that the auditory food signal in Experiment 10 would have failed to control food expectancy; systematic visual observations of every bird showed that food-related movement patterns were acquired to the auditory stimulus during the first phase of training.

The present failures to find blocking do not, of course, change the fact that blocking of autoshaped responding has been demonstrated in other experiments. But, it does appear that the blocking of autoshaped responding depends on the choice of stimuli, or on the conditions of their presentation, in ways that are not as yet understood. Enormous reductions in the (nonredundant) predictive value of the autoshaping stimulus can fail to show significant blocking. One is led to consider seriously the possibility that autoshaping does not depend in any fundamental way on the predictive value of the stimulus. A further suggestion that predictive value may not be the key to the acquisition of autoshaping comes from observations on the onset of the spacing effect.

Rapid Onset of Spacing Effect

When the incidence of keypecking on the first few acquisition trials is examined, it becomes apparent that the duration of the wait between the first and second autoshaping trials has a substantial effect on performance. Collecting results from the previously reported experiments, we find 18 subjects that were exposed to a 30-sec intertrial interval and 24 exposed to a 300-sec intertrial interval under comparable conditions. As shown in Table 8.6, with a long wait from the first to the second trial the percentage of birds making at least one peck increased by almost 40% from the first to the second trial whereas with a short wait, it decreased by 8%. The effect of trial spacing appears to be immediate.

The substantial effect of the very first intertrial interval raises a problem for an account of trial spacing based on predictive value of the autoshaping stimulus. For the account to succeed it is necessary to assume that the expectation of food in the next moment declines with time spent waiting after the first trial; food expectation must be lower after waiting five minutes than after waiting one-half min. This assumption cannot be rejected outright, but we think it implausible. Recall that before the first session, extensive training was given with variable interfeeding intervals (range of 12–132 sec). Would not this training result in a mean level of food expectation that was too stable to be altered substantially by the duration of the first posttrial wait?

A more acute problem for an account based on predictive value is raised by another observation. In Experiment 5 it was found that a very long wait (100 min) before the first trial had little effect on acquisition. It is not easy to see why the prevailing level of food expectation should be relatively unaffected by the duration of the wait before the first trial and yet be affected strongly by the duration of the wait after the first trial.

Conclusion on Spacing and Predictive Value

We have considered three facts that go against the hypothesis that acquisition of autoshaped keypecking is dependent on the ability of the trial stimulus to increase food expectation: (a) the temporal location of the trial in the interval

TABLE 8.6
Percentage of Subjects Making at Least One Peck

Intertrial interval	Trial number			
	1	2	3	4
30 (N = 18)	33	25	30	25
300 (N = 24)	22	61	67	67

between periodic feedings did not have the kind of effect implied by the hypothesis; (b) pairing a preestablished auditory signal of food with the autoshaping stimulus had only a minor, statistically insignificant, effect on acquisition; and (c) the large effect of the first posttrial wait and the small effect of a pretrial wait are difficult to explain on the predictive-value hypothesis.

As we have noted, the rationale for the scalar expectancy theory of autoshaping is that the acquisition of the autoshaped response depends on the extent to which the autoshaping stimulus increases food expectation over the level that prevails under the background stimulus conditions. Although the results we have reviewed do not support this assumption, scalar expectancy might still be correct in its basic assertion about the parameters of spacing that control the acquisition of autoshaping. The basic assertion is that acquisition depends on the ratio of the average time between reinforcers (referred to as C for cycle time) to the average trial duration (T) per reinforcer. In order to separate this generalization from its rationale in terms of increased expectations, or predictive value, I will refer to the *relative waiting time hypothesis*.

The relative waiting time hypothesis asserts, as does scalar expectancy theory, that the critical parameter for the acquisition of autoshaping is the ratio of the average waiting time per feeding in the trial stimulus to the average waiting time per feeding in the experimental setting. It does not assert, however, that this generalization reflects the role either of predictive value or of a reduction in the animal's expectation of future waiting time to food. According to the relative waiting time hypothesis, the important variable is the average length of time the animal has waited for feedings in the experimental setting in relation to the average wait in the presence of the trial stimulus. The relative waiting time hypothesis assumes, to put the matter informally, that in an environment where food is infrequent, a stimulus that signals its imminent arrival is excitatory even when food is already confidently expected from another source of prediction. If this view should prove to be correct, positive results in blocking experiments would require a new explanation; one not fundamentally tied to predictive values.

RELATIVE WAITING TIME HYPOTHESIS

Consider the arrangements shown in Figure 8.5. The center trial is referred to as a reference trial. The feedings that occur at other times (not associated with the reference trial) are referred to as context feedings regardless of whether, or how, they are signaled. In A, there are no context feedings, and we know that very rapid acquisition can be obtained. In B, unsignaled context feedings occur at a high rate; we know this results in slow acquisition. In both C and D the context feedings are signaled; in C by a stimulus distinctly different from the reference

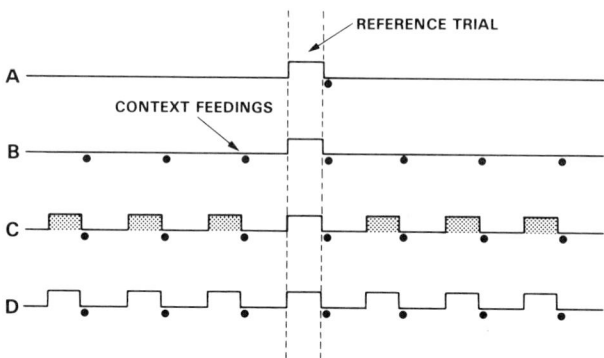

Figure 8.5. Four arrangements for autoshaping (see text for discussion).

trial stimulus, and in D by exactly the same stimulus as appears on the reference trial. Is the interference with the effectiveness of the reference trial due to context feedings the same or different in arrangements B, C, and D?

The simplest version of the relative waiting time hypothesis is that the effectiveness of the reference trial depends on the waiting time in the reference trial relative to the overall waiting time between feedings no matter whether, or by what stimulus, the feedings are signaled. This implies the equivalence of arrangements B–D. The first two experiments to be considered are concerned with the case in which the context feedings are signaled by a stimulus distinctly different from the reference trial stimulus (illustrated by C). The last experiment concerns the case in which the same stimulus is used throughout (illustrated by D).

Auditory Signaling of Context Feedings: Experiment 11

Each of three groups received the same first phase of training in which all feedings were signaled by an auditory stimulus. The reference trials were not introduced until the second phase. In the second phase, Group Signaled received context feedings that continued to be signaled by the auditory stimulus (corresponds to arrangement C in Figure 8.5); Group Unsignaled received context feedings with no auditory signal (arrangement B in Figure 8.5); and Group Control had no context feedings; only the reference trial (A in Figure 8.5). Eight subjects were assigned at random to each group. (Group Control here is the same as Group Control in Experiment 10. It is reported again to facilitate comparisons).

The details were as follows. Sessions were programmed on the basis of 100 13-sec intervals. In the first phase, in which all groups received feedings signaled by an auditory stimulus, 40 of these 13-sec programming intervals ended with a

3-sec feeding. Each feeding was preceded by a 10-sec burst of white noise. Intertrial intervals were equally often 26 or 39 sec in random sequence. There were 21 sessions in the first phase. In the second phase, all groups received 10 10-sec autoshaping trials (reference trials) with the red dot stimulus. Four of these trials were reinforced (terminated in 3-sec feedings). Trials were assigned at random to the 13-sec programming intervals but were not allowed to occur in adjacent intervals. In Group Signaled, 40 percent of the intervals not occupied by the autoshaping stimulus contained a 3-sec feeding, and all of these feedings were signaled by the 10-sec noise, as in phase one. These signaled context feedings were assigned entirely at random to the 13-sec programming intervals. In Group Unsignaled, the same context feedings occurred but without the auditory stimulus. It might be noted that for both Group Signaled and Group Unsignaled the average waiting time for food within the autoshaping trial stimulus was the same as the overall waiting time for food because 40% of both autoshaping trials and of all other 13-sec intervals contained a feeding. In Group Control, no context feedings were presented.

It was evident from observations of the birds in phase one that the noise had acquired signal value (see description of behavior in the first phase of Experiment 10). Acquisition results in the second phase are shown in Figure 8.6. The context feedings severely reduced the acquisition of autoshaped keypecking in Group Signaled as well as in Group Unsignaled. (Group Control versus pooled results for Groups Signaled and Unsignaled; $U = 8$, $p < .001$). Group Signaled showed slightly more keypecking than Group Unsignaled, but this small difference was far from significant ($U = 13$, $p < .16$). The same conclusion is reached when rate of pecking is used as the measure. Context feedings interfered with autoshaping no less when signaled by a previously conditioned stimulus than when unsignaled.

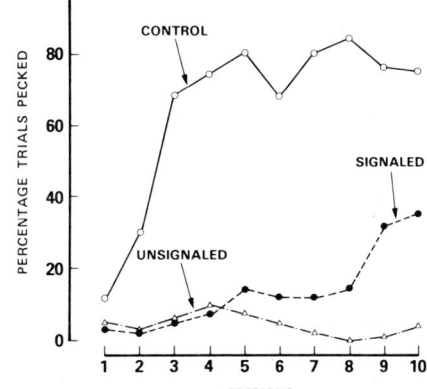

Figure 8.6. Percentage of trials pecked by session in Group Control (no context feedings), Group Signaled (signaled context feedings), and Group Unsignaled (unsignaled context feedings), Experiment 11.

Visual Signaling of Context Feedings: Experiment 12

The plan of this experiment was similar to that of Experiment 11 except that a visual stimulus presented on the autoshaping key itself, rather than an auditory stimulus, was used to signal context feedings. Training parameters were chosen to produce strong signaling in the first phase of training.

The first phase of training consisted of 10 sessions, each 620 sec (10.3 min) in duration. Midway in the session a single 8-sec stimulus was followed by a 3-sec feeding. For half of the subjects the red-dot stimulus was used to signal these feedings; for the remaining subjects it was the uniform lighting of the entire key with white light. The second phase of training consisted of 12 sessions. At the midpoint of each session there was a single reinforced, 8-sec trial (reference trial). The stimulus on this trial was a red dot for birds previously trained with the white key in the first phase; it was the white-lighted key for those previously trained with the red dot. In Group Signaled ($N = 10$) 30 3-sec context feedings were delivered at regular 20-sec intervals throughout the session. The context feedings were signaled by the first phase stimulus. Group Unsignaled ($N = 10$) received the same context feedings but the first phase stimulus was omitted. Group Control ($N = 8$) received no context feedings. The three groups were matched as closely as possible on the rate of pecking at the end of the first phase.

As was expected on the basis of other experiments in this laboratory, a higher rate of pecking was observed to the red dot than to the white key. For the last four sessions of the first phase of training the mean number of pecks per 8-sec trial on the red dot was 16.4 whereas on the lighted key it was 2.1.

The results of principal interest are responses to the reference stimulus in the second phase, and they are shown in Table 8.7. The mean results show that context feedings severely reduced acquisition to the reference stimulus in both Group Signaled and Group Unsignaled (Group Control versus pooled results for Group Signaled and Group Unsignaled: $U = 0$, $p < .004$ for the red test stimulus; $U = 7$, $p < .066$, for the white test stimulus). However, as in Experiment 11, signaled context feedings did not interfere less than did unsignaled feedings ($U = 42$, $p < .5$ based on pooled results for subgroups with different reference stimuli). The use of pecking rate as a measure leads to the same conclusion ($U = 33$, $p < .2$).

TABLE 8.7
Percentage Reference Trials Pecked, Experiment 12

Reference stimulus	Group control	Group signaled	Group unsignaled
Red dot	94	17	28
White key	77	32	37
Mean	85.5	24.5	32.5

In this experiment, the signaling of context feedings by localized visual stimuli resulted in autoshaped keypecks. Had signaling lessened interference, the possibility that it did so through stimulus generalization from the signaling stimulus to the reference stimulus would have to be considered. Because there was no advantage to signaled context feedings even under these conditions we can be especially confident that interference with autoshaping due to context feedings is not reduced by signaling the context feedings.

The effect of signaling the USs that occur outside of the CS on other forms of classical conditioning has received little attention. However, Rescorla (1972, p. 25 ff) reported an experiment on this question using the conditioned emotional response (CER) procedure with rats. One group received unsignaled non-CS shocks, another group received non-CS shocks signaled by a stimulus distinctively different from the CS, and a third group received no shocks in non-CS periods. In contrast to the present results, significantly stronger conditioning to the CS was found when the USs occurring in non-CS periods were signaled than when they were not signaled. However, the difference was small when compared with the far stronger conditioning that developed when no shocks were delivered in non-CS periods. The question deserves further study.

Context Feedings Signaled or Unsignaled by the Autoshaping Stimulus: Experiment 13

We turn now to a comparison of interference from unsignaled context feedings with interference from context feedings that are signaled by the autoshaping stimulus itself. Arrangements B and D in Figure 8.5 illustrate this comparison. In effect, the experiment asks whether the effectiveness of a reinforced trial for the acquisition of autoshaping is reduced when the percentage of feedings that are signaled is (drastically) reduced.

An 8-sec presentation of the red dot autoshaping stimulus, followed by a 3-sec feeding, occurred at the midpoint of 21-min sessions (reference trial). Every group received one unsignaled feeding (first feeding in the session) approximately one minute after the start of the session. In Group Control, the only other event in the session was the reference trial. In each of four experimental groups there were 30 additional 3-sec feedings per session spaced at 40-sec intervals. The sixteenth feeding occurred on the reference trial (the unsignaled feeding at the session start is ignored in subsequent descriptions of the procedure). The experimental groups differed solely in terms of the percentage of feedings that were signaled: Group 100—all 30 feedings signaled; Group 50—15 feedings signaled; Group 30—9 feedings signaled; Group 3—1 feeding signaled (the reference trial). There were 40 sessions of training. Four subjects were assigned at random to each group.

The mean percentage of reference trials with at least one peck is shown by

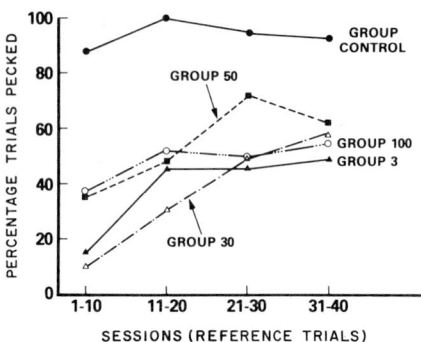

Figure 8.7. Percentage of reference trials pecked over 10-session blocks; Experiment 13. Group Control received only the reference trial. Other groups received a total of 30 feedings of which from 100% to 3% were signaled.

10-session blocks (one trial per session) for each group in Figure 8.7. Performance in Group Control, in which the only feeding occurred on the reference trial itself, was superior to that of any of the experimental groups (Group Control versus pooled results for all experimental groups: $U = 6$; $p < .013$). An early advantage for the groups with a higher percentage of feedings signaled was expected simply because these groups received many more trials per session than did those with a lower percentage of trials signaled. The early advantage was obtained. However, in later blocks of trials no systematic effect was obtained despite variations in the percentage of feedings signaled from 3% to 100%.

It is the case that the results in the experimental groups were highly variable; in each group, one or two subjects failed to reach the criterion of five consecutive reference trials with at least one peck; yet, each group contained at least one subject that pecked consistently at a high level. The medians of response totals over the last 10 reference trials were: Group 100—68.0; Group 50—36.5; Group 30—27.0; Group 3—49.0. Nonparametric analysis of variance of response totals by experimental groups did not approach significance (Kruskal–Wallis, $df = 3$; $.30 \le p \le .20$). For Group Control, the corresponding median response total was 225.0.

The results of this experiment showed that context feedings interfered with acquisition on the reference trial, and that the interference was no less when feedings were signaled by the autoshaping stimulus itself than when they were unsignaled.

Conclusion on the Relative Waiting Time Hypothesis

Although confidence must be tempered by the large amount of between-subject variability, the simple form of the relative waiting time hypothesis appears to be a good approximation to the facts: The effectiveness of a reference trial depends on the waiting time in the reference trial relative to the overall waiting time between feedings within the experimental setting. It is independent of whether, or by what stimulus, the feedings outside of the reference trial are signaled. This is the most important result of the present experiments. It is consistent with a simple version of the relative waiting time hypothesis because it means that the prevailing waiting time within a given experimental setting, against which the waiting time in the trial is "compared," depends only on the average wait between feedings without respect to the stimulus conditions that accompany them. The same generalization is implied by scalar expectancy theory. Moreover, the result is important because it goes against a widely held view of the role of contingency in conditioning. We will return to this point later.

Earlier in this chapter it was stated that the trial-spacing effect is due largely to the feeding rate, not to the rate at which the autoshaping stimulus occurs. But there are several indications that some role is played by the spacing of the autoshaping stimulus itself. The substantial effect of the length of the first intertrial wait, and the virtual absence of an effect due to the length of the wait before the first trial points to an effect of trial spacing. Further support for that possibility was found in an aspect, so far unmentioned, of Experiment 13. Considered in terms of reinforced trials only (rather than sessions, as in Figure 8.7, which entails varying numbers of trials for different groups), early acquisition was actually more rapid at lower stimulus presentation rates; that is, in groups with smaller percentages of feedings signaled. The effects of stimulus spacing as such, independent of feeding rate, requires more thorough analysis.

SUMMARY OF FINDINGS

1. Waits between feedings that are long in relation to the wait in the autoshaping stimulus are necessary for rapid, reliable acquisition of autoshaped pecking.
2. The duration of the wait that follows the first autoshaping trial has a substantial effect on responding, whereas the duration of the wait prior to the first autoshaping trial is quite ineffective.
3. A small number of long waits interspersed with clusters of closely spaced trials results in rapid, reliable acquisition.
4. The location of long waits in relation to autoshaping trials is not critical. For example, long waits are effective even when every trial is immediately preceded by a feeding so that the feeding on the trial itself always occurs after a very short wait.
5. The effect of a long wait depends on the background stimulus condition. A long wait in a setting (darkened chamber) radically different from the setting in which the autoshaping stimulus is presented (lighted chamber) is less effective in promoting autoshaping than is a wait in the same setting.

6. The effectiveness of an autoshaping trial appears to depend on how much time, on the average, the animal has already waited for a feeding rather than on the ability of the autoshaping stimulus to increase the expectation of food, or in other words, on its predictive value. This conclusion is based on the failure to block acquisition of autoshaping with an auditory stimulus that had become, through previous training, a signal for the imminent arrival of food, and on the absence of a systematic effect due to the location of the autoshaping stimulus in the interval between periodic feedings.
7. Acquisition to a given autoshaping stimulus is greatly retarded when extra feedings are presented at a high rate. The interference due to extra feedings is not reduced when the extra feedings are signaled by another stimulus even though that stimulus has been pretrained as a food signal.
8. Interference is not reduced when the feedings are signaled by the autoshaping stimulus itself. Over a very broad range of percentages, the effectiveness of an autoshaping trial in bringing about autoshaped pecking appears not to be lessened by a reduction in the percentage of feedings that are signaled.

RELATION TO THEORIES OF SIGNALING IN CLASSICAL CONDITIONING

We consider the relation of these findings to two theories of signaling in classical conditioning; Gibbon's scalar expectancy theory, and the Wagner–Rescorla theory. Gibbon's scalar expectancy theory has the advantage, for present purposes, of having been developed around temporal variables whereas the Wagner–Rescorla theory was centered on different phenomena. Nevertheless, with certain extensions, the Wagner–Rescorla theory yields some interesting implications for temporal variables.

Scalar Expectancy Theory

Certain of the present findings have led us to reject the hypothesis that the predictive value of the trial stimulus underlies the acquisition of autoshaped pecking. On the other hand, the generalization about the critical temporal variables that emerges from scalar expectancy theory—the generalization that was renamed the *relative waiting time hypothesis*—was found to be a good approximation to the main features of the present results. It is thought, however, that it needs to be supplemented by taking into account the greater effectiveness of widely spaced stimulus presentations when the feeding rate is not a variable.

The relative waiting time hypothesis is a radical one. Figure 8.8 shows a segment from trial sequences of four types. On the relative waiting time hypothesis, the trial in position 2 has the same effectiveness for the acquisition of

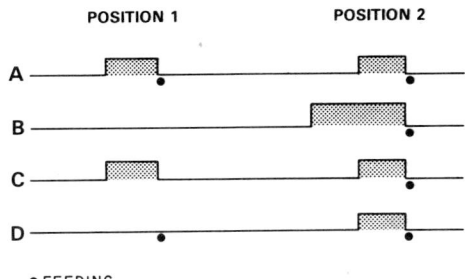

Figure 8.8. On the relative waiting time hypothesis the effectiveness of the trial in position 2 is the same in arrangements A–D.

autoshaped pecking in each of these sequences. In sequence B the trial duration is twice that in sequence A, but so is the interfeeding interval. If, as appears to be the case (See Gibbon & Balsam, Chapter 7, this volume), acquisition depends on the ratio of the waiting times, the trial in position 2 in A and B will have equal effectiveness. The equivalence of the Position 2 trial in C follows from the same reasoning. Note, however, that C involves partial reinforcement of trials, so the equivalence of C implies the absence of a partial reinforcement effect. Results reported by Gibbon, Farrell, Locurto, Duncan, and Terrace (1980), which are discussed by Gibbon & Balsam in Chapter 7 of this volume, are consistent with the absence of a partial reinforcement effect: The number of reinforced trials to acquisition was not significantly altered by removing feedings from even a large fraction of the trials. Finally, on the relative waiting time hypothesis, D is equivalent to the others because the removal of the stimulus at position 1 alters neither the waiting time in the trial nor the prevailing waiting time. The present finding of equivalent acquisition over large variations in the percentage of feedings signaled supports this implication of the relative waiting time hypothesis.

Wagner–Rescorla Theory

Application of this theory to the effects of spacing and duration of trials involves the following ideas (see Rescorla & Wagner, 1972):

1. The experimental setting always includes a background stimulus, A, that is present throughout the presentation of experimental stimuli. When a trial stimulus, X, is reinforced, both A and X are available for conditioning.
2. The AX compound gains signal value on a reinforced trial in proportion to the difference between the current signal value of the compound and the maximum possible signal value. The maximum is set by the nature and magnitude of the reinforcer. The signal value of the compound is equal to the sum of its component values.
3. These assumptions imply that the excitatory value gained by one element depends on the excitatory value of the other. In the limit, if one element

were conditioned to asymptote, the other would acquire no signal value on reinforced, compound trials. It is as though the fully conditioned element removed all surprise value from the reinforcer and thereby prevented further conditioning (Kamin, 1969).

Application of the theory to effects of trial spacing and duration rests on an additional assumption.

4. Intertrial periods can be viewed as a series of nonreinforced background stimulus trials. The unit duration of background stimulus trials is equal to the duration of the trial stimulus (see Gibbon et al., 1977).

From the fourth assumption it follows that for a given trial duration, longer intertrial periods result in more extinction on the background stimulus. Together with the first three assumptions this implies that the trial stimulus will receive a larger increment to its excitatory strength on reinforced trials. Shorter trial durations will have the same effect because there will be a corresponding increase in the number of (presumed) nonreinforced background stimulus trials in the intertrial period. It is obvious that the theory yields the prediction that it is the ratio of trial to intertrial durations, rather than their absolute durations, that governs acquisition. The theory therefore asserts the equivalence of the position 2 trial in arrangements A and B in Figure 8.5.

Gibbon et al. (1980) have argued that the equivalence of arrangements A and C in Figure 8.5 (i.e., the absence of an effect of partial reinforcement on the number of reinforced trials to acquisition) is not consistent with the Wagner–Rescorla theory. However, the clearest break between the relative waiting time hypothesis and the Wagner–Rescorla theory lies in their predictions about signaled and unsignaled feedings.

On the Wagner–Rescorla theory, unsignaled feedings should interfere with acquisition more than do signaled feedings. With an unsignaled feeding, the background stimulus receives all of the increment due to reinforcement whereas with a signaled feeding, the background shares the increment with the experimental signaling stimulus. The effectiveness of the position 2 trial in arrangement D, should, according to the Wagner–Rescorla theory, be less than in the other arrangements because this arrangement results in greater conditioning to the background. As we have seen, this appears not to be the case. Moreover, the use of a thoroughly pretrained stimulus to signal context feedings should virtually eliminate interfering effects from context feedings because a fully trained signal would prevent the background from acquiring excitatory value. Again, our results go against the theory; context feedings signaled by a pretrained stimulus do not interfere less with the acquisition of autoshaped pecking than do unsignaled context feedings. The relative waiting time hypothesis is in better agreement with present findings than is the extension of the Wagner–Rescorla theory to temporal variables.

Contingency in Classical Conditioning

It has become widely accepted that stimulus–reinforcer contingency, or correlation, is fundamental to the acquisition of signal value in classical conditioning (for a recent statement see Mackintosh, 1977). Even so, except for the work of Gibbon, Berryman, and Thompson (1974), not much attention has been paid to the question of what index of CS–US contingency would most closely reflect the acquisition of signal value. A commonly used index, and one that will serve the present purpose, is given by the difference between two conditional probabilities: the probability of the US given a CS, $P(US/CS)$, and the probability of the US given the absence of a CS, $P(US/noCS)$. Conditional probabilities can be converted to waiting times by the artifice of considering an extended CS to be composed of a train of molecular CSs of short unit duration. The average waiting time in CS is then inversely proportional to the probability of a US given the molecular CS. In this way an index of contingency based on a contrast between conditional probabilities can be recast in terms of a contrast between the average waiting time in the CS and the average waiting time in no-CS periods. It is important to see that this index contains a term that differs from the term in the index implied by the relative waiting time hypothesis. The latter contrasts the average waiting time in the CS with the average waiting time that prevails in the experimental setting; not with a waiting time based only on the no-CS portion of the experiment. To be completely explicit: If the relative waiting time hypothesis is expressed in probabilities it involves the contrast between $P(US/CS)$ and the $P(US)$, not between $P(US/CS)$ and $P(US/noCS)$ as in the index of contingency.

The contingency and relative waiting time indices make the same prediction for the noncontingent case. When the index of contingency is zero $[P(US/CS) = P(US/noCS)]$, the waiting time in the CS will be the same as the overall waiting time. When expressed in probabilities, that means that $P(US/CS) = P(US)$. From either formulation one would not expect the acquisition or maintenance of signal value. In the well known experiment on the role of contingency in autoshaping by Gamzu and Williams (1973), the contingency between CS and US was reduced to zero by presenting food in nonCS periods at a rate equal to its rate in CS periods. Under these conditions, autoshaped responding to a CS did not develop. If responding had already been acquired as the result of prior training on a contingent procedure, it was virtually eliminated by exposure to noncontingency. But, this result does not imply that the index of contingency captures the essential properties that make event sequences effective for generating, or maintaining, signal value. As we have just noted, for the completely noncontingent case, the relative waiting time index implies the same outcome as does the contingency index.

Although the two indices imply the same outcome under some conditions, there are others in which they imply very different outcomes. The relative waiting time index is not an index of CS–US correlation, nor of the predictive value of the CS, nor of the contingency between CS and US. To see that this is so we need only consider that (a) the relative waiting time index can change radically while the contingency index remains unchanged; and (b) the relative waiting time index can remain constant while the contingency index changes radically.

The first case occurs when the intertrial interval is varied. If, for example, the average intertrial interval is shortened, the contingency index remains unchanged while the waiting time in the CS draws closer to the overall waiting time, thereby reducing the contrast between waiting times that, according to the hypothesis, is required for the acquisition of signal value. In an important article, Gibbon, Locurto, and Terrace (1975) demonstrated that effects that might be erroneously assigned to a loss of contingency could arise from an increase in the rate at which the US is presented. It is necessary to separate the effects of a change in trial rate, or in US rate, from the effects of a change in contingency.

The second case, in which the index of contingency between the CS and US varies widely while the index of relative waiting time remains constant, was exemplified by Experiment 13. In that experiment, the percentage of USs signaled by the CS was varied from 3% to 100%, a variation that greatly changed the index of contingency but left the relative waiting time index unchanged. Otherwise said, the $P(US/CS)$ and the $P(US)$ were unchanged but the $P(US/noCS)$ was substantially changed. The results, as we have seen, showed no systematic effects on performance despite the major change in contingency; they therefore lend support to the view that the relative waiting time hypothesis is closer to capturing the critical property of event sequences for the development of signal value than is the contingency hypothesis.

Surprisingly, the experimental evidence on the role of contingency in other forms of classical conditioning is far from decisive. The experiments on contingency by Rescorla (1968) are the most substantial ones available, and they might at first appear to provide a clear demonstration of the role of contingency in CER conditioning. On close examination, however, they prove subject to another interpretation.

The first experiment involved three conditions: a contingent procedure in which USs occurred only during CS periods, and two noncontingent control conditions. One noncontingent control received shocks during both CS and US at the same rate as shocks were received during CS-only periods in the contingent group. The other noncontingent control received the same total number of shocks as did the contingent group, but the shocks occurred randomly throughout the session. Only the contingent group gave evidence of conditioned suppression to the CS.

The experiment certainly demonstrates that contiguity between CS and US is not sufficient for conditioning, and it provides a control to show that the failure of conditioning in noncontingent groups was not a consequence of variations in the overall rate at which shocks occurred. The experiment does not, however, demonstrate that excitatory conditioning depends on the extent to which $P(US/CS)$ exceeds $P(US/noCS)$; or, in other words, on CS–US contingency. As previously noted, when contingency is entirely removed the indices of contingency and of relative waiting time each lead to the expectation of no conditioning.

The second of Rescorla's experiments provides data on conditioning as a function of intermediate degrees of contingency that were obtained by varying the probability of US in the CS and in the absence of the CS. The larger the difference between these probabilities the greater was the conditioned suppression. Once again, and for reasons we have already discussed, this is not decisive evidence that contingency is fundamental to conditioning. Note, for example, that for a fixed shock rate in the CS, the overall shock rate is increased as the shock rate in nonCS periods is increased. Consequently, the data do not allow one to distinguish between the possibility that the critical terms for conditioning are the $P(US/CS)$ and $P(US/noCS)$ or, on the other hand, the $P(US/CS)$ and the $P(US)$, the terms implied by the relative waiting time hypothesis. The crux of the matter is that the results might have been no different if the shocks delivered in nonCS had been signaled by the CS, thereby leaving contingency unchanged. Such a result would be in accord with the present findings for autoshaping. The possibility that CER conditioning might yield a similar result is suggested by the findings of Stein, Sidman, and Brady (1958). They found that the duration of the CS relative to the nonCS period was highly correlated with the degree of suppression; in particular, for a fixed duration of the CS, the amount of suppression decreased as the time between presentations decreased. Rescorla's data themselves provide no basis for choosing the contingency formulation over the relative waiting time hypothesis.

Although the idea has been widely accepted, it has yet to be shown that CS–US contingency is the fundamental property of event sequences responsible for the acquisition of signal value in classical conditioning.

ACKNOWLEDGMENT

Experiments 1–8 are part of an unpublished doctoral thesis by R. A. Barnes (1976), supervised by the first author, entitled: "The effect of temporal spacing on the development of autoshaped key pecking in the pigeon" (McMaster University, 1976).

REFERENCES

Allaway, T. A. *Attention, information, and auto-shaping.* Unpublished doctoral dissertation, University of Pennsylvania, 1971.

Barnes, R. A. *The effect of temporal spacing on the development of autoshaped key pecking in the pigeon.* Unpublished doctoral dissertation, McMaster University, Ontario, 1976.

Blanchard, R., & Honig, W. K. Surprise value of food determines its effectiveness as a reinforcer. *Journal of Experimental Psychology: Animal Behavior Processes,* 1976, 2, 67-74.

Dweck, C. S., & Wagner, A. R. Situational cues and correlation between CS and US as determinants of the conditioned emotional response. *Psychonomic Science,* 1970, 18, 145-147.

Gamzu, E. R., & Williams, D. R. Associative factors underlying the pigeon's key pecking in autoshaping procedures. *Journal of Experimental Analysis of Behavior,* 1973, 19, 225-232.

Gibbon, J., Baldock, M. D., Locurto, C., Gold, L., & Terrace, H. S. Trial and intertrial durations in autoshaping. *Journal of Experimental Psychology: Animal Behavior Processes,* 1977, 3, 264-284.

Gibbon, J., Berryman, R., & Thompson, R. L. Contingency spaces and measures in classical and instrumental conditioning. *Journal of the Experimental Analysis of Behavior,* 1974, 21, 585-605.

Gibbon, J., Farrell, L., Locurto, C. M., Duncan, H. J., & Terrace, H. S. Partial reinforcement in autoshaping with pigeons. *Animal Learning and Behavior,* 1980, 8, 45-59.

Gibbon, J., Locurto, C., & Terrace, H. S. Signal food contingency and signal frequency in a continuous trials auto-shaping paradigm. *Animal Learning and Behavior,* 1975, 3, 317-324.

Kamin, L. J. Predictability, surprise, attention and conditioning. In B. A. Campbell & R. M. Church (Eds.), *Punishment and aversive behavior.* New York: Appleton-Century-Crofts, 1969.

Leyland, C. M., & Mackintosh, N. J. Blocking of first- and second-order autoshaping in pigeons. *Animal Learning and Behavior,* 1978, 6, 391-394.

LoLordo, V. M. Selective associations. In A. Dickinson & R. A. Boakes (Eds.), *Mechanisms of learning and motivation: A memorial volume for Jerzy Konorski.* Hillsdale, N.J.: Erlbaum, 1978.

Mackintosh, N. J. *The psychology of animal learning.* New York: Academic Press, 1974.

Mackintosh, N. J. Conditioning as the perception of causal relations. In R. E. Butts & J. Hintikka (Eds.), *Foundational problems in the special sciences.* Dordrecht, Holland: D. Reidel, 1977.

Perkins, C. C., Beavers, W. O., Hancock, R. A., Hemmendinger, P. C., Hemmindinger, D., & Ricci, J. A. Some variables affecting rate of key pecking during response-independent procedures (autoshaping). *Journal of the Experimental Analysis of Behavior,* 1975, 24, 59-72.

Rescorla, R. A. Probability of shock in the presence and absence of CS in fear conditioning. *Journal of Comparative and Physiological Psychology,* 1968, 66, 1-5.

Rescorla, R. A. Informational variables in Pavlovian conditioning. In G. H. Bower (Ed.), *The psychology of learning and motivation: Advances in research and theory.* New York: Academic Press, 1972.

Rescorla, R. A., & Wagner, A. R. A theory of Pavlovian conditioning: Variations in the effectiveness of reinforcement and nonreinforcement. In A. H. Black & W. F. Prokasy (Eds.), *Classical conditioning II: Current research and theory.* New York: Appleton-Century-Crofts, 1972.

Stein, L., Sidman, M., & Brady, J. V. Some effects of two temporal variables on conditioned suppression. *Journal of the Experimental Analysis of Behavior,* 1958, 1, 153-162.

Terrace, H. S., Gibbon, J., Farrell, L., & Baldock, M. D. Temporal factors influencing the acquisition of an autoshaped key peck. *Animal Learning and Behavior,* 1975, 3, 53-62.

Tomie, A. Interference with autoshaping by prior context conditioning. *Journal of Experimental Psychology: Animal Behavior Processes,* 1976, 2, 323-334.

Zeiler, M. Schedules of reinforcement: the controlling variables. In *Handbook of operant behavior.* W. K. Honig & J. E. R. Staddon (Eds.), Englewood Cliffs, N.J.: Prentice-Hall, 1977.

JOHN GIBBON 9

The Contingency Problem in Autoshaping[1]

INTRODUCTION

Pavlov understood that the conditioning phenomenon he studied depended very heavily on temporal contiguity in the training procedure. He observed that when a previously indifferent trial cue (T) preceded and overlapped in time the delivery of a biologically important event (S^*) that T came to evoke anticipatory behavior similar to that elicited by S^*. But if only a small delay was interposed between the cue and consequence (trace procedure), a profound retardation of conditioning resulted (Pavlov, 1927). After this early emphasis on temporal contiguity, it was natural that much subsequent research was devoted to the problem of identifying optimal temporal arrangements between cue onset and unconditioned stimulus onset, and between unconditioned stimulus offset and cue onset (ITI).

Elsewhere in this volume, Gibbon and Balsam (Chapter 7) and Jenkins (Chapter 8) treat the temporal arrangement problem for autoshaping in considerable detail. My purpose here is to enlarge on the implications of temporal relationships in the context of the contingency between cue and consequence embedded in these training paradigms. Essentially, I will argue that the emphasis on temporal relationships is quite appropriate and constitutes a portion of the total information contained in a contingency between signal and food.

[1] This work was supported by National Science Foundation Grants BNS76-01229 and BNS78-23616.

CONTINGENCY

A strong statistical association or contingency between two events A,B is said to exist when two requirements are met: (a) A must "predict," "imply," or "go with" B and (b) the absence of A, ~A, must predict or go with the absence of B, ~B. In the classical conditioning context, this means that a strong association between the trial signal and the reinforcer requires not only that T and S^* occur together but that the absence of S^* occurs in the absence of T as well.

This latter requirement has been the focus of much research following a seminal series of papers by Rescorla (1967, 1968, 1969) in which he argued that both of these predictive relations are learned in our traditional training procedures. He noted that the excitatory training procedure in which T and S^* are positively related was formally similar to an inhibitory training procedure in which T and S^* are negatively related. Excitatory procedures are those in which the cue is a reliable predictor of the presence of the reinforcer, and inhibitory procedures are those in which the cue is a reliable predictor of the absence of the reinforcer. The term "reliability" here is to be taken in the statistical sense to mean a level of confidence in the soundness of the predictive relation.

Rescorla argued that given this symmetry, an appropriate control condition for an excitatory or inhibitory contingency is one in which there is no statistical relationship between the two events. He called this condition the "truly random control." Rescorla studied a training regime incorporating this control in a CER paradigm with rats. The procedure had several variants, which are discussed below, but the common feature was that the rate or probability of reinforcement in the presence of the signal was equal to that rate in its absence.

These conditions may be diagrammed in the contingency space (Gibbon, Berryman, & Thompson, 1974) shown in Figure 9.1. The probability of S^* delivery given T is plotted on the ordinate and the probability of S^* delivery given the absence of T on the abscissa. The truly random control or noncontingent condition is then represented by any arrangement in which these two

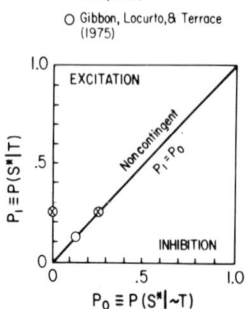

Figure 9.1. Contingency space representing excitatory and inhibitory conditioning procedures. The conditional probability of reinforcement given a trial signal (P_1) is on the ordinate and the conditional probability of reinforcement given the absence of the trial signal (P_0) is on the abscissa. Points along the rising diagonal represent noncontingent procedures in which the cue provides no differential information about reinforcement.

probabilities are equal. The locus of such points is the positive diagonal in the diagram. When the probability of S^* given the signal is higher than the probability of S^* given its absence, excitatory conditioning may be expected. Such procedures are those above and to the left of the positive diagonal. Inhibitory conditioning should result from the reverse of this inequality, exemplified in the diagram by points in the lower right half of the square. Along the rising left edge of the square, S^* events occur with some probability in the presence of T and never in its absence. Thus procedures along this edge represent partial reinforcement contingencies, with the continuous reinforcement case in the upper left-hand corner.

The distinction between partial and consistent pairing procedures at the edges and corners of the square has a parallel in the logic of implication. Gibbon et al. (1974) discuss these parallels and their relationship to a vast literature of association in comprehensive detail. My purpose here will be to inquire whether autoshaping procedures represented by points within contingency diagrams of this sort may be in some sense "collapsed." That is, I will describe "equally contingent" procedures that engender equivalent speeds of acquisition. These isocontingent conditions are derived from the "Expectancy Ratio" hypothesis in Scalar Expectancy Theory (SET; Gibbon, 1977; Gibbon & Balsam, Chapter 7). The conclusions drawn, however, might as easily be argued in terms of Jenkins's Relative Waiting Time hypothesis (Jenkins, Chapter 8). At the present level of development, the two accounts are virtually identical. Their predictions are exactly the same, but the spirit of the conceptualization differs. An attempt will be made later to distinguish them, but the body of the contingency analysis which follows is valid from either the Expectancy or Waiting Time point of view.

Autoshaping Contingencies

The contingency investigation has been adapted to the autoshaping procedure in a manner quite analogous to that developed by Rescorla for CER. Gamzu and Williams (1971) were perhaps the first to study the contingency problem in autoshaping. They studied two groups of birds, one that received response-independent food in the presence of the key-light signal and not in its absence (contingent group) and another that received food at the same rate, both when the key-light was lit and when it was dark. These two conditions are shown in the contingency square in Figure 9.1 by X's. The points were calculated assuming a "trial unit" of 10 sec for T (lit key) and $\sim T$ (dark key) periods. Reinforcement probability was, on this construction, .25 in the presence of T and zero in its absence for the contingent group (left edge) and .25 in the presence and absence of T for the noncontingent group (diagonal). They found that the noncontingent group did not acquire responding while the contingent group showed rapid acquisition of autoshaped pecking.

A later study (Gamzu and Williams, 1973) also found a failure to acquire for a group that was functionally a contingent group. For this group reinforcement was programmed at about one per 40 sec in the presence of the *dark* key and never in the presence of the lit key. Thus, the point on the left edge of the contingency square represents both of these conditions, yet one of them (lit key) showed robust responding and the other (dark key) showed no responding. We will see that the salience difference of the cues is not the only candidate for the explanation of the failure to observe responding to the dark key.

A subsequent investigation by Gibbon, Locurto, and Terrace (1975) studied conditions shown in Figure 9.1 by open circles. We replicated the contingent and noncontingent groups studied by Gamzu and Williams and added three others. In our adaptation of the procedure, the response key was always lit with one of two colors, and reinforcement was programmed with some probability at the end of each 10 sec lit-key period. In the reference condition the positive key color occurred one-fourth of the time and one of every four of these occurrences was followed by food. Food never followed the other (negative) color. The left-most circle represents two other contingent conditions we studied as well, with different results. When the positive trial occurred more frequently but with the same reinforcement probability in its presence, conditioned responding emerged slower (equal frequencies of positive color and negative color) or not at all (higher frequency of positive color than negative color). The contrasting noncontingent control conditions indicated by circles on the diagonal were those corresponding to Rescorla's high-density and low-density noncontingent procedures. For the high density case (circle plus X) reinforcement was added at a rate of one every 40 sec in the other of the two trial colors. For the low-density control (lower circle on the diagonal) reinforcements were redistributed across the two key colors so that the two conditional probabilities of reinforcement were equal, but *overall* reinforcement density was the same as that in the contingent condition. Our results paralleled those of Gamzu and Williams and Rescorla. Conditioning did not occur for either of the two noncontingent groups.

The noncontingent procedures defined in the contingency square are evidently the appropriate ones to contrast with procedures that do engender autoshaped responding. When the rates of food in the presence and absence of the trial signal are equal, conditioned responding does not emerge. However, the results of the contingent procedures are not homogeneous. When trials were infrequent, robust conditioning occurred, but when they were frequent, no conditioning occurred. Thus, a condition that eliminates associative responding is identified by the contingency analysis, but the conditions that generate it are not.

The additional variable required here is the frequency, or spacing, of the trial signal. Gibbon *et al.* (1974) organized the trial spacing variable as a third dimension in the contingency plot, which resulted in a tetrahedral volume for all possible training procedures. The three contingent groups that are not differentiated in Figure 9.2 are differentiated in the tetrahedral space. One purpose of the present analysis is to show that this third dimension, in a sense, is unnecessary. The trial spacing variable may be incorporated into a two-dimensional metric using scalar expectancy theory as adapted to the autoshaping situation (Gibbon & Balsam, Chapter 7).

The analysis that follows is restricted to contingency factors affecting acquisition. A theory for the later course of such learning is not developed here. Instead, I will concentrate on the limiting procedures for generating associative responding.

EXPECTANCY

The central idea behind the expectancy analysis is that subjects appreciate or value the signal inversely with its duration. One might think of expectancy in the signal as a subjective analogue of food rate. We have argued earlier (Chapter 7) that it is the average time that the signal is present per contiguous reinforcement that counts, and successive instants within each single presentation are undifferentiated. Expectancy in the signal is indexed by $h_T = H/T$ where H is a motivational parameter reflecting the value of the reinforcement occasion, and T is the average time that the signal is present between signal–food pairings. This subjective food rate is quite comparable—in fact, under some constructions it is proportional—to the probability of food given the signal, that is, to the ordinate in the contingency square (Figure 9.1).[2]

Expectancy of food in the signal is compared in SET with an overall cycle, or background, expectancy indexed by $h_C = H/C$ where C is the average time (cycle) between reinforcers overall. This background rate is what most powerfully differentiates the expectancy account from a contingency analysis. When the background food rate is high, the expectancy of food in the presence of the signal may not differ sufficiently from the background expectancy to engender responding. SET holds that the comparison between background and trial is made by taking a ratio of these two expectancy levels, $r = h_T/h_C = C/T$. When this ratio is sufficiently large, the procedure generates conditioned responding. Gibbon and Balsam (Chapter 7) present data to show that when the expectancy ratio is less than about 1.5–2.0, conditioned responding does not emerge, even though contingent arrangements may be in force.

[2]Breaking time into discrete "trial units," expectancy of food in the signal may be written, $h_T = (H/u)P(S^*|T)$ where u is the unit for calculating the conditional probability of S^* given T. This correspondence, however, is not in the spirit of the expectancy analysis since I believe it is unlikely that subjects adopt such a discrete time unit in assessing the food rate. This point is discussed in more detail later.

The abscissa variable in the contingency square, probability of food in the absence of the trial cue, does not explicitly enter into the background rate. Rather, food rates in the presence *and* absence of the CS are integrated to give an average background expectation. This expectancy value may be thought of as that appropriate to "ignoring" presence or absence of the signal. The cycle, or background expectancy is analogous to the unconditional food rate, $P(S^*)$, not the food rate conditioned on the absence of the signal. This difference is a profound one, which has several implications for association learning.

The Gibbon *et al.* (1975) contingency experiment is adapted to the expectancy framework in Figure 9.2. The top row shows three expectancy diagrams that correspond to the three contingent conditions. The reference condition is in the upper left panel. Expectancy in units of H is indicated on the left ordinate and time, in 10-sec periods, on the abscissa. The diagram shows one cycle comprising the time between two reinforced trials, with reinforcement indicated by filled circles on the abscissa. On the average, one in four 10-sec positive signals was reinforced, and reinforcement was never presented in the absence of the positive signal. The expectancy appropriate to the trial signal is therefore $H/4$, and this is indicated by the height of the vertical hatched bars representing positive trials in the figure. Signals occurred one-fourth of the time on the average, so that the average overall reinforcement rate was 1 reinforcer per 160 sec, or one per 16 10-sec periods. This background rate is indicated by the height of the diagonal hatching in the diagram ($h_C = H/16$). The other two contingent procedures studied maintained the same reinforcement rate in the signal ($h_T = H/4$) but varied the frequency with which the positive signal occurred. In the middle diagram the positive signal occurs half the time and thus, on the average, two positive trials are reinforced in 160 sec. The background food rate has therefore been doubled from that in the reference condition on the left. In the right-most panel, the positive signal occurs still more frequently (three-fourths of the time), and so the background food rate has been tripled above the reference condition.

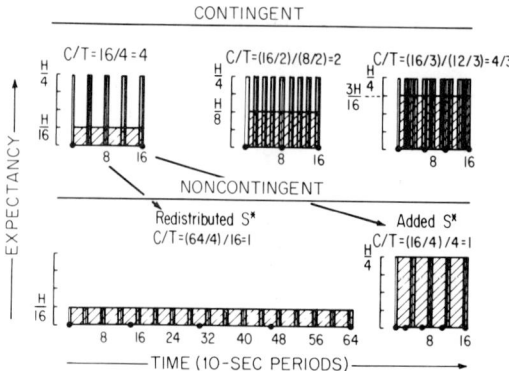

Figure 9.2. Expectancy diagrams for contingent and noncontingent procedures studied by Gibbon, Locurto, and Terrace (1975). The vertical hashed bars represent food expectation in the trial signal and the diagonal hashed area represents food expectation in the background. Circles represent food delivery.

SET regards subjects as comparing these two levels of expectation by taking their ratio. The C/T ratios shown above each diagram decrease as the positive signal is made more frequent. This is just another way of depicting the trial spacing effect analyzed previously. In accord with the requirement that the expectancy ratio be greater than or equal to about 2, responding did not occur for the group represented by the $C/T = 4/3$ ratio. This group corresponds very closely to the contingent group studied by Gamzu and Williams (1973) in which reinforcers were programmed only in the absence of the key-light. The failure to observe pecking to the dark key (positive signal) in their subjects therefore may be as readily explained by the unfavorable C/T ratio as by the salience difference between dark and lit keys.

The two noncontingent procedures are represented by the diagrams in the bottom row. On the left, the low-density noncontingent control is shown in which the overall food rate is maintained the same as that in the reference condition, but food occasions are programmed randomly in time. Since trials were scheduled with the same frequency (one-fourth of the time), on the average one out of every four reinforcers occurred contiguous with a trial signal. Thus, the average interval between two reinforced trials was 640 sec. In this interval, on the average, three additional reinforcers occurred not contiguous with the signal. Both the signal rate and the background rate were therefore $h_T = h_C = H/16$. Expectancy in the signal has been lowered to the background level for this condition, and subjects "see" no improvement in food rate in the cue.

In the diagram in the lower right, the high-density noncontingent control procedure is represented. In this procedure, food was added until the rate in the absence of the signal was equal to that in its presence. On the average, in 160 sec four reinforcers occurred, but three of them were contiguous with the (formerly) negative signal that occupies three-fourths of this time period. Thus, for this condition, the background food rate has been raised to that in the trial and, again, subjects see no improvement over their expectation of food overall.

Expectancy Metric

The critical variable that distinguishes SET from the contingency analysis is the background food rate. The two expectancies may be plotted orthogonally to produce an expectancy metric analogous to the contingency square. Within this space, excitatory, inhibitory, and noncontingent procedures may be specified. In Figure 9.3, trial expectancy is represented on the ordinate and cycle expectancy on the abscissa. The main diagonal represents conditions in which trial expectancy equals cycle expectancy ($r = C/T = 1$). Trial expectancy is proportional to the probability of food given CS, and background expectancy is proportional to the overall probability of food. When these two are equal, all statistical measures of association are zero (cf. Gibbon et al., 1974). Thus, the main diagonal here

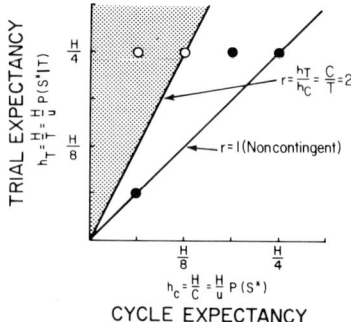

Fig. 9.3. Expectancy space. Trial expectancy on the ordinate is proportional to $P(S^*|T)$, with proportionality constant H/u where u is the time unit for calculating probability. Cycle or background expectancy on the abscissa is proportional to $P(S^*)$. Noncontingent procedures are those that hold these two values equal ($r = 1$), indicated by the rising diagonal with slope 1.0. Expectancy ratios greater than 1.0 are rays emanating from the origin with a steeper slope. The theory predicts excitatory conditioning for procedures above and to the left of the ray representing an expectancy ratio of about 2.0 (stippled area). Points in the figure correspond to the Gibbon, Locurto, and Terrace (1975) procedures diagrammed in Figure 9.2.

corresponds to the main diagonal in the contingency square. What differs is that now different signal frequencies are distinguished. The top row of points corresponding to an ordinate value of $H/4$ represents the three contingent procedures and the high-density noncontingent procedure in the Gibbon, Locurto, and Terrace study. The low-density noncontingent condition is represented by the lower point on the diagonal. The two open circles represent the groups that acquired and the three filled circles represent those that did not.

In this metric, constant expectancy ratios are represented by rays emanating from the origin. One appropriate to $r = C/T = 2$ is shown. This value of the expectancy ratio is close to (or perhaps a little above) the threshold for conditioning proposed by Gibbon and Balsam (Chapter 7). Expectancy ratios larger than $r = 2.0$ are represented by the hatched area above and to the left of this line, and so this region represents effective excitatory conditioning procedures. Procedures which, from a contingency point of view, may still possess a positive correlation between trial signal and food, may nevertheless not produce reliable acquisition. A case in point is the filled circle for the frequent positive signal condition to the right of the $r = 2$ ray, but above and to the left of the noncontingent $r = 1$ diagonal.

Figure 9.3 represents my proposal for an expectancy metric within which procedures that are effective and those that are not are specified by areas in a two-dimensional space. It incorporates food rate in the trial, the more traditional variable indexing contiguity of cue and consequence. But it also incorporates the trial spacing variable into cycle expectancy on the abscissa. A high frequency of trials results in a high background expectancy, and thus these conditions move closer to the noncontingent diagonal.

What is omitted here is the probability of food in the absence of the trial signal, the abscissa of Figure 9.1. I will argue that $P(S^*|\sim T)$ is not appreciated as such by subjects, at least early in acquisition, so that this potential third dimension is irrelevant to the power of the training procedures to engender associative responding. This is the sense in which the expectancy metric represents only part of the information contained in the correlation between signal and food. Correlations, such as ϕ, index the ratio of the difference between the probability of food in the presence and absence of the signal to a normalizing constant that is a direct function of the overall probability of food (cf. Gibbon et al., 1974, Equation 1). The *expectancy ratio*, however, is a direct function of just the normalized probability of food in the signal.

The expectancy metric of Figure 9.3 represents inhibitory training procedures in the area below the noncontingent diagonal. Here expectation of food is lower in the signal than overall ($h_T < h_C$). The traditional inhibitory procedures are those along the abscissa, in which S^* is presented only in the absence of the signal ($h_T = 0 < h_C$). The expectancy ratio has not been applied to acquisition of inhibitory control, but it is worth noting that inhibitory and excitatory procedures are *not* symmetric in the expectancy space, as they are in the contingency space. Points on the ordinate correspond to $r = \infty$ ($T = 0$ or $C = \infty$) which is not a realizable procedure, whereas points on the abscissa represent standard inhibitory procedures. An analysis of inhibitory contingencies is beyond the scope of this account, but it is tempting to speculate that this asymmetry may bear some structural relation to differences between excitatory and inhibitory learning.

The concept of inhibition reveals another perspective on the reduced information in the expectancy ratio. In any contingent procedure, there are potentially two distinct signals, as well as a background context. The absence of the trial signal is a potential inhibitory cue. It is a reliable predictor of a reduced rate of reinforcement relative to the background or the trial. It is the core of the expectancy view that this predictor is ignored with respect to acquisition of excitatory responding. The symmetry of the contingency space, and the correlational measures appropriate to it, do reflect all the information in contingency procedures, but animal subjects—with the possible exception of the statisticians—appear to use only one of the two predictive dimensions available.

In the remainder of this chapter I will examine, in more depth, the implication of this view for understanding the manner in which partial contingencies retard the formation of an association between signal and food.

PARTIAL CONTINGENCIES

Decreased Reinforcement of Trials: Partial Reinforcement

A traditional way in which to degrade the contingency between signal and S^* in classical conditioning procedures has been to program reinforcement only for some porportion of the trials. This operation in the autoshaping paradigm has some effect on the level of asymptotic responding but very little effect on the speed with which the association is acquired (Gibbon, Farrell, Locurto, Duncan, & Terrace, 1980). This failure of partial reinforcement to produce substantial retardation in acquisition is analyzed by Gibbon and Balsam (Chapter 7) in terms of SET. We argue there that in the traditional probability manipulation, when reinforcers are deleted for some proportion of the trials the result is longer time periods between reinforced trials *and* longer time periods between reinforcements overall. The result is that the numerator and the denominator of the expectancy ratio are increased by the same factor and as a result the ratio remains constant. This idea is depicted graphically in Figure 9.4. The top row shows an expectancy diagram for a reference condition in which the trial signal occupies one-fourth of the session and reinforcers are delivered at the end of every trial. This condition corresponds to the reference condition in the upper left panel of Figure 9.2 but with regular reinforcement of a longer signal. Two cycles are shown on the abscissa with reinforcement (filled circles) occurring at the end of each trial. Again, expectancy in the trial is indicated by the height of the vertical hashed bars and in the background by the height of the diagonal hashing. In this example, the expectancy ratio is 4, and the procedure would be expected to generate responding at an intermediate acquisition speed.

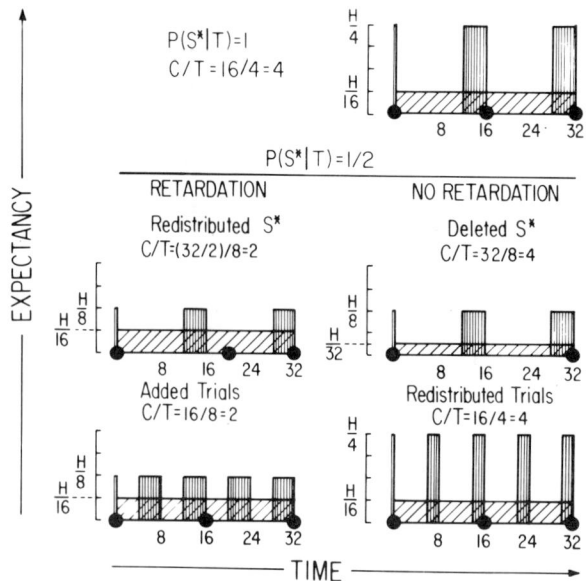

Figure 9.4. Expectancy diagrams for partial reinforcement. The reference condition with 100% reinforcement is in the upper right panel. Two methods of programming partial reinforcement that would be expected to produce retardation are shown in the left column. Two methods expected to produce no retardation are shown in the right column under the reference condition.

The four panels below represent four different ways in which probability of reinforcement, given the signal, might be reduced. Directly below the reference condition is the right hand column, two procedures are shown in which no retardation would be predicted from the expectancy point of view. The middle panel depicts the traditional probability of reinforcement procedure in which one of the reinforcers is simply deleted, but the temporal arrangements remain the same. According to Gibbon and Balsam's analysis, this operation reduces expectancy in the trial by one-half, since twice as much trial time occurs between reinforced trials. It also reduces expectancy in the background by half, since there is twice as much time overall between reinforcers. The result is a constant expectancy ratio ($C/T = 4$) and no retardation is predicted according to SET. In fact, the evidence summarized by us (Chapter 7) is quite strong that there is little or no retardation due to this operation. Moreover, a review of the literature comprising a variety of subjects and preparations (Gibbon et al., 1980, Table 2) shows that this manipulation produces retardation with just about the traditional significance-level frequency. That is, only about 1 in 20 experimental results show some retardation for the deleted reinforcers manipulation.

In the lower right panel, a second procedure in which reinforcement probability in the signal has been nominally halved is shown. This condition also produces no retardation. In this diagram, each trial may be thought of as comprised of two halves, one that goes unreinforced (at 8 time units and 24 time units) and a second that is followed by food (at 16 units and 32 units). This is what Gibbon and Balsam have called the "split trials" procedure, and in comparison with the appropriate reference group (top panel), retardation is not observed. Thus, both of these procedures are (superficially) procedures in which the conditional probability of reinforcement, given the signal, has been reduced. The results imply, however, that birds construe time rather than probability as the relevant variable and integrate between reinforcement experiences, producing equivalent food expectations for all three cases.

In the left column two procedures are indicated in which the conditional probability of reinforcement has been reduced in such a manner that retardation *is* predicted from the expectancy point of view. The first of these, labeled "Redistributed S^*," is the analogue for a partial contingency, of the noncontingent redistributed reinforcement case, (low-density noncontingent control in Figure 9.2). In the present example, overall food rate is maintained constant but food rate in the presence of the signal is reduced. Thus, the reinforcer delivered in the reference condition after the first trial (at 16 time units) has been moved to the following intertrial interval. Expectancy in the signal is dropped by half, but expectancy in the background is maintained the same, because on the average two reinforcers occur in 32 time units. This is the reason for the reduced effectiveness of the contingency in the redistributed noncontingent control. It reduces expectancy in the trial signal *without* reducing background expectancy.

In the lower left panel, another procedure is shown in which retarded acquisition would be expected. In this procedure, the overall background food rate is maintained the same, but unreinforced trials are simply added between pairings. This manner of decreasing reinforcement probability has been studied with autoshaping by Wasserman, Deich, Hunter, and Nagamatsu (1977) and has been shown to result in substantial retardation of acquisition speed. The reason is clear from the expectancy diagram. Since background food rate remains the same, cycle expectancy is constant but trial expectancy has been reduced by one-half. Thus, the C/T ratio here, as in the diagram above, is reduced, and retarded acquisition results.

Comparing the expectancy diagrams in the bottom row, it is clear that the integration between reinforced trial episodes produces very different results for different trial durations. When the trial durations are half of those in the reference condition, integration over cumulative trial time results in a constant expectancy ratio and no retardation. When trial durations are equal to those in the reference condition but their frequency is doubled, the expectancy ratio is halved and acquisition is substantially slower. This means that the failure to find an effect for diagrams on the right cannot be attributed to "inattention" to unreinforced signals, since then these two conditions would be equivalent. Unreinforced signals are noticed by subjects but integrated with the reinforced signal at the end of the cycle.

Increased Reinforcement of Background: Indifference between Signaled and Unsignaled Food

A second and now traditional manner of degrading a strong contingency is to program reinforcers at some nonzero rate in the period between trials. The extreme case is the high-density noncontingent condition (Figure 9.2). There, the food rate in the absence of the signal is raised to that in the presence of the signal. From a contingency point of view, this procedure is effective in eliminating conditioning because the absence of the signal is as good a predictor of food as the presence of the signal. According to scalar expectancy theory, however, this procedure eliminates conditioning because the background expectancy is equal to the trial expectancy.

Jenkins (Chapter 8) has devised a very strong test of the difference between these two accounts. He argues that if it is the increased background food rate that retards conditioning, then it should make no difference whether additional feedings are signaled or unsignaled. Yet, if they are signaled, the traditional view attributes any degradation of the contingency to the massing of trials; whereas if they are unsignaled, degradation must be attributed to a very different source, the increase in predictiveness of the absence of the signal. Jenkins's insight is that these two sources of retarded acquisition are one and the same from the point of view of the average time to food in the background. He arranged conditions to test this view in which for different groups, different proportions of reinforcers were signaled or unsignaled, while overall reinforcement density was held constant.

Expectancy diagrams for this situation are shown in Figure 9.5. Again, the reference condition (Figure 9.4) is the upper right-hand panel. Food is available at the end of each trial signal and never in the absence of the signal, and signals occupy one quarter of each cycle. The expectancy ratio is $C/T = 4.0$. The two diagrams in the bottom row depict the two ways in which added food occasions were programmed. For the condition represented in the lower left panel, a procedure analogous to partial contingencies studied by Rescorla (1968) is shown. Additional reinforcers are programmed in the absence of the cue, but all other temporal arrangements are held constant. This group acquired at a substantially slower rate than those exposed to the reference condition in the upper right.

The condition diagrammed in the lower right corner has the same overall reinforcement rate as that on the left, but now each additional reinforcer is preceded by a trial signal of the same duration. The conditional probability of reinforcement given the absence of the signal is zero for this group, whereas for the group on the left it is greater than zero. Both procedures, however, result in the same overall probability of food, which is higher than that in the reference condition. The important result was that the retardation produced by both procedures was equivalent. It made no difference to the degree of retardation, whether added food presentations were signaled or not.

Jenkins's demonstration of indifference between signaled and unsignaled added food, is perhaps the most damaging observation for any view of the role of

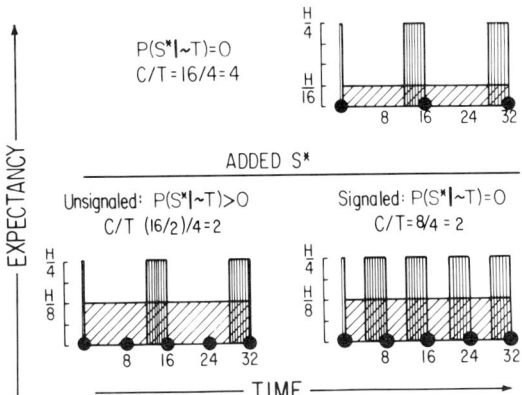

Figure 9.5. Expectancy diagrams for added reinforcement in the background. The reference condition is in the upper right panel (as in Figure 9.4.). Two methods of programming additional reinforcements are shown in the lower two panels: On the left, additional reinforcers are unsignaled; on the right, they are signaled.

contingency, as traditionally espoused, in the formation of association between cue and consequence. It means that the background excitation level controls the emergence of conditioned responding quite independently of the presence or absence of trial signals, provided at least a few signal–food pairings occur. It argues against alternative theoretical accounts that ascribe a special role to reinforcement in the absence of the signal.

RELATION TO RESCORLA–WAGNER THEORY

The powerful theoretical account developed by Rescorla and Wagner (Rescorla & Wagner, 1972; Wagner & Rescorla, 1972) deals at least implicitly with some of the contingency effects discussed here. For example, the noncontingent procedures are equivalent under both accounts. The Wagner–Rescorla equations result in some early value for the trial signal embedded in a background, but a subsequent rapid decline to zero under noncontingent training procedures. The associative competition axiom in the Rescorla–Wagner account holds that all stimuli present at reinforcement occasions, the explicit trial signal, and background contextual cues compete for a limited amount of excitatory strength. With continued reinforcement of background alone, background stimuli come to absorb all of the conditioned excitation under the noncontingent procedure. This means that the value of the signal for the subject declines over continued experience to zero and so no conditioned responding emerges.

Scalar expectancy theory also predicts no conditioned responding under noncontingent procedures, but for different reasons. In the expectancy view, conditioned responding reflects a differential expectation of food in the presence of the signal as against the background. When overall reinforcement rate is equal to reinforcement rate in the signal there is no differential expectation level to support responding to the signal. In a sense, a high background food expectation blocks responding to the keylight. The theory has been silent to date on whether this is a learning or a performance block. It may be that pretreatment with a noncontingent regime effectively prevents subjects from acquiring a food expectation in the signal (Lindblom & Jenkins, 1979) or, alternatively, food expectation in the signal may be acquired but may not be of sufficient magnitude to generate responding. In either case, behavior to the cue would not be observed, and at this level of analysis the two kinds of blocking look alike. The importance of the blocking phenomenon for the autoshaping situation is discussed in more detail later.

Trial Spacing

The trial-spacing effect common in classical conditioning procedures with other preparations has been analyzed in some detail from the expectancy perspective by Gibbon and Balsam (Chapter 7) and Jenkins (Chapter 8). The Rescorla–Wagner theory was not developed in a temporal framework, but the theory may be adapted to afford a prediction of the trial-spacing effect by viewing long intertrial intervals as occasions for extinction of the excitatory value of background contextual stimuli. Under this view, a subsequent compound of trial plus background has a lower value when the intertrial interval is long than when it is short, and the effectiveness of reinforcement is greater in the former than the latter case. This results from the competition between stimulus elements for associative strength. When the compound consisting of the aggregate of background plus signal is low, a greater increment accrues to both stimuli upon reinforcement.

This view of the greater effectiveness of a reinforcer when trials are spaced differs from the expectancy account in which reinforcers are thought of as equally effective, but the expectation they engender is reduced when it must be "spread" over a longer time period. Thus, as with the noncontingent procedures, the predictions are the same—spacing trials should facilitate acquisition—but the reasons are different.

Differences between the two accounts arise in quantitative as well as qualitative ways. For example, the size of the trial-spacing effects depends heavily on the salience of the background stimuli. Stephen Fairhurst and I (reported in Gibbon, 1976) have found that for Rescorla–Wagner theory to predict a substantial trial-spacing effect, the background salience must be an order of magnitude or so larger than the salience of the signal. This requirement is similar to the learning rate parameter results for trial and background that were necessary to achieve a reasonable prediction of the quantitative features of acquisition data studied by Gibbon and Balsam (Chapter 7, Figure 7.11). However, the salience differences in SET were not as pronounced. In this discussion, I will concentrate on qualitative differences between theories, and on qualitative grounds the Rescorla–Wagner account is consonant with the trial-spacing effect.

Trial Units

A fundamental problem for any probabilistic theory in which intermittancy is important is the definition of the "units" within which probability is assessed. In SET, we have seen that reinforcement probability is viewed essentially as 1.0 throughout. That is, because of the integration between reinforced trial episodes, accumulated trial time in this interval is always reinforced. In the Rescorla–Wagner model, however, extinction plays an important role for context and trial, and so there must be some structure to the paradigm that allows for a trial or background period to go unreinforced with a consequent reduction in value. If we regard the duration of the nominal trial—that signal just preceding a reinforcement occasion—as the trial "unit" defining reinforcement probability, then the Rescorla–Wagner equations predict that the value accruing to the signal rises to lower levels when the conditional probability of reinforcement given the signal is reduced. In the appendix to this chapter, a probabilistic version of the asymptote prediction for the value of the trial signal, V_T, when reinforced intermittently in the presence of a continuous background context is found as

$$V_T(\infty) = \left[1 + \left(\frac{1-P_1}{P_1} \right) \frac{\beta_2}{\beta_1} \right]^{-1}, \tag{1}$$

where β_1, β_2 are learning and extinction rate parameters, respectively, and $P_1 = P(S^*|T)$.

It is clear that this asymptote depends directly on the conditional probability of reinforcement in the signal. One might argue equally that it depends heavily on the trial "unit," since arbitrarily changing the size of the unit changes the magnitude of this probability. One consistent view would require some "minimal time unit" that subjects use for assessing reinforcement probability and would hold that all trial and cycle durations are scaled in terms of this unit. This would mean, for example, that conditions in which there is but one signal per reinforcer and all reinforcers are delivered in the presence of this signal would not necessarily imply that the probability of reinforcement, given T, is 1.0. Rather, $P(S^*|T) = u/T$ where u is the trial unit common to all durations. Just such a trial structure is required for the asymptote value in equation 1.

Difficulties with such a view are illustrated in Figure 9.6, which shows sets of

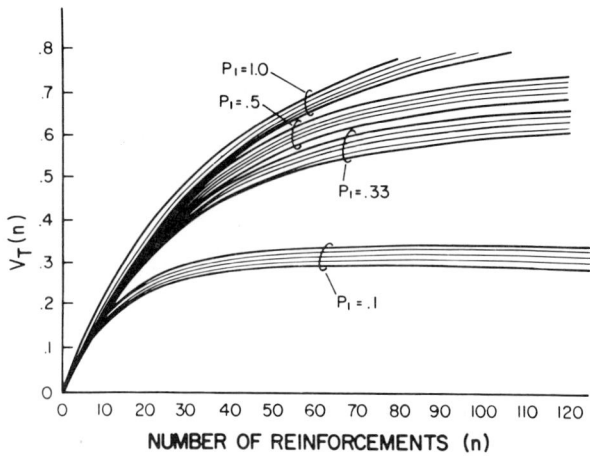

Figure 9.6. Growth of the value of the trial signal (V_T) as a function of successive reinforcements for the Rescorla–Wagner theory. The four sets of functions correspond to different conditional probabilities of reinforcement, given the signal $P_1 = P(S^*|T)$. Within each set corresponding to a given P_1 value, cycle-to-trial duration ratios (C/T) range from 1.5 (bottom function) to 11.0 (top function).

learning curves for the associative value of the signal under the Rescorla–Wagner assumptions at four different levels of the conditional probability of reinforcement given a trial unit (labeled P_1). The abscissa is the number of reinforcements or cycles. Within each group of curves, the top curve represents a cycle-to-trial ratio of 11 to 1, and the bottom curve a C/T ratio of 1.5 to 1. The learning rate parameters were those used by Rescorla and Wagner in their 1972 simulation of the contingency effect.

If we assume that conditioned responding emerges when the value accruing to the signal exceeds some criterion threshold, then several difficulties are apparent. First, it is clear that the threshold must be lower than the lowest of the value asymptotes, or else conditioning will not occur at some probability values. In this example, when the probability of reinforcement is .1, the threshold must lie below about .25. This means that the ITI effects are extremely small relative to the size of the effects in the data we observe. Consider, for example, the very small differences between abscissa values at which the $P_1 = .5$ curves would intersect a horizontal threshold line set at $V_T = .25$. Lower probability values would of course exaggerate this difficulty, though to our knowledge, .1 is about the lowest value that has been studied (Gibbon et al., 1980). Recently Stephen Fairhurst and I have explored other parameter choices. Assuming much more rapid conditioning to the background than to the trial, as was assumed in SET, a more robust ITI effect may be obtained. However, there remains a large probability effect that does not appear to be maskable by an adroit choice of parameter values. In the theory, probability controls strongly and time controls weakly, while in the autoshaping data, just the reverse is the case.

A modification of the Rescorla–Wagner equations that might handle this difficulty would allow the duration of the trial signal to modulate (perhaps equal) the trial unit. Several advantages would accrue from this conception. First, the fact that acquisition is constant at constant C/T ratios would be accommodated. It may be shown that the value functions in Figure 9.6 are constant for constant C/T ratios under this assumption. Second, if integration of unreinforced "segments" of the signal is incorporated into the unit, then the failure to find a robust probability effect when trials are "split" or when reinforcements are deleted (Figure 9.4) is also accommodated. A trial unit that gets rescaled with the actual trial duration programmed essentially holds reinforcement probability constant at the same value for any procedure.

However, a closer examination of this latter advantage reveals difficulties. The failure to find a probability effect requires that trials be integrated over the cycle between reinforced trial occasions. In essence, no trial "segment" goes unreinforced on this assumption. But then a problem arises for the trial-spacing effect. The same assumption cannot be extended to cover background "segments" as well. The reason is that if background "trial units" are represented as total cycle time, then probability of reinforcement is always 1.0 for both the cycle and the trials. What is required for the trial-spacing effect is that trial segments be integrated into a "unit", T, which then defines the number of *unreinforced* intertrial periods as $C/T - 1$. Integration must proceed over trial signals only, and cannot apply to the background cycle. Alternatively, extinction must never occur for trial segments and yet must always occur for unreinforced background segments exceeding the total trial duration. Thus the conception of trial structure required to accommodate both a large trial-spacing effect and no partial reinforcement effect is clearly a little strained. It does preserve, however, the associative competition feature, and thus suggests the route for a possible synthesis of SET and Rescorla-Wagner theory.

Blocking

The Rescorla-Wagner theory was developed in the context of the important findings on blocking in classical conditioning pioneered by Kamin (1969). The stimulus competition feature of the Wagner-Rescorla equations that is at the core of the blocking explanation has proved a very powerful analytic tool for understanding a variety of stimulus compounding effects. These effects have appeared most powerfully when two or more explicit stimuli are involved. In the autoshaping situation, blocking by pretraining an explicit excitatory signal which is later compounded with the autoshaping cue has not been reliably demonstrated (Jenkins, Chapter 8). Rather, a variety of workers (Hall & Honig, 1974; Mackintosh, 1973; Straub & Gibbon, 1977; Tomie, 1976a, 1976b, this volume, Chapter 6) have shown retarded acquisition to an autoshaping signal when that signal is presented in a pretrained context, relative to acquisition in a novel context.

At present it is not known why blocking by an explicit pretrained cue is difficult to obtain in the standard autoshaping procedure. Perhaps the punctate visual signal has some special biological status for birds, or perhaps the background context has some special status that overrides a concurrent pretrained cue. Whether problems with blocking make autoshaping different in some important respect from other classical conditioning preparations remains an open question. It seems likely at present that the status of the background as a potential blocker (and blockee) has not been studied as fully as it should be in the light of the important role the background plays in temporal effects. Lindblom and Jenkins (1979) have recently reported some provocative findings that suggest that under the noncontingent procedure the background may block initial learning about the signal but cannot absorb conditioned strength from a signal that has been pretrained. Rather, subjects that have learned to expect food in the signal inhibit the expression of that learning during a noncontingent regime but reveal an intact food expectation by responding when tested subsequently in extinction.

The expectancy account has not been elaborated with a stimulus competition feature precisely because of the ambiguities about the role of the background with respect to blocking discussed above. When a pretrained signal is presented in compound with the autoshaping cue, what is the background? If subjects may be induced, so to say, to consider the pretrained cue as the background, then it may block learning to expect food in the signal. If, on the other hand, the background remains available for comparison with the cue, irrespective of alternative signals concurrently present, then the failure to find blocking that Jenkins and others have reported may be expected.

These ambiguities evidently must be resolved by future theoretical and empirical work. All that is clear at present is that the stimulus competition feature of the Rescorla–Wagner account is not readily transported without modification into the autoshaping situation. The key to resolving these difficulties may lie in understanding the sense in which the background may be regarded as a "stimulus" like any other, or must be accorded a special status. Jenkins' important finding on indifference between signaled and unsignaled reinforcement reviewed in the next section strongly suggests the latter.

Background Alone

The stimulus competition axiom applied to the noncontingent procedure holds that background stimuli compete more effectively with the nominal cue when the background receives reinforcement in the absence of the cue. According to this view, reinforced background-alone occasions increase the value of the background while the trial signal remains unchanged. On subsequent compound, trial-plus-background reinforcement occasions, the aggregate value of the compound is higher with a resulting smaller increment to the trial signal.

This view of the mechanism by which a noncontingent or partially contingent procedure retards acquisition to the signal is severely strained by Jenkins's demonstration that the retardation produced by unsignaled reinforcers is no worse when these added reinforcers are themselves signaled. When reinforcement occurs only to the compound in the signaled case (Figure 9.5, lower right panel) the more favorable position of the background when it is reinforced alone (lower left panel) no longer obtains. Of the two conditions, reinforcing the background alone should therefore result in considerably more retardation. In fact, Jenkins's data say that there is no difference between the signaled and unsignaled conditions.

In terms of a blocking analysis, this means that the background cannot be "protected" in the autoshaping situation. Signaling additional reinforcers, which ought to prevent the background from competing as effectively with the trial signal, does not attenuate the deleterious effect of these additional reinforcers on acquisition speed.

Extinction

Another line along which the two accounts diverge is the way in which extinction is conceived. In the Rescorla–Wagner theory, nonreinforcement of some "trial unit" in the background is critical to differential excitatory strength accruing to the signal. In SET (and Relative Waiting Time) extinction in some sense cannot occur. Subjects integrate over the entire period between reinforced signals, so that this view is silent on how food expectation declines when reinforcement is omitted entirely. A tentative approach to this problem may be constructed along the lines of the observation by Gibbon *et al.* (1980) that extinction after autoshaping training proceeds at a constant rate per expected reinforcer. They found that when probability of reinforcement was varied for different training groups, after 15 days of conditioning, omission of reinforcement resulted in a decline in responding that was roughly constant per (previously) scheduled reinforcer. Groups differed in the starting point for the decline, but if response rates were normalized for their pre-extinction levels, the decline was roughly constant for constant omission of expected reinforcers.

This suggests that the way in which the rapid adjustment to new background levels is accomplished is on an expectation basis. When reinforcers that are expected at some interval are omitted, the associative mechanism establishing excitation in time adjusts. It does so, however, relative to the expected rate. It is the violation of this expectation that governs a change in expectancy—not the absolute frequency of reinforcement.

RELATION TO RELATIVE WAITING TIME

Jenkins (Chapter 8) has proposed an alternative construction that shares virtually all of the features I have outlined above but is couched in a different conceptual language. He argues that it is the relative waiting time for food in the trial and in the background that counts. If relative waiting time is indexed by the ratio of the time that the signal is present between reinforced signals to the average time between reinforcers, it is hard to see a difference between the two accounts. The ratio comparator of SET is simply more explicit than the relative waiting time proposal in stating the mechanism whereby these two time values are discriminated. Otherwise, the formal predictions are identical.

There is, however, a potential conceptual difference between the two views. SET in its emphasis on expectation, is oriented toward predicting the delay to reinforcement, rather than toward the wait since the last reinforcement. Relative waiting time has the opposite emphasis. Conditioning is a function of how long, on the average, subjects have already waited, rather than how long they expect to wait in the future. Although this conceptual difference appears to be a real one to us, it is not obvious how to test it. One possibility explored by Jenkins is to ask whether extensive pretraining on a *Fixed Time* (FT) schedule may retard acquisition. If it is expectation of food that governs the conditioning process, then time periods that evoke a high food expectancy might be expected to function as blocking stimuli in a subsequent autoshaping test. Conversely, if it is the average waiting time between feedings versus the average waiting time in the signal that counts, temporal blocking might not occur.

Perhaps unfortunately, the averaging of background expectancy assumed in SET invalidates this test. The background must remain undifferentiated even after many months of periodic reinforcement training. For example, in the SET account of standard Fixed Interval (FI) training, temporally discriminated time values are themselves compared with an undifferentiated background, and it is this feature of SET that predicts proportionality in response rates under FI (Gibbon, 1977). Since asymptotic temporally discriminated behavior requires an undifferentiated background, it seems unlikely that any pretraining procedure could alter this property. Background cycle times appear to be always averaged, and so a distinction between waiting and expecting is not possible from this point of view.

It is not clear to me, at present, how to forge a clean distinction between SET and Relative Waiting Time. A resolution may emerge from a clearer treatment of the background in the blocking paradigm or as a blocking stimulus itself, if reliable blocking of autoshaping may be demonstrated. Superficially, at least, an emphasis on waiting time in the background does not seem to fit as readily with a stimulus competition mechanism, as an emphasis on food expectation associated with a context.

However, the theoretical accounts are about as ambiguous as the data at the present level of development. Until the differences between the two are sharpened, they remain virtually indistinguishable except for an orientation in terms of what might be called "hope" or "excitement" (expectancy) versus "disappointment" or "frustration" (waiting).

APPENDIX A: RESCORLA-WAGNER THEORY

Rescorla–Wagner theory may be adapted to probabilistic trials and reinforcement as follows: Let $P = P(S^*|T)$ and let $S = P(T)$. There are then three kinds of "trials" or "events," $CT+$, $CT-$ and $C-$, corresponding to reinforced and nonreinforced trials plus background and (equal periods of) nonreinforced background alone. The associated (stationary) transition vector has corresponding probabilities of sP, $s(1 - P)$, and $(1 - s)$. These three events have associated value changes of

Event	Value change	Probability
CT+	$\Delta V_T = \alpha_T \beta_1 (1-V_{CT})$ $\Delta V_C = \alpha_C \beta_1 (1-V_{CT})$	sP
CT−	$\Delta V_T = \alpha_T \beta_2 (-V_{CT})$ $\Delta V_C = \alpha_C \beta_2 (-V_{CT})$	$s(1-P)$
C−	$\Delta V_T = 0$ $\Delta V_C = \alpha_C \beta_2 (-V_C)$	$(1-s)$

where α_I, $I = T,C$ are the saliences of the trial and background cues, β_J, $J = 1,2$ are the learning rates for conditioning and extinction, and $V_{CT} = V_C + V_T$. The asymptotes for conditioning and extinction are assumed to be zero and one. The expected value changes are then

$$E(\Delta V_T) = s\alpha_T[P\beta_1 - (P\beta_1+(1-P)\beta_2)V_{CT}], \quad (A1)$$

$$E(\Delta V_C) = \alpha_C(s[P\beta_1 - (P\beta_1+(1-P)\beta_2)V_{CT}] - (1-s)\beta_2 V_C). \quad (A2)$$

The expected number of C− events between trials (CT+ or CT−) is $(1-s)/s$, and the mean number of reinforced trials, say n, is related to the total number of events, m, by

$$n = \left(\frac{1}{sP}\right)m. \quad (A3)$$

The functions in Figure 9.6 were obtained by computer iteration of equations (A1) and (A2) to obtain $V_T(m)$, but plotted against n given by (A3).

A general closed form solution for $V_T(m)$ exists,[3] but its derivation is somewhat difficult and lies clearly outside the scope of this appendix. However, the asymptotes for both trial and background are readily obtained from (A1) and (A2) by setting these expected increments equal to zero. Since $s\alpha_T \neq 0$, setting $E(\Delta V_T) = 0$ gives

$$V_{CT} = \frac{P\beta_1}{P\beta_1 + (1-P)\beta_2}. \quad (A4)$$

Letting $E(\Delta V_C) = 0$, we have

$$s[P\beta_1 - (P\beta_1 + (1-P)\beta_2)V_{CT}] = (1-s)\beta_2 V_C. \quad (A5)$$

But substituting (A4) into (A5) makes the left side zero, and since $(1-s)\beta_2 \neq 0$ we must have

$$V_C(\infty) = 0, \quad (A6)$$

and so (A4) implies

[3] Gibbon, Manuscript in preparation.

$$V_T(\infty) = \left[1 + \left(\frac{1-P}{P} \right) \frac{\beta_2}{\beta_1} \right]^{-1}. \tag{A7}$$

(There is a typographical error in the statement of this result in Rescorla & Wagner, 1972 (p. 89) and in Rescorla, 1972 (p. 21). The denominator is a sum, not a difference.)

REFERENCES

Gamzu, E., & Williams, D. R. Classical conditioning of a complex skeletal response. *Science*, 1971, *171*, 923–925.

Gamzu, E., & Williams, D. R. Associative factors underlying the pigeon's keypecking in autoshaping procedures. *Journal of the Experimental Analysis of Behavior*, 1973, *19*, 225–232.

Gibbon, J. Scalar expectancy in autoshaping. Proceedings of the 47th Annual Convention of the Eastern Psychological Association, 1976.

Gibbon, J. Scalar expectancy theory and Weber's Law in animal timing. *Psychological Review*, 1977, *84*, 279–325.

Gibbon, J., Berryman, R., & Thompson, R. L. Contingency spaces and measures in classical conditioning. *Journal of the Experimental Analysis of Behavior*, 1974, *21*, 585–605.

Gibbon, J., Farrell, L., Locurto, C. M., Duncan, H. J., & Terrace, H. S. Partial reinforcement in autoshaping with pigeons. *Animal Learning and Behavior*, 1980, *8*, 45–59.

Gibbon, J., Locurto, C. M., & Terrace, H. S. Signal-food contingency and signal frequency in a continuous trials auto-shaping paradigm. *Animal Learning and Behavior*, 1975, *3*, 317–324.

Hall, G. & Honig, W. K. Stimulus control after extradimensional training in pigeons: A comparison of response contingent and noncontingent training procedures. *Journal of Comparative and Physiological Psychology*, 1974, *87*, 945–952.

Lindblom, L. L., & Jenkins, H. M. Responses eliminated by non-contingent reinforcement recover in extinction. Proceedings of the 20th Annual Convention of the Psychonomic Society, 1979.

Kamin, L. J. Predictability, surprise, attention and conditioning. In B. A. Campbell & R. M. Church (Eds.) *Punishment and Aversive Behavior.* New York: Appleton-Century-Crofts, 1969.

Mackintosh, N. J. Stimulus selection: Learning to ignore stimuli that predict no change in reinforcement. In R. A. Hinde & J. Stevenson-Hinde (Eds.) *Constraints on Learning.* London: Academic Press, 1973.

Pavlov, I. *Conditioned Reflexes.* Translated by G. V. Anrep. London and New York: Oxford Univ. Press, 1927. Reprint. New York: Dover, 1960.

Rescorla, R. A. Pavlovian conditioning and its proper control procedures. *Psychological Review*, 1967, *74*, 71–80.

Rescorla, R. A. Probability of shock in the presence and absence of CS in fear conditioning. *Journal of Comparative and Physiological Psychology*, 1968, *66*, 1–5.

Rescorla, R. A. Conditioned inhibition of fear resulting from negative CS–US contingencies. *Journal of Comparative and Physiological Psychology*, 1969, *67*, 504–509.

Rescorla, R. A. Informational variables in Pavlovian conditioning. In G. H. Bower (Ed.) *The Psychology of Learning and Motivation: Advances in Research and Theory.* New York: Academic Press, 1972.

Rescorla, M. E., & Wagner, A. R. A theory of Pavlovian conditioning: Variations in the effectiveness of reinforcement and non-reinforcement. In A. Black & W. Prokasy (Eds.) *Classical Conditioning II, Current Research and Theory.* New York: Appleton-Century-Crofts, 1972.

Straub, R. O., & Gibbon, J. Contextual blocking with a diffuse temporal stimulus. Proceedings of the 48th Annual Convention of the Eastern Psychological Association, 1977.

Tomie, A. Interference with autoshaping by prior context conditioning. *Journal of Experimental Psychology: Animal Behavior Processes*, 1976, 2, 323–334. (a)

Tomie, A. Retardation of autoshaping: Control by contextual stimuli. *Science*, 1976, 192, 1244–1246. (b)

Wagner, A. R., and Rescorla, R. A. Inhibition in Pavlovian conditioning: Application of a theory. In R. A. Boakes & M. S. Halliday (Eds.) *Inhibition and Learning*. New York: Academic Press, 1972.

Wasserman, E. A., Deich, J. D., Hunter, N. B., & Nagamatsu, L. S. Analyzing the random control procedure: Effects of paired and unpaired CSs and USs on autoshaping the chick's keypeck with heat reinforcement. *Learning and Motivation*, 1977, 8, 467–487.

Index

A

Additivity hypothesis, 14
Adjunctive behaviors, 97
Adventitious reinforcement, 4, 93–94, 114–115, 119, 121, 123
Anticipatory behavior, 226
Appetitive behavior, 39, 42
Appetitive object, direct versus indirect approach, 44–45, *see also* Detour problem
Arbitrariness of responding, 28
Associative inhibition, 198
Aversive fear conditioning, 262

B

Background conditioning, 287–291
Behavioral contrast, 208
Biconditional behavior, 55–97
Biological aspects of conditioning
  in autoshaping, 74–76, 87, 94
  in classical conditioning, 70–72
Biological constraints, 209–210
Biology of associations, 14
Blocking, associative, *see* Context-blocking
Blocking, nonassociative, 2
Blocking of conditioned response, 124–125
  surgical intervention, 124
  barriers, 124
  inaccessible food, 124
Botanizing of behavior, 92

C

Cats, classical conditioning, 38
Chicks, autoshaping, 3, 6, 30, 117, 125
Children, autoshaping, 3
Classical conditioning
  associative aspects, 70–71
  biological aspects, 70–72
  temporal factors, 71
Cognitive approach to associations, 23, 25
Comparative analysis of behavior, 38, 45
Conditioned Emotional Response, 183, 206, 275, 282–287
Conditioned inhibition, 140, 146, 154–155, 160
Conditional responses, *see* Conditioned responses
Conditional stimuli, *see* Conditioned stimuli
Conditioned responses
  approach–withdrawal, 35
  directed approach, 30, 75–76
  galvanic skin response, 230
  key approach, 34
  key contact, 34
  loop pulling, 115
  manipulation of objects, 35
  rearing, 120
  similarity to unconditioned response, 125
  species-typical behavior, 37–38
  types of, 6, 69
Conditioned stimuli
  animate, 36, 126

309

Conditioned stimuli *(Cont.)*
 associability with unconditioned stimuli, 35
 eliciting versus directing role, 41
 informativeness of, 62, 63
 lever insertion, 37, 115
 localizability of, 36, 201
 types of, 6
Constraints on learning, 25
Consummatory behavior, 39, 42, 65
Consummatory response, 2, 39
Context-blocking, 188–207, 247, 265–267
 auditory stimuli, 268
 blocking stimuli, 188, 203–204
 context conditioning, 188, 200, 206, 209
 intertrial interval effects, 203
 nonreinforced preexposure to context, 197
 unblocking, 204–205
 unconditioned stimuli, 197–198
 in background, 217–226, 280
Context feeding, *see* Context-blocking; Unconditioned stimulus in background
Contextual stimuli, 173, 221
Contingency
 role of, 285–305
 degradation of, 296
Contingency index, 281–282
Contingency space, 286–289
 isocontingency, 287
 tetrahedral, 289
Crows, autoshaping, 14, 37, 117
Cycle-to-trial ratio, 223–224, 228, 236–245, 280, 289–297
 absolute value of cycle, 240
 discriminability, 287
 integration of cycles, 231–236

D

Delay of reinforcement, 79, 121–122
Detour problem, 44, 45
Differential reinforcement of low rates, discrete trial, 88–90, 93
Differential reinforcement of other behavior, discrete trial, 86–90
Differential versus nondifferential reinforcement, 123, 127
Discriminative operant, 10
Dogs
 autoshaping, 3
 classical conditioning, 12, 38, 145
Dual-unit hypothesis, 108–112

E

Equipotentiality of association, 95
Evolutionary analysis of behavior, 38, 45
Expectancy, 46, 224–234, 265–269, 287–293, *see also* Scalar expectancy theory
 in background, 237–242, 249–250

F

Feature-negative discrimination learning, 146
Feedback hypothesis, 42–43
Feeding reactions, 67
Fish
 autoshaping, 3
 classical conditioning, 37
 instrumental conditioning, 80–82
Free-operant performance, 207–208

G

General activity, 240–241
 generative factors, 92, 97
General inattentiveness, 186–191
 versus attentiveness, 207
 competing instrumental responses, 192
 temporal factors, 192
Generalization testing, 207–208
Guinea pigs, classical conditioning, 38, 117

H

Hedonics, 4
Higher order conditioning, 139, *see also* Second-order conditioning
Hopper training, 256

I

Ingestive patterns, 65–68
Inhibition of delay, 152
Inhibitory association, 228, 293
Internal representation, 23
Intertrial interval effect, 2, 86, 194, 222–223, 280, 301
 fixed versus variable, 225
 lit key stimulus, 222
 response independent food, 222

L

Law of effect, 3, 8, 78
Learned helplessness, 183, 209

INDEX | 311

Learned irrelevance, 186–187, 194–197, 210
Learned laziness, 183, 186–187, 192–194
Learned releasers, 65–68
Learning functions, 240–242
Learning speed, 236–242
Learning versus performance, 21–24
Linear operator, 241–242
Lizards, classical conditioning, 37
Local interference in trial spacing effect, 257–260
Long waits, enhancement of acquisition, 261–265
Look–peck hypothesis, 40

M

Magazine training, *see* Hopper training
Massed training, 219–220
Minimal units, 10, 109
Motivation, 228–230

N

Negative autoshaping contingency, 58, *see also* Omission contingency
Negative transfer effect, 186–210, *see also* Context-blocking
 in autoshaping, 186–189, 207
Noncontingent reinforcement, 182
Nonspecific Pavlovian associative interference, 184

O

Object orientation, 41
Omission contingency, 2, 8, 10, 14, 45, 59, 81, 94, 102, 107
 conditioned reinforcement, 107
 fixed trial versus response terminated trial, 77, 108, 116
 multiple negative contingencies, 84–85
 naive versus experienced subjects, 103
 omission-analog procedure, 127–130
 pre-keypecks, 113–120, 125
 redirection of behavior, 119–121
 species differences, 117
 topography of responses, 111–112, 119, 126–127
 yoked control, 107
Origin hypothesis, 9, 13
Overshadowing, 246, 258–265

P

Partial reinforcement, 225, 293–298, *see also* Retardation of conditioning
 integration, 232
Peck duration, 83, 108–109, 119
 differential reinforcement, 110
Plasticity of responding, 26
Positive behavioral contrast, 14
Positive conditioned suppression, 118
Preparedness, 94, 95
Primates, autoshaping, 3, 38, 126
Primitive timing, 225–227
Principles of variation, 92
Pseudo-reflexes, 12
Psychobiology, integration with learning theory, 56
Psychophysics of association, 15, 71

Q

Quail, autoshaping, 3, 37

R

Ratio comparator, 224, 227, 230, 304
Ratio effect, *see* Cycle-to-trial ratio
Rats, autoshaping, 3, 6, 37, 115, 126
Reacquisition of autoshaping, 199
Relative waiting time hypothesis, 271–283
 extinction, 304
 partial reinforcement effect, absence of, 279, 287
 relation to scalar expectancy theory, 304–305
Representative stimuli, 42
Rescorla–Wagner model, 140, 152–176
 adaptation to probabilistic trials and reinforcers, 306–307
 blocking, 173–174
 contextual stimuli, 173–174
 contingency effects, 298–304
 extinction, 299
 inhibitory versus excitatory stimuli, 175
 and relative waiting time hypothesis, 278–280
 stimulus competition, 302–303
 trial spacing effects, 258, 278–280
 Unconditioned stimulus-absent procedure, 153, 156, 167, 175
 weighted sum rule, 157–158
Response elimination, response decrements
 differential reinforcement of low rate, 88–89
 differential reinforcement of other behavior, 86, 89

Response evocation problem, 24
  conditioned stimulus influence, 27
Response–reinforcer relation, 56, 76–80
  association, 28
  correlation and contiguity, 78, 90
Response sets, conditioned and unconditioned, 72
Response substitution, 120, 126
Response system, 120
Response terminated trial versus fixed trial, 58, 108, 116
Retardation of conditioning
  autoshaping
    competing response, 201, 205
    context-blocking, 188–210
    fixed versus variable intertrial interval, 225
    nonspecificity of conditioned stimulus, 185
    partial reinforcement, 233, 236
    transfer of training, 189, 205
    uncorrelated conditioned stimulus and unconditioned stimulus, 184
    unpredictable unconditioned stimulus, 190
    unsignaled unconditioned stimulus, 186, 258, 294–296
  instrumental conditioning, 184
  Pavlovian conditioning, 184–185
  response-independent reinforcement, 182, 183

S

Scalar expectancy theory, 224–230, 235, 242–247, 271, 277–279, 287–299
  partial reinforcement effect, absence of, 279
Second-order autoshaping, 2, 139, 140, 142
  conditioned excitation, 148
  conditioned inhibition, 146, 150
  contextual blocking, 173–174
  degradation of S1, 143–144
  generalization, 151, 158
  magnitude of unconditioned stimulus, 171, 172
  neural representation of unconditioned stimulus, 142
  partial reinforcement, 161–162, 164–168
  temporal factors, 149–150, 164
Second-order conditioning, 2, *see also* Second-order autoshaping
  heat reinforcement, 30–31
Self-control, 230
Self-reinforced behavior, 1

Shaping, 66
Shock-avoidance learning, 59
Sign-tracking, 6, 7, 63, 120
Simultaneous negative contrast, 172
Spaced training, 219–220
Species-specific defense reactions, 97
Species-specific responses, 13
Species-typical behaviors, 55
Split trials, 234–236
Stimuli
  directing function, 41–42
  generalization, 30, 33
Stimulus–reinforcer relation, 56, 61, 63
  in autoshaping, 61–76
  correlation and contiguity, 78, 285
  informativeness of stimuli, 61
  interdependence with response–reinforcer relation, 90
  predictiveness, 71
  respondent versus operant, 65
  versus response–reinforcer relation, 66–68, 73
  separation from response–reinforcer relation, 128–129
Stimulus–stimulus association, 23
  versus stimulus–response relation, 142
Stimulus substitution theory, 6–7
Stimulus substitution, 26, 29–33, 74–75
  drainage, 26
  Konorski's hypothesis, 32
Stimulus traces, 157
Superstitious behavior, *see* Adventitious reinforcement
Surrogate stimuli, 6–7

T

Taste aversion effect, 210
Temporal discrimination, 226–232, 243–246
  integration of signal and intertrial interval, 236
  predictiveness of signal, 243
Temporal factors in conditioning, 219–252
Temporal patterning of responses, 165, 169
Terminal and interim behaviors, 93
Topography of response, 2, 4
Transfer of training, 189, 205, 208
Trial spacing effect, 220–224, 255–283, 288–289, 299, *see also* Intertrial interval effects
  addition of unsignaled food, 257–260
  onset, 270
  predictive value of trial stimulus, 265–271

Truly random control, 190, 286
Two-factor theory, 1–2, 9, 108
   weaknesses, 108

U

Unconditional responses, *see* Conditioned responses; Unconditioned responses
Unconditional stimuli, *see* Unconditioned stimuli
Unconditioned responses, topography, 65
Unconditioned stimuli
   animate, 6
   availability of mate, 6
   cool air, 230
   duration, 228–230
   electrical stimulation of brain, 37
   food, 29
   heat, 6
   nondifferential pairing with conditioned stimuli, 63, 90
   non-reward, 33
   shock, 33, 230
   thermal stimulation, 30, 111, 125
   types of, 6
   water, 29, 126
   in bill, 30, 68

V

Variability of acquisition, 242–247

W

Weber's Law in animal time discrimination, 248

Y

Yoked control, 81, 87–93, 107, 117, 122